P9-CPZ-292
POMPEY PURSUES THE PIRATES
Adriatic Sea
CAESAR DRIVES OUT POMPEY
VILLAS
APPIAN WAY
BRINDISI
FORMIAE
NAPLES
MT. VESUVIUS
CUMAE
PUTEOLI
POMPEII
SPARTACUS
MT. AETNA
SICILY
TOMB of ARCHIMEDES FOUND BY CICERO
SYRACUSE

Elmer Davis says: "I can say little about this beyond a shout of approbation. Its great merit is that Haskell has seen politics, and politicians, in action."

Of all the great men whom the Roman Republic produced in its last decades, Marcus Tullius Cicero was, and has remained through twenty centuries, one of the most widely known and least understood. For Cicero's campaigns, many and vicious as they were, were fought not on the simple terrain of the battlefield but in the confused, often treacherous atmosphere of the courtroom and the political meeting. We know him today as the foremost orator of his time, equally great as essayist and as letter-writer. Few of us realize that much of his patriotic oratory was mere partisan politics, that in his own eyes he was an unimportant literary figure but a very great statesman—on both of which counts he was wrong.

This new life of Cicero is perhaps the first to show him as he really was, for it is the first by a scholar who has a real knowledge of practical politics. H. J. Haskell, editor of the *Kansas City Star* for many years, has looked upon several decades of American politicians in action, and there is not a trick of that tribe which deceives him, even when the practitioner was a politician in another republic now two thousand years dead. His picture of the great Roman, full, readable, and curiously timely, is a logical successor to his earlier distinguished study, *The New Deal in Old Rome.*

Also by H. J. Haskell

THE NEW DEAL IN OLD ROME

How Government in the Ancient World Tried to Deal with Modern Problems

" . . . something more than a notable contribution to the economic, political and social history of the Roman republic and empire, written in terms of contemporaneous events. It is a book of vital importance to the American people today. It should be a 'must' book for every student of modern affairs."

WILLIAM ALLEN WHITE

Published by Alfred A. Knopf

This was Cicero

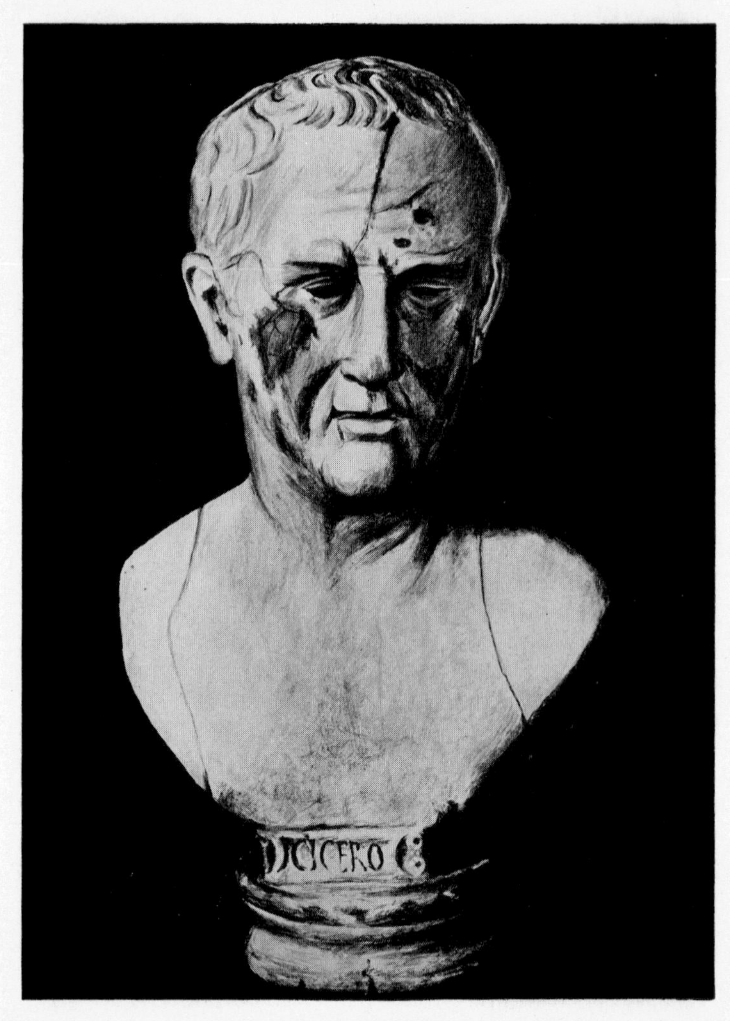

CICERO

The broad forehead furrowed by trouble, the face sensitive and rather disillusioned; in the studied melancholy a dash of the poseur. This Apsley House bust is probably the most surely authenticated of a group of five of the late Republic or early Empire that may have been copied from an original made from life. (Drawn by Richard F. Hunter with the permission of the owner, the Duke of Wellington)

THIS WAS

CICERO

MODERN POLITICS IN

A ROMAN TOGA

H. J. Haskell

NEW YORK 1942
ALFRED A. KNOPF

Manufactured in the United States of America.

FIRST EDITION

Published simultaneously in Canada by The Ryerson Press

To

A L H

WHO STARTED ME ON THE ROAD

AND HAS BEEN MY COMPANION

IN ITS ADVENTURES

PREFACE

THERE is only one reason, I think, for my presuming to add another Life of Cicero to the seventeen biographies in English listed in Appendix II. This has to do with politics. Cicero considered himself as primarily a politician. The political aspects of his career fall into the familiar and ageless pattern of political behaviour. Most of the biographers have not been sufficiently familiar with this type of behaviour to get the significance of much of the manœuvring of the Roman politicians of the first century B.C. I have constantly been horrified to find historians accepting political speeches as statements of fact. Cicero's denunciations of Catiline and Mark Antony are no more sober historical documents than the campaign speeches of American politicians.

In a former excursion into Roman history, *The New Deal in Old Rome,* I was impressed with the reappearance in modern America of many of the economic problems of ancient Rome. I was impressed as well with the persisting character of the social pressures that have compelled governments, ancient and modern, to adopt very similar measures in dealing with these problems.

In similar fashion appraising the political problems of the final century of the Roman Republic, I have found little change in the fundamentals of political behaviour in the last two thousand years. There seemed room for another study of Cicero that would take into account factors that had escaped the attention of biographers who were not familiar with politics in action.

As a Washington correspondent I long ago discovered that there were two aspects to every problem — the real aspect and the political. It is routine political behaviour to exaggerate and distort in order to gain advantage. The same technique bedevilled ancient Rome that bedevils modern Washington. The same irresponsible gossip seized and exploited for political purposes. The same manœuvring to put an opponent in a hole. The same attempts to twist and cloud issues. The same mixture of personal ambition with patriotic purpose. The same confusion as to when to compromise and when to fight.

In the century that led into the Empire, Italy was going through an economic and social revolution that had much in common with what the world has been experiencing in this modern age. The course of this revolution may be traced in the careers of the men who were involved in its progress. In the record of Cicero's life we may read how blind conservatism, failing to understand the significance of what was happening, resisted change in the hope of reconstructing the vanished past. Cicero was nobly devoted to freedom. He did not perceive that his freedom was the product of a political system working a simple social order with a fairly equable distribution of wealth; that with the sudden onrush of riches and poverty the old stability had collapsed, carrying with it the old democratic institutions.

Through his revealing letters we get a vivid sense of the reactions of a cultured man as his world crashed about his head, destroying him in its ruins. In dazzling contrast stands the tremendous figure of Julius Cæsar, whose soaring ambition carried him far beyond narrow personal aims into a far-reaching program of social reconstruction. In the end his plans were frustrated by the selfish stupidity of the society with which he had to deal.

America has not escaped the internal strains that proved so disastrous to Rome. There are lessons for the American democracy in the disintegration of what was called the Roman Republic.

So far as possible I have tried to base my judgments on contemporary sources and the accounts of the later ancient writers who followed contemporary writings now lost. Of course no amateur can work in this field without being under immense obligations to the scholars who have so thoroughly and competently explored it, even if he dissents from some of their conclusions. Most of the necessary material may be found in translation in the Loeb Classical Library without which this book could not have been written. Quotations from this series are used with the kind permission of the publishers. A few gaps in that Library are closed by volumes in the old Bohn Library.

In looking up points in the various lives of Cicero in English I have repeatedly observed with some pain the lack of any chronology. A fairly full chronological table of the Ciceronian period is supplied in the first Appendix. In the second is reviewed the literature for those who would read further, and in the third some of the moot points and controversial matters are discussed. I venture to commend to readers the lively comments and dissenting opinions of my learned advisers in the third Appendix.

I have been so fortunate as to obtain the help of three classical authorities who have read and criticized the manuscript of this book — Dr. Hubert M. Poteat, professor of Latin, Wake Forest College; Dr. Arthur T. Walker, professor of Latin, the University of Kansas; and Dr. Louis E. Lord, professor of Classics, Oberlin College. To these consultants, I am more indebted than I can say. They have been vigilant, patient, and tolerant. I should be less than fair if I did not include with these my wife, whose criticisms have helped me clear up ambiguities and have kept before me the point of view of those who are not familiar with the background of Roman history. But there are such wonderful opportunities for slips in a book of this kind that I can only hope no errors of consequence have got by.

In the course of my study the leading Romans of the last century of the Republic have become as vivid to me as the politicians I have known in Kansas City and Washington. I should like to think that these pages may make Cicero a real person to readers who remember him only vaguely as a name connected with certain exercises in Latin grammar of their college days.

H. J. Haskell

The Kansas City Star
March 15, 1942

CONTENTS

ILLUSTRATIONS

MAPS

This was Cicero

CHAPTER I

PROLOGUE OF GREAT NAMES

IT WAS a turbulent century into which Cicero was born, the last century of the Roman Republic. This restless and terrible century produced more men and events familiar to the modern world after the lapse of two millenniums than any similar period in the thousand years of Rome. Curiously the shining span of the long Roman peace that came with Augustus and the Empire near the beginning of the Christian era was far less distinguished in outstanding figures. Danger rather than safety developed personalities.

As a boy, Cicero could have talked with men of middle age who had known the two fiery reformers, the brothers Gracchus, and their mother, the great lady Cornelia, who had presented her sons as her jewels. He lived through the perilous times when the brilliant soldier Marius rolled back the last flood of German invaders who had threatened Rome and gave the capital security for five hundred years. When he was fifteen, Italy was swept by a fierce civil war that threatened to destroy the unity of the country and that took a heavy toll of its substantial citizens. In his young manhood he saw Sulla emerge as a general rivalling Marius and from safe obscurity witnessed the ferocious struggle for supremacy between these two military leaders in which the civil government all but disappeared. He was only thirty-three when Spartacus led the revolt of gladiators and slaves, and he may have ridden down the Appian Way between the miles of crucified prisoners after the revolt had been crushed.

As head of the state he suppressed an uprising of poor devils led by Catiline who were trying to obtain a redress of grievances. From Rome he watched the campaigns of Julius Cæsar that made Gaul and therefore France a part of European civilization. As a provincial governor in Asia Minor he heard of the growing hostility between Pompey and Cæsar and the impending armed conflict. " If it could only be managed without personal risk to yourself," a friend wrote him, " a drama of infinite entertainment is being staged by Fortune for your benefit." It proved indeed a tremendous drama, but in the end it engulfed both Cicero and his Roman correspondent. Just home from the governorship, Cicero shared the panic at the capital when Cæsar crossed the Rubicon. Both leaders were his personal friends and he spent anxious months trying to decide which to support. Finally casting his lot with Pompey, at the Macedonian port of Durazzo he received the news of the battle of Pharsalus, in which Pompey was overwhelmed by his mighty rival. In the Cæsarian dictatorship he met the haughty Cleopatra, whom Cæsar had installed in an elaborate villa outside of Rome.

Age cannot wither her, nor custom stale
Her infinite variety,

wrote Shakespeare in accordance with the tradition. Cicero took a different view. " I can't abide the woman," he confided in a letter to a friend.

The organizers of the great conspiracy against the dictator, republican fanatics and disgruntled nobles, excluded Cicero as too old and timid. But he welcomed the fatal ides of March and hailed the assassins as liberators. Later he was to lament that the " deed was done with the courage of men but the blind policy of a child " — that though Rome was rid of the tyrant, the tyranny remained.

The lean and hungry Cassius came within his orbit. He

corresponded, sometimes acrimoniously, with the noble Brutus, who was met by his evil spirit on the fatal field of Philippi. For a time he was a friend of the young military adventurer, Cæsar's great-nephew Octavian, who later was to organize and rule the Roman world under the name of Augustus. The best known of the Roman writers were his contemporaries, or were born in his lifetime — the poets Lucretius, Catullus, Horace, Virgil; the historians Sallust and Livy. And he made use of the magnificent library of the wealthy Lucullus, whose name has been handed down to modern times as the supreme epicure.

It would be hard to find another man since Cicero whose life covered such a period of conspicuous individuals and spectacular events. Fate cast him in an age when the Roman self-governing city-state was slowly disintegrating from its own success. Changes in the social structure were putting too great a strain on rigid political institutions adapted to a simpler time but now outworn. Without realizing it Cicero was living at the end of an era, the defender of the lost cause of the aristocratic Republic.

As the defender of this cause at the height of his power as chief magistrate of Rome he was challenged by the other great figure of his day. Cicero was submerged as Cæsar, the man of action, came to the front. The one fought a losing struggle to conserve the past. The other was forced by events and his own restless temperament to break from the past into a new order which he only dimly discerned. Cæsar won supremacy at the cost of alienating vital elements in the state. In the end his old antagonist was the spiritual although not the actual leader of the plot to which Cæsar fell a victim. His death released forces of disorder before which Cicero went down. Toward this double climax the conflict inexorably moved as Rome sought by trial and error to deal with problems which in new forms confront mankind today.

There is always danger in comparing figures in the ancient world with those in the modern. The intellectual, social, and economic gulf between them is too great. With due reservations it may be said that Cicero would have found himself no stranger in the House of Commons with Walpole, the elder Pitt, and Edmund Burke. For the moment it may help us to an understanding of the Roman's career to think of him as in some respects an English Whig of the eighteenth century. Like the Whigs he was less conscious of the misery of the submerged masses about him than he was of possible governmental oppression. One great quality he and the Whigs had in common: they were deeply concerned with political liberty.

CHAPTER II

A ROMAN VISITS EIGHTEENTH-CENTURY LONDON

IN THE great debate leading up to the framing of the American Constitution John Adams made his contribution from London, where he was stationed as minister. It was in a work entitled: *A Defence of the Constitutions of Government of the United States of America,* by which he meant the state constitutions. Adams produced an astonishingly learned and intelligent study of more than forty experiments in democratic government in the ancient and modern world and analysed the causes of their failure. The first volume, published in London early in 1787, was immediately republished in Boston, New York, and Philadelphia and circulated among the delegates to the Constitutional Convention. Adams's conclusion that liberty depended on a separation of the powers of government, legislative, executive, and judicial, " contributed somewhat," his grandson wrote, " to give direction to the opinion of the members." The work was discussed in newspapers and by delegates in the Constitutional Convention.

Letters showing the wide interest it aroused were written while the convention was in session by Benjamin Franklin, James Madison, John Jay, Benjamin Rush, Henry Knox, and Richard Henry Lee. Thomas Jefferson commented on it from Paris. As was manifest in a letter from Madison to Jefferson, there was prejudice to be overcome because Adams's proposals were supposed — mistakenly, to be sure

— to be embodied in the British Constitution, which was suspect to American democrats. Here Adams was able to make an effective appeal to Cicero. "As all the ages of the world," he wrote, "have not produced a greater statesman and philosopher united than Cicero, his authority should have great weight. His decided opinion in favor of three branches is founded on a reason that is unchangeable."

No American of the period would have thought of challenging Cicero's claim to statesmanship. Jefferson read the *De Senectute* every year. Josiah Quincy had three editions of Cicero, one in twenty volumes for the pocket, testifying to his devotion to Cicero as a defender of liberty. In his last sermon the Reverend Jonathan Mayhew, a clergyman of wide influence in the first half of the century, avowed that the chief sources of his ideas of civil liberty were Plato, Demosthenes, and Cicero. John Quincy Adams, lecturing at Harvard College in 1806, proclaimed the doctrine from Cicero that eloquence was the stay of liberty.

These high estimates of the Roman were general among John Adams's eighteenth-century contemporaries both in England and in the America that was part of the English intellectual world. Cicero spoke with such convincing force to that world because in many ways he belonged to it. Eighteenth-century England had much in common with Rome of the first century before Christ. In considering Cicero as a product of the society in which he lived we shall have a more vivid idea of the man if we make certain comparisons of ancient Rome with the England from which the American Republic emerged. We shall also have a better conception of the problems with which he had to deal.

An upper-class Roman of the first century B.C. would have found himself quite at home in eighteenth-century England. London, with a population of nearly a million, was larger than Rome, but not too much larger. Its narrow, crooked streets, cobblestone pavements, and sedan chairs borne by liveried attendants, would have reminded the Roman of his own capital. If his visit had been in the first third of the century he would have found the streets badly lighted at night, with the city government merely trying to supplement sporadically the lanterns or candles hung out before their doors by private citizens. He would have recalled that Rome had been lighted in the same way on that glorious night when Cicero as consul had announced that Catiline's fellow conspirators had been put to death and the city saved from fire and revolution. An unimaginative fellow, he probably would have reflected that, after all, the old Roman way of using torches carried by attendants answered all purposes. Gas lighting of streets, introduced in London in 1736, would of course have baffled him. Nothing like that was known even in the glittering world metropolis of Alexandria.

Besides, he would have asked his London friends whether it was not generally unsafe to venture out at night, assuming that the few night watchmen were as worthless in London as they were in Rome. Were not highwaymen about, and perhaps reckless young hoodlums who might wantonly attack inoffensive pedestrians? Stories of the escapades of London's Mohock gang of high-born rowdies who terrorized the streets at night would not have surprised the Roman visitor. He might even have been able to match the accounts of matrons enclosed in barrels and rolled down hilly streets. Outrageous, he might have commented, but what could be done about it? Experience had demonstrated that it was dangerous to free institutions to quarter regular troops within the city. Londoners would have agreed. Social organizations develop slowly. In spite of disorders and extensive rioting in the capital, the possibility of establishing an effective civilian police system did not occur to the Roman of the first century before Christ. The Englishman began to realize the possibility only in the middle of the eighteenth century. It was not until the sixth year of our era that the organizing ability of Augustus provided Rome with a fire and police department of seven thousand men. It was not until 1829 that Robert Peel set up the London metropolitan police, who were to be endearingly nicknamed "Bobbies" or "Peelites" from their founder. This disposition to poke fun was to crop out in imperial Rome, where the firemen were to be called "the little bucket fellows," and where it was to be regarded as a fine joke to bring them running on a false alarm from the smoking kitchen of some house where an elaborate dinner was being served.

The Roman visitor would have shaken his head over the state of the English roads. "Your coach and six," he might have said, "seems very grand. But I hear you need the six horses to pull the coach over your muddy roads – and at that the coach sometimes bogs down. Your Great North Road doesn't compare with our splendidly paved highways – our Great North Road, the Flaminian Way, for instance, or the Aurelian or Appian Way or many others I might mention. Julius Cæsar once travelled more than seven hundred miles from Rome to Geneva in a hired carriage in eight days. Nothing approaching that time could be made on your roads in England."

Strolling westward on the Strand to the districts to which the great nobles were moving, the Roman would have found himself among familiar scenes. The new houses on Piccadilly and in Cavendish, Hanover, and Grosvenor Squares he would have had to admit were more substantial and elaborate than the residences of the Roman nobility. But he would have insisted that the fashionable quarter on the Palatine was rapidly overtaking the best that London could show. As to public buildings he would have been rather quiet. The marble age of Augustus was still in the future.

The splendid country seats of the English nobility would not have astonished him. Did not Lucullus have a magnificent place at Tusculum? Was not the lovely Bay of Naples surrounded by noble houses? Was not a mere professional man like Cicero able to maintain seven villas for his varying moods? Did not the famous lawyer on one occasion entertain Cæsar and his staff, with a guard of two thousand men, at his villa on the bay?

These sumptuous estates with their fountains, colonnades, gardens, fishponds, gymnasiums, libraries, picture galleries, and statuary would have compared favourably, in the Roman's opinion, with the elaborate places of the English peers.

Social life in London and the prominent part taken by women the Roman would have perfectly understood. His English friends might have warned him that the life was rather dissolute, with great moral laxity and much hard drinking. The state of religion, they might have added, was deplorable. In the best circles the church was regarded as a necessary state institution, but religion itself was politely ignored. They could have proceeded with a bill of particulars on all these points designed to impress the presumably unsophisticated visitor from the past.

The ravishing Georgiana, Duchess of Devonshire, for instance, was leader of the smart set. Her greatest friend was her husband's mistress, Lady Elizabeth Foster, a member of the household. The Duchess had three children by her husband, one by Lord Grey. The Duke had two by Lady Elizabeth. Included in the family were two children of Lady Bessborough, sister of the Duchess, by Lord Granville Levison Gower. The children were brought up together to become social leaders, and the " Devonshire House girls " were much sought after. The Harleys, children of the Countess of Oxford, were of such uncertain parentage that they were known as " the Harleian miscellany." Great confusion existed in Lord Melbourne's household. According to gossip, the second son of Lady Melbourne, who was to become Victoria's prime minister, was the child of Lord Egremont; another the son of the Prince of Wales. " The vices," a lady wrote, " are wonderfully prolific among Whigs. There are such countless illegitimates, such a tribe of children of the mist."

Naturally the great ladies used their influence politically.

Promotions in the diplomatic service and in the peerage often were attributed to some liaison which a lady used to her neglected husband's advantage. Lord Melbourne became a viscount as a reward for his wife's friendship with the Prince of Wales.

As for hard drinking, it was the accepted thing. A statesman was proud to be known as a one-bottle, two-bottle, three-bottle man. Lord Oxford, a minister of the crown, was reported to have gone drunk into the presence of the Queen. The brilliant Lord Bolingbroke spent many of his nights drinking. Dr. Johnson remarked that the decent people of Lichfield got drunk every night and nobody thought the worse of them. The father of the future statesman Sir Robert Walpole used to insist when they were drinking together that the son should always take two drinks to his father's one. This on the moral ground that a befuddled Robert would be spared the demoralizing experience of realizing how drunk his father could be.

Christianity in eighteenth-century England the Roman's informants would have described as less a belief than a convenience, an excellent expedient for keeping the lower classes in their place. The son of a respectable family had his choice of professions, the army and the church. It was a matter of personal preference. No religious qualifications were expected of the young man who decided to take Orders. The choice of vicars lay largely with the landed gentry. Livings could be bestowed upon favoured relatives or offered for sale. We hear of one extravagant young man who took a charge in Suffolk as an honest way to pay his debts. "Here he became a great favourite with the country gentlemen by whom his society was much sought; for he kept an excellent hunter, rode well up to the hounds, drank very hard. He sang an excellent song, danced remarkably well, so that the young ladies considered no party complete without him."

The aristocrats supported the Church of England precisely as they supported other solid English institutions. Their religious beliefs were their private affair. They might be deists like the third Earl of Shaftesbury or they might be agnostics, although that designation did not come into vogue until the next century, or they might be urbanely indifferent. "No, my Lord," Melbourne replied to an invitation by the Archbishop of York to attend evening service; "once is orthodox, twice is puritanical." And on one occasion he stamped out of church after listening to a sermon directed against prevalent vices, exclaiming: "Things are coming to a pretty pass when religion is allowed to invade a gentleman's private life."

To all such recitals the Roman could have responded with an understanding smile. Conditions in the last age of the Roman Republic were very similar. There was the dashing and fascinating Clodia, for instance, descendant of a great family and for a year first lady of Rome as the wife of a consul. Her magnificent Palatine mansion was frequented by all the radical young nobles of the capital. The "burning eyes of Clodia" dazzled the young poet Catullus, and he addressed passionate lyrics to her under the name of Lesbia — "Let us live and love, my Lesbia." He was only one of many. Her affairs were notorious. Still she maintained her position and Cicero attended her salons although later he called her "the Medea of the Palatine." "Known to us only through her enemies," a modern scholar has written, "the very bitterness of their onslaughts testifies to the greatness of her personality, a personality of which none can read without feeling its power and intensity, though but one or two facts of her life are to be seen, and that fitfully, through the virulence of her foes, like a wild revel in the night revealed by flashes of lightning."

There was the high-born Servilia, a social leader and a power in politics. A minor indiscretion involving her was much laughed about in Rome. At the trial of the Catilinarian conspirators she sent a love letter to Cæsar in the Senate. Her strait-laced half-brother Cato suspected the letter had to do with the conspiracy and said so on the floor. It was moved that the letter be read aloud. Cæsar handed it to Cato, who recognized his sister's handwriting. So he threw it back to Cæsar exclaiming: " Take it, you sot! " and went on with his speech. Gossip made Cæsar the father of Servilia's famous son, Marcus Junius Brutus, who finally joined in the conspiracy against the great man's life. Circumstances were against this particular bit of scandal, but the affair was not worth arguing. Cæsar, like others of his contemporaries, was irresistible to the ladies. He is credited with having given Servilia a pearl worth $300,000.

Servilia had a strong-minded daughter-in-law, Porcia. There is every reason to suppose the two women struggled for the soul of Marcus Brutus before he was brought into the conspiracy. The mother naturally would try to keep him loyal to Cæsar. The wife, with the republican training of her stern father, Cato, undoubtedly incited him to resist the dictator. In any event, she was the only woman who was allowed to know of the proposed political assassination in advance.

The important role played by women is suggested by Cicero in a letter written three months after the murder. The conspirators amid gathering clouds held a conference at Antium attended by Servilia, Porcia, and Tertulla — the last-named the half-sister of Brutus. There plans were considered and Servilia offered to get a senatorial decree modified to meet the wishes of Cassius.

Of a wholly different type was the lovely Julia, daughter of Cæsar and wife of Pompey. Her husband, twenty-three years her senior, was so devoted to her that he neglected his public duties in order to be with her in their country houses and at the seaside resorts of Italy. She was a strong influence in keeping her father and husband together politically and it was not until after her premature death that the break between them came.

Her successor as Pompey's wife, Cornelia, also young and attractive, was distinguished for her knowledge of literature, music, geometry, and philosophy. When her husband, defeated by Cæsar at Pharsalus, sought refuge in Egypt, where he was murdered, she accompanied him — an example of a high-minded, cultured, and loyal woman.

Another *grande dame* who took a hand in politics was Cæsar's wife, Calpurnia. Immediately after her marriage she used her influence to have her father elected consul, to the enormous disgust of this same Cato, who protested it was intolerable that women should be permitted to name commanders of armies, governors of provinces, and other high officials — a protest, someone has suggested, in the spirit of Napoleon's question: "Since when did the Council of State meet at Madame Récamier's?" Society attributed to another lady, celebrated for her wit, beauty, and political influence, the appointment of Lucullus to the important eastern command. Still another attractive woman was Sempronia, mother of Decimus Junius Brutus, one of Cæsar's marshals, and a friend of that problem child of the aristocracy, Catiline. She could sing and dance, was well read in Greek and Latin literature, could write verses, engage in witty conversations, and break men's hearts. Another to be mentioned, but with raised eyebrows, was the terrible Fulvia, several times married, who as the wife of Mark Antony in the time of a bloody purge ordered the execution of her personal enemies without consulting her husband. She it was whose attempted flirtation with the rising young Octavian drew from the future Augustus a bit of very improper verse.

The forerunner of the modern suffragettes appeared in Rome in the person of Hortensia, daughter of a leader of the Roman bar and a masterful person in her own right. Perhaps she gained courage for her exploit from a successful feminist movement of the previous century, when the matrons of Rome blocked the approaches to the Forum and importuned the men to vote for the repeal of an obnoxious law regulating their dress and their ownership of gold. Finally they rushed the Assembly: "And when accordingly the law was speedily repealed," the ancient chronicler says, " they straightway put on some ornaments there in the Assembly and went out dancing."

The occasion for the suffragette protest headed by Hortensia was a decree by the government imposing a special tax on fourteen hundred of the richest women of the capital. The women marched to the Forum, forced their way in, " the guards dividing to let them pass," and Hortensia addressed the Three who dominated the state. Her plea is the first that history records against taxation without representation. " Why should we pay taxes," she demanded, " when we have no part in the honours, the commands, the statecraft, for which you contend against one another with such harmful results? " Horrified at this feminine presumption, the Three ordered the guards to put the ladies out. But the spectators raised such an uproar that the guards desisted and the Three discreetly announced they would take the matter under advisement. The next day they compromised by exempting a thousand of the fourteen hundred from the proposed taxation.

Another famous lady was Octavia, sister of Augustus and the successor of Fulvia as wife of Antony. " A wonderful woman," Plutarch calls her, and beautiful. Her devotion to her errant husband was the talk of Rome. She succeeded for a time in averting an armed struggle between him and her brother. Even after Antony had fallen for the charms of Cleopatra, his loyal wife gathered money and soldiers in Italy and set out with them to help her husband in one of his Asiatic campaigns. A message from him reached her in Athens directing her to return to Rome although he accepted the help she had furnished. After his death his children by Cleopatra were taken into her home by the compassionate Octavia.

Cleopatra herself was a flaming soul who flashed across the Roman scene, influencing history and leaving destruction in her wake. A Queen, of course, and a Greek. But her type was familiar in the Italian capital.

OCTAVIA, SISTER OF AUGUSTUS

Octavia was the wife of the roistering Mark Antony during his affair with Cleopatra. A wonderful woman and beautiful, Plutarch calls her. Observe her twentieth-century hair-do. (From a bust in the museum at Carthage, North Africa)

High society was chiefly concerned that the conventions be preserved. It would have accepted the admonition of the American financier to one of his younger associates who had become involved in a scandal. "But," the young man protested, "I only do openly what other people do behind closed doors." "My dear sir," the upholder of decency replied, "that is what doors are for." Even so practising a Puritan as Cicero could speak publicly of the escapades of a young scapegrace friend with the tolerance of a Lord Chesterfield writing worldly advice to his son.

Most middle-class Romans no doubt led virtuous lives according to the practices of the time. The double standard of morals was conventional. But the Roman visitor to London would have known that the aristocracy constituted a little world of its own in which departures from the old way of life were so common as to attract scant attention.

As for drinking in eighteenth-century England, the Roman could hardly have been shocked. Cæsar was abstemious, but the fact that this was remarked upon showed it was rather unusual. The great Marius had ended his life in a prolonged drunk. There were scandalous reports of the drinking parties of Sulla after he had laid down his dictatorship. Cato at times would spend a whole night over his wine. Mark Antony was a terrific drinker. Cicero was blameless in his habits, but we have a letter that he wrote to a friend about a dispute at dinner over their wine in which he speaks of returning home "at a late hour comfortably mellow." It was reputed to be the high ambition of his irresponsible son to outdrink Antony. He was so successful that on one occasion he caused a minor scandal by throwing a drinking cup at a distinguished general. Long drinking parties after formal dinners were common. While Italian wines were not so potent as the liquors served in England, continued drinking could send the guests staggering into the streets prepared for any wild adventure.

It would be misleading to suggest that the primitive religious practices of the Roman people were at all analogous to the Christianity of the eighteenth century. There was nothing in Italy comparable to the Church of England. At the same time a Roman in London would have noticed certain aspects of religious observances that would have seemed familiar. Thus he would have found the practice in country parishes of "beating the bounds" with peeled wands, "when the minister accompanied by his churchwardens and parishioners would deprecate the vengeance of God, beg a blessing on the fruits of the earth, and preserve the rights and properties of the parish." This would have reminded him of the May festival on Roman farms, with its procession of sacrificial victims that made the rounds of the fields, ending with the sacrifice of animals and the prayer to a god to protect the products of the land.

The relation of religion to the English state, and the attitude of the upper classes to religion, would have seemed even more familiar to our Roman. Religion in Rome was a more important part of the government than it was in the England of the Georges. The primitive superstitions that survived among the people made them anxious that nothing be undertaken in either private or public life without the assurance that it would not be displeasing to the unseen powers. The Romans set great store by the priestly colleges that were charged with looking after this important aspect of their affairs. The Assemblies could be prevented from meeting or could be adjourned by a simple announcement by the magistrate of unfavourable omens, a valuable weapon in the hands of the aristocracy.

Skepticism had long been growing among the intelligentsia. A remark by a sturdy Roman statesman of the second century before Christ, the Cato who was the great-grandfather of Cicero's contemporary, was widely quoted. "I wonder," he said, "that a soothsayer doesn't laugh when he sees another soothsayer." The philosophic Greek historian Polybius, writing in the same century, defended religious superstition on grounds that would have appealed to Lord Melbourne. Religion, he remarked, would not be necessary in a state made up wholly of wise men. " But as every multitude is fickle, full of lawless desires, unreasoned passion, and violent anger, the multitude must be held in check by invisible terrors and suchlike pageantry." He added that the Romans of his time were foolish in undermining such beliefs.

But undermined they were with the spread of the Greek enlightenment. Early in the first century B.C. the official head of the state religion, the chief pontiff (*pontifex maximus*) taught his law students that there were two sorts of religion, one philosophic and adapted to the intellect, the other traditional and not so adapted. The philosophic religion he held was not fitted to be the religion of the state since it might be demoralizing to the mass of the people.

By the time of Cicero the Roman intellectuals were generally agnostics, although they might profess some vague form of pantheism. That did not prevent their upholding the state religion. Cicero was proud to be chosen a member of the dignified board of augurs, the experts on omens, in which he had no belief, and Cæsar spent a fortune to be elected *pontifex maximus.* It may fairly be said that the attitude of the great nobles of Ciceronian Rome toward the state religion was very similar to the attitude of the aristocracy of Georgian England toward the established church. There might be something to it, of course. An interesting subject for speculation if one cared for that sort of thing. In any event, it was a useful instrument for control of the lower classes.

The discussion of religion might have prompted the visitor's English friends to bring up the apparent lack of the humanitarian spirit among the Romans. " If you will pardon my frankness," one of them might have said, " the Romans of your century seem to have been singularly brutal. How could cultivated men have tolerated the gladiatorial combats? When you had conquered King Jugurtha you starved him to death in prison. Your massacres under Marius and Sulla were horrible. The mere fact that Antony could have had the severed hands and head of Cicero nailed up above the rostra seems to indicate an innate coarseness covered by a thin veneer of Hellenic refinement."

"I have no defence of such ghastly deeds," the visitor might have replied. "All I can say is that the course of history seems to justify your comment on the thin veneer of civilization. Only I might remark that this unhappy situation is not confined to my countrymen. If you will permit me to ignore your own capital for the moment, I am told that Paris represents the fine flower of cultural life. Yet in the memoirs of Casanova I read that in the middle of the present century a criminal was publicly tortured to death in the Place de Grève and that great ladies gathered in parties where they could overlook the scene and hear the poor wretch's screams. I believe heads of rebels were nailed on Temple Bar in 1745 and there allowed to decay; that the execution of criminals in London is a great popular amusement; that their bodies are sometimes left to rot on public gallows. I hear that your great legal authority, Blackstone, enumerates one hundred and sixty capital offences. By contrast I think you will find your own classical scholars writing of the criminal code of the Roman Republic as the mildest ever known. English popular sports are brutal, if not so brutal as our gladiatorial exhibitions. In fact, I suspect you will find future historians writing that humanitarianism was really a product of the nineteenth century. From my own acquaintance with human nature I would not be sure that even our terrible mass murders might not be duplicated from time to time in the twentieth century and beyond."

One contrast might have struck the visitor. Roman society was founded on slavery. There were no slaves in England. A great establishment in Rome might have two hundred slaves. No noble family could maintain its social standing without a retinue of cooks, waiters, room servants, porters, ladies' maids, footmen, palanquin-bearers, copying-clerks, stewards, tutors, and other household attendants — all slaves. White, and some of them well educated and generally well treated, but still without civil rights, and liable to be punished or sold if they incurred the master's disfavour. But perhaps the different status of the English servants might not have impressed him as important. Every great family in London had its army of menials who were paid only a pittance, with no provision for their comfort. Little more attention was given their welfare than was given to the welfare of the slaves in well-appointed Roman households. To English high society the wretchedly poor did not matter. Quite the same way in Rome.

CHAPTER III

AND FINDS HIMSELF AT HOME

THE STRIKING similarities in the social structure of Rome and England would have prepared the Roman for similarities in the field of government where on the surface they seemed not to exist. England was a monarchy with a king and court. While the House of Hanover ruled by the Act of Settlement — that is, by the will of the people expressed through Parliament — the crown was hereditary. Rome regarded itself as a self-governing commonwealth, a republic. Traditionally the very name of king was detested. Two consuls were elected annually by a popular assembly, each with a veto on the other so that kingly power should not be usurped by one ambitious man. In its social and political position in the state the House of Lords was very like the Roman Senate. But although the House of Commons and the Roman Assemblies were supposed to represent the people, they were wholly different in make-up. The representative principle as applied to the House of Commons was foreign to an Assembly which long had been frozen in the form of a town meeting.

In spite of surface differences the visitor would have discovered fundamental likenesses in the two forms of government. Each was the result of a long process of development. The English Constitution, like the Roman, was a composite of laws and practices. Polybius, keen analyst of Roman institutions, remarked that the Romans had not reached their form of government " by any process of reasoning, but by the discipline of many struggles and troubles, always choosing the best in the light of the experience gained in disaster." The same description might have been given of the English Constitution.

In both cases custom and the Constitution favoured control of the government by an aristocracy. England was really ruled by the great Whig houses, Rome by the great nobles. The aristocratic monarchy of eighteenth-century England was not far removed from the aristocratic Republic of Rome of the first century before the Christian era.

A group of Whig nobles had been the driving force in the Glorious Revolution of 1688 and later had established the House of Hanover on the British throne. These families included the Bentincks, headed by the Duke of Portland, the Campbells by the Duke of Argyll, the Cavendishes by the Duke of Devonshire, the Pelhams by the Duke of Newcastle, the Russells by the Duke of Bedford, the Grenvilles by Earl Temple, the Stanhopes by Earl Stanhope and the Earl of Chesterfield — all names known and respected throughout Britain. Such families with their connections by intermarriage formed a powerful network over the Kingdom and for a half-century dominated the government. Even after the Whig rule was broken, the aristocratic tradition persisted. A modern investigator reports that in the hundred and twenty-five years preceding the first Labour government of 1924, of the three hundred and six men reaching cabinet rank, one hundred and eighty-two, or sixty per cent, were hereditary titled aristocrats. So in Rome. One of the two consuls elected every year was invariably from a noble family. With the rarest exceptions, both were. Among these families a small group, corresponding to the great Whig houses, emerged as dominant. In something under two hundred years down into the second century before Christ Mommsen has listed sixteen Roman families that furnished one hundred and forty of the two hundred patrician nobles who attained consular rank. The Cornelii, Valerii, Æmilii, Claudii, Fabii, Manlii, Postumii, Sulpicii, corresponded to the English Pelhams, Cavendishes, Bentincks, and the rest.

If he had discussed the matter with a congenial English friend the Roman undoubtedly would have justified the attitude of his countrymen. "The memory of great ancestors," he might have said, "and the desire not to suffer a great name to fade become an incentive of the most powerful kind. A structure of society like that of Rome, which brings the upper class into such political prominence that they usually furnish the candidates for election, has at least the advantage of saving the nation from government by speculators, adventurers, and demagogues, which is the gravest of all the evils to which a commonwealth is liable. With such politicians in charge the foreign policy of the country would be in danger of being directed by men who sought only for notoriety or for the consolidation of their tottering power and who might plunge the nation into wars that would speedily lead to national ruin. In home politics institutions which are lost in the twilight of a distant past might, through similar motives, in a few months be recklessly destroyed. To minds ambitious only of notoriety, careless of the permanent interests of the nation, and destitute of all real feeling of political responsibility, a policy of mere destruction possesses an irresistible attraction. From these extreme evils a country is for the most part saved by entrusting the management of its affairs chiefly to the upper classes of the community."

The Englishman would have agreed. Indeed, the words just attributed to the Roman are taken almost verbatim from W. E. H. Lecky's defence of aristocratic government in his *History of England in the Eighteenth Century* — the century that was Lecky's intellectual habitat. The sentiments expressed in them are implicit in the writings of Cicero. They certainly belonged to Rome as well as to England. Both countries were essentially conservative. In both the glorious past was venerated. In both the families that had guided the national destiny through periods of storm and stress were highly respected. Only a comparatively few persons were beginning to appreciate the selfishness, meanness, and inherent incompetency of an oligarchy based on hereditary succession. It was assumed in both the Rome of the first century before Christ and the England of the eighteenth century that members of the aristocracy had a natural right to the high offices of state. In both countries the people generally resented the ambitious intrusion of one of their own number into the sacred precincts of the governing class. In Rome it had become an axiom of politics that Providence always sent a great noble to the head of the poll. In an English county there might be rival candidates, each sponsored by a great family. The family's head might ride at the front of a cavalcade to the poll, hats streaming with ribbons of yellow or blue. His son or nephew aspiring to represent the constituency would address the electors: "Gentlemen, I offer myself. . . ." He might be cheered by supporters or he might be pelted with clods by members of the faction attached to the rival house. But he knew if he was defeated it would be by a candidate of his own class and not by some low-born outsider.

The methods by which the two aristocracies exercised control were very similar. In both England and Rome it was necessary for the nobles to dominate the popular legislative bodies. In each case the foundation of power, as has just been suggested, was social prestige. In England the situation was set forth in the old rhyme:

God bless the squire and his relations
And keep us all in our proper stations.

In Rome even the brilliant Cicero was ill at ease when he addressed a Roman of distinguished ancestry. His stilted letters to great nobles show his obsequious embarrassment.

But social prestige was not the sole reliance. More practical methods were at the command of the aristocracy of both countries in the very structure of government. In Britain the rotten boroughs constituted a major scandal until they were swept away by the Reform Bill of 1832. A considerable minority of these constituencies electing members to the House of Commons were the private property of the peers. The great parliamentary influence of the mediocre but industrious Duke of Newcastle was founded to a considerable extent on the fact that as one of the largest landowners in England he owned more members of the House than any other statesman. In other boroughs the few voters organized themselves into close corporations and offered their representation in the Commons to the highest bidder. There were regular borough-jobbers. Lord Chesterfield, applying to one to obtain a seat for his son for twenty-five hundred pounds, was informed that the demand had exhausted the supply. Rich nabobs from the East and West Indies had bulled the price to three or four thousand and none was left. Thus for many years before the industrial revolution it was generally possible for the great landed families, through the boroughs which they owned or could buy, to exercise a strong influence in the House of Commons.

In Rome the same ends were differently attained. While the Senate, dominated by the great families, was in theory a consultive body, in practice it came to direct the course and form of legislation and so was much more powerful than the House of Lords. Nevertheless final legislative authority lay in the two Assemblies. These had different structures and somewhat different functions. The differences in Cicero's time had become technical rather than practical. They need not concern us here. The organization and procedure of both played into the hands of the nobles.

The Assembly which did most of the legislating was based on thirty-five districts: four of them within the city, sixteen in the immediate vicinity, and fifteen in the suburban territory. Those Italians throughout the peninsula who were Roman citizens were registered in the various rural districts. If they desired to exercise the franchise, they had to go to Rome to vote; and Rome was a longer journey from southern Italy than Washington is from the Pacific coast. Besides, each district voted as a unit. If there were one hundred thousand voters in the capital, they could cast only four votes in the Assembly, one for each municipal district. This set-up left control to the voters registered in the thirty-one outlying districts. Farmers and business men from the towns, if they cared to travel to Rome, could have taken charge of legislation. Most of them ordinarily could not spare the time. So normally there was a slim attendance of outside voters. This gave the nobles their opportunity. Most of them were landowners, with the privilege of registering in any district where they owned land. In addition each family had numerous retainers and dependents who were registered with them in the rural districts. With these voters, who could be depended on to attend the Assembly whenever the word was passed, the nobles usually could be sure of carrying a majority of the thirty-five districts and so of determining the action of the Assembly.

The process of voting was simple. An informal open-air meeting (the *contio*) was held, at which the presiding magistrate explained the measures that were to come before the Assembly and invited officials and prominent citizens to discuss them. This was the only opportunity for debate. Then the meeting reconvened as the Assembly. The presiding officer stated the question and the voters separated into thirty-five groups by districts. Adjoining the place of meeting were enclosures, one for each district. After all the voters had gathered in the enclosures they filed out, giving their votes to tellers stationed on either side of the exit. A majority determined the vote of the district, which was at once reported to the magistrate in charge. The votes of eighteen or more districts carried or defeated a bill.

In the circumstances it was difficult to obtain a large attendance even when important questions were up. Cicero once remarked in a speech that he had seen a law enacted with only five voters to a district present, and some of these voted in other districts than those in which they were registered.

But there were occasions in both London and Rome

when the aristocratic control slipped and the legislative bodies got out of hand. In fact, in the House of Commons it was regularly necessary for the government to buy additional votes for hotly contested measures. "As for your rascals in the House of Commons," George I said to Walpole, "manage them as you please. I don't interfere with them." This minister once boasted that the defeat of a certain proposal had cost only nine hundred pounds. Of a group of M.P.'s he remarked: "All these have their price," and he complained that he was obliged to bribe members not to vote against, but for their conscience.

In the middle of the eighteenth century a member refused to take the leadership in the House of Commons unless the prime minister let him know how the secret-service fund was distributed. Without information as to which members were taking bribes he would be handicapped in dealing with the House.

Very similar conditions prevailed in Rome. In close votes in the Assembly certain districts might hold the balance of power and it was necessary to control these with money. There were even decayed noble houses that financed themselves on occasion by selling the votes of their retainers. Bribery was so common that a discussion of it and the means to circumvent it is given a conspicuous place in the very practical candidate's handbook that was sent to Cicero when he was running for consul by his younger brother Quintus. On one occasion Rome was upset by reports that the African prince Jugurtha had been able to bribe the Senate. Sallust, the historian who recounts the affair, says Jugurtha had a conviction that at Rome anything could be bought. He adds that when Jugurtha left the city he looked back at Rome in silence and finally said: "A city for sale and doomed to speedy destruction if it finds a purchaser." Sallust's picture and reports may have been overdrawn. Nevertheless money played an important part in emergencies in consolidating the authority of the nobles and their rich business allies over the Roman government.

If the House of Commons in spite of all the aristocratic controls proved completely intransigent because of a wave of public opinion, the House of Lords could finally exercise the veto power over legislation. If the Roman Senate disliked a bill, it could annul the legislation on the technical ground that the measure had been improperly passed. It could find that the meeting of the Assembly had been in the face of unfavourable omens. It might allege that intimidation had been used. It might discover other violations of the Constitution.

Another curious although minor parallel may be noted. " The theory of the statesmen of the first half of the eighteenth century," Lecky observes of the British system, " was that the electors had no right to know the proceedings of their representatives and it was only after a long and dangerous struggle which was not terminated until the reign of George III, that the right of printing debates was virtually conceded." The Roman senators of the first half of the first century before Christ had a similar opinion. The sessions of the Senate were not open to the public, although at times crowds listened at the doors. When Cæsar first became consul he fell into a bitter controversy with the Senate. Its unreasonable attitude forced him to appeal to the Assembly, which anyone might attend. Presumably in order to keep the public informed of the jockeying in the Senate, he introduced shorthand reporters and ordered that their record of the proceedings be published. Publication was by the posting of bulletins in the Forum. Out of these *Acta Diurna*, " Daily Doings," developed the Roman equivalent of the modern newspaper. Reporters circulating in the Forum copied the senatorial records, added bits of news and gossip, and sent their work to out-of-town subscribers.

For all these political similarities, a significant difference might have impressed the man from Rome. The Whig nobles were a high-living, hard-drinking lot, but their abounding energy overflowed into the public service. They took their obligations seriously. The great man felt a duty to the people who lived about his estates. He might be lord lieutenant of his county, responsible for order and generally determining the appointment of the magistrates. As a member of the governing class he might be a cabinet member, with a son in the House of Commons and another in the diplomatic corps. If he was summoned to London on public business he expected to respond as a matter of course. He was always self-confident and sometimes competent.

In the earlier days of Rome the same sense of responsibility permeated the old families. The great nobles and their ancestors had served the state in all its high offices. There was a time when the Senate was made up of ex-magistrates pre-eminent in experience and ability. With the flood of unearned wealth from eastern conquests the upper class had become soft and enervated. There was a general neglect of senatorial duties and indifference to public affairs except when the aristocrats felt that some of their prerogatives were being threatened. The "fishpond brigade," the indignant Cicero had called the indolent nobles who preferred a luxurious life on their country estates to the business of government in the capital.

Speakers in the Senate often found themselves addressing almost empty benches. Important resolutions sometimes went through with only a handful of members present. The thin Senate became such a public scandal that a law finally was enacted providing that for special-privilege legislation, which the Senate shared with the Assembly, at least two hundred of its six hundred members should be required for a quorum. In certain other cases also a quorum rule was imposed. The old governing class was becoming increasingly unequal to its job.

Thus, as we have seen, there were striking similarities between the Rome of Cicero and Georgian England: in physical conditions, in social life and modes of thought, in the fundamental structure of government. Republican Rome is not to be considered a museum piece, something far away and long ago. On the contrary, it was the product of a social order with which the England of the elder Pitt and the America of John Adams were quite familiar. Its major problems were those that already were beginning to develop in England and later were to develop in America from the transformation of an economy of agriculture into an economy of business.

There are modern historians who write of the moral laxity, the decay of the old standards of family life, the dissolute manners, the widespread political corruption of the last years of the Roman Republic as if these were unique instances of social depravity. They find in these defects the cause of the downfall of the Republic. Their indignation does credit to their moral sense. From the standpoint of historical judgment it leaves something to be desired. In retrospect the evils that confronted the English reformers of the eighteenth century seem almost as formidable as those that confronted the Roman reformers nineteen hundred years earlier. Yet one society was able to carry through into the liberal monarchy of the nineteenth century. The other failed in its task and was submerged by a growing autocracy that eventually extinguished freedom. The reasons for success in the one case, failure in the other, are a fascinating challenge to the student of history.

CHAPTER IV

THE COUNTRY BOY OF ARPINUM

MARCUS TULLIUS CICERO was born on January 3, 106 B.C.,[1] near Arpinum in the Volscian mountains, some sixty miles southeast of Rome. By taking the Naples line from Rome to Frosinone, the modern traveller follows the general course of the ancient Latin Way which Cicero took when he journeyed to his ancestral home. Thence the Sora autobus conveys him close to his destination. This is a small island in the delta of a mountain stream, the Fibrenus, where it joins the river Liris, coming down from the Apennines. A few hundred yards before it reaches the Liris, the Fibrenus, cold and clear as a Rocky Mountain brook, divides into three small branches enclosing two tiny islands. One of these branches is an artificial canal. There was only one island in Cicero's day. At the eastern end of the southern island stands the ancient monastery-church of S. Domenico. On this site or adjacent to it on what is now the northern island was the villa of Cicero. In the crypt of the church are sixteen marble columns which may have been taken from the villa. One arch still stands of the ancient bridge by which Cicero used to cross the Liris when he came from Rome.

The Fibrenus is still shaded by the poplars and alders under which Cicero loved to walk. A few miles away are hills and mountains which become lofty to the north and

[1] Except where otherwise specified all Roman dates are B.C.

are snow-capped in winter. Less than a mile to the south of the mouths of the Fibrenus the Liris divides around the island of Isola, with handsome cascades some eighty feet high. Three miles downstream, on a hill above the Liris, is the modern Arpino, Cicero's Arpinum, a town of four thousand inhabitants, still proudly conscious of its illustrious sons, Marius and Cicero, and of a third attributed to it by legend, Agrippa, the great minister of Augustus. Their busts are on the façade of the Tulliano high school, which faces the main piazza of Arpino.

In his treatise *On the Laws* Cicero has left a charming account of his birthplace. The book is cast in the form of a conversation. The participants are Marcus Cicero, his younger brother Quintus, and his devoted friend, business agent, and publisher Atticus, three years his senior and brother-in-law of Quintus. At the time assigned to the conversation the friends may have been in their late forties or early fifties. As they talk they are strolling along the Liris and it is assumed that the occasion is the first visit of Atticus to his friend's country villa. Both Marcus and Quintus have written poetry. The quick sensitiveness of Cicero, his response to the beauties of nature, the poetic side of the man, are revealed in his remarks, some of them put into the mouth of his brother.

Atticus opens the conversation by pointing to a grove in which stands an ancient oak and inquires whether this is not the grove and " the oak tree of Arpinum " of which he has read in one of Marcus' early poems, the " Marius."

" Yes, my dear Atticus," replies Quintus, " that oak tree lives and will live for ever; for it was planted by the imagination. No tree cared for by a farmer can be so long-lived as one planted by a poet's verses."

" How is that, Quintus? What sort of planting is it that poets do? "

" What sort of planting? Ah, need I tell you, Atticus, that so long as Latin literature shall live there will always be an oak tree on this spot called ' the Marian oak '? "

Cicero's idea of the immortality of verse is familiar to us through later writers. Horace uses it when he speaks of his poems as constituting " a monument more lasting than bronze." In one of the sonnets Shakespeare has the same thought:

> *Not marble, nor the gilded monuments*
> *Of princes, shall outlive this powerful rhyme.*

But the prosaic Atticus is not satisfied. He wants to know whether the incident connected with the oak tree in the poem is fact or fancy. He is inclined to sympathize with those hard-headed persons who insist that a poem about a historical character such as Marius should stick to facts.

Marcus is impatient with such a pedestrian outlook. Persons, he says, who expect a poet to be as careful of the truth as a witness in court are merely displaying their ignorance. They would take all the poetry and romance out of the legends that are the heritage of Rome. The poet is not supposed to be a historian. The standard for history is truth, for poetry pleasure.

The mention of history impels Atticus to suggest that Cicero might well undertake a history of Rome. Marcus replies he is too busy; he has only " odds and ends of time." Then it occurs to his friend that in the present " odds and ends of time " he might give his views on his specialty, the civil law. Thus by pleasant and informal steps Cicero leads up to the theme of his book. He continues the popular nature of his treatise by the fiction of a walk along the river in the course of which he gives delightful glimpses of the setting of his boyhood home.

" We might walk here by the Liris," says Atticus, " in the shade along its bank."

" Very well," Cicero replies, " your beloved Plato used to discuss problems while walking in cypress groves and forest paths. We might do the same, strolling among these stately poplars on the green and shady riverbank."

The discussion proceeds until they reach the delta of

CICERO'S ISLAND BIRTHPLACE NEAR ARPINUM

The painting by Richard Wilson, eighteenth-century British landscape painter who lived for several years in Italy, shows Marcus and Quintus Cicero and Atticus beside the Liris looking at the Marian oak. Beyond them is the bridge to the island formed by two branches of the Fibrenus, where stands the remodelled farmhouse in which Cicero was born. (Courtesy of the Findlay Galleries, Inc., Chicago)

the Fibrenus. Atticus then suggests they have walked far enough and that they should cross to a little island just beyond them where they might sit while they finish the conversation. This is the island where Cicero was born, although the book assumes that Atticus is ignorant of the fact.

" By all means," says Marcus. " That island is a favourite haunt of mine for meditation, reading, and writing."

Atticus is enthusiastic over its rustic beauty. He cannot get enough of the place, he says, and he wonders how Cicero can go anywhere else when he is able to get away from Rome.

" Indeed," his host replies, " whenever it is possible for me to be out of town for several days, I do come to this lovely and healthful spot." He explains that it is his birthplace, his " fatherland." " Yonder you see our homestead as it is now – rebuilt and extended by my father. As he was an invalid he spent most of his life in study there. It was on this very spot in a small cottage that I was born while my grandfather was alive. So I have a lingering attachment to the place."

They leave this island and walk up the little stream for a mile to another island which today roughly answers the description given by Atticus: " Really nothing could be more charming. It cuts the Fibrenus like the beak of a ship, and the Fibrenus, divided into two parts, flows swiftly past and then comes quickly together again, leaving only enough space for a wrestling-ground. Then after accomplishing this, as if its only function were to provide us with a seat for our discussion, it plunges into the Liris."

The same coldness from its mountain source that travellers notice today was remarked on by Atticus. " I never have come upon a river which was colder," he says. " I could hardly bear to put my foot in it."

A fragment of the book preserved by a later writer tells how the friends in the late afternoon of the Italian summer decide to leave the island and go back to the shady bank of the Liris. " Now that the sun is no longer straight above us and our place here is not wholly shaded by these young trees, would it not be better to go down to the Liris and pursue our discussion in the cool shade of the alders? "

Thus in a serious treatise on government Cicero provides us with a vivid picture of the surroundings in which his boyhood was spent, with glimpses of a spirit keenly aware of the loveliness of trees and rushing streams. In the letters of his later years he constantly goes affectionately back to his boyhood home —

A rugged soil, yet nurse of hardy sons;
No dearer land can e'er my eyes behold.

So he writes to his friend Atticus, quoting from the *Odyssey.* His villa there, he says, is so remote that it gives him shelter from the bores who flock about him when he is accessible. One hot September day he writes to his brother Quintus in Britain that he has escaped from Rome — " I never remember greater heat " — to refresh himself at Arpinum and enjoy the loveliness of the river. " In Rome there is no time to breathe." A few weeks after the death of his beloved daughter Tullia he writes to Atticus from Arpinum that he has gone there " to find streams and solitary spots, the easier to keep up my spirits." But the violent and persistent rains have kept him indoors. So he occupies himself — for he is always a tremendous worker — in revising one of his philosophic treatises, the *Academics.* Two days later he tells Atticus that the three historic characters who conduct the discussion in the book are inappropriately cast. It is " more learned than anything that they would seem likely ever to have dreamed of." So he is recasting the treatise to put the words into the mouths of more accomplished men.

His neighbours in the little town are close to his heart and he looks after their affairs. The community gets its public revenues from lands it owns in the province of northern Italy. On one occasion he writes to his friend Marcus

Junius Brutus, governor of the province, telling him of the situation and of his especial interest in it. The letter is to let the governor know that a commission has been sent from Arpinum to visit the town's estates, collect the rents due, and " generally to investigate and provide for the management of the whole property." He hopes " in the name of our friendship " that the governor will facilitate the business. To emphasize his own concern he informs Brutus that he has consented to allow his son and nephew to be chosen the chief magistrates of Arpinum for the year in order to put the municipality's affairs in order.

While Roman snobs referred scornfully to his country origin — " an alien resident in the city of Rome " — Cicero always took pride in the place of his birth, and indeed in the country towns of Italy generally. In one of his cases in court the attorney against him, a brash young chap running for office, taunted him with being a " foreigner."

" Why have you called me a foreigner? " Cicero demanded.

" You come from a country town."

" I admit it," replied the distinguished attorney. " From a town from which salvation has twice come to this city and state." His reference, as all his hearers knew, was to the salvation of Rome first by Marius of Arpinum from invasion by the Germans, and second by Cicero himself from the conspiracy of Catiline. And he went on to warn the lawyer-candidate not to call his rivals foreigners or he would be " buried beneath foreign votes."

Cicero sprang from one of the old and well-to-do families of Arpinum, and his roots drove deep into the soil. But his was a provincial name not known in the capital and when he first ran for office some of his friends urged him to change it. He refused. " I will make my name," he proudly replied, " more glorious than the great names of Rome " — a precedent for General Junot's famous answer to the inquiry about his ancestry: " *Moi, je suis mon ancêtre.*"

The family came from the upper middle class and was

in more than comfortable circumstances. It belonged to a social order — the Equestrian, of which I shall speak later — which included citizens with property worth at least $20,000. Even today this would be a modest fortune for a farmer of one of the American prairie states. According to tradition Cicero's father was proprietor of a fuller's establishment, the equivalent of a modern laundry. In later years the Arpinum estate included tenant farms, some of which may have been part of the original homestead.

The grandfather, also named Marcus Tullius, whose property Cicero inherited through his father, another Marcus Tullius, was a thorough-going conservative, as were all solid Roman citizens. In his time the Greek language and culture were becoming fashionable in high society. The old gentleman detested the Greeks. Syrian slaves were coming on the market from Greek dealers. " Our people," the elder Cicero grumbled, " are like the Syrian slaves; the more Greek they know, the greater scoundrels they are."

Any innovation he found obnoxious. When his brother-in-law introduced a measure to reform the voting system of Arpinum the elder Cicero's vigorous fight against it attracted attention in Rome. He discovered a kindred spirit in one of the conservative consuls. " Marcus Cicero," said the official, " I could wish you had chosen to dedicate your efforts to the national welfare with the same spirit and energy you have shown in the affairs of a small town."

Any change was to be resisted. The typical Roman of the day would have approved Tennyson's lines:

> *A land of settled government,*
> *A land of just and old renown,*
> *Where Freedom slowly broadens down*
> *From precedent to precedent.*

Cicero speaks of his semi-invalid and studious father as a wise and excellent man and refers to his earnest perseverance in the education of his sons. His considerable acquaintance with some of the leading citizens of Rome testifies to his intelligence and standing. Marcus recalled years later some of his father's conversations with him and his brother. The qualities of the " good man," for instance, were discussed in the home.

The older Cicero lived to see his son the leader of the Roman bar and a rising star in politics, although he died when Marcus was only thirty-eight and before he had attained his supreme ambition, the consulship. There has been comment on the fact that Cicero mentions his father's death in a single sentence in a letter to Atticus: " My poor father died on November the 27th." But it is quite possible, as has been suggested, that the death had been announced in a previous letter now lost and that in this letter Cicero was merely giving the date, perhaps in reply to an inquiry by Atticus.

Cicero does not mention his mother Helvia in any of his writings now extant. Plutarch, from whom we learn her name, says she was well born and lived an unblemished life. Her son Quintus gives a glimpse of her matronly thrift in a letter to Marcus' secretary, Tiro. Slaves, he says, often used to steal wine from their masters' casks. His mother would seal all the casks, the empty as well as the full. If any was found empty and unsealed she would know the contents had been stolen.

In after life Cicero showed the effects of his father's training in his interest in ethical problems. His mother's carefulness made little impression. He was often careless about money.

We know nothing about Marcus' boyhood in his country home. There may have been elementary schools in Arpinum. Plutarch indeed describes Cicero as the youthful prodigy of a school. But as a biographer Plutarch displays some of the highly moral characteristics of Parson Weems in writing of George Washington, and the story of the hero-worship of young Marcus suggests the cherry tree and hatchet incident reported by Weems.

The schools of republican Italy were private, not public. The Republic was too thoroughly imbued with laissez-faire to establish a system of public education. Roman leaders would have joined with Governor Berkeley of seventeenth-century Virginia in thanking God " we have no free schools," and with Herbert Spencer of nineteenth-century England in referring to free public education as the entering wedge of " the coming slavery " of socialism.

A century before Cicero's time Polybius, then a resident of Rome, criticized the lack of a public-school system. Quoting the criticism in one of his books, Cicero replies that the Romans did not care to have an educational system " fixed by law or artificially established, or uniform in all cases." His argument is precisely that urged in the United States against establishing a federal department of education with a member of the cabinet as its head.

This does not mean that elementary schooling was neglected. There are frequent references to schools in the legendary annals of Rome. It was on a passage in Livy that Macaulay based his lines:

And blithely young Virginia came smiling from her home;
Ah! woe for young Virginia, the sweetest maid in Rome!
With her small tablets in her hand, and her satchel on her arm,
Forth she went bounding to the school, nor dreamed of shame or harm.

The children were taught the three R's at home or in private schools, conducted usually in Cicero's time by a Greek slave or freedman who charged a nominal fee. While there are no statistics on literacy, it seems a fair assumption that the people generally could read and write. Polybius says that in the Roman armies the watchword was inscribed on a wooden tablet which was passed around. When Hannibal captured Tarentum, according to Polybius he ordered the inhabitants to write their nationality on the doors of their houses, to distinguish them from the Romans. Evidently soldiers and townspeople alike had at least the rudiments of an education.

Other evidence of general literacy is found in tombstone inscriptions and in scribblings on walls. Excavations at Pompeii, which was overwhelmed by the eruption of Vesuvius a little more than a century after Cicero's death, have revealed approximately fifteen thousand such wall scribblings. "Everybody writes on the walls but me," one of them reads. Alphabets are scratched on the lower parts of the walls that could be reached by children. Some of them are written backwards as well as forwards. Maxims and other school exercises appear. Similar scribblings have been found elsewhere in the Empire, including far-off Britain. The evidence prompts an English historian to conclude: "There is reason to believe that in the lands ruled by Rome education was better under the Empire than at any time since its fall until the nineteenth century."

True, these scribblings belong to the century after Cicero. But when Cicero visited his Pompeian villa, presumably he saw the same sort of scribblings on the walls of buildings that have been revealed by the excavations.

The chances are that Marcus and Quintus followed the practice of many well-to-do Roman families and studied under their father, who gave them the rudiments of an education together with the training in the fundamentals of Roman citizenship that was traditionally stressed in family life. Perhaps it was to this period that Marcus referred when he wrote regretfully later: "We learned the Law of the Twelve Tables in our boyhood as a required formula, though no one learns it nowadays." The Law of the Twelve Tables, the first written code of Roman law, was venerated in the great days of the Republic as the Catechism was venerated in America a hundred years ago.

But the time came when Cicero *père* felt his sons needed the instruction that could be obtained only in the big city. He bought a house in the capital.

CHAPTER V

HE MOVES TO THE BIG CITY

THE HOUSE which the elder Cicero acquired was in keeping with the substantial position of the family. It was on the Carinæ, the southwestern slope of the Esquiline Hill near the present Church of S. Pietro in Vincoli, which all travellers visit to see Michelangelo's huge statue of Moses, double-starred in Baedeker. " Carinæ " means " keels " and the name came from buildings that looked like the keels of ships, evidently designed by an architect of modernistic tendencies. A writer two centuries later refers to the district in the old days as being " the most fashionable quarter of the capital." This was hardly true at the time the Cicero family took up its residence there. The region was beginning to show the signs of social decay with which we are familiar in American cities. The period was one of transition, and ambitious families were anxious to move over to the swankier neighbourhood on the Palatine. The famous Pompey lived on the Carinæ. But he wanted larger grounds, which he acquired on the east side of the modern Corso, extending up the slope of the Pincian Hill, where he built a finer house. After Pompey's death Mark Antony took over the Carinæ house until he could obtain a suitable mansion on the Palatine. When Cicero had become famous and as soon as he could afford a more pretentious house — as soon, that is, as he could borrow the money — he moved into the fashionable quarter. The estate cost him $175,000. In one of his letters he refers with pride to the call made by a great

Roman lady upon his wife in the new home. The house on the Carinæ went to his brother Quintus, who eventually became sufficiently affluent to rent the place and follow Marcus to the Palatine. We have the record of another young blade, Cælius, a friend of Cicero's, who rented a house on the Palatine at a bargain in order, Cicero says, to be near the Forum and the more easily " to visit us at our houses and to receive visits from his friends." The most luxurious place on the fashionable hill was that bought by Clodius, a suspiciously wealthy politician, for $750,000; a price, Pliny says, worthy of the madness of kings.

Still there was good society in the modest neighbourhood of the Carinæ when the Cicero family went to Rome. The family's most remarkable neighbour, although the Ciceros did not know it at the time, was young Julius Cæsar. He came of a decayed noble family whose home was in the adjacent low ground of the Subura, which was largely given over to shops. Later, when Cæsar had become a distinguished statesman and general engaged in the conquest of Gaul, his enemies tried to terminate his Gallic command. Cicero helped block the move by a strong speech in the Senate in which he referred to his long acquaintance with Cæsar and " that period of familiarity and intimacy " between Cæsar and Marcus and his brother " from the time that we were all young men " – probably, that is, when the Ciceros lived in their modest home on the Carinæ and Cæsar around the corner.

The world capital to which Cicero went as a boy was not the magnificent city of Augustus and the Empire. But its reconstruction was to begin in his lifetime under the master builders Sulla, Pompey, and Julius Cæsar. It is estimated that in the last three decades of the Republic more money was spent on public buildings than had been spent in the previous four centuries. As the Greek geographer Strabo wrote in the reign of Augustus: " The early Romans made little account of the beauty of Rome because they were occupied with other greater and more necessary matters;

whereas the later Romans, and particularly those of today and of my time, have filled the city with many beautiful structures." If the lad Cicero had climbed the low Capitoline Hill, a hundred feet above the Tiber, he would have looked out on the Forum and the great city extending beyond. World travellers would have found it drab in spite of its white walls and red tile roofs. Some of the cities of the East were much more splendid. But Rome would doubtless have impressed the boy from the country.

Most of the dwellings and shops were constructed of sun-dried brick, usually protected from the weather by a coat of whitewash. After the republican period came concrete walls faced with kiln-baked brick for the more pretentious buildings. These walls were sometimes covered with marble slabs, to which Augustus referred when he wrote near the end of his career that he had found Rome brick and had left it marble — or, more accurately, marble veneer. The streets were crooked and usually not more than twelve or fifteen feet wide. The more important were paved with stone blocks. High tenements, to which I shall refer in a moment, gave a canyon-like effect. Across the valley on the Palatine the young Cicero would have seen the show places of the nobility. A few such houses he might have noted on the other hills upon which Rome was built. The poor, as always, swarmed in the low ground.

The buildings in the Forum, most of them old, were not yet the fine edifices of the next century. The most imposing of the public buildings was the ancient Temple of Jupiter on the Capitoline. It was to burn a few years later and to be replaced by a more elaborate structure. Outside the city he would have seen the broad meadow of the Campus Martius, the Field of Mars, lying in the upper loop of the great letter S made by the Tiber. This was an athletic field and a voting-place of the popular Assemblies. Writing early in the next century, Strabo gives a pleasant description of the Campus, green with grass throughout the year and of such size that it afforded space simultaneously for chariot races and other equestrian sports and "also for that multitude of people who exercise themselves by ball-playing, hoop-trundling, and wrestling." The Circus of Flaminius already stood there. Later, in Cicero's lifetime, Pompey was to erect on the Campus the first stone theatre of Rome; in its adjoining hall Cæsar was to be murdered.

On the island in the Tiber close to the Capitoline the boy would have observed the Temple of Æsculapius, the God of Healing, a sort of primitive hospital. Just below it he would have been thrilled to recognize an ancient wooden bridge, the Pons Sublicius. He would have recalled the legend of how Horatius kept the bridge in the brave days of old when Lars Porsena of Clusium with "false Sextus that wrought the deed of shame" moved on Rome at the head of the Tuscan host and was blocked at the Pons Sublicius by the "dauntless Three" headed by Horatius, until the bridge could be hewed down by the city's defenders. Descending from the hill, Cicero could have passed through the old cattle market and have come to the chief amusement place of the city, the huge Circus Maximus, where the horse races were run. Retracing his steps around the base of the Palatine, he would have entered the Forum, the centre of business and public life. Here he would have found the old Senate house, the rostra from which in after life he was often to speak, the law courts, the banking and mercantile houses. It was a place of bustling crowds. The eastern entrance, spanned by the Arch of the Fabii, was a veritable bottleneck. In one of his speeches Cicero refers to being "knocked about in the crowd at the arch."

By the last century of the Republic Rome had become a meeting-place for people of all nations and it was a cosmopolitan throng that jostled in the Forum. Later writers enumerate the various classes of people who frequented it: scholars, painters, animal-trainers, rope-walkers, astrologers, magicians, shrewd and shifty Greeks and Syrians, black Numidians, and Gauls wearing those queer trousers that scandalized all sensible Romans, who knew that the toga was the proper garb of civilization.

But it was not only in the Forum that the boy Cicero would have found crowds. The narrow streets were jammed with the population of the great city. One of the writers to whom I have just referred tells of his experiences when out for a walk: " We are blocked by a surging crowd in front and by a dense mass of people pressing in on us from behind. One man digs an elbow into me, another a sedan pole; one bangs a beam, another a wine cask against my head. My legs are beplastered with mud. Huge feet trample on me from every side and a soldier plants his hobnails firmly upon my toe." One hundred and fifty years before the Ciceros moved to Rome a great lady was caught in a traffic blockade. A Roman fleet under her brother's command had suffered heavy losses in a severe defeat in the first war with Carthage. She was overheard to say that she wished her brother was still alive and able to lose another battle so that some of the superfluous people could be cleared off the streets. Plebeian magistrates, deficient in a sense of humour, brought her to trial for the remark and she was fined. The traffic problem finally became so acute that the use of trucks in the daylight hours was severely restricted.

For a stranger or even an old resident to find his way about in the labyrinthine maze of the Roman streets presented difficulties in broad daylight. At night the unlighted and unmarked streets must have been baffling. In his novel of Roman life and manners in the next century Petronius tells of the struggles of three friends to reach their inn after a jolly dinner party. They had no torch and it " was midnight, as silent as a grave, and we had no hope of meeting anyone with a light." They stumbled about for an hour, cutting their feet on rough flints and broken pottery. But one of the party had taken the precaution to go over the route the day before and indicate the way by chalk marks on pillars and columns. Finally they picked up the markers, which showed white in the inky darkness, and so were able to reach their destination.

The city was extremely noisy. Complaints have come down to us about the bawling of hucksters, the cries of beggars, the banging of hammers, the clatter of wagons at night, so that only the wealthy in their secluded homes could sleep. Presumably noise was regarded as one of the necessary evils of city life — noise and the inevitable stenches.

The Rome of Cicero's day was abundantly supplied with water from four celebrated aqueducts. "Veritable rivers," Strabo remarks, "flow through the city." The Greeks, he adds admiringly, had nothing like them or like the remarkable system of sewers. Visitors may still see on the left bank of the Tiber the mouth of the great Cloaca Maxima, constructed more than two thousand years ago.

The drains served the double purpose of carrying off storm waters and sewage. The dwellings had primitive latrines — seats above a channel flushed with water. Usually the connection was with a cesspool, though some were connected with the main sewers. These private water supplies were confined to the ground floors. The upper floors of apartments were indescribably filthy. We hear of public comfort stations a century later. It is reasonable to suppose that they existed in Cicero's time. They were much like the comfort stations on the boulevards of Paris, but were provided with marble seats. There were sewer connections, and the odours from the manholes must have been offensive. Besides, if we may judge from modern Rome and Naples, there were plenty of men who did not trouble to go to the comfort stations, and we can imagine the resulting smells.

Refuse and slops were emptied into the streets. The householder was responsible for cleaning the street in front of his premises under the supervision of a commissioner of public works. It was easier to depend on the rains to do the job.

Worst of all were the public cemeteries where the poor were buried without cremation. The largest potter's field was on the Esquiline, near the present Piazza Vittorio Emanuele, not far south of the Terminal Station. Bodies of slaves, beggars, and prisoners and carcasses of beasts were dumped into uncovered pits. The stench was intolerable. In the early Empire Mæcenas, prime minister for Augustus, had the whole cemetery buried under a blanket of earth twenty-four feet deep, upon which he laid out gardens. So great was the improvement that it was celebrated by his friend Horace in verse:

And now we breathe a purer air
And walk the sunny terrace fair,
Where once the ground with bones was white —
With human bones, a ghastly sight.

Ciceronian Rome must have stunk. There is no other word. But human beings accustom themselves to what they regard as necessary discomforts and it is quite possible that the ancient capital was little more odoriferous than London and Paris before nineteenth-century sanitation. The prevalent indifference to public hygiene may be inferred from a remark of Cicero's that the site of Rome was "salubrious in a pestilential region." He probably referred to the scourge of malaria in the surrounding plain. But the malaria-bearing mosquitoes infested the city and Cicero must have been familiar with the three temples to the Goddess of Fever upon which the people depended in lieu of quinine. Even the eminent were not spared. The frequent illnesses of the Emperor Augustus have been diagnosed by a German physician as attacks of malaria.

A great cosmopolitan centre such as Rome necessarily was supplied with plenty of gambling-places and bawdy-houses. The taverns in the city and indeed throughout Italy had a bad name. For travelling the well-to-do liked to have their own lodges where they could spend the night. If that was impossible they tried to arrange their journeys so as to stay with friends. An inscription from a provincial town cites a traveller's bill that includes twelve cents for a night with a chambermaid. A poster found at Pompeii notifies the passer-by that three young women are attached to the establishment. Similar customs prevailed in the capital.

Rome was a city of violent contrasts. A few thousand wealthy nobles and members of the upper business class lived luxuriously. The masses were submerged in extreme poverty. There was a large foreign element, including slaves, freedmen, and descendants of slaves. The size of the population can only be guessed. Estimates run from six hundred thousand to upwards of a million, with perhaps two hundred thousand slaves.

A city of the size of Rome would require of course not only a large amount of food, but housing, clothing, furniture, and other necessaries of life. We lack government reports and Chamber of Commerce statistics, but there is evidence of intense business activity, small-scale industry, trade with the outside world, banking and financial operations. Wheat was imported from abroad by sea and brought up the Tiber to the warehouses on the river at the base of the Aventine. It was processed in large bakeries. The entire procedure is pictured on the monument of a proud baker near the Porta Maggiore. If Cicero as a boy had been attracted into such an establishment he would have seen the grain cleaned and sifted, then ground by horses in a mill, the dough kneaded by a machine turned by a donkey, and the loaves baked and distributed. There must have been a multitude of small shops making textiles and clothing, and manufacturing and repairing military equipment. In industries where capital was required, as in tanning leather, treating and cleansing cloth, and producing luxury furniture and plumbing equipment, an incipient factory system developed. There were extensive yards to furnish the sun-dried brick and the tile required for houses.

Inscriptions indicate that most of the workmen were slaves. Still there is evidence of the existence of numerous guilds of free workmen, like the Worshipful Companies of old London. The Carpenters' Guild, for instance, was important. More than forty guilds of professional craftsmen have been identified. Presumably the names of certain streets, such as Shoemakers Street, Harness-Makers Street, Glass Street, indicate districts of small independent industries. Outside of Rome, but connected with the capital by many ties, specialized industries developed. There was almost mass production of pottery, the famous Arretine ware, at Arezzo, one hundred and twenty-five miles northwest of Rome. One factory employed forty designers, and its products went all over the world. Capua, something more than one hundred miles to the southeast, became the centre of copper and bronze manufacture. Puteoli, near Naples, became a large iron centre. Imports from foreign countries poured into Puteoli and Rome – metals, wool, hides, leather, ivory, spices, glassware, rugs. There were exports of wine, olive oil, and pottery. But the balance of trade was maintained to a large degree by tribute and interest on loans from the provinces.

Wages were kept close to the subsistence level by competition from slave labour and by the small output that could be produced without the help of machines. The standard of living was extremely low. Professor Tenney Frank estimates that a labourer might earn twenty cents a day. The wheat for his bread was furnished by the government at a fair price, and after the year 58 as a dole. Meat was beyond his reach, but vegetables were so abundant that meat was not missed. He could afford cabbages, beets, turnips, chestnuts, figs, lentils, and cheese and a little cheap wine and olive oil. He wore no shoes, and his tunic probably did not cost more than a dollar a year. A room in a slum tenement might be had at a dollar and a half a month. In short, his condition was probably not very different from that of the poor man in the slums of Rome or Naples within the memory of men still living. Games were provided free and there were public baths with an admittance charge of a fraction of a cent. A great gulf separated the very few rich from the very many poor. While the well-to-do furnished daily hand-outs to a multitude of hangers-on, the situation lent itself admirably to politicians who were ready to exploit human wretchedness for their own ends.

It must be borne in mind that the best people regarded trade and manual work as low — "unbecoming to a gentleman," as Cicero wrote to his son. "All mechanics," he said, "are engaged in vulgar occupations." Wholesale trade he thought respectable, but agriculture was best of all. Here spoke the authentic voice of a society long dominated by the landed gentry.

This mental atmosphere was not conducive to the development of industry. There were other obstacles in addition to the general attitude of high society. The Roman roads had been extended in the later years of the Republic, but except for certain articles the cost of land transportation was prohibitive. Fuel was expensive and the national temper not inventive. With an abundant supply of cheap labour, the incentive to devise labour-saving machinery was lacking. It was difficult to obtain capital for industrial purposes. The corporate form of doing business was familiar but regarded with distrust and its field was limited. The Romans believed in individual responsibility. They were as suspicious of big business as many Americans are today. The organizing of corporations to engage in industry was forbidden. However, joint-stock companies were permitted to handle public contracts for roads, public buildings, the operation of mines, and in certain provinces tax-collections. There was prejudice against government in business although the government intervened at times when the contractors proved inefficient or dishonest. Besides, the principle of rotation in office was fundamental in the Roman Republic. With official terms usually limited to one year it was impossible to develop trained staffs of public servants competent to take charge of public works.

A century before the birth of Cicero a law had been

enacted that virtually barred senators from direct participation in foreign trade. Senators and their sons were forbidden to own ships of seagoing size. The purpose was to prevent members of the governing class from having private financial interests that might influence their public policy. Also they were prohibited from taking state contracts. One result was to force the noble families to invest more largely in landed estates. Another was to expand the market for the shares of the joint-stock companies organized by the business men. These shares were traded in widely in the exchanges in the Forum. " One may almost say," Polybius writes, " that everyone is interested in these contracts and the work they involve."

How extensive these interests were is indicated in a famous speech of Cicero's. In the province of Asia — western Asia Minor — there had been a bloody uprising and a general massacre of the Italian business men and their families settled there. It was proposed to entrust Pompey with the command against King Mithridates, who had instigated the uprising. Supporting the proposal, Cicero spoke of the " vast sums invested in the province." " Coinciding with the loss by many people of large fortunes in Asia," he said, " we know there was a collapse of credit in Rome owing to the suspension of payments. It is impossible for many individuals in a state to lose their property and fortunes without involving still greater numbers in their own ruin. The system of credit and finance which operates at Rome in the Forum is bound up with and depends on capital invested in Asia. The loss of the one inevitably undermines the other and causes its collapse."

Investments were not confined to Asia. All the newly acquired provinces attracted Roman business men. On another occasion Cicero remarked, doubtless with considerable exaggeration: " No Gaul ever does business independently of a citizen of Rome; not a penny changes hands in Gaul without an entry in some Roman account book."

Banking operations, which generally meant money-lending, were carried on by the financiers of Rome on a considerable scale. Money was lent not only to individuals, but to provincial cities to meet their requirements for tribute money and other purposes. Interest rates were often extortionate and sometimes led to open scandals.

The men involved in these transactions and those of which Cicero was speaking constituted only a fraction of the population. The great bulk of the inhabitants of the capital, as I have said, lived in poverty. Because of the congestion in a large city without transportation facilities, the housing problem was particularly acute. Most of the people had to live in apartments or tenements, as is explained by Vitruvius in the standard work on architecture of the time, " because of the greatness of the city and the unlimited crowding of the citizens." Some of the apartments for the well-to-do were expensive. Cælius, of whom I have spoken, rented an apartment for $1,500 a year before he moved to the Palatine. The poor had to live in crowded tenements five or six storeys high.

The building restrictions as described by Vitruvius evidently were influenced by the landlords, who desired to build as cheaply as possible. But he suggests that there were fine views to be had from the upper storeys and that the people in general had " excellent dwellings." This rosy account is not borne out by Plutarch, who says the tenements often burned or collapsed. People lived, a satirist wrote later, " in perpetual dread of fires and falling houses and the thousand perils of this terrible city." Strabo speaks of building going on " unceasingly because of collapses and fires," and mentions the fact that the Emperor Augustus was obliged to restrict the height of buildings to seventy feet. Plutarch tells a curious story of Crassus, the richest man in Rome. Crassus collected a fire brigade of five hundred trained slaves. It was his practice to go to fires and buy for a song houses that were burning and those in the neighbourhood that were threatened. Then his slaves would put out the fire. So, says his biographer, " the greater part of Rome at one time or another came into his hands." This successful speculator had an interesting business theory, familiar in our day, that there is no money in rental property. Apparently he would promptly sell at a profit the houses and lots he had acquired at distress prices. " He used to say that men who were addicted to building would ruin themselves soon enough without the help of other enemies."

The first stirring of discontent among the underprivileged masses had begun to show itself in politics a few years before Cicero's birth. Violent outbursts became ominously frequent. These were not recognized by the well-to-do for what they were: the symptoms of a deep-seated social malady.

The poor hardly existed for the circle to which Cicero belonged except as a mob which could be stirred to rioting by some demagogue, and as a political force whose members could be held in line for wealthy patrons through the dispensing of household charity. When Cicero got into politics we shall see the problem that confronted him and other politicians in dealing with those to whom he publicly referred with great respect, but privately regarded as extremely undesirable citizens who unfortunately had to be reckoned with. It was necessary to keep them alive by charity. But so far as their welfare was concerned these people no more entered into the life and thought of the upper classes than they entered into the life and thought of the aristocratic society of eighteenth-century England or of certain parts of society in twentieth-century America.

CHAPTER VI

DINING OUT WITH FRIENDS

FROM THE physical and business aspects of Rome we may turn to its intellectual background. Like the aristocratic English society the society of Rome of the first century B.C. to which Cicero belonged was civilized and urbane. It was the first really urbane society of history. Unlike Greek society, women as well as men moved freely in it. The similarities to modern times are so great that we must not forget the differences. Roman culture had developed only recently under the Greek influence that had come flooding in during the second century before Christ. It was a far newer society than that of the great Whig families of England. Many of the ideas and customs that the English took for granted would have been wholly foreign to the Romans. Many of the practices accepted by the Romans, or that occasionally cropped out, had long since faded from English life. The mass of the people were still grossly superstitious. In the last two hundred and fifty years of the Republic ancient writers cite human sacrifices on four different occasions to propitiate the unseen powers. The practice was abolished by law in 97, when Cicero was nine years old. Nevertheless Roman writers of the first century of our era imply that "these horrid rites," as the elder Pliny calls human sacrifices, continued in private.

Still in considering Roman superstition we should not forget the Salem witches or that the execution of witches in England was not forbidden until early in the eighteenth century. Even in the twentieth century human sacrifices have been reported from the backwoods of America. High culture and gross superstition have co-existed throughout human history.

On the general subject of the latent brutality in a society externally civilized we must include the ghastly massacres in the Roman civil wars and the gladiatorial combats. Late nineteenth-century British historians were shocked by the record of wholesale murders and proscriptions. They were sure that civilization had left these horrors behind because, as Anthony Trollope wrote in his *Cæsar*, "the coming of Christ has changed all things." The vast brutalities of twentieth-century Europe were beyond their imagining.

Gladiatorial combats in the Forum, the Circus Maximus, and later in the Colosseum, were introduced into Rome in the middle of the third century before Christ. They were a survival from the primitive religion of the Etruscans, Rome's immediate neighbours to the north. After a nobleman's death his retainers and slaves killed one another in fights at the funeral ceremonies so he would have a proper escort to the lower world. In Rome these combats rapidly developed into great and bloody public spectacles. But they were complacently accepted as any customary practice is accepted.

Even so humane and cultured a man as Cicero could write: "A gladiatorial show is apt to seem cruel and brutal to some eyes, and I incline to think it is so as now conducted. But in the days when it was criminals who crossed swords in the death struggle, there could be no better schooling against pain and death, at any rate for the eye." In somewhat similar vein Boswell quotes Dr. Johnson as saying: "I am sorry that prize-fighting is gone out. . . . Prize-fighting made people accustomed not to be alarmed at seeing their own blood or feeling a little pain from a wound." National softness was abhorrent to both the Roman and the Englishman.

Augustus, the brilliant world-organizer, felt it necessary to cater to popular tastes in the customary way. It is recorded that he usually watched the games in the circus, " even in company with his wife and children." Whenever he was present he " gave his entire attention to the performance " for two reasons, the chronicler says. Not only did he frankly confess his " interest and pleasure in the spectacles," but he recalled that his predecessor Cæsar, who seems to have been bored by them, was widely criticized for reading and writing while the performances were in progress. Only one flicker of pity came from Augustus. He forbade the practice of forcing the gladiators to fight to the death. Under his ruling the vanquished were allowed to appeal to the crowd for quarter, which sometimes was given to popular favourites.

Another unfortunate influence in Rome and Italy was the existence of slavery. It not only kept down wages, as I have said previously, but tended to demoralize masters and mistresses. On the great estates in the country districts slaves were cruelly treated. In the capital the treatment was generally humane. Some of Cicero's most sympathetic letters are to a former slave, his valued secretary, Tiro. Public sentiment did not countenance harsh treatment, and slaves were constantly given or allowed to buy their freedom. Under the developing enlightenment of the imperial period the legal position of the slaves was progressively improved. But the " peculiar institution " had bad repercussions in Rome, as in America.

Bearing on the culture of the age was the comparative newness of Latin literature. There was a much longer native literary tradition behind the English society of the eighteenth century than behind the Roman society of Cicero. Its cultural background was thin. The first Latin poet died less than a century before Cicero was born. He was followed by a small group of writers, the poet Ennius, whom Cicero often quotes, the dramatists Plautus and Terence, whom American students read in college, and a few others. But in comparison to the Greek writers who were read in Rome, the Latin authors constituted only a handful. A scholar has gone to the trouble of listing the Greek and Roman writers referred to by Cicero. There were one hundred and sixty-seven Greek to only twenty-nine Roman. We must think of Ciceronian society as having a predominantly foreign literary tradition.

The first really cultivated social group in Rome, known to us as the Scipionic circle, antedated Cicero by only half a century. It gathered about the famous soldier, statesman, and literary gentleman, the younger Scipio, who destroyed Carthage. Polybius, who was with him at the time, records that the general turned to him and, grasping his hand, exclaimed: " A glorious moment, Polybius; but I have a foreboding that some day the same doom will be pronounced on my own country." A later Greco-Roman historian, Appian, says that Scipio wept over the destruction of the city and quoted the lines from the *Iliad:*

> A *day will come when sacred Troy shall perish*
> *And Priam and his people shall be slain.*

We may turn aside for a moment to recall that his forebodings were justified. A little more than five centuries later St. Jerome wrote a moving letter from a little monastery cell in Bethlehem telling a friend of the catastrophe. " The Roman world," he wrote, " is falling. . . . The wolves of the north have been let loose from their remotest fastnesses and have overrun great provinces. . . . The city which has taken the whole world captive is itself taken. The great city is swallowed up in one vast conflagration. Who could believe it; who could believe that Rome, built up through the ages by the conquest of the world, has fallen; that the mother of nations has become their tomb? " His account of what happened at the time was exaggerated. Eventually almost every detail was to come true.

Scipio's father, Æmilius Paullus, conqueror of Macedonia, had brought back to Rome a Greek library, the first we hear mentioned in the capital. The boy was educated with a love for literature which was not extinguished by his public service. A proud aristocrat, in later years Scipio made his home a centre of culture and of cultivated conversation where the most distinguished men in Rome met to talk over ethical, political, and literary problems. A Stoic philosopher from Rhodes was one of its shining lights, along with Polybius and others, including Terence, whose appealing line is still quoted: "I am a man, and nothing human is alien to me."

It was of this comparatively recent development of culture that Cicero was a product — a culture necessarily spotted and with conspicuous gaps, but, for all that, surprisingly modern. Perhaps we shall get a more vivid impression of the best society of the Ciceronian age if I reconstruct a small dinner party that was given many years after the family of Cicero had moved to Rome and after Cicero himself had served as consul. It will furnish an idea of the intellectual climate of the last century of the Republic. The dinner was given by Cicero's friend Lucullus, who is known to us chiefly by his reputation as a gourmet. In reality he was much more than that. Lucullus was a brilliant soldier and a cultivated man whose library was famous. His military career in the Near East had been ended by an intrigue in Rome and he had been superseded by Pompey. After Pompey had returned from the war he and Cicero, loitering in the Forum, came upon Lucullus. In spite of the inevitable bad feeling between the rival generals Cicero suggested that he and Pompey would like to dine with Lucullus that afternoon and take pot-luck.

"A dinner party," said Cicero, "is my delight. There I talk on any subject that comes up and, believe me, I can promise you some good laughs no matter how blue you may be feeling. I'm not nearly so interested in the food as I am in lively conversation."

With true Roman courtesy Lucullus consented. His guests were curious to see what sort of dinner their host would have when he was not expecting company. They insisted that he should not talk with his servants about it. Plutarch, who relates the incident, says that Lucullus outwitted them by ordering dinner in the Apollo room. Each of his many dining-rooms had its standard of service, and dinner in the Apollo room meant an elaborate meal.

From a description given somewhere by Cicero of a gathering at a nobleman's home we may imagine the scene: the guests announced by a servant and courteously conducted to seats by their host; then walking back and forth in lively conversation; the host showing them the piece of sculpture for which he had paid $50,000; apologizing that he was unable to obtain the original of the famous painting of a flower girl and so had had to content himself with a copy, which gossip said had cost him $2,400; then suggesting as it was winter that they retreat to the sunniest part of the lawn; and finally in the later afternoon taking them in to dinner.

We have no record of the conversation. But as Pompey was being blocked in desired legislation by some of his rivals, including Lucullus himself, we may assume that a fragment of the dinner-table talk ran something like this, with the words attributed to Cicero taken almost verbatim from his writings:

"I see," says the host somewhat maliciously, "that Metellus and Cato are giving our friend Pompey some trouble in the Senate. What do you think of them, Cicero?"

"Metellus?" replies Cicero. "Oh, Metellus isn't a human being. He's a seashore, an empty void, a desert waste. As for Cato, he has more honesty than judgment or ability. By the way, Pompey, I suspect you are beginning to wonder whether out of sight isn't out of mind. People forget you when you are long out of town. That was brought home to me years ago when I was a youngster. I was finance officer for the western district of Sicily. Thought I'd done a rather good job. Got the wheat supply off to Rome on time. Made it a point to be civil to the Sicilian financiers, fair to the merchants, and all that. I believe I was unusually popular in the province. When I came home I thought I'd be

INTERIOR OF A ROMAN HOUSE

This is the handsome drawing-room (atrium), the central apartment of the house. The furniture was scanty. (The photograph is of a Roman house of the Augustan period constructed for the Augustan Exposition held in Rome, 1937–8.)

swamped with honours. On the way I broke the journey at Puteoli just at the height of the season. Gentlemen, I nearly passed out when somebody asked me on what day I had left Rome and whether there was any news. When I answered I was on my way back from my provincial assignment the fellow said: 'Why, of course. How forgetful of me! You come from Africa, don't you?' 'No,' I answered rather coldly, 'from Sicily.' Then another chap cut in as if he pitied the other's ignorance. 'What!' he said. 'Don't you know our friend has been finance officer for the eastern district of Sicily?' It was the western district and I gave up. Made myself just one of those who had come down from Rome for the bathing.

"But I'm talking too much. One shouldn't monopolize conversation at a dinner table. There ought to be give and take. Let's hear what you two have to say. Pompey, how do you find things in Rome since your return?"

"I don't like the trend. When I got back from the East I demobilized my troops. Now I think it probably was a mistake. Soldiers are an argument that the Senate listens to. You know Crassus says no man can be considered rich unless he can maintain an army at his own expense. I'm coming to believe that the same thing applies to a politician if he's to be successful."

"Oh, that insufferable Crassus," Cicero interrupts. "He's a poor fish. By the way, have you been around to see Cato lately?"

"Yes," replies Pompey, "but the maid said he was out. I didn't believe her, but I came away."

"Well," Cicero comments, "such things have happened. Remember the story about the poet Ennius? A friend called on him one day and the maid said he wasn't home. But something told the visitor she was lying. A few days later Ennius called on his friend, who shouted from within the house that he wasn't there. 'What?' says Ennius. 'Don't I know your voice?' 'You're an impudent fellow,' rejoins the friend. 'When I asked for you I believed the maid when she said you weren't home. Won't you believe me when I tell you the same thing?'

"I must say, though, that I'd hate to be caught in anything like that. Nothing stays with a man like his mistakes."

And so the cheerful talk goes on. As the guests leave, Cicero compliments Lucullus on his library. "Books," he says, "are great companions. My books are always at leisure for me. They are never engaged."

I have often speculated on how the men at this dinner party and Cæsar, another great gentleman, would have fitted into a modern evening. Quite well, I fancy. Certainly their dignified bearing, their grave courtesy, their vitality, their wide interests, their witty conversation would have marked them as distinguished guests in any company. In particular Cicero and Cæsar would have been centres of attraction. Both of them were bilingual. They could speak Greek, the fashionable language of the day, as few Americans can speak French. Cicero often threw Greek phrases into his letters to Atticus. Many years ago an English clergyman translating the letters turned the Greek phrases into French with a surprisingly modern effect. "A problem in *la haute politique*" — in high politics; "what you have done for me is not a mere *pis aller*" — a mere makeshift; "I am speaking absolutely *à la lettre*" — absolutely literally.

Cicero and Cæsar would have been at sea in any scientific discussion; so would eighteenth-century Englishmen. Our assumption of inevitable social progress would have been alien to their thinking; but no more alien than to the thinking of the eminent historian of *The Decline and Fall of the Roman Empire*, who believed the Golden Age was in the past, not in the future. While they would have been familiar with monotheism and while they could have discussed the arguments for immortality, in which neither of them believed, they would have been baffled by many of our assumptions based on the Christian religion. Perhaps some modern who had been reading John Buchan's *Oliver Cromwell* might have referred to Oliver's last testament, which begins: " Lord, though I am a miserable and wretched creature, I am in covenant with Thee through grace," and continues: " Thou hast made me, though very unworthy, a mean instrument to do Thy people some good and Thee service."

Cæsar, we may imagine, would have been politely puzzled. " Your great soldier and administrator," he might have observed, " was evidently one of those queer religious zealots. I knew some of them, Jews, whom I favoured in Palestine. I must say I never found such fanaticism in any distinguished commander of my time. To be sure, both Alexander the Great and I used the idea of our divinity, but we used it for political purposes. We knew better. And to turn to an example from your Christian age, Napoleon, I recall, sent a pious encyclical to the French bishops. But he must have had his tongue in his cheek when he expressed his appreciation of the God of Hosts who so evidently protected the French arms. Oliver seems sincere. I wonder what practical effect his religious zeal had on his conduct. I remember that when he had the garrison at Drogheda put to the sword he reported it was 'a righteous judgment of God upon these barbarous wretches.' Then he went on: 'It will tend to prevent the effusion of blood in the future.' That last I understand. I did the same thing in my Gallic campaigns because I thought severity the most effective way to shorten the war. Oliver's piety about the slaughter seems hypocritical to me. His real reason was a military one. But I suppose I do not understand your religious development."

Rome, as Lecky somewhere remarks, produced many heroes but no saints. The background of centuries of the Christian religion, which in unnumbered ways affects unconsciously even modern skeptical thought, was of course lacking in the Roman civilization. This would have been an important factor in differentiating the mental outlook of the cultured society of Rome of the first century before Christ from the thinking of eighteenth-century England or twentieth-century America.

CHAPTER VII

HE STUDIES LAW

CICERO WAS a sensitive, gifted lad of boundless ambition. When the family moved to Rome it was his purpose, as it was the purpose of every upper-class youth, to prepare himself for a public career perhaps culminating in the glittering prize of the consulship. This, however, the aristocracy had reserved for members of noble families. It was almost unheard of for a man outside the charmed circle to crash the gate. But to a lad of Cicero's temperament nothing was impossible. He had a superb self-confidence that showed itself in a vanity that must have been a bit trying to his friends and that infuriated his enemies. In later life he recalled to his brother that from boyhood he had passionately cherished the aspiration – here he quoted Homer – " far to excel and alone be a leader of others." We may imagine that young Marcus often walked from his home to the Forum at twilight when it was deserted to gaze at the rostra and the Senate house and picture himself holding a crowd spellbound by his oratory or thundering in the Senate. Then his eye would wander up the slope of the Palatine as he wondered whether some day he might own one of those palatial mansions on its summit, with fashionable Rome at his feet.

To the career that Cicero had in mind the law was the stepping-stone. The courts in the Forum were open to the public. Any advocate who made a name for himself could be sure of attracting a crowd to hear him plead his case.

In this way he could become known to the voters and if he caught their fancy he could count on their support when he ran for office. For the subordinate offices, not for the consulship. For that, as I have said, noble birth was almost essential, with military distinction a great asset. The career of Marius, the soldier who had risen from the ranks, was a conspicuous exception. Cicero, with no military aptitude, could not expect to win political success by service in the field. He could only hope that if he became favourably known to the public the way to the highest office might open to him. There were no law schools in Rome. In nineteenth-century America it was the custom for boys aspiring to the bar to read law in the office of some successful practitioner. The procedure in Rome was somewhat similar. Cicero tells of this phase of his training in one of his books. Scævola, the augur, was the greatest lawyer of the day. " My father," Cicero writes, " introduced me to him immediately after I had put on the garb of manhood [that is, when he was sixteen years old] and directed me so far as possible to stay with the old gentleman. So to profit from his legal skill I made it a practice to memorize many of his learned opinions and many of his epigrammatic sayings." Scævola was the son-in-law of Lælius, one of the men prominent in the old Scipionic circle to which Cicero in later life often looked back as representative of the Golden Age of the Republic, and we may imagine that his legal instructor often talked to him about the cultured men who made up the circle. His friend Titus Pomponius, later known from his long residence in Athens as Atticus, was a fellow student at this time, although he soon abandoned law for business.

After Scævola's death two or three years later Cicero attached himself to another Scævola, a relative of his first teacher, and also eminent in the law. Jurisprudence was a family inheritance of the Scævolas, and a story has been handed down about the father of this second teacher to illustrate his remarkable memory. The elder Scævola was fond of a game very like backgammon in which men were moved on a board in accordance with the throws of dice. It was a game in which chance was compounded with skill. One day on his way to the country Scævola went over in his mind the moves by which he had lost a game. In the course of this review he hit on the move that had ruined him. So elated was he by the discovery that he rushed back to town to tell his opponent, who agreed that he had put his finger on the fatal move. Most of us today have known old-fashioned lawyers, devotees of chess, who might have done the same thing.

In later life, when Cicero had achieved distinction at the bar, he wrote several treatises discussing his conception of the broad training necessary for an advocate, and an appraisal of the more distinguished Roman lawyers and orators. His conclusions were the result of his wide reading of Greek authors and of his own experience. But he must have developed his general ideas fairly early, for it is remarkable how soon he began working along the lines which he laid down in his maturity.

To understand his ideas of a proper legal education it may be helpful to make a brief survey of the procedure of the courts before which a Roman lawyer practised in Cicero's day. "Law," James Bryce once said, "is Rome's great gift to the world." It was a peculiarly Roman contribution. To only a slight extent did the Romans build on the legal experiences of other peoples. They had the same genius for justice that the Hebrews had for religion. There is no evidence that they knew anything of the earlier codes of Egypt, of Hammurabi of Babylon, or of the Hittites. They were familiar with Greek procedure. But essentially the great Roman law developed out of Roman experience. In the middle of the fifth century before Christ the common law was codified and published in the famous Twelve Tables. Tradition assigns two or three possible borrowings from the laws of Solon. But all the laws set forth in the Tables are characteristically Roman. It is impossible to look over the fragments of these laws that have been preserved without being impressed with the modern flavour of their neat and concise language — thirty days of grace allowed for a debtor to settle after judgment has been pronounced; careful provision for the distribution of an estate whose owner dies without making a will; appointment of a guardian for an insane person or a spendthrift.

The Roman law was broadened in the middle of the third century in a revolutionary way, but still in response to practical experience. By this time many foreigners were doing business in Rome. It was observed that they brought and acted on conceptions of law that differed from the Roman. So the Senate set up in addition to the regular court a Strangers' Court to harmonize the alien laws with the domestic. This required a review of the underlying principles of justice. Broad moral concepts were thus injected into the Roman system which made it possible later for Roman law as well as the Roman peace to dominate the civilized world. Two centuries after the establishing of the Strangers' Court Cicero set forth its fundamental principles in a famous paragraph: "True law is right reason consonant with nature, world-wide in scope, unchanging and everlasting. . . . We may not oppose or alter that law, we cannot abolish it, we cannot be freed from its obligations by any legislature, and we need not look outside ourselves for an expounder of it. The law does not differ for Rome and Athens, for the present and for the future, but one eternal and unchanging law will be valid for all nature and for all times. . . . He who disobeys it denies himself and his own nature."

It was this philosophy that infused the American Declaration of Independence as formulated by Thomas Jefferson — the philosophy of the "unalienable" rights of man. This doctrine has been superseded by modern experimentalist ethics. But its practical results remain. A commentator on Cicero is quite justified in saying that his statement of the principle of natural law has "wrought greater progress in jurisprudence for nearly two thousand years than any other written statement of the same length."

The Ciceronian exposition was developed further two hundred and fifty years later by the great jurist Papinian, who enunciated the central principle that the law was not the will of the autocrat but "the common engagement of the state." This conception spread over Europe and England. In the middle of the thirteenth century Henry de Bracton, author of the first comprehensive treatise on English law, relied in his work on Roman legal principles and especially on the central principle of Papinian. At the beginning of the seventeenth century John Cowell, who was to become regius professor of the civil law at Cambridge, announced that years of study had convinced him that "our common law, as we call it, is nothing else than a mixture of the Roman and the feudal." This theory has been vigorously combated, but modern historical research is swinging toward Cowell and Bracton in emphasizing the indebtedness of the common law of England to the principles of Roman jurisprudence. We may enlarge Bryce's reference to law as Rome's great gift to the world by saying that law was Rome's great contribution to the good life.

Like the English common law the Roman law was a growing organism. It developed not only by legislative enactment but by judicial interpretation. Every year on assuming office the judges announced by edicts what their rulings would be in given cases. The edicts became "the living voice of the civil law." These supplemented and interpreted the law and by Cicero's time had taken the place of the Twelve Tables in the education of Roman law students.

Perhaps it was one of the defects of their qualities that the Romans' instinct for law and justice made them inveterate litigants. They were always suing and being sued. The old American threat: "I'll have the law on you," must have been familiar in republican Rome. The stern elder Cato, remembered to this day for the phrase attributed to him:

" Carthage must be destroyed," was sued more than fifty times, and he was constantly suing other people. As litigation increased, it was necessary to create additional courts. By the time Cicero was practising, there were two civil and six criminal courts in Rome with elective judges. Each criminal court specialized in some particular field of the criminal law.

The jury wheel was prepared by the presiding judge. The names of the prospective jurors were recorded in an *Album*, or White Book. In English procedure peers skilled in law are known as the " law lords " and sit in certain cases as a court of last resort. In Roman procedure all the senators on duty in the capital were regarded as law lords and their names were inscribed in the *Album*. Early in Cicero's career the four hundred senatorial jurors were supplemented by an equal number drawn from two other divisions of the upper classes: the wealthier business men and perhaps business men of lesser means. The wheel usually included more than a thousand names.

Jurors for any particular case were selected from the *Album* by lot. Challenges were allowed to both sides and the ordinary jury in a criminal case included from fifty to seventy-five men. It is evident that the large Roman jury more nearly approached a public meeting than the modern jury of twelve men, so that oratorical training was emphasized in the education of an aspirant to the Roman bar.

A curious procedure is related that illustrates the resourcefulness of a Roman official in preventing tampering with the jury in important cases. Pompey, who happened at one time to be temporarily sole consul, applied the procedure to all the political trials of his year. We have specific information about one of these, the trial of a turbulent politician, Milo, for felonious assault in a hot election campaign in which his chief opponent had been killed. A part of the general *Album* was assigned to each court. The court before which this case was brought had an *Album* with three hundred and sixty names. All three hundred and sixty were summoned to hear the evidence. Then on the last day of the trial eighty-one were chosen by lot and the rest dismissed. The eighty-one listened to the speeches of opposing counsel, after which each side struck off fifteen names and the remaining fifty-one gave the verdict. Evidently it would not have been worth while to bribe a few of the original three hundred and sixty, for the chances were that those bribed would not be on the final list that gave the verdict.

Civil cases were usually heard in the great basilicas that lined the Forum; criminal cases in the open air. In these latter cases a preliminary proceeding took place before a judge and jury to determine whether there was a cause of action and if so to choose the prosecutor. There was no public prosecutor and the complaining witness usually was authorized to conduct the prosecution. If there was reason to suppose he might be in collusion with the accused person, or if some more vigorous applicant appeared, the complainant might be passed over and another man designated to conduct the case. He could have assistants if he so desired. So too the defendant might appear for himself or he might be represented by counsel, with several assistants. As in Great Britain today and less definitely in the United States, there were two classes of lawyers, the office consultants and the pleaders in court. In British procedure the consultants are called attorneys or solicitors; the trial lawyers, barristers. In Roman, there were learned jurisconsults, and advocates who might be consulted by the lawyers who appeared in court.

While Cicero was pre-eminently a trial lawyer, his speeches in court verify the assumption that might be made from his industry, his natural ability, and his long training that he was well versed in all branches of jurisprudence. It could hardly have been otherwise, for he was not only the leading corporation lawyer in Rome, but the leading criminal lawyer as well. Nevertheless it was sometimes useful to him to adopt the pose of ignorance. "You must speak to the level of your audience," he writes. On occasion he would poke fun at the learned jurisconsults and the way they made the law an intricate matter so they would have to be called in as specialists. The gentle irony against his profession in one of his famous pleas in court still makes delicious reading. Cicero was defending a consul elect, Murena, on the charge of election bribery. His client probably was guilty, so it was highly desirable to divert the jury's attention from the legal aspects of the case.

The contestant for the consulship was a man learned in the civil law. "You seem to be caressing your knowledge of the law as if it were your little daughter," says Cicero, turning to him. But there can be no dignity, he continues in "so hair-splitting a science." The law, he says, used to be kept an unpublished mystery so its practice should be the monopoly of a select few. After the Tables had been published the lawyers were angry "because they were afraid lawsuits could be conducted without their assistance," so they "invented certain legal formulas that they might still have a part in every transaction" — an indictment that has persisted to the present day. Suppose, proceeds Cicero, there is a dispute over the ownership of land. You might suppose that one contestant would appear in court with the simple claim: "The Sabine property is mine." The other would protest: "No, it is mine," and the trial would then begin. Not at all. The lawyers have to pump up the case into complex legal form: "A property which is situate in the district which is designate as Sabine. This I, in accordance with the law that governs Roman citizens, affirm to be my property." And so on. In short, legal technicalities had developed in Rome almost to the Himalayan peak of absurdity that they reached in America about the turn of the century when the supreme court of Missouri upset the verdict in a murder case because the prosecutor in his indictment had written: "against the peace and dignity of state," instead of "against the peace and dignity of *the* state."

Evidently Cicero was disparaging legal learning in order

to appeal to the prejudices of the jury. Not only was there the prevalent feeling, as he says in one of his later essays, "the more law, the less justice," but also there was considerable contempt for all higher education among the new rich of Rome. He mentions somewhere a lawyer who "desired not so much to be thought unlearned as to hold learning in contempt." In conducting the case against the corrupt provincial governor Verres, who had plundered his province of art works among other things, Cicero deliberately affects ignorance of sculpture and sculptors, although he was himself a collector. One of the stolen statues was a Cupid by Praxiteles. "I learnt the artist's name," he apologizes, "in the course of my investigations as prosecutor." Then there were statues of the Muses. "The sculptor," Cicero gropingly inquires, "who was he? Now who did they say he was? Oh yes, thank you" — when somebody prompts him — "Polyclitus."

In the next century the novelist Petronius has the self-made nabob in his book propose to include in his epitaph the lines: "He died a millionaire — Yet he never attended a lecture on philosophy."

But to get back to the procedure in a criminal case. The trial was opened with a statement by the prosecution, followed by the presentation of the defence. The evidence was then introduced, the witnesses were cross-examined, and there were final pleas by each side in the form of give-and-take arguments by opposing counsel. The judge gave no charge to the jury but he might comment in the course of the trial. One such comment quoted by Cicero has been made famous by a mistranslation. The words involved were "*Cui bono?*" often translated: "To what good?" or more liberally: "What's the use?" In fact the words had a quite different meaning as used by a severe Roman judge in murder trials. He would ask repeatedly, Cicero says, who had a motive for the crime, and would admonish the jurors to inquire: Whom would it benefit? For whose good was it done?

The case was decided by a majority vote of the jurors who probably were not allowed to consult before returning the verdict. Rules of evidence in a Roman court would outrage modern lawyers. Hearsay testimony was admitted and great weight was given to the character of the accused. Often affidavits from absent character witnesses were used. The trial lawyers were given their head. No objection could be raised to evidence as irrelevant, incompetent, and immaterial. Cicero was an unscrupulous advocate. In reading his denunciatory legal and political speeches we have constantly to bear in mind that facts meant little to him in driving home a point. Indeed he delicately hints at this in the treatise *On Moral Duties.* " It is always the business of the judge in a trial," he writes, " to find out the truth; it is sometimes the business of the advocate to maintain what is plausible, even if it be not strictly true."

The latitude allowed a Roman trial lawyer is beautifully illustrated in one of Cicero's most famous speeches. It was in defence of the Greek poet Archias, who as his tutor had done much to inspire in Cicero as a boy that love of literature that distinguished him throughout life. Archias had early acquired Roman citizenship. As an incident in a political feud against the family of Lucullus, with whom Archias lived, his citizenship was challenged. Cicero was able to produce witnesses to the enrollment of Archias as a citizen. But this was only a minor part of his case. He knew his jury and he sought successfully to play on the patriotic pride of its members by pointing out that the Greek poet had done much and could do more to spread the fame of Rome in Greek, the polite universal language. The bulk of his speech is devoted to a lively and delightful discussion of the part of literature in life.

" I would ask you," he says at the outset, " to allow me, speaking as I am on behalf of a distinguished poet and a consummate scholar, before a cultivated audience, a most austere jury, and the presiding judge, to enlarge somewhat upon enlightened and cultivated pursuits, and to employ what is perhaps a novel and unconventional line of defence to suit the character of one whose studious seclusion has made him a stranger to the anxious perils of the courts."

A lord chancellor of England, Lord Brougham — remembered today for the carriage he designed — has commented that "Cicero's speech for Archias, which is exquisitely composed, but of which not more than one sixth is to the purpose, could not have been delivered in a British court of justice." It was perfectly admissible in a Roman court.

Laxity permeated the whole judicial procedure in Rome. The prisoner at the bar found himself on trial for his general conduct and reputation. Particularly were the political bearings of his case taken into account. Thus, in defending a provincial governor, Flaccus, charged with malfeasance in office, Cicero makes little effort to meet the specific charges. He cites the services of the accused in helping expose the conspiracy of Catiline, and says: "Jurymen of good sense and high character have always, in giving their verdict, taken into consideration what was demanded by the interests of the community, public welfare, and the exigencies of the state." In the same way in defending a successful candidate for consul on the charge of having secured his election through bribery, Cicero falls back on general considerations of the public welfare. The accused man, Murena, had defeated Catiline for the consulship. His attorney successfully appealed to the jury on the peril to the state should Murena be disqualified and Catiline seated.

While the dangers of this kind of procedure have been recognized and guarded against in British and American jurisprudence, public opinion and juries are still susceptible to the irrelevant arguments that were employed in Roman courts.

There was a clerk of the court, the *scriba,* who would be called upon to read documentary evidence, and shorthand reporters might be present, probably in the hope of selling copies of speeches that they had taken down in the expectation of a demand for them. At least a famous lawyer of the next century complains of the careless mutilation of some of his pleas by these commercial stenographers.

Because of the practices of the courts and the latitude allowed a Roman lawyer, we are not surprised to find Cicero stressing in his later writing the need of a broad liberal education for the aspirant to the bar. Speaking of oratory in general, he remarks that in his opinion " no one can hope to be an orator in the true sense of the word unless he has acquired knowledge of all the sciences and all the great problems of life." As for the lawyer, he should be trained in philosophy, mathematics, music, literature, and public speaking. He should have the wit, grace, learning, and urbanity of the well-bred man. Roman mathematics, it may be observed, was rudimentary. It was confined, Cicero remarks, to the practical purposes of measuring and reckoning. History, he says, should not be neglected. " To be ignorant of what happened before you were born is to live the life of a child for ever." And in another work he adds this noble tribute to history: " Witness of the ages, light of truth, life of memory, teacher of life, messenger of antiquity " — phrases that bring to mind in form and feeling some of Charles W. Eliot's fine lapidary inscriptions. I cannot forbear quoting for comparative purposes the original draft of the Eliot inscription on the Washington post office before it was revised by President Woodrow Wilson: " Carrier of love and sympathy — Messenger of friendship — Consoler of the lonely — Bond of the scattered family — Enlarger of the common life." These words might have been written by Cicero.

As a boy the future lawyer followed the principles that he expounded later. His temperament and inclination started him on the course that he ever ardently pursued. In his defence of Archias he says the earliest recollections of his boyhood clustered around the poet. " He first fitted my back for the burden and my feet for their destined path." Poetry was one of the things at which the boy tried his hand. In an earlier chapter I have referred to his poem on Marius.

Plutarch says he tried to write five hundred verses in a night. It was a common failing of Romans of his day. "Cæsar and Brutus wrote poems," Tacitus sourly observes, "not better than Cicero, but more fortunately, for fewer people know that they did it."

In the humanities the Greeks were the pre-eminent teachers. "We Romans," Cicero wrote in later life, "have gone to school in Greece; we read their poets and learn them by heart, and then we think ourselves scholars and men of culture." A Greek philosopher named Philo was a refugee in Rome in Cicero's boyhood. "Filled with enthusiasm for the study of philosophy," Cicero says, "I gave myself up wholly to his instruction." Later he worked with another Greek philosopher, the Stoic Diodotus, whom afterward he took into his home, and who died there. He found another Greek teacher, Molo of Rhodes, who, he tells us, was "famous as a pleader." Whenever opportunity offered in the distractions of the civil wars which closed most of the courts in Rome he hung about the Forum to listen to the most distinguished Roman orators. Every day, he says, he wrote and read and took notes.

The boy's studies were interrupted by the war in Italy between Rome and its allied cities and states which resorted to arms to gain the prized Roman citizenship. In this war he served with the northern army under Pompey's father, when his long friendship with Pompey may have begun, and later in the southern army under Sulla. But war was not for Cicero. He was essentially a man of peace and his military campaigns left little imprint upon him. After his army service he returned to Rome and continued his education. It was a severe regimen that he laid out for himself. In one of his later speeches he tells of the heavy price that must be paid for success. "A man," he says, "must renounce all pleasures, avoid all amusements, say farewell to recreation, games, entertainments, and almost to intercourse with one's friends." This was the course to which his ambition drove him. "I spent my days and nights in study of every kind," he writes, and his record bears out his statement. He prepared and delivered declamations in both Latin and Greek. The Greek he needed, he tells us, because the foremost teachers were Greeks and they could correct his faults better if he spoke their language. "It was my ambition," he writes, "not (as most do) to learn my trade in the Forum, but so far as possible to enter the Forum already trained."

During a good part of these student years the city was torn in the struggle of military leaders for supremacy, a matter to which I shall return later. The nobles and the well-to-do were chiefly involved in the murders that attended the reigns of terror of the rival generals, and the young student, absorbed in his work, paid surprisingly little attention to what was going on. Rather objectively he disapproved. He was a humane man with the old Roman devotion to liberty. A few years later he was to express publicly his disapproval of Sulla's dictatorship and to utter the fervent hope that no second dictator would ever seize the government. One reform, however, in Cicero's own field was carried out by Sulla. The judicial system was reorganized and permanent courts were set up in place of temporary commissions. "Then for the first time," he writes in his reminiscences, "I began to take public and private cases."

Cicero was now twenty-five years old. One plea in court dating from his first year at the bar has come down to us. It was in a civil case involving a dispute over the ownership of real estate in the Roman province in southern France. He tells of his timidity on this occasion, when he was pitted against Hortensius, a leader of the Roman bar. When he was asked to take the case he says he protested he would be so nervous he might not be able to utter a word. He was persuaded when his prospective client's kinsman explained to him that the case turned on one simple point: Was it possible that a court order could have reached southern France, six hundred and forty miles from Rome, in less than three days?

Cicero made the most of this point in his plea to the jury. " If we suppose," he argued, " that someone started running from the court immediately the order was issued, the journey of six hundred and forty miles must have been accomplished in less than three days. Incredible! A winged messenger! Lucky man to possess such messengers, or rather flying horses! " This early effort shows the clearness of exposition and liveliness of style that made Cicero such a successful trial lawyer. We do not know whether he won the case. But he was sufficiently proud of the speech to see that it was published. The next year his first real opportunity came in an important political trial of one Sextus Roscius of the country town of Ameria.

CHAPTER VIII

HIS FIRST BIG CASE

ONE LATE afternoon in the year 80 the dinner parties in the great houses on the Palatine were stirred by reports from the law courts. That young chap from the country, Marcus Tullius Cicero, had won the celebrated Sextus Roscius murder case about which Roman society had been gossiping. What interested the fashionable diners-out was not merely the verdict of acquittal. Everyone took it for granted that the accused man was innocent and the charge against him a frame-up. What especially intrigued them was that this twenty-six-year-old lawyer had dared challenge a powerful member of the autocratic regime then ruling Rome under republican forms. In the entourage of the dictator Sulla was an unscrupulous Greek who was trying to railroad Roscius to death or exile in order to cover up a shady financial transaction. It was this man whose anger Cicero had braved by appearing in the case. Naturally the incident was the subject of dinner-table conversations.

The verdict was reassuring. It showed that the courts remained independent. After all, the dictatorship undoubtedly was only a passing episode. Rome was still a republic with a proud history reaching into a past as remote as is the discovery of America from the present age. To the gay residents on the Palatine Roman institutions doubtless seemed as permanent as American institutions seem to us today. To be sure, for a century there had been disquieting symptoms which finally had required the strong hand of Sulla to control. The large slave population in Rome and Italy was a cause of anxiety. The frequent wars in which Rome had been engaged had yielded a multitude of captives who had been sold as slaves and put to work in town and country. There always was a chance that they might turn on their masters, as they already had turned twice in Sicily and as they were to turn in the great insurrection headed by Spartacus a few years later. Many farms had been devastated in the long invasion by Hannibal near the end of the third century, and large numbers of farmers, the backbone of the Roman armies, had been killed in battle. The census returns indicate that one third of the Roman citizens had been lost. Local capital to restore the devastated farms was lacking and many of them had been bought up by speculators and finally had found their way into the hands of gentlemen farmers in Rome. This situation had been aggravated by the wars of the second century and by the loss of life and destruction of property that had attended the recent war of the Italian allies.

To accentuate the farm problem cheap wheat had begun to come in from Sicily and Africa. Along the coastal region accessible to water transportation Italian-grown wheat could not compete with Sicilian. The situation was to a degree comparable to that in the United States when the opening of the Western lands ruined farmers in the Eastern states. Grapes and olives could be grown profitably, but they required more capital than the small Italian farmer possessed. Slave labour could be advantageously used on livestock ranches in the interior, and here too the small operator suffered. Impoverished farmers drifted to the towns and the capital to be supported by odd jobs and by charity from the rich. As a result of these factors there had been a progressive deterioration of the middle class, which had been the strength of the agrarian Republic.

The wars of the third and second centuries that had borne so heavily on the farm population had brought sudden wealth to the shrewd business men and the ruling class in Rome. Spoils of conquest flowed in and there were many opportunities for exploiting the conquered lands. In the late eighteenth century and early nineteenth England surmounted a somewhat similar crisis through the industrial revolution. The progress of industry helped build a strong middle class. Rome lacked industries, and the newly acquired riches could not be widely redistributed through productive enterprises in wages, salaries, and ownership profits. Wealth accumulated in a comparatively few hands and was spent in luxurious living by a slave-owning oligarchy. The door of opportunity was closed to the mass of the people. Their standard of living was anchored at a low level. The poor protested, an ancient historian writes, that poverty prevented their rearing children. As a result, by the latter part of the second century a social cleavage had developed and the structure of society, once firmly united, was being split wide open.

Popular discontent found expression in two far-seeing and brilliant young noblemen. Tiberius Gracchus and his younger brother Gaius had great personal qualities and became for a time the idols of the populace. In the three brief years in which they served as tribunes, first Tiberius in 133 and later Gaius in 123–122 proposed a remarkable program of social and economic reform. Their most important effort was directed toward stopping the disappearance of the small farmer, the mainstay of the middle class, by restoring the public domain to a multitude of owners. With this attempt to revive farming as a way of life they made headway, but not enough to accomplish their purpose. The most celebrated measure associated with the Gracchan period was worked out by the younger brother. The price of wheat, the staple of Roman diet, was subject to violent fluctuations. Gaius Gracchus undertook to stabilize the price at a fair level at government expense. This project was liberalized later until wheat was furnished free by the state.

Up to the age of the Gracchi Rome always had settled

class conflicts by reasonable compromise. Now for the first time the great tradition was sharply interrupted by appeal to armed force. The brothers were killed successively in riots instigated by men of wealth who believed their property interests were menaced by the young reformers. Historians have speculated on whether this break with tradition was due to the dilution of the old stock by Oriental elements that had come to Rome, freed slaves from Greece and Asia and their descendants. How much importance should be attributed to this racial mixture is impossible to determine. Perhaps in the last century of the Republic the melting-pot lacked time to do its work. Very many of the new-comers were under the handicap of their slave origin and of the absence of the tradition of self-government. But in the murder of the Gracchi it must be borne in mind that the rioting was instigated by upper-class conservatives. Sudden riches may demoralize their possessors just as progressive poverty may make its victims desperate. The increasing tension in the state may be amply accounted for by social and economic changes. The poor felt themselves oppressed and became defiant. The rich became arrogant.

" It is probably the secret of British strength," a German writer has said, " that revolutions in England are invariably made by conservatives." And the Frenchman Maurois remarks that the prudence of the British aristocracy and the political shrewdness of its leaders " made possible the transformation of a country gentlemen's club into a great national assembly." Here the Roman oligarchy conspicuously failed.

As the last century of the Republic wore on, another fundamental difficulty developed. For the defence of the expanding Roman domain it proved necessary to supplant the old short-service conscript army of citizens with a professional standing army. For a livelihood after their term of service was over the soldiers needed bonuses and farms. These needs the government was not prepared to meet. When spoils from conquered provinces were mounting,

Rome had welcomed the opportunity in 167 to abolish direct taxes. There was no treasury surplus for the veterans. To tax themselves for the benefit of a lot of ex-service men was unthinkable to members of the ruling class. The soldiers had to look to their commanders for means of support when they should retire to civil life. Their loyalty was to their generals, not to the state. It needed only the realization of his power by an ambitious field marshal to bring a military dictatorship.

In the twenty years preceding the trial of Sextus Roscius two outstanding commanders had emerged. The first, Marius, was a man of the people. Like General Grant he was a good soldier but a stupid statesman. A military hero, defender of Italy against German invaders, he had entered politics as the champion of the commoners and the business interests against the aristocracy. The other, Sulla, a brilliant reactionary aristocrat, was the darling of the nobles. In the clash of arms between these rival holders of great commands the voice of the law, as Marius remarked, could not be heard. The struggle began with the attempt of the Marian party to replace Sulla with Marius as commander in a war that had broken out with King Mithridates in Asia Minor. At the head of his legions Sulla seized Rome, and Marius fled. When Sulla left for Asia the next year, Marius returned to the capital and carried out a massacre of aristocrats. Marius died shortly afterward, and when Sulla came home victorious four years later, he fought his way to Rome against government troops. There he took a terrible revenge on the business men and political leaders who had supported his rival. Several thousand of the best-known names of Rome were on his proscription lists.

Lacking in imagination and insight, Sulla thought he could re-establish the old order. With his authority as consul and dictator he had revised the Constitution to give lasting control of the state to the great families operating through the Senate. The aristocrats drew a long breath. At last their troubles were over. The wretched common people had been put in their place. The best of all possible governments in the best of all possible worlds had been restored. As soon as the dictator's iron hand should be withdrawn the government might be expected to continue to function by the nobles and for the nobles as it had before those impractical reformers, the Gracchus brothers, had upset the complacency of the Palatine dwellers a half-century earlier. There is no evidence that it ever occurred to the aristocrats that the underlying weaknesses of Rome had been left untouched, that the ancient system was no longer adapted to the needs of the times and was on the verge of collapse. They could no more see into the future than could the French aristocrats of the old regime.

There were, of course, unpleasant features in the dominance of an autocrat even though he was using his temporary power to restore the rule of the great families. But what would you? One can't have everything. Such a beneficent revolution as Sulla's inevitably attracts undesirable hangers-on. A dictator is bound to have his favourites. Some of the men about him were terrible. This upstart Chrysogonus, for example, the real prosecutor in the Roscius case. The fellow was an ex-slave who had wangled himself into the good graces of the dictator. Cashing in on the connection, he had accumulated wealth. Then to the horror of the old families he had acquired a residence among them in the fashionable Palatine quarter. This was almost more than they could bear.

There was sympathy too for Sextus Roscius, even though he was a simple farmer unknown in Roman society. After all, his father, for whom he was named, had been a leading citizen of Ameria, fifty miles north of Rome. In the dangerous years of the civil wars he had been a valued supporter of the aristocratic cause. He had been often entertained in the capital by some of the distinguished families.

The elder Roscius had been murdered while on his way home from a dinner party in Rome. Presumably the murder had been instigated by two relatives who had hoped to come into possession of his landed estates. They had made a deal with Chrysogonus to have the name of the murdered man listed among the enemies of the regime. His thirteen farms had then been ordered confiscated by the state and put up at auction. One of the relatives had obtained three of the thirteen. The other ten had been bid in by the second relative acting as agent for Chrysogonus. In the circumstances nobody else had cared to bid.

The people of Ameria had been outraged and the town council had sent a protesting delegation to Sulla. Chrysogonus had met the delegates, had promised to see that restitution was made, and then had undertaken to clear his title by having the younger Roscius assassinated. The son had fled to Rome and had taken refuge in the home of a great lady Cæcilia Metella, an old friend of his father's. This had not deterred the avaricious young Greek. Counting on his political influence and on the general fear of antagonizing so powerful a favourite of the dictator's, he had instigated the charge that Roscius had murdered his father.

With the influential family of the Metelli and some other aristocratic houses taking an interest in the case, the Palatine dinner parties must have been familiar with the background. There probably had been indignation over the affair. It was hardly prudent to permit this indignation to go beyond the conversational stage.

In the absence of a regular public prosecutor an experienced lawyer of bad reputation had been accepted by the court to handle the prosecution. In spite of the concern of some of the nobles it was not easy to find a lawyer willing to risk antagonizing the regime by undertaking the defence. Nobody cared to stick his neck out. Finally an idealistic youth of the aristocracy, not old enough himself to appear in court, had appealed to the young lawyer from the country. At this time Cicero was not a particularly attractive figure. A spindling fellow, he afterward described himself, with a long, thin neck, who spoke in a nervous monotone. But he was a hard worker, clever and resourceful, and, as has been noted in a previous chapter, with an unusual training for the bar.

Why did Cicero undertake this difficult and dangerous case? Not primarily, we may assume, because of an altruistic desire to defend an innocent man. Cicero was a lawyer, and under the code of his profession he took cases as they came. He was ready to appear for a scoundrel, if necessary. Of more consequence was the prestige the successful defence of Roscius would give a young attorney. In a Rome dominated by the great houses, the doors of advancement, as I have said before, were barred against the "New Man," the man without noble ancestry. In a later speech he mentions this difficulty. "We are aware," he says, "with what jealousy, with what dislike, the merit and energy of New Men are regarded by certain of the nobles; that we have only to shut our eyes for a moment to find ourselves caught in a trap; that we must never relax our vigilance and never take a holiday." If Cicero could show both outstanding courage and ability by taking this conspicuous case and winning it he might make a dent in the stone wall of aristocratic exclusiveness. Who could predict what might not happen? With such a start he might eventually break into the inner circle of the proud old families.

It had been a difficult decision for the young man. He was always in the habit of weighing the arguments on both sides before he made up his mind. In this case on the one side was the undoubted danger of inviting reprisals from Chrysogonus, and perhaps from Sulla. On the other was his natural sympathy for a man on trial for his life under an unjust accusation. If worst came to worst he might depend on the protection of the great families who were interested in his client. But most important of all, here was his chance to emerge from obscurity and to become one of the most talked-of lawyers in Rome. Many years later in his treatise *On Moral Duties* Cicero wrote about this very case. "Briefs for the defence," he says, "are most likely to bring glory and popularity to the pleader, and all the more so if it falls to him to lend his aid to one who seems to be oppressed and persecuted by the influence of someone in power. This I have done on many occasions; and once in particular in my younger days I defended Sextus of Ameria against the power of Lucius Sulla when he was acting the tyrant." In view of his standards and his later record and statements I think we shall not be unfair to Cicero if we assume that ambition was probably the determining factor in his decision to defend Sextus Roscius.

His opening speech at the trial shows the qualities of the keen jury lawyer, the qualities that before many years were to carry him to the top of his profession. The situation needed delicate handling. Cicero faced a jury drawn from a panel of senators. The implications of this fact require a word of explanation. A half-century earlier the provincials had found it difficult to get justice against corrupt governors from the senatorial class, who were tried before senatorial jurors. As part of his reform program the younger Gracchus had taken the jury courts from the senators and had turned them over to the upper-class business men. Like many well-intended reforms this one had failed to produce the expected results. Honest governors who tried to restrain the rapacity of corrupt business contractors in the provinces were now in danger of being cited before juries of prejudiced business men on trumped-up charges. Control of the courts was of economic importance and the senators were anxious to regain their lost prerogatives. In the Sullan restoration the courts were turned back to them. This was the situation at the time of the trial of Roscius. Scandals resulted and a few years later the system was changed to that described previously with the jurors chosen from three social classes. But now Cicero had to deal with a senatorial jury.

In his defence of Roscius it was necessary for him to criticize the Sullan regime and to do this so adroitly as not to offend the jurors who were sitting in the case as beneficiaries of Sulla. Obviously too the jury would not be disposed to bring in a verdict of acquittal that might get its members into disfavour with the regime. Thus it was the job of counsel for the defence in presenting the case to draw a sharp line between the subordinate Chrysogonus, who was responsible for the attempt to get rid of Roscius, and the principal Sulla, upon whose favour the lieutenant was relying. Cicero must condemn Chrysogonus without seeming to reflect upon Sulla. In spite of these handicaps he had to make such an effective presentation of the case both to the court and to the spectators that a verdict of acquittal would be forced upon even a reluctant jury which might not want to incur the odium of outraging public opinion.

The speech, still extant, shows the skill with which the young attorney handled the whole situation. He begins by apologizing for his youth and lack of experience. But because of his very obscurity, he says, he may undertake a case from which more distinguished lawyers might shrink because of its hazards. Outlining the story, he soon mentions the name of Chrysogonus. This startles the prosecutor, who expected only a timorous and vague defence and has been joking with friends. The man jumps to his feet, and on the third mention of the name he sends out messengers to let Chrysogonus know what is happening and perhaps to get his advice. Meanwhile Cicero becomes increasingly outspoken. He appeals to the prejudice of his senatorial jurors by reminding them of the effrontery of this former Greek slave in acquiring a palace on the Palatine. Sulla, he says, with affairs of state upon his shoulders, cannot be expected to know what his subordinates are doing. Like Jupiter he presides over a vast universe and he cannot be expected to pay attention to details. Men return thanks to the god for blessings from his hands, while they do not blame him for the incidental hurricanes and floods that may destroy them. " And so it is with Sulla."

The young defence counsel builds a damning case against Chrysogonus in behalf of his client and ends with an appeal which we may take to heart today. Rome, he says, is sick from the cruelties of the civil wars and the purges. He begs the jury to take a stand for justice and decency. "The daily spectacle of atrocious acts has stifled all feeling of pity in the hearts of men. When every hour we see or hear of an act of dreadful cruelty we lose all feeling of humanity."

A universal experience, as the modern world has reason to know.

A great crowd had assembled at the trial, and the jury met its expectations by a verdict of acquittal. Cicero left the court no longer an obscure young attorney. He was thereafter a man to be reckoned with.

CHAPTER IX

POST-GRADUATE WORK AT ATHENS

IN A fragment of autobiography written when he was sixty years old Cicero dates the beginning of his brilliant career from the defence of Sextus Roscius. " It won such favourable comment," he writes, " that I was thought not incompetent to handle any sort of litigation. There followed then in quick succession many other cases which I brought into court, carefully worked out and, as the saying is, smelling somewhat of the midnight oil."

But he was far from robust, his health had been impaired by his heavy work, and his voice was giving him trouble. His friends and physicians urged him to abandon his profession. This he would not do. He concluded, however, that a long rest would restore his health and that further study might give him better control of his voice and improve his delivery. He resolved to make the grand tour and visit the famous centres of the ancient Greek civilization in Athens, Asia Minor, and the island of Rhodes. With his brother Quintus and a cousin Lucius he set out for Athens.

It was a congenial group of travellers. Marcus was devoted to his cousin as well as to his brother. When Lucius died eleven years later, Marcus wrote of the grief he felt and of the loss to him in both his public and his private life. Quintus Cicero was four years younger than Marcus, who brooded over him with an older brother's solicitous affection. A man of some ability but with no spark of genius,

Quintus was to have a considerable public career. He served as commissioner of public works, judge, and governor of the province of Asia. As one of Cæsar's generals in Gaul, on one occasion he was publicly commended by his chief, and on another mildly criticized by him for lack of caution. He had literary ambitions, tried his hand at verse, and once wrote to his brother from the Gallic campaign that he had produced four tragedies in sixteen days. Were they translations, Marcus inquired, politely asking to see them. The two exchanged brotherly admonitions. Quintus regarded Marcus as too much of an idealist to be a practical politician, and when the older brother was running for consul wrote for him an elaborate *Handbook of Politics* as a guide for his campaign. It was Marcus' turn when disquieting reports reached Rome of Quintus' handling of the Asiatic governorship. The younger Cicero was noted for his violent outbursts of temper. There were murmurings that though he was honest he was arbitrary and cruel and that his trusted freedman Statius was corrupt. Marcus wrote him frankly about his faults and told him of his lieutenant's arrogance. Later when Marcus was governor of the province of Cilicia he took Quintus with him as his military chief. But when leaving for home he confided to Atticus that he dared not leave Quintus in charge; he would always be anxious as to what his impulsive brother might do.

Curiously Quintus, who in public was so violent, in private was quite subdued. His wife, Pomponia, sister of Atticus, had him cowed. The henpecked husband, however, was as familiar a phenomenon in ancient times as in modern. Plutarch cites the Greek statesman Themistocles as complaining that while the Athenians governed the Greeks and he governed the Athenians, his wife governed him, and their son governed her. Cato was moved to bring a similar charge against the Romans, who, he said, governed the world but were themselves governed by their wives. In a letter to Atticus Marcus tells about a painful luncheon at Quintus' country house. Pomponia had taken offence because Quintus had sent Statius on ahead to make the arrangements. " I'm only a stranger here," she exploded before all the guests. Her husband had no come-back. Marcus continues the story. " ' There you are,' says Quintus to me. ' That's what I have to put up with every day.' You may say that didn't amount to much. It amounted to a good deal. She irritated even me, she had answered with such uncalled-for acrimony in word and look. I concealed my annoyance. We all took our places except her. Quintus sent her some food from the table, which she refused. In a word, it seemed to me that my brother was as good-tempered and your sister as cross as could be, and I have left out a lot of things that irritated me more than they did Quintus. . . . Quintus came to me the next morning and told me she would not sleep with him, and when he was leaving she was as cross as when I saw her. I don't care if you tell her that to my mind she behaved with a lack of courtesy that day."

Looking in on this family spat two thousand years later, we may guess that the trouble went back to Quintus' favourite servant. Pomponia among others could not put up with Statius, and she had her tantrum when he appeared to look after things. A glimpse of his overbearing temper is given in Cicero's correspondence. " How often," Marcus writes his brother, " do you suppose Statius in conversation with me has used with the utmost naïveté such expressions as: ' I could not agree to that,' ' I lectured him,' ' I argued with him,' ' I cautioned him.' . . . The mere appearance of a freedman or slave possessing such influence cannot fail to be utterly undignified." Apparently Quintus, for all his blustering, was easily bossed. When he had escaped from Statius and had wriggled out from under the thumb of his wife by divorce, undoubtedly someone else was ready to take him in charge.

Freedmen were to become an increasing problem in Rome. Clever slaves were able to worm their way into their masters' confidence. If they were lucky they would finally be given their freedom and remain in charge of their former masters' affairs. Often they were arrogant, greedy, and unscrupulous — traits which they usually were able to conceal from their patrons by their usefulness and flattery. It would be interesting to know what became of Statius. His dark figure merely stalks briefly across the scene and then fades out.

Athens, which the Ciceros reached in the year 79, when Marcus was twenty-seven years old, was the great centre of graduate study in philosophy and literature. Other cities, Alexandria in Egypt and Pergamum in Asia Minor, with their famous libraries, one with seven hundred thousand volumes, the other with two hundred thousand, might be more attractive for scientific research than the Greek capital. But the brilliant achievements in literature, philosophy, art, and architecture associated with Athens were destined to draw scholars there for a thousand years.

The three young men from Rome were to find their boyhood friend Atticus already established in the city. He had inherited $100,000 from his father and had withdrawn from Rome some six years before the visit of the Ciceros to escape from the partisans of Sulla. It was more than twenty years before he returned to Italy. This young expatriate, who was to become such an integral part of the elder Cicero's life, is a fascinating personality. A many-sided man, keen in business, of cultivated tastes, genuine kindness, a sympathetic and understanding mind, Atticus had shed all illusions and looked out with clear vision upon the weaknesses and foibles of mankind. A cultured and charming exterior gave no inkling of the hard acquisitive instinct behind it. To his original patrimony was added a legacy of $500,000 from a grasping uncle with a reputation for charging even relatives one per cent a month for loans. This large capital enabled him to become one of the leading financiers of his day.

Money-lending was regarded with disdain in the Roman world and the leading practitioners preferred to cover up what they were doing. Atticus acquired a large estate on the picturesque western coast of Greece overlooking the Ionian Sea and liked to pose as a country gentleman. But his lending operations were on a scale that could not be concealed and there was abundant gossip about him. It was said that when he was about to sell out some unfortunate debtor who could not keep up his payments, he would console the victim with the admonition that this should prove a lesson that might prevent his being ruined in the future.

Later Cicero used to poke gentle fun at Atticus for his methods. He writes about his friend's "siege" of a town that owed him money; an unsuccessful siege, incidentally. He tells how he met an attempted touch by their common nephew, Quintus. "I took then something of your eloquence," he writes. "I didn't answer him." While Atticus could be grandly generous in public affairs, like many another rich man he was thrifty, even penurious, in his personal living. In his later years he had a fine house in Rome. But his biographer, Cornelius Nepos, who says he had personal knowledge of Atticus' affairs, asserted that the financier had held his personal expenses to $150 a month. Cicero ribbed him on his parsimony. Once when Atticus was to read one of Cicero's works at a dinner party, the author urged him to serve a decent meal. "I don't want your guests," he wrote, "to vent their spite on me."

The gifted but careless statesman and man of letters found in the astute financier not only a devoted friend but an indispensable business agent. He looked after Cicero's property, collected his rents, acted as his banker, advanced him money when he was pressed for funds – his normal condition – executed commissions for the purchase of art objects, patiently listened to troubles, gave him good advice, and made allowance for his outbursts of temper.

The obligation was not all on Cicero's side. Atticus was the first important publisher in Rome. He had a corps of skilled slaves who made copies of manuscripts to be sold. Naturally Cicero, the most distinguished writer of the day, headed his list of authors. "There are no hands in which I would rather have my writings than in yours," Cicero wrote him. On another occasion, referring to the publication of a minor speech, Cicero complimented Atticus on the "magnificent start" he had made on the sales, and added: "Henceforth when I write anything I shall leave it to you to advertise it." The Latin word for "advertising" that he uses, *præconium*, comes from *præco*, "a public crier," and means literally "a crying out in public."

The publication of Cicero's works must have brought returns. Probably they were moderate. Editions were comparatively small. There were no copyright laws and popular books might be pirated in cheap and slovenly form. We do not know whether Atticus paid Cicero royalties. It has been suggested that they may have had some partnership arrangement. In any event the author-politician probably profited much more politically than financially from the sale of his writings.

Cicero was demonstrative in his affection. "I love Atticus like a brother," he says. When in trouble he found solace in letters to his friend. "A sick heart," he writes on one occasion, "not only robs me of sleep, but will not allow me to keep awake without the greatest pain. I have begun to write to you something or other without any definite subject, that I may have a sort of talk with you, the only thing that gives me relief." It is a tribute to the personality of Atticus that not Cicero alone, but most of the great ones of the time were on terms of intimacy with him. Whether these intimacies were suffused with the emotion that would have converted them into real friendships it is difficult to say. Certainly Atticus was able to maintain an extraordinarily objective attitude toward them all. He never allowed one friendship to get in the way of another.

His Epicurean philosophy was supposed to afford him conscientious grounds for abstaining from politics. At least the doctrine furnished a convenient excuse and he worked it overtime. Cicero saw through the subterfuge. In his book

On the Laws, in which Atticus is represented as one of the speakers in a conversation under the trees beside a brook, to which I referred in an earlier chapter, Cicero starts an argument against the Epicurean view. Atticus doesn't care to defend his position. "I don't mind admitting you are right," the author has him reply, "for, thanks to these birds that are singing and to the murmuring of these brooks, I'm not afraid that any of my fellow disciples may overhear me."

With philosophical detachment the millionaire watched the *comédie humaine* unfold before him in a series of bloody conflicts. Privately he held strong views on current issues. He would urge others to action, but he remained quiescent. Publicly he always refused to take sides. Through some strange charm he made his refusal respected. We get glimpses of this charm from his biographer. He spoke Greek and Latin with elegance and grace. He was familiar with literature and philosophy and amused himself with writing a chronology of Roman history. His taste in art was impeccable. His wide interests and discriminating conversation made him a universal favourite. When Sulla visited Athens he found the youthful Atticus so attractive that he wanted him constantly by his side. In his old age Atticus was equally fascinating to the young Augustus. Men found his judgment so objective and sound that his advice was sought by political rivals. His financial help was freely given to those in need, and often to those on the losing side. His clear judgment was untouched by moral indignation. There can be no doubt that he was sincerely devoted to Cicero for more than thirty years. But he dispassionately observed the events leading to the murder of his old friend and saw no reason why this untoward and regrettable happening should disturb his friendship with the men who were responsible for the deed.

In his later years he pleaded age as well as philosophy as a reason for standing aside. "I have taken my discharge," he wrote at the age of sixty — the Roman military age limit — when Cæsar started civil war by crossing the Rubicon.

Theoretically he believed in the Republic rather than in a dictatorship. But no issue seemed to him worth fighting over. As so often happens with men who pride themselves on their realism, he confused ideals with illusions. How Cicero tried to justify to himself his friend's strange apathy appears in a letter to Atticus. " I have never thought," he writes, " that there was any difference between you and me, except our choice of a career. A touch of ambition led me to seek for distinction, while another perfectly laudable motive led you to honourable ease. But in the real glory which consists in uprightness, industry, and piety, there is no one I place above you."

Others made the same excuses for him. Even the fanatical patriot Brutus, who had taken part in the assassination of Cæsar as a public duty, did not blame Atticus for his neutrality. Brutus wrote him a burning letter. It was directed not at Atticus personally, but at the general indifferentism of the age, an indifferentism with which the twentieth century has been familiar.

" Believe me," Brutus wrote, " we are too much afraid of exile, death, and poverty." An excitable young man, the recipient of the letter doubtless thought; sincere, but violent. At the end of the civil wars Atticus could have made the response of the Abbé Sieyès when asked what he had done during the Terror. " What did I do? " repeated Sieyès. " I lived."

A unique record of the friendship of Cicero and Atticus has come down to us in approximately four hundred letters from Cicero to his friend. The first was written eleven years after the renewal of their acquaintance at Athens and the last about a year before Cicero's death. No letter from Atticus is included in the correspondence, but often we may infer what he had written from Cicero's replies. Quotations from him are cited by Cicero in one of his letters. He wrote gracefully and used occasional Greek expressions, as Cicero often did. In addition we have some four hundred letters written by Cicero to his brother and to other friends.

Then there are letters to Cicero, nearly one hundred of them. Cæsar wrote to him, and Pompey and Antony and the conspirators against Cæsar — Cassius, and Marcus and Decimus Brutus. The correspondence with Augustus was suppressed. With perhaps a few exceptions the letters were not written for publication. The possibility of publishing some of them, however, occurred to Cicero late in life. A year and a half before his death he wrote to Atticus: "There is no collection of my letters, but Tiro has about seventy, and some can be got from you. Those I ought to see and correct and then they may be published." Apparently he never had time for the correcting. His secretary assembled the general correspondence and published it after Cicero's death. He may have retained copies of some of the letters. Others he probably obtained from the persons to whom they were sent. Atticus is generally credited with getting together the letters that had been sent to him. These were not published, however, until after the middle of the first century of the Christian era. We hear of as many more known to the ancients that have not survived. That Cicero should have taken the pains to write so many letters is the more remarkable when it is borne in mind that there was no postal service. The letters had to be sent by private messengers or by the messenger service of the joint-stock companies operating in the provinces.

It is a revealing and amazing correspondence. Many public men have been great letter-writers — Napoleon, Jefferson, John Adams, Macaulay, Theodore Roosevelt, to mention only a few of the old familiars. In sheer interest and fascination Cicero ranks in the top group. It has been the fortune of few men to know all the distinguished personalities of a great age and to have at the same time the gift for informal, vivid, sensitive literary expression. The reader who takes up the letters for the first time, either in the old Shuckburgh translation or in the Loeb Classical Library, has something of the feeling of Keats when he first looked into Chapman's Homer:

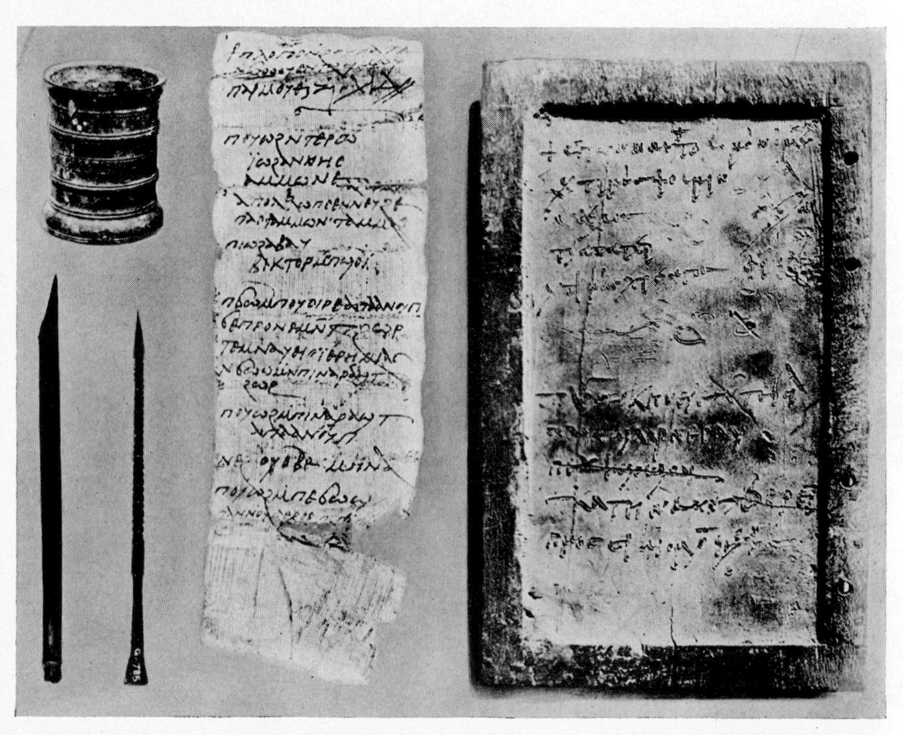

ROMAN WRITING MATERIALS

Cicero probably wrote his letters with a reed pen (lower left), on paper made from the papyrus plant (middle of page). The ink that filled the well (upper left) was made of lampblack and gum. When busy he used dictation. The tablet (right) was usually a thin piece of wood covered with wax. The writing was scratched on the surface with a stylus (next to pen). Schoolchildren used the tablet, and it was available for short letters. (Tablet and ink bottle, courtesy of the Metropolitan Museum of Art. Papyrus, pen, and stylus, courtesy of the Royal Ontario Museum, Toronto)

Then felt I like some watcher of the skies
When a new planet swims into his ken.

Here is a man who tells of entertaining Cæsar at one of his country villas and of their conversation about literature, who gives his impressions of Cleopatra, who recounts a conversation with Pompey, who reports a conference with the conspirators who killed Cæsar, who retails in lively fashion the social and political gossip of the world capital. Perhaps the most fascinating part of the correspondence is that in which he reveals himself in all his complex aspects — his indecision, timidity, courage, depression, exaltation. It is a record of glaring faults and shining virtues in conflict in a human soul. Writing to mere acquaintances Cicero was on guard. In letters to his intimates, Quintus and Atticus, he concealed nothing. "I saw a complete picture of you in your letter," his brother writes to him. To Atticus he says: "I talk to you as I do to myself."

In modern times Alexander H. Stephens, Vice President of the Confederacy, poured out his innermost thoughts in letters to his half-brother Linton. Many of them showed such vanity that out of consideration for the great man's reputation Linton destroyed them. Fortunately no such editing mars Cicero's self-painted portrait. We see him as we see Cromwell, wart and all.

It is interesting to observe the effect of the letters on the great humanist who rediscovered them after they had been lost for centuries. In 1345 Petrarch found the letters to Atticus, Quintus, and Marcus Brutus in the cathedral library at Verona. It was the great event of his life. When he had looked them over he addressed a letter in Latin to Cicero, dated "in the 1345th year after the birth of the God whom you did not know." The human weaknesses of the Roman, revealed in the letters, shocked the scholar, who had judged him by the dress parade of some of the orations and philosophical works. "I have listened to you, Marcus Tullius," he wrote, "as you talked of many matters, as you lamented many ills, as you threw upon many subjects the transforming light of your intelligence, and I, who had long known what sort of guide you were to others, have at last understood what sort of man you were to yourself. . . . I grieve at your lot, my friend, I feel shame and pity at the thought of your great mistakes. . . . What profits it to teach others, of what profit is it to speak always of the virtues in the most fitting language, if meanwhile you do not listen to yourself?"

Six months later, however, Petrarch had recovered from the first shock and was able to take a more lenient view. He addressed a second letter to Cicero, apologizing for the severity of the first. "It was your life with which I found fault," he wrote, "not your talent or your eloquence. In fact, I wonder at the one, I am lost in admiration of the other. And yet in your life I find nothing lacking save steadfastness and the love of repose which belongs of right to a philosopher's life, and a desire to avoid civil wars. . . . I feel a compassion for you in view of your life, I congratulate you upon your genius and your eloquence. O most exalted father of Roman eloquence, not I alone but all of us who are adorned with the beauties of the Latin tongue render you our thanks; for we refresh our fields from your streams, we frankly confess that we have been directed by your guidance, aided by your opinions, and illumined by your light; that, finally, under your auspices, so to speak, we have gained the power and inspiration to write, however small it may be."

The first letter by Cicero that has been preserved, a letter to Atticus, was written in 68, when Cicero was thirty-eight years old, in the early part of his public career. Only eleven letters represent the next four years. The important years 64 and 63, covering his candidacy for the consulship and his year in office, are a blank. Atticus was in Rome at this time and there was no reason for their corresponding. Half of the letters cover the last four years of Cicero's life. The last was written in July 43, six months before his death.

From the letters it is possible to construct a fairly complete life of Cicero for the twenty years succeeding his consulship. And not his life alone. The correspondence gives us a more intimate view of the Roman scene in the closing years of the Republic than we have of the life of any European capital down to comparatively modern times.

Cicero's acquaintance with Atticus was renewed at Athens, as we have seen. That venerable university centre, like Oxford and Cambridge, was made up of colleges, although at Athens they had no organic union. Each of the four famous schools of philosophy except the Stoic had started with an endowment of private property — perhaps a house and grounds. In some cases bequests were left for their support. Presumably revenues were supplemented by fees. We hear of one distinguished teacher who charged $180 for his course, which lasted three to four years. Cicero tells us that he spent six months in graduate work in philosophy and public speaking. Apparently Atticus and Cicero's brother and cousin attended some of the lectures with him. Writing many years later, Cicero tells of his student days in Athens with a nostalgia that would appeal to any modern college graduate reflecting fondly on his Alma Mater. He recalls an afternoon stroll with his student friends after the morning lecture "in the building called the School of Ptolemy." They proceed to the grounds of the Academy, founded by Plato. He is reminded of the founder, who made a practice of holding discussions in the Academy grounds; of other famous scholars "who used to sit on the very seat we see over there." On the walk they had seen the village of Colonus "and it brought to my imagination Sophocles, who lived there." They had passed Epicurus' Gardens, and he speaks of the pictures of Epicurus on the drinking cups of students. "All over Athens," he adds, "there are reminders of eminent men in the actual places where they lived." It was all a glowing and memorable experience to the enthusiastic young Roman, and one he always cherished.

Like many an American college boy Cicero had his first

religious experience while away at school. Later, at the time of the death of his beloved daughter Tullia, he had a much more profound experience. Probably it would be extreme to call this first religious experience a conversion in any modern sense. He does not refer to it in his letters. In fact the only reference to it is in his treatise *On the Laws*, written more than a quarter of a century later. Here he reminds Atticus that while they were together at Athens they were initiated into the Eleusinian Mysteries. "Among the many excellent and indeed divine institutions which your Athens has brought forth and contributed to human life," he continues, "none, in my opinion, is better than those Mysteries. . . . We have learned from them the beginning of life and have gained the power not only to live happily, but also to die with a better hope."

Looking back over the years, Cicero may have attached more importance to his youthful experience than it deserved. Still it is interesting to have this testimony of the religious value of rites that we might naturally dismiss as products of gross and fantastic superstition. The Eleusinian Mysteries had some of the characteristics of a modern revival meeting. They took place in a magnificent temple erected by Pericles at Eleusis, twelve miles from Athens. Each year after a long period of preparation the Mysteries culminated in a divine drama representing the sorrowful search of the goddess Demeter for her lost daughter Persephone, who had descended into the lower world, and the mother's joy at finding her. From bits of description we learn that the drama started in darkness, which contributed to the painful suspense of those to be initiated. Then a dazzling light suddenly was thrown on the shrine of the goddess. This is the familiar technique of certain spectacular latter-day evangelists. By sensitive observers the physical thrill is translated into a moral emotion. It is surmised that the ceremonies at Eleusis pointed to comfort in the trials and sufferings of life and to reward or punishment after death. "You are not to ask for reason in the religious feeling," says Renan.

"The spirit bloweth where it listeth; and if it chooses to attach the ideal to this or that, what have you to say?" At least in retrospect the Eleusinian Mysteries seemed to Cicero to have brought him comfort and religious inspiration.

In his later years Cicero was at times preoccupied with religious speculation. But with him, as with Romans generally, philosophy rather than theology was related to problems of conduct. He was an upright man; far more so than most of his associates. It is impossible to follow his career and read his revealing letters without believing that for the most part he tried to do his duty as he saw it, even though Duty to him was not the stern Daughter of the Voice of God. That does not mean that he always succeeded. He was very human. Often he did not listen to his own precepts. Besides he had to a high degree that faculty for self-deception with which we all are familiar. Frequently he had trouble in making up his mind. But when he had done so, he felt himself invariably right, his opponents invariably wrong. Like Metternich after the Congress of Aix-la-Chapelle, Cicero might have written: "I cannot help saying to myself twenty times a day: 'Good God, how right I am, and how wrong they are! And how easy this reason is to see — it is so clear, so simple, and so natural!'" Like many conspicuous American politicians he could convince himself he was acting in accordance with disinterested public motives when in reality personal feelings and prejudices were animating him. Still he had a lofty conception of the moral code that was expressed in his later writings. "You could fancy sometimes," said Petrarch, "that it is not a pagan philosopher but a Christian apostle who is speaking." In his *Confessions* St. Augustine attributes his conversion to a book of Cicero's now lost, the *Hortensius*. "This book," he writes, "quite altered my affections, turned my prayers to Thyself, O Lord, and made me have clean other purposes and desires. All my vain hopes I thenceforth slighted; and . . . I thirsted after the immortality of wisdom." While these religious and philosophical writings belong to his mature years, we may find their origins in Cicero's student days in the East.

After six months of strenuous work in Athens the young lawyer visited teachers of oratory in Asia Minor and then proceeded to Rhodes to visit the instructor Molo, under whom he previously had studied in Rome. "He was distinguished," Cicero writes, "not merely as a practical advocate and composer of speeches for others, but was particularly skilful in criticizing and correcting faults. He made it his task to repress if possible the redundance and excess of my style, which was marked by a youthful impetuousness and lack of restraint, and to prevent it, so to speak, from overflowing its banks." The effective restraint of his delivery is remarked by Plutarch, who reports that Cicero used to ridicule loud speakers "who shouted because they could not speak, like lame men who get on horseback because they cannot walk."

On the way home from Rhodes we learn from Plutarch, not from Cicero himself, that he stopped to consult the oracle at Delphi. That historic spot under the Shining Rocks of Mount Parnassus overlooking the lovely olive groves of the valley toward Itea held a strange fascination for the ancient world down to the middle of the fourth century of the Christian era. While Cicero consulted the oracle as everybody did, it is doubtful whether he took its prophetic counsels seriously. Certainly his mature judgment held them "in the utmost contempt," as he wrote later. The gossipy Plutarch reports that the oracle advised him to "make his own genius and not the opinion of the people the guide of his life."

The two years abroad quite restored his health. He returned to Rome "almost a changed man." "The overstraining of my voice had abated," he says, "my style had lost its frothiness, my lungs had grown stronger, and my bodily frame had moderately filled out." In short he was on the way to becoming the handsome man whose appearance attracted favourable comment from his contemporaries.

We may still study his mobile face in the fine portrait busts that have come down to us from antiquity. There are five of these. The most surely authenticated was acquired by the first Duke of Wellington for Apsley House, his home in London. The other four are in Italy. A familiar bust in Madrid has been ruled out by archæologists as a modern copy. Of those in Italy the best are in the Vatican and Capitoline museums in Rome and in the Uffizi Gallery in Florence. In these we may see Cicero as he was in his later years, the hair beginning to thin, the broad forehead furrowed by trouble. The face is sensitive and rather disillusioned. In its studied melancholy is more than a dash of the poseur. The expression is in striking contrast to the fuzzy bewilderment of Pompey, and to the hard, incisive intelligence and drive of Cæsar, as shown in their portrait busts.

It had been a rich and fruitful vacation. The ancient culture to which Cicero had been exposed coloured his whole subsequent life. Perhaps he wore it a little conspicuously at first, like a Phi Beta Kappa key. According to Plutarch, he had to overcome the political handicap with the voters of being regarded as " a Greek and a scholar." But his ambition was equal to surmounting even the obstacle of a higher education. With an unusual natural endowment, thorough training for his profession, and a mind broadened by travel, he plunged into the glittering career that he saw opening before him.

CHAPTER X

HE BECOMES A MAN OF FAMILY

CICERO WAS now twenty-nine years old. The dictator Sulla had died in retirement during the young lawyer's absence in the East, and the field of law and politics seemed open without the limitations that had been imposed by an autocratic government. Because of his reputation Cicero was at once sought out to handle some " conspicuous cases," as he calls them, and he could look forward to increasing success at the bar which would further his political ambitions.

It was probably in this busy year that Cicero took the time to set up a household in proper Roman fashion. Undoubtedly his marriage was the customary one of convenience. Terentia, the young woman of his choice, perhaps ten years his junior, came of a family of standing. Its social prestige is evidenced by the fact that her half-sister had been chosen for the select company of the Vestal Virgins. Malicious gossip later connected the sister's name with that of the reckless Catiline. While the scandal was disproved by a formal trial, we may imagine that Terentia had it treasured up against Catiline when the famous conspiracy charge broke a few years later. The bride brought to Cicero a dowry of some $20,000. In addition she owned rental property in Rome and some woodland near the city. About this time, Plutarch says, Cicero inherited $18,000 more – he does not tell the source — so the young couple could live "in a genteel and at the same time a frugal manner." Their daughter Tullia was born probably the next year and their son Marcus eleven years later.

Because Cicero is revealed to us so intimately in his letters, the story of his married life, culminating after thirty years in divorce, has been more widely discussed than the married life of any of his contemporaries. For many years there was real affection between husband and wife, which finally faded. In appraising the record we must remember that we do not have Terentia's side of the story. Even Plutarch probably had to depend on prejudiced Memoirs written by Cicero's loyal secretary.

We may gather, however, that Plutarch probably was right in saying that Terentia was "a woman of imperious temper," and her masterfulness fretted Cicero in a perfectly human way. But her firmness complemented his indecision. "You are more courageous than any man," he once wrote her with sincere admiration. Still, he complained that she intervened in his political affairs far more than she allowed him to intervene in affairs at home. A practical, thrifty housewife, she undoubtedly found her brilliant, moody, and improvident husband extremely trying at times. Nevertheless in the first two decades of their life together she tried to do her part. Cicero writes of her to Quintus as the "truest of helpmates." In the same letter he speaks of their children. Of their daughter Tullia, to whom he was devoted: "how affectionate, how modest, how clever! The express image of my face, my speech, my very soul." And of little Marcus: "the prettiest boy, the very joy of my heart." Terentia and Tullia, he says, are his "two sweethearts." To the children he was always the devoted father.

It is a normally pleasant and congenial household that is here pictured. But its head was conspicuously indifferent to feminine charm. His interests and preoccupations were such as appeal especially to men. It is impossible to read his letters without noticing how small a part women, except his daughter, play in his life. In a letter written when he was sixty he speaks with some embarrassment of a dinner party at which one of the guests was an actress, the mistress of Mark Antony. "I had no suspicion," he says, "that she would be there." After a word to show that as a man of the world he was not shocked he hastens to add: "As for myself the fact is that that sort of thing never had any attraction for me when I was a young man, much less now that I am an old one."

Different ages of course have different standards of taste. The coarseness of the Elizabethan age is offensive to modern ears. This coarseness would have seemed quite natural and unobjectionable to cultivated Romans. Yet Cicero's personal taste in such matters was more nearly modern than Roman or even Elizabethan. In his entire correspondence there are surprisingly few passages that we find offensive. There is none so coarse as to impel translators to let it stand in the original Latin — a device that is occasionally forced upon the embarrassed scholars who have made translations of such typical Roman writers as Catullus, Petronius, Martial, Juvenal, and Apuleius.

Malicious gossip found little opportunity to exercise itself on Cicero. Plutarch suspects, but with insubstantial evidence, that Terentia was jealous of the fascinating Clodia. Another historian hints at possible scandal involving a woman whom Cicero refers to as "an intimate friend." The evidence is all against the truth of the reports. But the affair, slight as it is, helps to an understanding of his difficulties with Terentia. Cærellia was a clever lady of means, considerably older than Cicero. They had a common interest in philosophy. One of his famous treatises was his work *On Theories of Ethics*. While Atticus had the manuscript in the hands of his copyists for publication, Cærellia borrowed it and had a copy made for herself without Cicero's knowledge. Cicero refers to the incident casually in a letter to Atticus, remarking that she was "prompted of course by her love of philosophy." He adds that he isn't finding fault with anyone, for he had neglected to tell Atticus that the book was not yet ready for circulation.

Cicero was sixty-one years old at the time. There is no reason to suppose there was any romance between the two. Chronically hard up, he had borrowed money from her as he borrowed from other friends. Atticus sent him word that he was indiscreet. Presumably the incident might cause talk. The cautious banker suggested that he might make over some doubtful notes to the lady. But Cicero demurred at doing so until he could learn more about the solvency of the persons whose notes would be involved. The correspondence between Cicero and Cærellia was published later. Presumably they wrote to each other on philosophical and literary subjects. Unfortunately the letters are lost.

Terentia lacked Cærellia's education and intellectual interests. In his letters to his wife Cicero never discusses the subjects that really concern him. A pious woman, in fact a Fundamentalist in religion, Terentia must have found her husband's urbane skepticism hard to bear. In a letter written in profound depression when an unhappy turn of politics had banished him from Italy, Cicero laments that " neither the gods whom you have worshipped with such devotion, nor men whom I have ever served, have shown the slightest sign of gratitude toward us." In a later letter he makes a concession to her religiosity. He has obtained relief from an attack of indigestion. " My relief was such," he writes, " that I fancied some god or other had cured me – probably Apollo or Æsculapius. Please be good enough to pay him your pious devotions as you always do."

We may trace the outline of this famous marriage in the twenty-odd letters from Cicero to his wife that have survived, letters that gradually shorten into brief notes. The first was written from Brindisi when he was on his way into exile. His only wish then, he tells her, is to see her as soon as possible and he adds, with the theatrical Latin temperament, " to die in your arms." But shall he ask her to come – " a woman of weak health and broken spirit? . . . Am I to be without you, then? I think the best course is this: If there is any hope of my restoration, stay to promote it and push the thing on. But if, as I fear, it proves hopeless, pray come to me by any means in your power. Be sure of this: if I have you I shall not think myself wholly lost." He ends by calling her "most faithful and best of wives." Very likely Terentia had heard this sort of thing before and did not take her husband's emotion too seriously. Later he laments that "a woman of your virtue, fidelity, uprightness, and kindness should have fallen into such troubles on my account." Again he shows his appreciation of her help in looking after his affairs in Rome and in working for his recall from exile. "I see you eagerly undertaking labours of every kind," he writes. "I fear you cannot endure them. Yet I see that everything depends on you. Attend carefully to your health." He begs her to remember that "nothing is or has ever been dearer to me than you are." And in closing: "Good-bye, my dear Terentia, whom I seem to see before my eyes, and so am dissolved in tears."

These endearing letters were written after twenty years of married life. Only a few months later, however, after his return to Rome from exile, comes the first intimation of trouble. It is merely an inference to be drawn from the omission of Terentia's name in two successive letters to Atticus. "My monetary affairs," Cicero writes in one of them, "as you know, are in an awful mess, and there are some private matters which I won't commit to writing. I am devoted to my brother Quintus as his extraordinary affection, virtue, and loyalty deserve." The second letter ends with a reference to causes of anxiety that he does not care to mention and with the statement: "My brother and daughter treat me with affection." In the light of subsequent events the failure to speak of Terentia along with Quintus and Tullia is significant.

No further hints of trouble find their way into the correspondence for several years. Just what lay behind the cooling of affection we do not know. The letters speak of money matters. Still we are justified, I think, in assuming that the disputes over money would not have proved serious if there had not been a background of growing incompatibility—to use a word that figures in many American divorces. Like other Roman women of means Terentia managed her own property with the help of an agent. To this agent Cicero entrusted the management of his affairs during a later absence from Rome while he was governor of Cilicia. At Athens on his way home he got a statement from the agent that showed that certain profits on which Cicero was depending had disappeared. "No more of that fellow for me!" he writes Atticus in a rage. "He's a slicker." He still does not blame his wife for the dishonesty of her agent. The same day he writes to her as "dearest, sweetest Terentia," and a month later she meets him at Brindisi.

The next year civil war broke out between Cæsar and Pompey. After long hesitation Cicero picked the loser and crossed the Adriatic to Pompey's camp on the Macedonian coast. From here he writes to Atticus about his daughter's dowry due to her new husband. While he does not mention names he evidently suspects his wife of holding back three thousand dollars that was to have been paid on the dowry account. There has been, he says, "culpable carelessness." If he had known he never would have permitted the money to be held back. On what are the rents of his farms being wasted?

After Pompey's defeat and death Cicero returned to Brindisi, where he had to wait nearly a year before getting Cæsar's permission to go back to Rome. In a very brief note he replies to his wife's letter of welcome and her offer to do anything she can to help him. "What you can do," he writes, "I cannot think. It's no use your starting on a journey at such a time as this; and I don't see what good you can do me if you do come. Good-bye." This was only two years after he had addressed her as "dearest, sweetest."

The other letters of this period show the same matter-of-fact indifference. While it is evident that he does not wish to see Terentia he writes with enthusiastic affection of the visit of their daughter; of her "perfect excellence and unsurpassed gentleness." Meanwhile he sends long letters to Atticus. The first direct criticism of his wife is in a letter to his friend written while he was still waiting in Brindisi. "As to Terentia," he says, "I omit lots of other things, for what can one add to this? You wrote to her to remit to me by a bill of exchange $500, saying that was the balance in my account. She sent me $400, saying that was all the balance. If she purloins so trifling an amount you can see what she has been doing in the case of larger sums." One other reference in a later letter to another friend perhaps applies to Terentia. He speaks of nothing being safe "from treachery within my own walls."

To Terentia Cicero continues to write brief notes, very brief indeed, each with a formal admonition to take care of her health. The final letter, dated in October 47, speaks of his impending arrival at his villa at Tusculum: "See that everything is ready there. For perhaps there will be several others with me and we shall stay for a considerable time, I think. If there is no basin in the bath, have one put in; and so with everything necessary for supporting life and health. Good-bye." The business-like tone of this letter has been compared to that of Mr. Pickwick's note to his landlady briefly suggesting "chops and Tomata sauce" for dinner, which Serjeant Buzfuz found so difficult to construe into language of affection in the famous breach-of-promise action of Bardell *v.* Pickwick.

The divorce was announced the next year. In the last century of the Republic divorce involved no legal formalities. Affection between husband and wife was regarded as an essential part of marriage and as necessary for its continuance. If affection disappeared either might give notice of a desire to dissolve the bond. No judicial decree was required; a formal notification was sufficient.

Plutarch gives a summary of the reasons assigned by Cicero for his action: that his wife had neglected him during the war; that she did not come to him during his long wait at Brindisi; that his house had been bereft of its furniture to pay the many debts which she had contracted. Terentia, Plutarch says, denied the charges, as well she might if we may judge by the letter from Brindisi in which Cicero clearly intimated that he did not wish to see her.

Anyone who has followed divorce proceedings in American courts knows that it is proverbially difficult to arrive at the facts from the conflicting testimony that usually is offered in a contested case. Under the impact of emotion perfectly innocent happenings often are distorted beyond recognition. We do not know, for instance, why Terentia withheld the payment on Tullia's dowry. She may have had a good reason. The charge of pilfering $100 from her husband's balance may have been based on misinformation as to the amount of the fund. In view of Terentia's long devotion to Cicero and the trust he always imposed in her, it is hard to believe that in the end she suddenly became dishonest. No experienced newspaper reporter, I suspect, would hold that the available evidence warrants a judgment as to where the weight of blame lay. All we may say is that under the stress of stormy years impatience, misunderstanding, and suspicion developed. The sensitive Roman would have understood Browning's lines:

Oh, the little more, and how much it is!
And the little less, and what worlds away!

Very likely the little less accumulated in family differences and led to the final break. It was not easy to disrupt the long companionship. A few months after the divorce Cicero speaks of the recent wounds which he cannot touch without cringing.

But there were unsentimental realities ahead. Alimony was not recognized in Roman law, but in the upper circles there was usually the little matter of the repayment of the dowry to be considered. The Roman *dos* was not precisely the same as the French *dot* or the English dowry. It was the contribution the wife brought to the expenses of the household. It did not belong to the husband although he had the use and administration of the property and was accountable for it if the marriage terminated in his wife's divorce or death. She had no claim to it if she was the party at fault in the divorce. But for forfeiture of dowry the fault must be a serious one, such as adultery or drunkenness. Cicero charged neglect and extravagance. There was no charge upon which he could have resisted repayment of the dowry and in fact his only resistance came from lack of funds. He felt aggrieved at the agent she appointed to see to her interests; he wrote that she was acting high and mighty, and asked Atticus and Tiro to look after the matter, nobly insisting that if there was to be any mistake "I would rather that I had reason to be dissatisfied with her than she with me." But with young Marcus about to go away to college at Athens, Cicero found it difficult to raise the money to satisfy Terentia's claims. In a letter to Atticus two years later there is a reference to the dowry as still unpaid. Then Terentia slips out of the correspondence. Cicero's subsequent marriage to a young woman, followed speedily by a divorce, will be considered later. Terentia must have been at least fifty years old at the time of her divorce. A few years after their marriage Cicero had remarked in the first of the letters to Atticus that his wife was suffering from a severe attack of rheumatism. Her health continued to be an object of real or conventional solicitude up to the last. So we are intrigued by a bit of information from the elder Pliny in his pioneer encyclopædia, published in the next century. In a chapter devoted to famous cases of advanced age appears the brief entry: "Terentia, wife of Cicero, lived one hundred and three years." Poor health proved a great aid to longevity.

The lady is involved in a final piece of gossip, recorded nearly four centuries after her death. The church father St. Jerome says she married Sallust, the historian, and subsequently Messala Corvinus, a courtly patron of letters and politician. These remarriages, however, are not known to Plutarch or to any of the earlier writers. Authentic history ends with the divorce and with Terentia still trying to collect what was due her from her former husband.

His daughter Tullia, whom he often calls by the affectionate name of Tulliola, was the grand passion of Cicero's life. Affectionate references to her run through his letters. "My pet Tulliola" sends love to Atticus. Her father must plan to be at one of his country places at a certain time for the games, because Tullia wants to see them. When he returns from exile it is "my dear Tulliola" who meets him at Brindisi. He refrains from speaking out on some scandal in Rome because "my little girl, who is unwell, was afraid of my offending" an influential politician. "My little girl" was then twenty-two years old. Later her ill health causes him "acute agony."

Every parent will sympathize with the problems that his daughter's affairs of the heart presented to her anxious father. As a child she was betrothed to a boy of good family, C. Piso Frugi. In accordance with the Italian custom of early marriages she was married while a mere girl in the year of her father's consulship. The marriage must have been a social equivalent of a White House wedding in Washington. Five years later, during her father's exile, Tullia and her young husband, recently elected a finance officer, made an appeal to one of the consuls on Cicero's behalf. Piso died the following year, and it was as a widow that Tullia travelled to Brindisi to meet her father. The next year she married again and Cicero mentions the fact that the expenses incident to the wedding, including the dowry, had swallowed up the money he had set aside for travelling. The second marriage shortly ended in divorce.

Tullia's third matrimonial adventure proved still more unfortunate and contributed greatly to her father's distress. While Cicero was serving as governor of Cilicia an eligible young man journeyed out to the province to ask for his daughter's hand. Meanwhile Tullia had fallen in love with a brilliant and utterly unscrupulous young aristocrat, Dolabella, and had obtained her mother's approval. Cicero's letter to his wife and daughter telling of the suitor who had visited him did not reach Rome until the betrothal to Dolabella had taken place, and the father had to make the best of what he knew was a bad business. His correspondence shows him struggling to convince himself that after all the profligate son-in-law might prove satisfactory. A friend writes him consolingly from Rome that " certain blemishes " in Dolabella's character undoubtedly would disappear as the young man grew more mature, and that others would be removed by " your society and influence and by the modesty of Tullia." To this Cicero makes the paternal reply that " what is done is done and heaven prosper it! " The marriage took place in his absence and his worst fears were realized. After four unhappy years there was a divorce. The daughter's troubles drew the father closer to her and her premature death at the age of thirty was a crushing blow to Cicero.

His younger child, Marcus, was born in July 65. The father announced the event briefly to Atticus in a letter devoted to politics. " I have to inform you," he writes, " that on election day I had an addition to my family in the shape of a baby boy; Terentia doing well." We find him like most fond parents regarding the boy with prejudiced eye, indulging and spoiling him. Young Marcus is his " sweet little Cicero." When the boy is six years old he is allowed to add a greeting in Greek to a letter to Atticus, to show off his accomplishments: " Terentia sends compliments and [then in Greek] Cicero the little greets Titus the Athenian." The next letter ends in the same way with a Greek sentence displaying the precocity of the child: " Cicero the philosopher salutes Titus the statesman." It was a false alarm. The boy developed into an athletic fellow, a man-about-town, but never a philosopher.

At the age of eleven Marcus with his cousin Quintus was put under the tutelage of a teacher of rhetoric. When Cicero went to Cilicia as governor he took the two boys with him, accompanied by a tutor. One of them, he writes back to Atticus, "needs the curb, the other the spur." Atticus hardly needed to be told that it was young Marcus who needed the spur.

In the civil war Marcus accompanied his father to Greece to join Pompey, and although he was not yet sixteen he was appointed to the command, probably honorary, of a squadron of cavalry. Later Cicero mentions the fact that in this army service his son won praise for his skill in horsemanship, javelin-throwing, and every form of military exercise. After Pompey's defeat and death the cousins, then nineteen, were introduced into politics by Cicero, whose influence obtained their election as commissioners of public works in the ancestral town of Arpinum. Young Marcus was now anxious to join Cæsar, who was fighting in Spain. His father dissuaded him and after the fashion of many modern fathers insisted that he go to college, which meant Athens, to study philosophy, for which the boy, now twenty years old, was entirely unfitted.

While Cicero was cramped for money at this time, he insisted that his son have an allowance sufficient to maintain the dignity of the family of a former consul. Atticus, who always acted as his financial agent and banker, was instructed to set aside the rents from certain of Cicero's properties in Rome, amounting to four thousand dollars a year, to keep the boy supplied. Young Cicero was extravagant and we find him complaining of his niggardly allowance. The prudent agent of Atticus in Athens dealt out the money to him "very sparingly and stingily." Apparently he was following instructions, for we find Cicero, moved by his son's complaints, remonstrating to Atticus that it was not becoming that Marcus should be held down.

Meanwhile, as was to be expected, the boy was not making a scholastic record to be proud of. One of the university authorities wrote Cicero that his son was getting on fairly well, "just at present" and "so far." The disquieting implications did not escape the father and he thought of running over to Athens. But he got consolation from another professor, who spoke well of Marcus, though not convincingly. Here a very fatherly note creeps into the correspondence. " I am glad to be deceived in this matter," he writes to Atticus, " and am not sorry to be credulous."

The cause of the trouble is evident. Marcus was much more interested in having a good time in Athens than in learning philosophy. We hear from Plutarch that one of the professors was a wild fellow and that Cicero believed he was leading his son into dissolute habits. He forbade the boy to associate with the man. Young Marcus at once wrote his father's secretary a penitent letter saying that while the professor had been very useful, he had given him up. " I wouldn't shilly-shally about the business for fear my making a fuss would cause my father to harbour some suspicion." The boy has turned over a new leaf and is working his head off with other professors. " I have hired a residence next door to one of them (Bruttius) and as far as I can with my poor pittance I subsidize his narrow means." I suspect that every father with a son away at college would recognize in this letter the familiar technique leading up to what is commonly called a touch.

The university life of the young student was broken off by the civil war that followed the murder of Cæsar. Brutus appeared in Athens and recruited officers for the republican army. Among the volunteers were Marcus Cicero and the future poet Horace, a fellow student. He fought at Philippi and probably ran away as young Horace confesses he did. After the war Marcus returned to Rome; and Augustus, perhaps to make amends for acquiescing in the murder of Cicero, made the son augur and allowed him to serve the unexpired term of a consul. After the death of Antony, Cicero's great enemy, the young man was given the revenge of being allowed to announce the news and to post the announcement on the rostra " where formerly his father's head had been fixed."

Later he served as governor of Asia and high commissioner to Syria. To what extent his official career was due to favouritism on the part of Augustus, and how far to his own merits we do not know. He was doubtless a hearty and convivial fellow and the legends of his drinking impressed antiquity. Seneca says he ruined what little memory he had by drunkenness. Perhaps some of the difficulty was due to paternal indulgence in his bringing up. Certainly he had no spark of his father's industry and genius.

Here, then, is Cicero's family, vividly pictured in the letters and records — the brilliant, sensitive, mercurial, extravagant father; the managing, practical, pious, pedestrian mother; the intelligent, perhaps blue-stocking, susceptible daughter; and the indulged, dull, athletic, good-fellow son, living on his father's reputation — a family pattern as familiar in America today as it was in Rome two millenniums ago.

CHAPTER XI

THE PLUNGE INTO POLITICS

THE YEAR after his marriage Cicero entered upon his political career. He was now thirty years old. This was the minimum age at which a Roman could be elected to public office, which he therefore could hold at the age of thirty-one. A regular succession of offices was fixed by law, and it was necessary to hold the first and third to qualify for the consulship. The first was that of finance officer under the Treasury department (*quæstor*). The next was that of commissioner of public works (*ædilis*), for which the minimum age was thirty-seven. It was desirable but not essential to hold this post on the way up. At forty a man could be judge (*prætor*) and at forty-three consul. In each case he would be elected the preceding year. The Romans took every precaution to prevent an official from building up his power by perpetuating himself in office. The equivalent of the American third-term issue was dealt with in the law of succession. The term of office was one year and the holder was ineligible for re-election to the same office for ten years. Such a restriction is familiar in American procedure. In the state of Missouri, for instance, a governor may not succeed himself, but is once more eligible four years later at the expiration of his successor's term. As a further precaution under the Roman system it was provided that two years must elapse between the end of a term and the assumption of the next higher magistracy. This provision was a salutary protection for the public against a dishonest or oppressive magistrate. A magistrate could not be prosecuted for official misdeeds during his term. The two-year interval before he could seek immunity in another office provided an opportunity to call him to account for any derelictions.

The finance office to which Cicero aspired in itself conveyed no great distinction. The growing business of the state had recently required an increase in the number of these treasury officials to twenty. Eight or nine of them were needed in Italy. The rest were assigned to the provinces. The old families were extremely jealous of the consulship. They insisted on keeping this highest office in their own hands. The subordinate offices did not greatly concern them. Naturally there always were young aristocrats coming up through these offices with an eye on the consulship. But ambitious men of promise and wealth outside the old families were not barred from election as finance officers, commissioners of public works, or judges. The importance of the position of finance officer lay in the fact not only that it was the first step toward the consulship, but that at the end of his term a finance officer became automatically a life member of the Senate.

If young Marcus Cicero at the outset of his political career had reviewed understandingly the political record of the previous half-century he would have found it shot through with disquieting aspects. In a previous chapter we have observed the frequency with which the civil government had been submerged. Three times in the twelve years immediately preceding Cicero's entrance into politics Rome had been taken by armed forces. In his boyhood the financiers had forced a law through the Assembly by crowding with drawn daggers about the speaker's platform. On a later occasion an Assembly had been compelled by military pressure to repeal legislation enacted only a few days previously.

Very likely these periods of anarchy and martial law seemed to the young politician merely a series of unrelated emergencies — regrettable indeed, but isolated and not likely to recur. Five years later the presence of troops outside the capital was to assure the election of their two commanders to the consulship. But for the most part the next quarter-century was to provide an interlude in which the forms of constitutional government were to be fairly well observed, although for several years there was to be a veiled dictatorship of three powerful politicians — the First Triumvirate. Throughout the period there was plenty of evidence that volcanic forces were seething beneath the surface. It was not, however, until repressed and growing tensions were released when Cæsar crossed the Rubicon in 49 that the full implications of the previous uneasy years became apparent.

Favourably known as he was at the bar, Cicero had no difficulty in being elected a finance commissioner. Sicily at that time was divided into two administrative districts and Cicero was assigned to the western district, with headquarters at the bustling port of Lilybæum, the modern Marsala. Lilybæum, on the westernmost point of the island, is only ninety miles from Cape Bon, the nearest point on the African coast. It had been the Roman base of naval operations against Africa and in time of peace was the natural port for the shipment of goods between Sicily and Africa. The young finance commissioner took pride in doing a good job, in conducting his office economically, and in leaving his post with the high regard of all those with whom he had had official business.

In a speech made in Rome after his return he mentions with satisfaction some of his achievements. He had kept the grain supply moving to Rome under difficult circumstances. To brokers he had been affable, to merchants just, in dealing with contractors a gentleman, "scrupulous in financial integrity toward the provincials." At the end of his term he had made an address in which he told the people of Lilybæum to feel free to call on him for service in Rome if the occasion should arise. Five years later the call came in an appeal for help against an outrageously oppressive governor, and Cicero made good his promise.

A characteristic incident that he relates shows the broad cultural interests of the man. The most famous personage in the history of Sicily was Archimedes, the Isaac Newton of antiquity, one of the great scientists and inventors of all time. The story of his experience with the bathtub is familiar. When he stepped into the tub the overflowing of the water displaced by his body suggested an important line of scientific inquiry in the field of hydrostatics. In his excitement he leaped from the tub and raced home without his clothes exclaiming: "*Eureka, eureka!* I have found it, I have found it!" Syracuse was his home and there he was killed when the Romans captured the city in 212. The story runs that he was so interested in drawing a mathematical figure in the sand that he paid no attention to the questions of a soldier, who ran him through without knowing who he was. The Roman commander was genuinely grieved by the great man's death and directed that he be given an elaborate funeral. In accordance with his expressed desire his tomb was marked by a sphere and a cylinder to commemorate one of his brilliant mathematical discoveries.

Among other achievements Archimedes had constructed two planetariums to show the motions of the stars. These had been taken to Rome after the fall of Syracuse. With his quite un-Roman intellectual curiosity Cicero had been fascinated by them. "A remarkable feat," he somewhere writes, "that Archimedes was able with a single motor to reproduce all the unequal and different movements of the heavenly bodies." Persons who have visited modern planetariums will agree.

Before leaving Sicily the young official made a devout and sentimental journey to Syracuse at the other end of the island to search for the forgotten grave of the distinguished Greek scientist. He tells of the quest in his *Tusculan Disputations*. The fact that the tomb had been marked with a sphere and a cylinder was known to him. With a party of prominent Syracusans the finance officer visited an old cemetery. There, in a wild thicket, he noticed rising above the bushes a small column on which was the figure of a sphere and a cylinder. Slaves opened a path to the grave with sickles. When the visitors reached the tombstone they found an inscription on it with only half the lines still legible. "So you see," Cicero writes, "one of the most famous cities of Greece, once indeed a great school of learning as well, would have been ignorant of the tomb of its most creative citizen had not a man of Arpinum pointed it out."

This sensitive feeling for the builders of civilization crops out in a kindred incident many years later. When Cicero, now one of the most distinguished men in the Roman world, was proceeding to his post as governor of Cilicia he stopped in Athens. An influential Roman in exile had recently acquired through action of the town council a building site upon which stood the ruins of the house of the famous philosopher Epicurus. This landmark was to be torn down to make way for a modern building. Apparently the new owner had given up his building plan, but he had got into a row with the Epicurean Society and refused to relinquish the site so that the ruins might be preserved. The head of the society appealed to Cicero to intercede with the owner, who had left Athens. We have the tactful letter which the proconsul wrote in response, asking the purchaser to instruct his agents to inform the town council that its action under which he had obtained the site might be rescinded with his consent.

It was on his return from his Sicilian assignment that Cicero had the deflating shock to which I referred in discussing a possible dinner-table conversation at the home of Lucullus. He learned that nobody had missed him. The lesson of the incident was not lost on the keen young Roman politician. He tells about it in a speech several years later. He realized, he says, that the ears of the Roman people were somewhat dull, but their eyes keen and alert. So from that time on he took care that he should be seen every day. "I lived in the public eye; I haunted the Forum; neither my doorkeeper nor sleep prevented any clients from getting to me for consultation." He cashed in on this policy whenever he ran for office.

By this time Cicero's reputation as a lawyer was established. By birth he was affiliated with the big-business interests and they naturally sought out the industrious, intelligent, and eloquent young pleader. Ambition combined with his restless temperament to make him a glutton for work. "Not even when I had nothing to do," he remarked afterward, "did I do nothing. I worked on my speeches on festivals and holidays. Absolute leisure was a thing I never knew."

He was not exaggerating. The perfectly incredible amount of work he did is testified to by his writings that have survived. I have made a rough computation that indicates these would fill thirteen volumes of one hundred thousand words each — and the surviving writings are only part of his literary product. It must be borne in mind, too, that his writing was done during a busy public and private career, except for two comparatively brief periods when he was in retirement. Few men in history have left such a monument to their industry.

Virtually all that we know of his next few years is that he was devoting himself to his law practice, with incidental excursions into politics. In his entire public life the imperfect records indicate that he was employed in sixty-nine criminal cases, of which he won forty-four and lost ten, with the outcome of the rest uncertain. Seven of ten civil suits were successful. In forty-two pleas to the Senate he scored sixteen successes and seven failures; in nineteen cases the result is not of record. In eighteen addresses to the people he succeeded on seven occasions; as to the rest we do not know.

Cicero's method of preparing his speeches has been recorded by a professor of rhetoric of the next century, Quintilian, the first public instructor in Rome to be paid from the state treasury. According to Quintilian, Cicero wrote out in advance the most vital parts of a speech, especially the beginning, and committed them to memory. The rest he outlined in his mind, and trusted to improvising when necessary. Many of his speeches he published after delivery. In this he was helpd by shorthand reports. But he took the opportunity to revise them and so to circulate them in the shape in which he wished them to appear. Several of his most famous speeches never were delivered but were published as if they had been spoken.

We learn from Cicero himself that, accomplished orator though he was, he invariably was frightened when he got on his feet. "I am always very nervous when I begin to speak," he remarked. Only once, however, did he really collapse from fright, and that was when hostile soldiers dominated the Forum. He must have put great dramatic force into his speeches. We have Quintilian's comment that there was "such weight" in his words that his audiences "felt ashamed to disagree." Webster, Gladstone, Bryan, and other effective speakers had the same power. When Webster thundered: "If the Whigs take this position where will *I* go?" his hearers shrank back shuddering. Where *would* Daniel Webster go?

In his famous treatises on the art of oratory Cicero frankly discloses his calculated methods of appealing to his hearers. The orator, he says, must give information, impart æsthetic pleasure, and finally stir the emotions. Reading his speeches with this technique in mind, we may still admire the lucidity and dramatic effect with which he marshalled his facts. As to æsthetic pleasure, he had a superb command of the language and a sensitive ear. His apparently unconscious rhythm, his balanced sentences, his thunderous climaxes carried his hearers away. On the emotional side we may postpone for the moment his use of invective and glance at his general method. This involved stirring up contempt for his opponents, ignoring the issues in a bad case by centring on personalities, and resorting to the cheap tricks of the trade by introducing to the jury the weeping child, father, or mother of the defendant. From the number of times Cicero used this last device it must have gone over in great shape with Roman juries. Further, he developed skill in clouding the issues when it was advantageous to do so. On one occasion he diverted attention from a charge of election fraud by dwelling on the fact that his client was a military man such as the times demanded. Again he carried the jury off its feet by ignoring his client and eulogizing Pompey, who had nothing to do with the case. According to Quintilian, Cicero once boasted of throwing dust in the eyes of the jury. These methods did not offend the moral sense of the times. Indeed, they are extensively practised in America today.

Cicero prided himself on his perorations which he counted on to carry his audiences with him. They usually display the same straining for effect that we find in eighteenth- and nineteenth-century orators who were influenced by the Ciceronian style. The Roman would have approved the ending of William J. Bryan's appeal to the Democratic convention in 1896: "You shall not press down upon the brow of labor this crown of thorns. You shall not crucify mankind upon this cross of gold." In his later years Cicero found his mastery of words had lost its old effectiveness. The simple directness of Cæsar had turned the tide from the elaborate and artificial Ciceronian periods. A new school of speakers had sprung up to whom Cicero seemed dreadfully old-fashioned.

It may be inferred from his voluminous writings on the subject that Cicero regarded the practice of law and speechmaking as an art and himself as a supreme artist. While his opinion of himself as an orator of the first rank has been widely accepted down to the present time, it is hardly justified. Cicero was too consciously the artist, his artistry was too obtrusive, too lacking in sincerity for him to be placed in the top flight of public speakers. In a letter to Atticus he writes half humorously, half seriously about his calculated effects. He had been trying to impress Pompey with a speech made before the Senate. His familiar purple patches, he flatters himself, had been employed with real success. " Ye gods," he exclaims, " how I showed off before my new listener, Pompey! Then, if ever, my flow of rounded periods, my antitheses, my constructive arguments stood me in good stead. In a word, loud applause! . . . You know how I can thunder on a subject like that. This time my thunders were so loud that I forbear to say anything more about them. I suspect you heard them over in Epirus."

Undoubtedly this technique was admirably adapted to the spirit of the times and to the emotional Latin temperament. The fact that Cicero was in constant demand in the courts and that he was generally successful testifies to his effectiveness but not necessarily to his supremacy in the general field of oratory.

Cicero's letters to Atticus, so simple, so natural, so human, belong in the eternal literature. Some of his less pretentious addresses when he was not consciously trying to make a great impression may still be read with pleasure. In many of his speeches are passages that show a breadth of learning, a familiarity with literature both Greek and Latin, an appreciation of art, an urbanity beyond praise. But these were not the speeches and passages in which he took the most pride. There were times, as his admiring brother said, when he showed such passion of look and gesture " that I thought some power was rendering you unconscious of what you did." In these outbursts when he took down his hair and turned himself loose — in short, when he thought he was most sublime — we find him tiresome, even ridiculous. Some of his violent speeches, like the *Second Philippic*, once greatly admired, are simply terrible.

To Cicero both as lawyer and as political speaker might be applied the language that Disraeli used regarding Gladstone: " A sophistical rhetorician inebriated with the luxuriance of his own verbosity and gifted with an egotistical imagination that can at all times command an interminable and inconsistent series of arguments to malign an opponent and glorify himself."

The speeches in which the orator specialized in invective require especial attention. Undoubtedly they did not give the offence to those who heard them that they give to modern readers. Quintilian has preserved a grossly coarse attack upon a distinguished prisoner at the bar by an advocate of Cicero's time. Then he exclaims admiringly: " Could you find anything more plausible in imagination, more vehement in censure, or more vivid in description? " Manners change. Queen Victoria would have been horrified at the language used by Queen Elizabeth. The Rome of Cicero was not far removed from the coarseness of Roman frontier life. Its culture was spotted. In some respects it was urbane, in others crude. This has been true in all ages. Cicero might exclaim to an opponent: " Now do you see, beast, now do you perceive what people complain of in your brazen face? " But in seventeenth-century England Coke called Raleigh " a spider of hell " and added that " there never lived a viler viper." In nineteenth-century America the revered but ruffled Horace Greeley shrieked at a man with whom he disagreed: " You lie, villain."

Invective in Rome was a favourite indoor and outdoor sport. When a Roman reviled an opponent he was not necessarily making accusations that he expected to be believed. He was merely getting his disapproval off his chest. In the imperial period there was a general law against libel and slander. Whether any such law existed in Cicero's time is uncertain. In the earlier years of the Roman Republic we learn of three instances in which a playwright and two actors were cited for slander. These cases all involved a state-owned theatre, and public officials doubtless felt they were entitled to protection. In the Senate, the Assemblies, and the courts the greatest freedom of speech was customary. It is surmised that a law enacted under Sulla penalizing injuries included injuries to reputation as well as injuries from personal violence. If so the law was rarely if ever invoked. It was easier for the slandered person, especially if he had political influence, to get back at his enemy by trumping up some accusation against him in a politically dominated court. If Cicero felt any restraint in his invectives from the possibility of a proceeding against him for slander I have been unable to discover it.

Public men were expected to be able to take it, and we occasionally find Cicero on agreeable terms with politicians whom he had scandalously denounced in previous speeches. The custom of the country warns us not to take too literally some of Cicero's famous denunciations, especially those against two of his dearest enemies, Catiline and Mark Antony. Nevertheless, with all allowances made, there is evidence that Cicero went beyond the accepted licence of his times and hurt his influence with Roman audiences. As the years passed they came to appreciate how personal feeling influenced the speaker and how unreliable were his statements under such conditions. One of his most violent attacks, for instance, was partly motivated by the fact that his opponent had made fun of his poetry as the real cause of his exile. Some boasting lines in a poem on his consulship greatly amused Roman critics for many years:

Oh happy fate of Rome, to date
Her birthday from my consulate.

When these were criticized Cicero couldn't take the joke. "That monster said," he exclaimed, "that I got into trouble not from my conduct but from my verses!" If the Romans had any sense of humour a chuckle must have swept over the Senate at these words.

Dio Cassius, a celebrated historian of Rome, writing two and a half centuries later, comments that while Cicero himself "always spoke immoderately to all alike, he could not bring himself to accept similar frankness from others." Dio may be prejudiced against Cicero. But the great orator was so sensitive, so impulsive, so lacking in restraint that I suspect Dio is right when he says: "Cicero made many bitter enemies by always employing an unbridled and excessive frankness of speech." Perhaps even Quintus found his brother's eloquence at times a bit trying. When asked why he had shrunk from public speaking he is reported to have replied that one orator in a family was enough.

In the schools Cicero continued to be used as a model even after his vogue had passed. Quintilian refers to him as the "perfect orator," a man whose name was "not the name of a man, but the name of eloquence itself." This would naturally be the judgment of a professor of rhetoric.

Turning from his professional life to his personal habits we come upon revealing traits. Cicero was one of those expansive men who are not greedy for money, but who love to gratify their taste for luxurious living. "It is a man's mind, not his money-chest, that is called rich," he once wrote. "Though your coffers be full, while I see you empty I shall never consider you wealthy." Still he was not blind to the advantages of an ample money-chest.

While Cicero did not rank with the multimillionaires of his day he was exceedingly well to do until troubles piled up in his later life. From his earliest years he never suffered from poverty. His father had means so that the sons did not have to go to work as youngsters, but could be taken to Rome to be educated for a profession. Marriage bettered Marcus' financial position. Terentia was not a great heiress but her dowry must have been of substantial help to the family, and her apartments in Rome brought some $5,000 a year in rentals. On this basis their value has been estimated at $65,000. As time went on Cicero was able to make productive investments. For these and for the extravagant scale on which he lived he needed a considerable income. In one of his highly moral moods he exclaimed: "Ye gods, when will men understand what treasures are found in economy!" Himself he never understood. He spent large sums on statuary for his country place at Tusculum and his town house in Rome. Pliny tells of a table of fragrant African wood, still preserved a century later, for which Cicero was supposed to have paid $25,000.

His income did not come from holding office. Roman

public officials received no salary, which proved an unhappy incentive to dishonesty and extortion to those on duty outside the capital. In his governorship of the province of Cilicia Cicero insists he was scrupulously honest. Yet in his year of foreign service in some way he managed to pick up $110,000 which he lent to Pompey for the war with Cæsar and probably never recovered. Just how he accumulated this considerable sum is still a matter of speculation. A Roman governor was not expected to meet his expenses out of his own pocket and the government always made him a generous allowance of money. Funds were provided for the payment of troops and staff, and for food, transportation, and clothing. While in general the unexpended balance was to be refunded, in certain cases savings reverted legitimately to the governor. With Cicero it is a moot point whether the savings could have reached the amount he mentions, or whether they were supplemented from the sale of war captives in spite of his protests to the contrary.

In any event the chief source of his income must have been his law practice. This, in spite of an old law of 204 that forbade the acceptance of legal fees in any guise. It was the theory of the law that members of the aristocracy were bound to furnish legal advice free. The effect was to prevent a poor man from entering the profession and to keep it as a monopoly for the well-to-do. Up to recent years there was an analogous situation in England, where members of the House of Commons used to serve without pay. Until a salary provision was made, poor men were almost barred from the House.

In the last century of the Roman Republic the law against fees had become a dead letter. No penalty attached to its violation and there were many ways to get around it. Clients undoubtedly found they could obtain better service from a lawyer if he knew his efforts would command some substantial expression of gratitude; not a fee, of course, or even a gift, but what is delicately called an honorarium.

Sometimes the able counsel needed a loan, and if he neglected to repay it the grateful client did not complain. If the lawyer was in politics and did not happen to be pressed for funds his services might be rewarded by political support. In his prosecution of Verres, corrupt governor of Sicily, described in the next chapter, Cicero repeats the ex-governor's boast that he systematically divided the spoils three ways — for the lawyers who would be needed to defend him, for the jurors who would try him, and for himself. The fee provision does not shock the prosecutor and that Verres' chief counsel had accepted a fee he mentions only with a smile.

The old law did not embarrass Cicero. In Rome he did as the Romans did. Only once does he mention the statute in his correspondence, and then jokingly. Still, he was sensitive on the matter of compensation. It was not pleasant for a man whose family had finally achieved its ambition of joining the nobility to be open to the gibes of opponents on the score of commercialism. Cicero liked to assume in the grand manner that he was above selling his legal services and he went to some pains to spread the legend. Plutarch took it seriously from Tiro, and Quintus Cicero fell in line in his political *Handbook*. But Dio implies that in the crisis that drove Cicero into exile his clients failed to rally to his support because they felt they had discharged their obligations to their lawyer with their fees and owed him nothing more.

In an unguarded moment Cicero himself admitted in a speech that his law practice gave him " moderate wealth." When the report got about that he had accepted $100,000 from a client — a " loan," of course — toward the purchase of his mansion on the Palatine, he passed it off as a joke. There are many references in his writings to cities that were devoted to him and whose interests he represented. Presumably he was paid for his services by the municipalities as well as by various business syndicates for which he appeared. His influence and talents were outstanding and he saw no reason why he should not cash in on them.

A curious Roman custom played into the hands of the legal profession. Rich men were accustomed to advertise their friendship with the great and the near great in their wills. They would leave substantial legacies to prominent persons. It would be natural for a man of wealth to encourage the devotion of his attorney by holding out the prospect of a legacy in addition to immediate compensation. The year before his death the contemptuous accusation was made against Cicero that no inheritances had come his way. He retorted grandly that his legacies had amounted to a million dollars. That would have meant an average annual income of $30,000. It happens that he somewhere speaks of this precise sum of $30,000 a year as suitable for a gentleman's income, and he seems to have lived on the scale suggested. But in general the legacies he mentions from time to time are so small and his exultation over one of moderate size is so great that we may assume he was exaggerating the amount of the bequests. The bulk of his income probably came in various ways from living clients.

His finances were often in confusion. Frequently he did not know where he stood. But if he was hard pressed today he expected that tomorrow he might be flush with some unexpected legacy. On one occasion he tells Atticus he has $30,000 in the bank which prompts him to buy some gardens. When he was in funds he would lend money generously to his friends without inquiring into their solvency. One instance is probably typical. He had endorsed a note for a man named Cornificius who defaulted payment. The creditor applied to Atticus, who acted as Cicero's financial agent. Cicero replied to an inquiry from his friend that he knew Cornificius was rich, but he had a son, and, come to think of it, Cicero was uncertain whose note he had endorsed. In fact he couldn't remember having endorsed any note. But the transaction dated back a good many years and of course he might be mistaken. Doubtless there were many times when the methodical Atticus was driven frantic by his friend's carelessness, but he was devoted to Cicero and he never lost his patience.

With his extravagant tastes as measured by his income, Cicero was a fearless borrower. He had to be. He was always in the banks that lined the Forum. His letters are a Who's Who of Roman bankers. Apparently his debts did not greatly disturb him. When he had borrowed to buy the great house on the Palatine he wrote jokingly to a friend: "I am so heavily in debt that I am eager to join a conspiracy if anybody would let me in." The reference was to the conspiracy of Catiline, which was suspected of having as one of its aims the scaling down of obligations.

One of his debts, however, he took seriously. When he was on good terms with Cæsar he had borrowed $40,000 from him. Then in a shift of politics he was on the other side. This occasioned him great embarrassment and he wrote to Atticus that the debt must be paid. "It is an ugly business," he says, "to owe money to a political opponent." And he speculates on the possibility that after he makes a speech in the Senate against Cæsar the great man's agent may call on him to pay up.

By a curious contradiction in traits Cicero, who was so careless in large financial transactions, was careful in small matters. He tells of prodding his gardener on the Palatine until he had a profusion of cut flowers, some of which could be sold in the ancient equivalent of the modern gorgeous flower market on the Spanish Steps. His show place at Tusculum included orchards and a truck farm. He writes to Tiro to stir up another renter for it in order to keep the present farmer on his toes. Why, he says, even before he had improved the place a former gardener, that rascal Helico, used to pay him $50 a year. The agricultural features of the estate were important enough to warrant Cicero's paying an irrigation tax. He inquires of Tiro about the water supply from an aqueduct between Tusculum and Rome.

There were rental properties connected with his ancestral

place. Later in life he speaks of going to Arpinum " to settle the small rents of my farms," and at the beginning of the civil war between Cæsar and Pompey he writes to his wife that if the cost of living advances too much in Rome she can retire to the Arpinum homestead, which will support her and her household attendants. He refers to the " managers " of his estate at Cumæ as if it included several farms from which he presumably derived income.

Our most definite information about revenues from his villas has to do with his property at Puteoli on the Bay of Naples. A share in this estate was left him with others by a banker, Cluvius. The banker had had difficulty in collecting loans which he had made to cities in Asia and Cicero had interceded on his behalf with the governor. His gratitude was shown in his will. The place at Puteoli included shops, and the investment possibilities impelled Cicero to buy out the other heirs. The shops were dilapidated. Sending for an architect to put them in repair Cicero wrote: " Two of my shops have fallen down and the rest are cracking. Not only the tenants but the very mice have migrated." So successfully did he handle the business that he wrote to Atticus that the revenue the first year was $4,000 and he hoped to bring it up to $5,000.

In acquiring villas in the country Cicero was following the prevailing mode. It was the custom of Roman gentlemen to have country places to which they could retire from the heat of the capital. Cicero loved the ancestral home near Arpinum, but as a rising politician he needed several villas to make the proper impression. As soon as he was able, a few years after his return from Sicily, he bought a villa near Formiæ, seventy-five miles down the coast, and the one at Tusculum near the modern Frascati, only fifteen miles from the city. While we do not know the site in spite of the positiveness of the modern guides, the Tusculan villa probably stood on a hillside about fifteen hundred feet above the plain, where it commanded a view of Rome and of the sea. His snobbish aristocratic neighbours, he admitted years afterwards to Atticus, were annoyed at the intrusion of this parvenu. Their disapproval did not disturb him. He always knew his worth and often talked about it.

It is pleasant to observe the enthusiasm with which he writes to his friend about the works of art which he had commissioned Atticus to pick up for him in Greece. In the first letter which has been preserved he says: "Anything you see suitable for my Tusculan villa I should be glad if you would procure for me, only don't put yourself to any inconvenience. The truth is there is no other place that gives me such complete rest after all my worries and hard work." A few weeks later he was asking for appropriate art objects for the hall. "I am so delighted with my Tusculan villa," he adds, "that I never feel really happy until I get there." For some trifling statuary for the gardens he arranged to pay $1,000.

Several years later we find him complaining to a friend whom he had commissioned to buy some statues and who had bungled the job. "I know those Bacchantes," he protests. "If I had wanted them I would have specifically asked you to get them. And a statue of Mars! What do I, a pacifist, want with that?" But he would like some pictures for his new reading-rooms at Tusculum. Paintings, he says, give him especial pleasure.

Cicero's love of beautiful things constantly crops out in his correspondence. "I write this," he says in a letter to his brother, "before daybreak by the carved wood lamp stand, in which I take great delight." Later he admits to Atticus that while he is immensely pleased with his property at Tusculum and with his estate at Pompeii, they have overwhelmed him with debt.

As Cicero became increasingly prosperous he added to his villas until he finally owned seven, together with several small lodges where he could stay the night in travelling back and forth. He was fond of the sea. The old homestead was in the Volscian mountains, and the Tusculan villa had only a distant view of the Mediterranean. But the others were scattered along the shore between Rome and Pompeii. One villa was at Antium, thirty-five miles south of Rome, where, as he wrote, he could read, fish, or watch the waves roll in. This he sold, perhaps when he bought a place at Astura, not far away. Then came the villa near Formiæ. Beyond this was Cumæ, near the fashionable resort of Baiæ. The next was the inherited estate at Puteoli, where on a famous occasion he entertained Cæsar with a large retinue. The seventh was at Pompeii.

Cicero was not always successful in finding seclusion for his work in these retreats. From the villa near Formiæ he confided his troubles to Atticus. Writing, he says, is impossible. His villa is so crowded with visitors from Formiæ that it is a public hall rather than a private house. Most visitors leave early. But two long-winded fellows have places next door on either side. " One of them," he writes, " almost lives in my house. He even declares that his reason for not returning to Rome is that he may spend whole days with me here philosophizing! Which way am I to turn? For you see with what bores I am pestered."

Nevertheless his country places were an essential part of his life and he loved them all. " My dear villas, those jewels of Italy," he calls them proudly and fondly in a letter to Atticus. Perhaps to him the jewels sparkled more brightly when he could make them pay their way.

CHAPTER XII

LEADER OF THE ROMAN BAR

THROUGH ALL these busy years at the bar Cicero never forgot the goal of his ambition, the consulship. When he was approaching the age of thirty-five he had to make an important political decision – whether to stand for commissioner of public works or for tribune. Neither office was an essential preliminary to the consulship. But the tribunes had originated as the champions of the commoners, the plebeians, and had been historically associated with them, whereas election as a commissioner of public works meant admission of the magistrate's descendants to the nobility. As Cicero's connections had been with the business crowd he obviously needed to build himself up with the old families whose support was virtually essential for election to the consulship. We do not need the confirmatory evidence of Dio to understand Cicero's decision for the public-works commissionership.

Just at this time while the candidate was doing his best to keep on terms with all factions, he was put on the spot by his friends in Sicily. In 73 a rapacious Roman politician, Verres, had been sent as governor to the island. Ordinarily his term would have been one year, but because of exigencies in Italy it had been prolonged to three. He had spent his time plundering the province and in the course of his plundering was guilty of many acts of extreme cruelty. At the expiration of his term in 70 the Sicilians appealed to Cicero to prosecute him and obtain restitution.

It was a delicate situation for the young aspirant for office. Verres had influential connections in Rome and there was little interest in the capital in provincial affairs. As Cicero remarked later: " In the bustle of life at Rome it is almost impossible to attend to what goes on in the provinces." If Cicero should take the case he knew he would be giving offence in important quarters while people generally might be indifferent to his exposures. There were counterbalancing considerations. Cicero was a man of humane instincts and he must have been really moved by what his Sicilian friends had suffered. This fact could hardly have been decisive. After all he was a lawyer who took clients as they came. The very next year without turning a hair he defended a similar though humbler criminal charged with extortion and misgovernment in a province. Under the Roman legal code he was quite justified in doing this. Under the modern practice important law-breakers have no difficulty in finding counsel to defend them. But we may assume that in the case of Verres the young lawyer was delighted that his professional duties coincided with his natural inclinations.

In accepting the case Cicero knew that he could count on the backing of Pompey, then one of the consuls and perhaps the most powerful man in Rome, who was at outs with the aristocracy. Beyond this was his knowledge that the trial might be made into a celebrated case. Verres was to be defended by Hortensius, at that time the leading lawyer of Rome. If Cicero could best Hortensius his prestige would be vastly enhanced. This consideration of prestige I suspect was decisive in this case as it had been in the case of Sextus Roscius.

Accordingly Cicero applied to the court for appointment as prosecutor. Here he had to overcome the claims of another aspirant put forward by Verres — a finance officer who had served under Verres in Sicily and on whose friendship the accused man might count. In the preliminary proceeding Cicero succeeded in exposing the collusion so successfully that he won the appointment. Before a criminal trial could proceed the prosecutor had to take oath that he had adequate grounds for bringing the charge and was not actuated by malice. If a jury by a large majority found the accused innocent the prosecutor was liable to be put on trial for malicious prosecution before the same jury. Cicero took no chances. He obtained permission to collect evidence in Sicily so he could be sure of maintaining his own position as well as of making an impressive showing at the trial.

Meanwhile Verres was employing all his resources, quite in the modern custom, to discredit the prosecutor and to postpone the proceedings until the next year, when he might count on a friendly court. An accusation of extortion was suddenly brought against another provincial governor whose trial was set before that of Verres. Apparently the purpose was to prolong the hearings in this other case so that Verres' trial would go over to the next year. The trick was circumvented. But Verres used his influence in Sicily to throw obstacles in the way of Cicero's gathering of evidence. One magistrate, for instance, made the technical excuse, in attempting to withhold evidence, that Cicero had addressed the court in Greek—the prevalent language in Syracuse—instead of in Latin. Nevertheless he was able to return in fifty days with the necessary witnesses and documentary evidence. Money was lavishly used, but to no avail, in an attempt to defeat Cicero for commissioner of public works in the July election.

The trial was set for August 5. Verres still had hope of dragging the case along by taking advantage of numerous holidays so that no verdict could be reached in that year. Under the ordinary procedure the prosecutor would have opened the case by a long speech reviewing the evidence, which might last several days. But ten days later the first set of holidays was to begin. Cicero avoided the temptation of a great oratorical display. He opened the proceedings with a brief speech and then began the examination of witnesses. Man after man testified to such a series of acts of appalling cruelty and rapacity on the part of Verres that the court more than once had to take a recess to keep the infuriated crowd of spectators from lynching the defendant. After nine days Hortensius threw up the case. Verres withdrew into voluntary exile at Marseille and the court ordered his possessions sold to provide restitution to the Sicilians. Unfortunately he had concealed so much of his loot that probably little was recovered. Retribution overtook him twenty-seven years later. He fell a victim in the proscription instituted by the reigning coalition in 43, because, as Pliny writes, Mark Antony coveted some of his "specimens of Corinthian brass," part no doubt of his Sicilian plunder.

Only two short speeches in the case of Verres were actually delivered, the first the pleading by which Cicero obtained the right to prosecute, and the second the introductory speech at the trial. Five others were published in order to complete the record. In spite of allowances that must be made for an eloquent prosecutor's customary exaggerations, the outcome of the trial and Verres' confession of guilt establish the general soundness of the charges.

The prosecution was so brilliantly conducted that it has remained a model for lawyers of succeeding ages. In his essay on Warren Hastings, who was impeached in London in 1788 for misconduct in India, Macaulay recalls the parallel. In the audience to hear Edmund Burke's opening speech was Edward Gibbon, historian of the Roman Empire. Macaulay says that he must have "thought of the days when Cicero pleaded the cause of Sicily against Verres." Lawyers may still study with profit the Verrine orations for the vividness of the incidents narrated, for the transitions from humour to pathos, from discussion of Greek sculpture to the recital of cruelties to Roman citizens, from light touches to outbursts of passionate indignation. Today the speeches remain great oratory.

The effectiveness of Cicero's pleading and the dreadful administration of the governor he denounced have combined to create a wrong impression of provincial government under the Roman Republic. It is not fair to regard Verres as a typical Roman governor. In spite of dishonest officials the Roman provinces in general were probably better governed than they had been under native rulers. Polybius, writing in the previous century, was able to say that the ascendancy of Rome was " the best thing Fortune ever did to the world." There had been a deterioration in the character of the governors. They were so far from Rome and the supervision of the central government was so lax that they were under great temptation to misbehave. But Cicero, later an honest governor, wrote to his brother as if he was enunciating a platitude that the first duty of a governor was to see to the welfare of the governed. Under the Empire the provincial government was greatly improved. But as one historian has remarked, Augustus had merely to enforce the laws of the Republic and to replace amateurs with experienced men.

One political factor in the trial should perhaps be mentioned, for it was not overlooked by Cicero. The jury was made up of senators. The Roman administration was proposing a reform of the jury system to admit to juries business men not of the senatorial order. Cicero kept reminding the jurors that they, too, were on trial, for the public was watching to see whether a senatorial jury could be trusted. While this jury proved honest its just verdict did not save the old jury system. In spite of the conviction of Verres the reform measure went through.

Apparently the Verres case was so flagrant that Cicero's prosecution of it did not give deep offence to the old families. Three years later the prosecutor was elected judge after two postponements of the election due to serious riots, the ominous significance of which he perhaps did not realize.

During the eight years between Cicero's return from his finance office in Sicily and his election as judge political tensions in Rome had been increasing. In the year 73 had come the famous slave insurrection in southern Italy under the gladiator Spartacus. The political generals sent against him had failed and the insurrection finally had been suppressed by Crassus and Pompey, both of whom had been lieutenants of Sulla. Then they had marched their troops on Rome and under military pressure had obtained consulships, to which they were legally ineligible at the time. Still retaining their soldiers outside the city to impress the Senate, they had proceeded to liberalize the reactionary Sullan Constitution in accordance with campaign pledges made to win popular support in the election. Once more the civil authorities had given way before the threat of force. Still the constitutional tradition was strong and both consuls retired to private life at the end of their term.

Three years later a plague of pirates who were sweeping the seas and interrupting the grain supply gave Pompey his opportunity. Although the old families disliked him because of his revision of the Constitution, the shortage of grain imports compelled them to acquiesce in his appointment to a great command to deal with the pirates. So complete was the public confidence in Pompey and in his ability to restore the interrupted flow of grain that immediately upon his appointment the price of wheat went off. He more than met expectations, and his success in clearing the seas of pirates led to his promotion to another great command.

For several years the government had been engaged in the Asiatic war against Mithridates previously referred to. Lucullus was in charge, but after brilliant successes his campaign had bogged down. His generous treatment of provincials in reducing extortionate interest rates and clamping down on the exactions of the tax-collecting syndicates had alienated the business men of Rome. They were able to bring about his replacement by Pompey. The command was conferred upon him in 66 by the Manilian Law, proposed by a tribune, Manilius. Because of the extensive military and political powers it bestowed, the proposal was bitterly opposed by the senators, again in vain. Cicero, now a judge, made his first political address to the people in the preliminary session of the Assembly — his famous oration for the Manilian Law, which is still read in American colleges. Another supporter of the bill was Julius Cæsar, then a rising young politician who had returned the previous year from serving as finance officer in Spain. Though he came of one of the oldest and most aristocratic families of Rome, his sympathies had been against his class. Perhaps as a boy he had been influenced by his admiration for the great commoner Marius, his uncle by marriage to his Aunt Julia. His first wife was the daughter of a popular leader and he had incurred the enmity of Sulla by refusing to divorce her at the dictator's command. The stodgy nobility had no attraction for his daring spirit. But as yet he was an unknown quantity in Roman politics.

We have what was perhaps cynical contemporary opinion reflected in Dio as to the motives animating Cæsar and Cicero in their support of the proposal of Manilius. The people, Dio says, were so strongly for the bill that it was certain to pass. The merits of the measure, he thinks, did not concern its two prominent supporters. Cæsar rushed in because he saw the people were much stronger than the opposing senators, and he wished to set a precedent for conferring similar powers on himself later. Cicero, with his candidacy for the consulship in mind, wished to create the impression that he could turn the scales to whichever party he might favour. And he adds the acid comment that Cicero " was accustomed to play a double role and would favour one party and then the other to the end that he might be courted by both." In other words, he used tactics familiar to politicians down to the present time, as we shall see in more detail in the next chapter.

Any observer of the American political scene recognizes the problem. To be successful in public life a man cannot go about speaking his mind freely on all occasions. Such a course risks alienating blocs of voters unnecessarily. I recall a brilliant United States senator who was defeated for re-election by a narrow margin. In the political autopsy that followed, his managers agreed that rather unthinkingly he had alienated the school-teacher group, the remnants of the Ku Klux Klan, and a small but compact faction within his party. The support of any one of these blocs would have put him over. But while the successful politician must have votes and at times must make compromises to get them, he is in danger if he compromises on important principles, or if his technique becomes too obvious. In the long run it is harmful for a man in public life to get the reputation of being too political, of sacrificing too much in order to hold office. Such a reputation undermines public confidence.

While Dio's comment on the reason for Cicero's support of the Manilian Law is wholly unfair, I believe his criticism of the "double role" reflects a widespread feeling concerning Cicero that developed subsequently and that greatly impaired his influence. This feeling is suggested by an incident reported twenty years later. A well-known playwright was looking for a seat in the theatre. Cicero called to him: "If we weren't so crowded here, Laberius, I would make room for you." "I'm surprised, Cicero," Laberius retorted, "that you haven't room. You usually sit on two stools." Undoubtedly Cicero's reputation gave point to the gibe. He was a patriot and a politician. As a politician he was so slick at times that he slipped.

In advocating the cause of Pompey Cicero knew he was on the popular side and that he was putting the powerful business crowd under fresh obligations to him. He was offending the aristocrats, but perhaps not too seriously. On balance his course promised political profit. Happily, reasons of state marched with political advantage. Pompey was the outstanding and natural choice for the eastern command. Cicero had a sincere admiration for him and in later years came to look upon him as the one military man who might be trusted to use his power to preserve the Republic rather than to destroy it.

But in spite of the fact that there was no alternative to granting extensive powers to Pompey, there were general forebodings as to the eventual use he might make of them. Only seventeen years earlier Sulla had returned with his army from the East, had established himself as dictator at Rome, and had taken terrible vengeance on his enemies. Might not Pompey follow his example? The shadow of this great fear fell across Rome and dominated the course of politics in Pompey's absence. A complicated political drama now began to unfold. In the absence of newspaper reports and contemporary records many of the details remain obscure. We may find the clue in the lack of statesmanship in the ruling class, the growing discontent of the poor, the inadequacy of the old institutions of government, and the fear of a military dictatorship with Pompey in the background at the head of a successful army in the East.

The disgruntled senatorial aristocracy struck first. The chief backing for Pompey as consul and then for his great commands had come from the People's Party. The aristocrats took advantage of Pompey's absence to bring legal proceedings on trumped-up charges against some of the opposition leaders. While the proceedings failed they added to the tension at the capital. The fear of Pompey extended beyond the group of his aristocratic opponents. It was shared by Crassus, who had got on badly with Pompey during their joint consulship and who evidently feared what might happen to him if his former colleague should return at the head of troops. Events had forced him to look to the People's Party for support and he undertook to build himself into a position where Pompey would not venture to attack him. In doing this he enlisted the support of Cæsar, whose political abilities were evident and who needed a wealthy political angel to help him further his own ambitions. Other figures flit across the stage, but in the background the multimillionaire boss and his clever young lieutenant pull the strings, with Cicero absorbed in his approaching candidacy for the consulship and oblivious of much of what was going on behind the scenes.

One of the minor figures who was presently to burst into notoriety was L. Sergius Catilina, known to us as Catiline. He was of an old patrician family, a dare-devil, magnetic, with qualities of leadership that far outran his rather limited abilities. A reckless fellow no doubt, of striking appearance. A hostile critic writes of his pallid complexion, his blood-shot eyes, his gait now fast, now slow; his face and his every glance showing the madman that he seemed to be to the men of property whom he later attacked. Slanderous stories of his early life were circulated by his enemies, although he was cleared by the courts of the various charges brought against him. One of the stories, repeated apparently with credence by modern historians, is that he murdered his wife in order to be free to marry a lady universally despised by " good men," and then at her insistence murdered his stepson as a preliminary to the marriage. We catch a glimpse of this supposed female fiend in a letter of Catiline's to an old friend. The glimpse is not in accordance with hostile tradition. Catiline speaks of her generosity in paying off certain obligations and commends her affectionately to his friend's care. In view of the habitual recklessness with which slanders were circulated in Rome it requires extreme credulity to accept these stories of Catiline at face value, especially when it is recalled that in spite of them he was twice elected to public office.

After Catiline's death Cicero, the bitterest of these enemies and the most reckless in his charges, admitted in a speech that his former foe had " many marks of the most eminent virtues," that he was conspicuous for his energy and military skill, and that many fine men were among his active political supporters. The implication was that he had fooled all these good citizens. There had been a time, the speaker added, when even he himself had been deceived and had thought well of the man. Evidently Catiline's reputation as a villain came late and probably as a political smear.

Catiline had been elected judge, had then served as governor of the province of Africa, and had returned to Rome in the year Pompey was given the great command, expecting to run for consul. Charges had been brought against him for extortion in his governorship, but the formal legal proceedings that would have disqualified him probably were not instituted until the next year. The consul in charge of the election had a certain discretion in submitting the names of candidates, and after consultation with leading senators he refused to submit Catiline's name. Perhaps this action was taken because of the African scandal. But it is hard to believe that senators who were ready to condone the flagrant offences of a Verres would have been outraged by anything Catiline might have done during his provincial career. It is more likely that Catiline's candidacy was thrown out by the senators because they recognized that it was promoted by Crassus and Cæsar in order to strengthen their position against both Pompey and the aristocracy.

Under a strong personal grievance Catiline thereupon joined with other disgruntled politicians in a plot to seize the government by a *coup d'état*. Their scheme, known as the first Catilinarian conspiracy, was frustrated by senatorial vigilance.

While Crassus and Cæsar had failed to control the consulship they made certain political gains in the uneasy year 65. Crassus had been elected censor, in which position he could put pressure on the Senate by virtue of the censorial power to purge the House of unworthy members. Cæsar had been elected a commissioner of public works and now set out to win popularity by staging gladiatorial shows of the utmost extravagance, in which he doubtless had the help of his wealthy senior partner. In the consular elections of the year Catiline was again held ineligible, this time because his enemies had brought the formal legal proceedings that disqualified him as a candidate. His acquittal, which followed soon after the elections, was certain to bring him into the field the next year, when Cicero planned to run.

For the moment Crassus and Cæsar marked time, hoping for a more favourable turn of the wheel of politics. Cicero, looking to future political fences, appeared as counsel for the defence in the cases of two popular favourites, former tribunes, who had offended the aristocrats.

CHAPTER XIII

THE NEW MAN CRASHES THE GATE

FOR AN able young man who had achieved distinction at the bar, election to the lower offices of state – finance officer, commissioner of public works, judge – presented no great difficulties. Cicero complacently mentions the fact that he had filled each of these offices at the lowest legal age. But the grand prize would be different. The old families, as I have said, regarded the consulship as their exclusive property, and conservative opinion among the people supported this attitude. "The commons," writes Cicero's contemporary, the historian Sallust, "could bestow the other magistracies, but the nobles passed the consulship from hand to hand within their own order. No New Man was so famous or so illustrious for his deeds that he was considered worthy of that honour and the office, so to speak, was considered as sullied by such an incumbency."

In a speech soon after his election as consul Cicero boasted: "I am the first New Man after a very long interval, almost more remote than our times can remember, whom you have made consul." This was not quite accurate. In the previous half-century one soldier and two or three commoners of social distinction had slipped in. But Cicero was the first New Man for a generation. The difficulties were fully recognized by Cicero and his brother Quintus – a practical politician, as we shall see presently – and they made careful preparations for the hard fight which they saw ahead.

Americans familiar with their political history recall the slow and uncertain way in which factions in the early years of the Republic developed into parties. Roman political development went through much the same stages. The beginnings of a party system appeared after the second great war with Carthage, nearly a century and a half before Cicero. A few nobles who were moderate liberals organized a group that corresponded in some ways to the Whigs of eighteenth-century England. They were in opposition to the reactionary Tories of the time. But a popular leader, Cato the censor, organized an attack on the aristocracy that drove the two groups together. The conservative senatorial crowd came to call itself complacently the Best Men (*Optimates*), while the coalitions that opposed it were called the People's Party (*Populares*). These were not well-organized parties in the modern sense. They had no caucuses, no platforms. But the Best Men, the Tories, always could be depended on to close ranks in support of property and the established order.

It would be a mistake to consider the People's Party the democratic party of Rome. Occasionally, as when the Gracchus brothers were its leaders, it had a really democratic program for the benefit of the people generally. More often it was headed by ambitious politicians, usually by nobles, who had been shut out by the governing group and who hoped to ride into power by espousing measures that might be expected to attract popular support. Fundamentally they stood for a career open to the talents, especially their own talents. Ordinarily they could make an issue of the inefficient government of the stodgy senatorial oligarchy. In general they were merchandisers of policies that would appeal to the people. As the conservative position was monopolized by the Tories the popular leaders were forced to become innovators and to an extent progressives.

Appraising this situation, Sallust writes cynically of those who were defending the rights of the people and the others who were defending the prestige of the Senate. "Under pretence of the public welfare," he says, "each side was working for its own advancement."

In the time of Cicero and earlier the political situation was complicated by a group of well-to-do men who under the Gracchi had been recognized as a special social order between the top crust of nobles and the lower level of the common people. As already has been pointed out, gorgeous openings for making money by exploiting the provinces had come with the expansion of the Roman domain in the second century before Christ. Most of these opportunities were at least nominally closed to the senators by law, although many of them were silent partners in the business syndicates. So energetic business men took charge of the enterprises that promised large profits. Their common economic interests drew them together to take a hand in politics although most of them refused to stand for office since membership in the Senate would have embarrassed them in conducting their business. Under these circumstances they looked for political leadership to sympathetic senators with business connections, like Crassus.

The situation was much like that contemplated by François Guizot in trying to reconstitute French society in the 1840's under the "green umbrella" monarchy of Louis Philippe. Guizot believed there was need of a governing aristocracy that would be essentially conservative. Progress then must depend on the business men who should be freed from political responsibility. These men had their own interests and private affairs and asked merely to be let alone to concern themselves with these affairs in freedom and security. The government would be conducted by a hereditary nobility.

In Rome the Guizot idea was carried so far that the business men were not liable to prosecution for corruption and bribery. In at least two famous trials Cicero tried laboriously to justify this immunity. Politics, he argued, gave distinction and glory. If the members of the business order voluntarily " renounced the honours and advantages of public life, then they ought to be relieved of its responsibilities," including the responsibility of being honest in their dealings. Cicero knew better. In a letter to Atticus he speaks of the " shamelessness " of their case. But as general counsel for the business interests he felt it necessary to defend their privileges.

In his efforts to build divergent elements in the state into a compact democratic party, Gaius Gracchus had realized the importance of enlisting the support of this influential business crowd. We do not know their number. Guesses from various data in ancient writers run from ten thousand to thirty thousand. The lower number seems the more probable. Quintus Cicero speaks of the group as comparatively small. But each business man had numerous dependents, debtors, and extensive business affiliates, so he might be worth as many votes in an election as a modern precinct captain. With his keen political instinct Gracchus set out to increase the effectiveness of his possible allies by uniting them into a class-conscious group. Here he made a successful appeal to tradition.

In the earlier days of the Republic the cavalry had been recruited largely from men who could furnish their own horses and equipment. A modest fortune was therefore necessary for membership in this élite branch of the armed forces. Before the motorization of modern armies several of the larger American cities had cavalry troops of rich young men of social standing, much after the Roman fashion. In Rome, as time went on, the cavalry was recruited elsewhere. The men of means who formerly constituted it were engaged in business in the capital or in the provinces. Gracchus organized the business men with a fortune of $20,000 or more — the precise amount may have been fixed a little later — into an order that took its name from the old Roman cavalry. It was called the Equestrian Order, or, more simply, the Knights.

The scheme was much as it would be in England if a successful business man on attaining a certain fortune should automatically be admitted to knighthood and become Sir John Jones without waiting for the formality of being knighted by the sovereign. It probably was Gaius Gracchus with his keen appraisal of human vanities who gave the new order certain outward signs of distinction — a gold ring, a narrow hem of crimson on the tunic, and, of all things, the right to a block of reserved seats immediately behind the senators in the theatre. But the astute tribune realized the necessity of tying the business men to him by something more substantial than the right to a gold ring and a conspicuous seat in the theatre. He put through a law providing that the contract for the collection of taxes in the new province of Asia should be put up at auction in Rome. The state would accept the highest offer and only the financiers had sufficient resources to bid. Also he gave them the coveted and unhappily valuable right to exclusive service as jurors in the courts; or at least in the chief court that mattered — that dealing with extortion in the provinces.

Previously this court had drawn its jurors from the senators. As the provincial governors were men of senatorial rank, they could expect to be favoured by a senatorial jury if and when they were accused of malfeasance in office. A juror might hope some day to be a governor, so he was not disposed to be severe with any governors who were brought before the court in which he was sitting as a juror. Cicero cites cases of governors who escaped punishment through the leniency of senatorial jurors after the court had been given back to them by Sulla. Gracchus probably thought he was instituting a salutary reform in turning over the extortion court to the financiers and traders.

Many complex problems could be brought under the jurisdiction of the extortion court. The governors had wide discretionary powers over the validity and payment of loans made to towns in the provinces. The interest rate might be assailed. A law passed by the Assembly limited the rate to

12 per cent. The Senate had attempted by resolution to grant higher rates in certain cases. The governor might have to decide whether such senatorial resolutions were valid. It may well have seemed to Gracchus that in cases brought before the court in Rome involving governors the senatorial juries might be prejudiced. Unfortunately the reforming tribune did not reckon with the effect of economic interest on juries of knights. A scandalous case is reported in the year 92 in which the financiers at Rome deliberately framed an honest governor who refused to yield to dishonest demands of the traders and financiers, brought charges against him, and sent him into exile. Thereupon he retired to the province which he was accused of mistreating and was received with the greatest warmth and hospitality. There were other instances in which the business men united to ruin honest provincial governors who protected their people from extortion from Rome. For many years after the death of Gracchus the control of the jury courts was a frequent source of friction and ill feeling between the financiers and the aristocracy.

Other definite economic interests drove the upper-class business men into politics. Some of these interests were in line with the public welfare. The financiers and great merchants were concerned in the maintenance of order both at home and abroad, in the safe-guarding of shipping from pirates, in the stability of credits. The extensive network of banking and trading naturally required protection by the government, which occasionally brought clashes between the two upper classes. While many nobles were silent partners in the financial and trading operations of the business men, the great families still cherished the traditional contempt of a landed aristocracy for men in trade. It was a nuisance for the governing nobles to have to send out an expensive punitive expedition to suppress a provincial uprising, or to fit out a fleet to clear the sea of pirates. Such demands were made on occasion by the traders for purposes with which the nobles were not immediately concerned.

It was to the interest of the business crowd to extend the domain of Rome with the opportunities that territorial expansion gave for making money. But the Senate was not keen to take on additional responsibilities for governing the lands that might be acquired by conquest. It hesitated to increase the number of magistrates needed for new dependencies. For a cultivated man Rome was a much pleasanter place of residence than some provincial capital. Cicero, punctilious statesman though he was, objected strenuously to being sent out for a year as governor of the province of Cilicia. It was such a bore to have to be away from the exciting political and social life that centred in the Roman Forum! " I cannot tell you," he wrote to Atticus from his province, " how terribly I miss life in Rome and how intolerable to me is the boredom of life here." In another letter to a young friend in the capital he exploded: " The city, the city, my dear Rufus — stick to that and live in its full light! Residence elsewhere, as I made up my mind early in life, is mere eclipse and obscurity to those whose energy is capable of shining in Rome."

When Cicero was ready to run for the consulship one political fact had been established by events. Usually the old families could carry enough of their dependents with them to give them control. But if the people were disaffected and badly split up, the business men might hold the balance of power. When they joined the nobles the coalition could be sure of controlling the Assemblies and the government. But if a considerable bloc of the people were united behind some ambitious popular leader, the business men could ally themselves with him and turn the Tories out — unless, as in the case of Sulla, the nobles had an army at their back. Repeatedly in the last uneasy decades of the Republic the business influence swung the government from one side to the other. After the death of the second Gracchus the business men were content to allow the nobles to run the government. But when Roman business men were killed in an uprising in Africa and the Senate showed lack of energy in dealing with the situation, the knights united with the commons to displace the mediocre noble commander with the competent commoner, Marius. Then when the politicians about Marius became too radical to suit the business interests, they united with the conservative senators in crushing the Marian leaders. So it went until the civil authority was submerged by military dictatorships. And in the end it was the business men who came out on top in furnishing the administrators for the Empire.

There were times in nineteenth-century America when the business men had a similar influence in controlling the government. Conspicuous instances were in the election of 1888 when the protected industries brought about the defeat of President Cleveland for re-election on a pledge of tariff reform, and again in the free-silver campaign of 1896 when the bankers, especially the thousands of country bankers, lined up their customers for William McKinley and the gold standard. In England the same sort of thing happened in the repeal of the corn laws in the 1840's. A combination of manufacturers and merchants had become convinced, and rightly, that the national welfare as well as their own economic interest required the breaking down of the protective-tariff system. The most powerful support for the system came from the ruling class of landed gentry, who insisted on high protection for wheat. Famine in Ireland played into the hands of the free traders. Sir Robert Peel, who had become prime minister for the Conservative Party on a pledge to support the corn laws, conscientiously reversed his position and carried a bill for their repeal with the help of the business representatives in the House of Commons against the opposition of two thirds of the members of his own party.

Cicero lacked statesmanlike imagination of the first order. But he was a shrewd observer of surface currents in politics and when he became consul he was to adopt a fundamental policy based on the experience of previous decades. That policy was to cement the political union of the two upper orders, the nobles and knights, in control of the government.) So long as the two orders worked together they could be certain of blocking revolutionary proposals that might win the support of the lower classes, and good conservative citizens could sleep peacefully. How early he formulated this aim the scanty evidence does not disclose. He mentioned the harmony of the orders as desirable in a speech made the year before his canvass. Evidently the idea dominated his actions during his term of office, and thereafter the " harmony of the orders " was one of his favourite phrases. But as a candidate it was his first obligation to get himself elected and he surveyed the situation from that standpoint. While his lower magistracies had made him first a member of the Senate and then had set his family in line for the nobility, he belonged by birth to the upper business class, which at this time was at outs with the Senate. On his own account he had challenged the aristocracy by his prosecution of Verres, and he had gone along with the business men in supporting the great command in the East for Pompey against the opposition of the nobles. Still he had been fairly moderate in his position and had taken care not to give needless offence to the old families. Impatiently as he often expressed himself at the indolence and frivolity of some of the great aristocrats, he looked up to them and was anxious to be accepted by them on equal terms.

With the mass of the people he had little sympathy. Under the stress of bad economic conditions they were deteriorating into a proletariat who a century and a half later were to be stigmatized by a great satirist as interested only in " bread and games," or, as a modern writer has put it, " a free lunch and the movies." Many of them sold their votes and they were readily stirred to rioting by any eloquent demagogue. Schooled as most Romans were in the let-alone doctrine of economics, Cicero had no conception of any constructive program for their betterment. Politically they had to be reckoned with, but he had no confidence in their political judgment. Like the old-school British Liberals

Cicero was devoted to political liberty. He did not see — no man of his day saw — how political liberty could be made the driving force of economic improvement.

Politics is politics in every age and clime. In Rome a canvass for office was called "handshaking" (*prensatio*), which illumines Roman campaign methods. Preparing for the election of 64, Cicero began his campaign in 65. In a letter to Atticus at Athens written in July of that year, the candidate sketches the situation for his friend. His expected rivals he mentions by name; a pretty poor lot and not formidable, except two — Gaius Antonius, uncle of Mark Antony, and Catiline. Both, he was to learn later, had the formidable support of Cæsar and Crassus. At the time he was ignorant of this important political fact. Catiline's trial was approaching; Cicero was convinced of his guilt and expected that the verdict would bar his candidacy unless, to use his words to Atticus, the jury found "the sun does not shine at noon."

In view of later developments it is interesting to discover in his next letter to Atticus that he considers undertaking Catiline's defence. He thinks the prosecutor is sympathetic and that the jury will be reasonable. "I hope," the letter continues, "that if he is acquitted he will be more closely united with me in the conduct of our canvass; but if the result be otherwise I shall bear it with resignation." For some reason this plan did not come off. In passing judgment on Cicero's attitude, however, we must bear in mind that while extortion in the provinces was publicly deprecated in Rome, the practical men of the time were disposed to wink at it unless, as in the case of Verres, it was too flagrant to be condoned. Their view was much like that of a prominent Missouri attorney and legislative lobbyist early in the twentieth century who protested that, after all, the bribery of legislators was "a conventional crime." Catiline was acquitted without Cicero's help, and before long in a sudden access of moral indignation the candidate discovered that his rival was then and always had been a thoroughly disreputable character. Such abrupt reversals of opinion under the exigencies of politics still take place.

In canvassing for the highest office in the state Cicero realized the handicap he was under as a new man. For all his demonstrated ability he was certain to be frowned on by the old families as an upstart. A related difficulty not only was to prove an obstacle to his election but was to haunt him and hamstring his efforts throughout the rest of his career. This was his lack of important family connections, which, as I have suggested in an earlier chapter, were as essential in Rome as they were in Georgian England. Noble Roman houses connected by marriage cooperated to obtain offices and power.

Sulla, for instance, had married a daughter of the Metelli, a family with a brilliant record in the service of the state. Its heraldic badge was an elephant, commemorating a victory against the Carthaginians. With its extensive connections and influence this family gave its powerful backing to Sulla and contributed to his success. The family of Cicero's contemporary, Cato, had ramifications throughout the nobility. The members of the clan could be depended upon to close ranks against any politician who threatened its interests. Even the fanatical patriot Marcus Junius Brutus refused to join with political associates against the man who had married his half-sister. As a public official Cicero was greatly handicapped by family weakness. "I was destitute of relations and not fortified by any extensive connections," he complains in one of his speeches. He could not depend on the support of armed forces. In default of these his lack of family connections left him in his later years a lonely and pathetic figure striving against overwhelming odds and forced to subordinate himself to other men more fortunately situated.

A side light on political technique is given by his remark to Atticus that he is hoping for the success of one of the candidates of the current year in order that he may be disposed of and not come up for election the next year in competition with himself. This man, he writes, has been commissioner in charge of the repair of the Flaminian Way. His success in completing the job would make him popular with the voters. What happened we do not know. In any event he was not a candidate in 64.

Other phases of his canvass Cicero confides to Atticus. The province of northern Italy, he writes, has considerable voting power and he expects to apply to the Senate for authorization to tour the province at public expense in September and meet influential men who might be expected to journey to Rome to vote in the consular election the next year. The expenses of a senator with such a roving commission were paid by the provincials, who often were scandalously imposed upon by these official junkets. Of the attitude of the nobility toward his candidacy he is still uncertain. As soon as he learns more about it he will let his friend know. The influential Pompey is in the East and won't be home for the election, but perhaps Atticus will do some electioneering among members of his staff who may be passing through Athens.

An awkward situation has developed in his law practice. One of his important clients was a rich and cantankerous uncle of Atticus, for whose goodwill and estate Atticus was always fishing. The uncle has asked Cicero to appear for him against an influential politician who is a great friend of another ward leader. These two politicians the candidate regards as among the key men in his campaign and he can't afford to offend them. He has explained his embarrassment to his client and has pointed out why he cannot take the case. "Your uncle," he writes, "has seemed to take this somewhat less courteously than I could have wished." He is sure Atticus will understand the delicacy of the affair in view of his need not only of retaining but also of acquiring "all possible sources of popularity."

This last sentence indicates Cicero's realization of the problem that confronted him. To win the hard fight that lay ahead of him as a new man, he understood he must pick up support from all sides — from the nobles if possible, from the business men, and from the mass of the people. But party lines were not closely drawn. No candidate was the nominee of any political organization. By doing a delicate piece of tight-rope walking and meeting each group separately he might be able to convince influential men of all factions that he was their friend and could be depended upon to promote their interests.

We are fortunate in having a keen analysis of the situation made by his politically minded brother Quintus. With a younger brother's solicitude for his brilliant elder's ignorance of the ways of the rude world, Quintus prepared for him a *Handbook of Politics.* This has come down to us, a perfectly candid pamphlet of some eight thousand words. Any American city boss would recognize with approval its fundamental principles.

"Every day as you go to the Forum," Quintus writes, "you should say to yourself: 'I am a new man; I am a candidate for the consulship; this is Rome'" — a city with a heterogeneous population. Marcus' reputation as a brilliant pleader at the bar, his brother believes, will offset to a large extent the fact that he doesn't belong to an old family. Also he may count on the support of the important tax-collecting syndicates, nearly the whole business group, many Italian towns, his numerous legal clients, some of the popular political clubs, large numbers of young men who admire his ability as a speaker, and his personal friends. But these political elements must not be taken for granted. They must be cultivated. Agents should be sent to men of high rank to assure them — and here he identifies himself with his brother — "that we always have been at one with the Conservatives in our political sentiments; that we never have been demagogues, and if we ever have seemed to incline to the side of the People's Party we did so in order to conciliate Pompey [a reference to Cicero's speech in support of the proposal to give Pompey the command in the East] that we might have his great influence actively enlisted in the canvass, or at least not opposed to us." But presumably out of hearing of the Conservatives the common people should be reminded that Marcus always has been their friend and that he has spoken up for their favourite, Pompey, and for others to whom they are devoted. These manœuvres are known in modern politics as playing both ends against the middle.

It must be frankly realized, Quintus observes, that Marcus will encounter the jealousy of politicians who have failed to reach the consulship and that many of the commons feel that the highest office in the state should not go to a man of unknown ancestry. The loyalty of friends must be cemented by kindness and attention. Even humble members of his household, freedmen and slaves, must not be overlooked. Nearly all the talk that forms one's public reputation emanates from domestic sources and it would be harmful if men connected with the household should be disaffected and spread poison. In canvasses for office, this practical politician continues, men are chiefly moved by three considerations — kindness received, hope of favours to come, and personal affection and good feeling. "By very small favours men are induced to think they have reason for giving support at the polls."

Marcus is admonished to lay out his campaign systematically. "The first and most obvious thing is that you should embrace the Roman senators and business men and the active and popular men all up and down the line. After that review the entire city, every district and neighbourhood. If you get the help of the leading men in every part of the city they will bring you mass support." This is the strategy of every successful American city politician.

The voters outside of Rome must not be neglected. Quintus advises his brother to lay out a political chart of all Italy and learn it by heart, precisely as a candidate for governor of an American state becomes familiar with every congressional district. Local leaders are to be sought out and their active co-operation obtained. Then the political mentor returns once more to the city of Rome. The great mass of the voters are in the capital or are able from there to control the country votes. So the candidate must spend most of his time in the city, call men by name, and solicit their votes personally. An ingratiating manner is imperative.

Further, a man running for office is always asked to promise favours. Quintus urges liberal promises. If at all possible, promises should be made even if they cannot be kept. The unexpected often happens and perhaps the successful candidate will not be asked to make good. In any event he can act in accordance with his better judgment. He may have to give offence. But it is better to give the offence after the election than before. During the campaign he would better not commit himself on public questions. If he takes sides he is bound to give offence. This kind of political behaviour is observed in twentieth-century candidates in the United States. Platitudes often are safer than opinions.

Finally, bribery unfortunately is common in Roman elections. Quintus apparently assumes that his brother is too impractical to use money. But he is a competent prosecutor and he should let it be known that he is on guard and it will be too bad for anybody who tries to buy the election. There is another piece of political tactics that is accepted as conventional in Rome to which Marcus may resort. " See that some new scandal is started against your competitors for crime or looseness of life or corruption such as is in harmony with their characters."

This last admonition as well as the others, Marcus took to heart. A little later he seized the opportunity in a speech in the Senate to attack his two chief rivals. It is called the speech *In the White Toga* (*In Toga Candida*). A glistening whitened toga was the proper garb of a man running for office and the word " candidate " is derived from *candidatus*, " clothed in white." In this speech he lashes his opponents, especially Catiline, with every charge he could lay his tongue to. Posterity probably has taken the invective much more seriously than it was taken by the Roman audience.

Cicero's handicaps as a candidate for the consulship were so great that in spite of his ability and all the practical admonitions of Quintus the outcome was in grave doubt. But a fortunate combination of circumstances developed by the time of the election in the summer of 64. As a result the nobles plumped for him, holding their noses, and he came in at the head of the poll. Antonius edged out Catiline for second place and so became his colleague. What these circumstances were and how they profoundly affected Cicero's year in office and his whole subsequent career, we have now to see.

CHAPTER XIV

CÆSAR KEEPS HIM GUESSING

ANY PERIOD of rapid economic change is bound to produce distress. A few shrewd men reap large profits. The mass of the people are unable to adjust themselves to changing conditions and are submerged.

In a previous chapter I have sketched the general course of events in which the small farmers in many regions — the sturdy Italian middle class — were squeezed out and flocked to Rome to join the urban proletariat. In the early part of the first century before Christ, during Cicero's boyhood and early manhood, a severe depression developed. Many farms were devastated in the war between Rome and the Italian cities and in the protracted slave insurrection. Business men were hard hit by the war in Asia Minor, where they had large investments. While the historical records are scanty, we may catch glimpses of what was going on from financial measures taken by the state. These are familiar to modern times. First the currency was devalued. " Coins fluctuated so much in value in that period," Cicero complained later, " that no one could tell what he was worth." Then came a revolt against payment of interest, in which the judge who sided with the debtors was killed by a mob of creditors. Finally, under stress of the collapse of credits due to the Asiatic trouble, debts were scaled down 75 per cent.

In the years immediately preceding Cicero's candidacy for the consulship the depression continued, with growing indebtedness and with stringency in the money market. That there was much speculation in the provinces is suggested by a law enacted three years earlier forbidding the lending of money to provincials. Incidentally the business men never forgave the magistrate, Gabinius, who proposed the law. As a result of their hostility they gave him a bad name which has lasted to the present day. The farm problem was becoming acute. The settling of discharged veterans on farms has been a familiar method of dealing with soldiers at the end of wars. In the United States the Homestead Act of Civil War days served this purpose. In the last century of the Roman Republic Sulla had confiscated vast areas of farm land in Italy and had distributed it among one hundred and twenty thousand of his veterans. The dispossessed farmers naturally were in trouble while many of the war veterans proved poor managers and became heavily involved in debt. This procedure of Sulla's proved an agricultural disaster and his purge of business men had produced uncertainty and economic distress in Rome. Even well-to-do farmers apparently were overextended as they were in America in the early 1920's when the bottom dropped out of the market. In a speech early in his consulship Cicero tells of farmers eager to sell who can find no buyers although they would be "glad to get rid of their land under any terms." In his book *On Moral Duties,* written many years later, Cicero remarks that "indebtedness was never greater" than in the year of his consulship and that "measures for repudiation" were never more strenuously advocated.

It was in this time of economic stress that the consular elections of 64 were held. While Catiline belonged by birth to the nobility, he had identified himself with the People's Party headed by Crassus and his sub-boss Cæsar. There is no evidence up to this time that he had been concerned with the condition of the underprivileged. It was personal ambition that motivated him. But he was deeply resentful toward the Tories for frustrating his attempts to win the consulship. I suspect it was personal resentment that transformed Catiline into a reformer, as it has transformed men since his day. He became acutely aware that the interests that had mistreated him were mistreating the mass of the people. With increasing clearness he saw that the aristocrats were a bad lot. Thus the frustrated patrician was set on the way to make himself leader of a left-wing party with a far more radical program than that of the People's Party led by a millionaire land speculator. This development was to come to a head the next year. Meanwhile the Old Guard viewed him with suspicion — a reckless, ungovernable fellow, backed by the leaders of the opposition, a dangerous radical and not to be trusted in critical times.

The circumstances, as I have said, were fortunate for Cicero. Under normal conditions his candidacy would have been wrecked by the hostility of the aristocrats to an outsider. Of course he had the business interests with him and he could count upon some support from the little people. Later in recognition of this support he assured the Assembly in a speech shortly after he took office that he expected to be the guardian of the interests of the masses; in short, to be a people's consul (*consul popularis*). But there is no reason to suppose that in addition to the business crowd he had enough of the people with him to swing the election against the opposition of the aristocracy. This fact he failed to recognize. In later years he used to boast that the old Roman Constitution was not narrowly exclusive, that true merit was recognized under its provisions, that careers were freely open to the talents; in short, that under the admirable Roman system any boy of parts, though of humble birth, might hope for the highest honours. In reality it was not quite that way. Cicero's case was altogether exceptional. Faced with the necessity of defeating Catiline, the old families plumped for the brilliant popular attorney. By temperament, tastes, and convictions he belonged with the Conservatives. In modern America he would have been a vestryman in a fashionable Episcopal church, outraged by the Bolshevists who wanted to unionize industry. The aristocrats knew his value to them in the emergency. After the emergency was over they frequently showed their contempt for the talented upstart.

Cicero was elected along with the inconsequential Antonius — "a man," brother Quintus had observed, "afraid of his own shadow." Cicero was so much the abler and more aggressive that he dominated the government for his entire term. With political astuteness he helped assure his primacy by sweetening his colleague with a deal under which Antonius was assured of the profitable governorship of Macedonia at the end of his term — a position for which he proved wholly unfitted.

With his election as consul Cicero had now reached the summit of his ambition. But he at once ran into political difficulties engineered by his opponents that must have taken much of the joy out of life. For the first few months of his consulship the Crassus-Cæsar coalition made the going hard. Cæsar was the genius of the combination, and no one familiar with the political game as it is played today can fail to admire the technique of this master Roman politician. His manœuvres were directed primarily against the aristocrats in order to build up the People's Party against a possibly hostile Pompey. Cicero, who had won Tory support in the campaign, was necessarily under the guns. In his subsequent military commands Cæsar's strategy was based on violent surprise attacks. It was precisely this strategy that he used in the earlier part of Cicero's consulship. His opponents never knew what Cæsar would do next or where the next attack would hit. With his quick and resourceful mind he was always one move ahead of his conservative adversaries. Cicero must have torn his hair over the unexpected thrusts of the opposition leader who was constantly forcing the fighting, taking the initiative away from the consul, and putting him on the defensive. In the next few months Cæsar brought off three — possibly four — major attacks in rapid succession, each violent and unexpected.

His first move was to put the people's consul on the spot by a land bill under which it was proposed to relieve poverty at Rome by settling some of the surplus population on farms purchased by the state. This was the only sort of practical relief measure possible in an economy predominantly agricultural. Cæsar believed in the method and resorted to it later when he became consul. Administration of the project was to be concentrated in a board of ten men. To all such measures from the time of the Gracchi the aristocrats had been sullenly opposed. Cicero felt obliged to come to the front for his aristocratic supporters. In an address to the Assembly caucus he began adroitly in the customary technique of politics by saying he had hoped to be able to favour the bill but on careful examination had regretfully concluded it was too dangerous. It concentrated authority in a way that might be inimical to Pompey, that great champion of the people. He hinted that the measure was drafted in the interest of wealthy landowners, who would be able to unload unprofitable estates on the public treasury, and he appealed to the people not to exchange the delights of urban life for a drab existence of hard work on farms. It required two speeches to the preliminary sessions of the Assembly and one to the Senate to block the bill. His speeches lacked candour; in short, they were thoroughly political. But they were accounted oratorical triumphs since they carried the people with him for the moment against their own interests. In the long run, after the audiences were out from under the spell, the speeches may have produced an unfavourable reaction and contributed to the popular hostility that gradually developed against him.

Three years later, when party politics was not involved, Cicero supported a somewhat similar measure modified to make it a bit more palatable to the big proprietors — "For, as you know," he wrote to Atticus, "the strength of our party lies in the rich landed gentry." His expediency was in line with what he was now convinced was a policy of fundamental importance: to unite the aristocracy with the business interests. To bring this about he was ready to make any compromise, to go any lengths. Like modern politicians he was prepared to advocate what seemed to him lesser evils in the interest of what he believed to be the greater good.

Although rebuffed by the failure of his bill, Cæsar was at once ready with another move against the governing class. It was directed at the use of martial law against political offenders. Under the mild Roman judicial procedure a man convicted by a jury of a capital offence was not put to death. He was allowed to go into exile. But in times of extreme peril the Senate was empowered to issue " the last decree " that " the consuls see to it that the state suffer no harm." This was virtually to declare martial law, under which the death penalty might be inflicted. The first use of this stern decree in a civil disturbance was in the time of the Gracchi. It had been used later and was a powerful weapon that the Senate might employ with devastating effect against its enemies. With another bitter election coming on, Cæsar may have thought it well to demonstrate to the aristocrats the popular feeling against the resort to martial law. He took a curious method to do this. Thirty-seven years previously a popular tribune, Saturninus, had been killed by a mob incited by senators after a declaration of martial law. A slave who claimed to have been the assassin was rewarded with citizenship. An aged senator, C. Rabirius, who had been with the mob, was living in Rome. Cæsar had him brought to trial for the murder in order to demonstrate that a decree of martial law could not legalize the killing of a Roman citizen. After preliminary skirmishing a procedure was arranged by which the case was carried directly to one of the Assemblies sitting as a court. Cicero spoke on behalf of the accused. But the proceedings were ended by a technical trick. From ancient times during sessions of the Assembly, which included all men of military age, a red flag displayed on the Janiculum Hill across the Tiber indicated that no hostile forces were in sight. If an attacking party of

Etruscans was sighted the flag was hauled down. This was a signal for the Assembly to cease deliberations and fly to arms. The ancient custom persisted far into imperial times and the Assembly was adjourned by the lowering of the red flag on the Janiculum. This device was used to stop the trial of the alleged murderer of Saturninus, and the proceedings were not renewed. Presumably Cæsar believed he had impressed a lesson on the senatorial Old Guard. If so, events were to demonstrate that he was mistaken.

In building up his power and the power of his party against the return of Pompey, Cæsar overlooked no bets. As the next step to the consulship he announced his candidacy for judge. If elected, however, he would not take office until the next year. Meanwhile an unexpected opportunity arose for him to drive home a third attack on his political opponents. The highest ecclesiastical office in the state, that of chief pontiff, had become vacant by the death of the incumbent. It carried large political powers and was held for life, usually by some venerable and distinguished member of one of the governing families. Although he was only thirty-nine years old, and an agnostic, Cæsar determined to run for this religious office with its prestige and authority. Two old gentlemen were candidates against him, one of whom tried to buy him off with the offer of a large sum of money. He contemptuously refused. He was ready, he said, to borrow more than the amount of the offered bribe to win — and presumably he did. When he left home on the morning of election day, Plutarch tells how his weeping mother kissed him good-bye. He felt he could not return to face his creditors if he lost. " Today, Mother," he said, " you will see me either chief pontiff or an exile." He was overwhelmingly elected.

Another political move, although not identified with Cæsar, sounds so suspiciously like him that we may assume that it was his fourth attack on the administration. It was a proposal to restore civil rights to the sons of those who had been proscribed by Sulla — mostly business men. It was a popular measure and a belated act of justice. But the nobles had been overridden by Pompey and Crassus in the repeal of much of Sulla's legislation. They would not stand for another assault upon it. Once more Cicero came forward to oppose any further undermining of the Sullan settlement.

He had been kept so busy resisting the projects of Cæsar that he had been able to get through only one constructive measure of his own. It was to limit the abuses of the senatorial junkets at the expense of the provincials, of which he himself had taken advantage in his canvass for the consulship. But he insisted that the privilege had been grossly misused and he proposed to do away with it. The complete reform he could not get adopted. But he did succeed in having the senatorial joy rides limited to a year.

As the months passed, the economic tension increased to panic proportions. The business men and nobles were taking no chances. They had elected their man consul. But they had not overlooked an almost equally essential official. Cases of indebtedness were brought before the superior civil court, and the financial interests had taken care to see that a dependable reactionary was made its presiding judge. At the beginning of his term the judge was accustomed to post an edict setting forth the legal principles on which he proposed to operate. While efforts had been made from time to time to modify the old law under which a creditor might seize the person as well as the property of the defaulting debtor — in other words, efforts to abolish imprisonment for debt — the ancient law and custom were there for a harsh judge to revive. This apparently was what the judge did at the beginning of the year 63. At least a protest from debtors later in the year asked that the Senate " restore the bulwark of the law of which the present judge's injustice has deprived us." The cruel procedure in the debtors' court helps explain later developments. It played into Catiline's hands when he renewed his candidacy for consul in the middle of Cicero's term.

Everyone who has studied Latin is familiar with Cicero's

def. of Cat

orations against Catiline, the first beginning with the familiar words: "*Quo usque tandem abutere, Catilina, patientia nostra?*" ("How long, Catiline, will you abuse our patience?") From the orations students get the impression that Catiline was a very wicked man. It is doubtful whether they are made to realize what the trouble was all about. A politician may be a villain, but it is well to understand what is in the back of his head, what really prompts his villainy. The reputation of Catiline has suffered for two thousand years because we have only the writings for the prosecution. The defence must be patched together from fragmentary evidence. The result has been a distorted account of what really happened.

Napoleon, who had had considerable political experience, confessed himself baffled by the conventional histories of the Catilinarian conspiracy. He could not comprehend, he remarked while in exile on St. Helena, the story of Catiline as it has come down to us. In his opinion, however great a wretch Catiline may have been, he must have had some object which had not been cleared up. "The Emperor," the memoir-writer reports, "was disposed to regard the affair as that of a faction which, finding its purposes defeated, accumulated upon the head of its chief all the wild accusations which are put forward on such occasions." In referring to "wild accusations" Napoleon showed insight. It is absurd to accept at face value the charges brought by any politician's bitter enemies.

Who were Catiline's supporters? Cicero lists them with a rather jaundiced appraisal of each group, in his second oration against Catiline. In general they are people in economic distress and heavily in debt. And in general the conservative consul has one remedy to propose — he would put the debtors through the wringer. This is a familiar remedy. It was proposed to President Hoover in 1932, early in the great depression. Possibly it might have been the solution. But the President took the position that the social structure would not stand up under such drastic deflation. Cicero had decided views on the subject and he set them forth later in sound advice to his spendthrift son. There are those, he writes, who think they should not be required to pay rent. "Why so? In order that when I have bought, built, kept up, and spent my money upon a place, you may without my consent enjoy what belongs to me? What else is this but to rob one man of what belongs to him and to give to another what does not belong to him? And what is the meaning of an abolition of debts, except that you buy a farm with my money; that you have the farm and I do not have my money?"

Holding sincerely, as he did, these views, we can understand Cicero's feeling toward the followers of Catiline. First among them, he says, are the men who are heavily in debt although they have large properties — land poor, we would call them — which they perversely refuse to sell. He forgot that a few months before in arguing against the land bill in a speech I have just mentioned he had said there was no market for farms and the owners wanted to unload on the government. He has a solution for these unworthy people. He will offer them, he says, a cancellation of their debts; but a cancellation "by the auctioneer." Second come the insolvent office-seekers who hope to improve their fortunes by getting government jobs. Third are two groups of farmers. The first is made up of Sulla's veterans who had been settled on farms and had failed to make things go, which was to be expected in view of their long absence from farm work while in the army, combined with the agricultural depression. But Cicero is sure they put up extravagant buildings and tried to live luxuriously — which must have sounded a sour joke to the hard-pressed veterans. The second group includes other impoverished farmers, embracing those dispossessed to make room for the veterans. Both groups, he says, hope for a dictatorship and a redistribution of wealth. Fourth are the lazy ne'er-do-wells, shiftless and always in debt. They can never get their heads above water and they might as well die peacefully as die in a revolt involving de-

CICERO DENOUNCES CATILINE IN THE SENATE

From a steel engraving by the celebrated humorous artist John Leech, who illustrated The Comic History of Rome *by Gilbert Abbott à Beckett, published in London in 1852. Leech was on the staff of* Punch *for twenty-three years. His Cicero-Catiline engraving is of course a caricature of the House of Commons.*

cent citizens in their ruin. Still another group of Catiline's supporters is mentioned by Sallust, wealthy historian of the conspiracy. It is made up of impoverished men from the country who have flocked to Rome and joined the city proletariat to live on odd jobs, cheap wheat, and charity. A reprehensible crew.

In Roman elections, without party platforms, we can only guess at the measures Catiline proposed. The ordinary radical remedy of the times was a cancellation of debts — the "clean-slate" policy, it was called. It is possible Catiline talked of a reduction of debts such as had been carried out a few years before with general approval. The only definite proposal of which we may be sure is the one already cited — the remonstrance against the court's harsh treatment of debtors. It is likely, however, that Catiline was appealing to all the discontented elements, and stories soon were circulated that he planned to resort to violence.

At about this time Catiline's powerful former backers, Crassus and Cæsar, fade out of the picture. Conspicuously Cæsar, whose restless activities had dominated the scene for the first six months of the year, suddenly becomes quiescent. A little later we find the two politicians quietly slipping useful information to their former opponent. It is likely they had become convinced that Catiline was too violent, self-willed, and erratic to be a serviceable agent and his favouring of debt-reduction would have made no hit with Crassus, the largest creditor in Rome. In addition the acute conjecture has been made on plausible grounds that intimations had come that Pompey was not irreconcilable to the leaders of the People's Party, but was open to a deal. If this conjecture is correct it would go far toward explaining the attitude of Crassus and Cæsar through the rest of the year. With hope of coming to terms with Pompey they would be under less pressure to back so undependable a fellow as Catiline and could afford to play a waiting game.

The change in attitude followed soon after the return of one of Pompey's officers, Metellus Nepos, to run for tribune. He may have been the intermediary for negotiations. It is significant that about this time a bill was enacted with Cæsar's approval granting special honours to Pompey when he should return from the East. Also a few months later the first act of Cæsar after he had become a judge was to propose to remove an old aristocratic leader from an assignment to rebuild the great Temple of Jupiter on the Capitoline and to transfer the honour to Pompey. These events happening in succession add plausibility to the theory of the deal just mentioned.

My own impression is that if there were negotiations they were with Cæsar and that Crassus did not share his lieutenant's confidence that they could be carried through. On purely political grounds Cæsar was fairly sure of the outcome. The Big Boss was not so readily convinced, although he may have trusted Cæsar's judgment sufficiently to believe it was no longer necessary to oppose Cicero and that he might be discreetly helped. Just the same, until the situation should be definitely clarified Crassus thought it prudent to move with his family out of town when Pompey landed at Brindisi the next year. Later events justified Cæsar's intuition that the Great Man could be handled.

But the considerations that affected Crassus and Cæsar brought no comfort to the senatorial party and Cicero. In the face of a financial crisis they had to meet the challenge of a popular leader who in their view was menacing the whole economic and social life of Rome. The situation was so threatening that in advance of the election a new law against bribery was hurriedly put forward. It is quite possible that one of the purposes of the law was to prevent wealthy men like Crassus from paying the expenses of country voters who could not otherwise afford to come to Rome to vote. This proposed law provoked violent discussions and in the debates that preceded the election Catiline used what Horatio, speaking to Hamlet, called "wild and whirling words, my lord." First he was reported to have told those who were down and out that they could not trust the promises of the fortunate; that he who would be a leader of the unfortunate must himself be identified with them as unfortunate. The inference was that he was himself bankrupt. This probably was demagogy, as we have a subsequent letter from Catiline to a personal friend speaking of his solvency. In a speech a little later he is reported by Cicero to have said that " if his plans were set on fire he would extinguish the flames not with water but with general ruin " — that is, by pulling down buildings in the path of the flames.

With the election approaching, some of Catiline's supporters from the country had arrived in Rome headed by Manlius, an old officer of Sulla's. Cicero heard reports that he was to be ganged and perhaps murdered on the day of the election. He obtained action by the Senate postponing the balloting, probably in order to gain time to obtain more evidence of the plot. The next day before a crowded house he failed to submit further evidence but called on Catiline to explain his words about extinguishing the fire with general ruin. Whereupon his enemy exclaimed: " There are two bodies in the state, one feeble with a weak head " — by which he meant the senatorial party led by Cicero; " the other sturdy but headless " — the mass of the people. " This body," he added, " if it deserves my support shall not lack a head as long as I live." Evidently by this time he had concluded that the People's Party headed by Crassus and Cæsar did not represent the mass of the people and he was attempting to build up a third really democratic party of which he should be leader. According to Cicero the Senate groaned at this outburst of the champion of the underdog but did nothing, and Catiline " flung himself out joyously triumphant," although the indignant Cicero contended he should not have been allowed to leave the Senate chamber alive.

It is quite possible that Catiline's hatred of Cicero had reached a point where he would not have stopped at murder, although the consul had no evidence which he could submit to the Senate. The election was held, but the Senate had not been sufficiently impressed to furnish Cicero with protection. He appeared on election day ostentatiously wearing a breastplate. Dio, who may here be a prejudiced chronicler, says this was partly for his own protection, partly to impress the people with the desperate character of Catiline. Friends gathered about him as a bodyguard. But there was no disorder.

Once more Catiline was defeated in the election. But by this time Rome was so aroused by the rumours of plots and uprisings that a financial panic ensued, with a flight of gold and silver from Italy which the government took means to stop, just as the export of gold from America was forbidden at the time of the banking panic of 1933. At the same time frightened creditors began to call in loans. Property was so depreciated that it was impossible to realize on it and ruin threatened. The panic was checked by a big banker, Quintus Considius, whose outstanding loans totalled $750,000. He gave notice that he would not press the borrowers for either principal or interest. This action quieted the excitement. His service was similar to that rendered by J. Pierpont Morgan in the American panic of 1907 when call money skyrocketed to 150 per cent. Under Morgan's leadership a pool of $25,000,000 was raised to be lent at 10 per cent, which made it possible for the situation to be worked out.

CHAPTER XV

CATILINE LEADS A DEBTORS' PROTEST

UP TO this time Catiline had been resorting only to constitutional methods to relieve the plight of the debtors. If he had been elected consul as leader of a third party representing the underprivileged he might have assumed it would be possible to obtain the repeal of the harsh and objectionable legislation under which the person as well as the property of a debtor could be seized. Upon his second defeat, however, it was evident that relief could not be obtained by normal political means. Cicero and other ancient writers say that he resolved upon a conspiracy to set fire to the city and to overthrow the government by violence. This would have been a desperate gamble even for so reckless a man as Catiline. An alternative course has been suggested which seems inherently more probable.

Catiline sent his lieutenant Manlius to Fiesole, near Florence, and other supporters to various parts of Italy to gather together the ruined farmers and down-and-outers from the capital and make some sort of dramatic demonstration which might impress the Roman oligarchy and induce it to do something to alleviate their condition. On occasion in earlier Roman times the common people had seceded; that is, had withdrawn from the city, in order to enforce their demands on the nobility. Something of this sort seems to have been in the minds of the poor fellows who looked to Catiline as their leader. This is indicated by one of the few fragments of evidence we have from their side.

There were reports that Catiline had begun to scrape together arms for his country followers. Accordingly the Senate sent troops to Fiesole under the command of a former consul and general, Marcius Rex. To this commander Manlius addressed a moving appeal — the sort of appeal that the Massachusetts Committee of Safety might have addressed to General Gage when he was on the point of sending the expedition to seize the magazines at Concord in 1775 or that General Putnam might have addressed to Sir William Howe before the battle of Bunker Hill on the basis of the guarantees of the British Constitution.

"We shall call gods and men to witness, General," Manlius wrote, "that we have taken up arms not against our fatherland, or to bring danger upon others, but to protect our own persons from outrage. We are wretched and destitute. Many of us have been driven from our country by the violence and cruelty of the money-lenders, while all have lost repute and fortune. None of us has been allowed, in accordance with the usage of our forefathers, to enjoy the protection of the law and retain our personal liberty, after being stripped of our patrimony; such was the inhumanity of the money-lenders and the judge. Your forefathers often took pity on the Roman commons and relieved their necessities by senatorial decrees. . . . Often the commons themselves, prompted by a desire to govern or incensed at the arrogance of the magistrates, have taken up arms and seceded from the patricians. But we ask neither for power nor for riches, but only for freedom, which no true man gives up except with his life. We implore you and the Senate to take thought for your unhappy countrymen, to restore the bulwark of the law of which the judge's injustice has deprived us, and not to impose upon us the necessity of asking ourselves how we may sell our lives most dearly."

This appeal evoked the reply that if the suppliants wished to ask anything of the Senate they must lay down their arms and come to Rome. Knowing the Senate, they naturally refused.

There are other bits of evidence that the movement for the revision of debt legislation was regarded by those who took part in it as merely a reasonable and legitimate protest. The Senate offered liberal rewards to any who would give information about the " plot." There was not a single response. Doubtless the debtors honestly believed they were engaged in an above-board enterprise and that there was no plot. At the last Catiline was urged by his friends to enlist recalcitrant slaves, but he refused. It may be assumed he thought of himself as leading the cause of free men.

How then are we to account for the attempt to obtain arms for the debtors and for the armed conflict that came a few weeks later? Reviewing the course of events in the last two months of Cicero's consulship, we may fairly infer that Catiline and his followers began to discover that they were being manœuvred into the position of rebels and so took what steps they could to defend themselves. The implacable antagonism that had greeted their efforts to win relief by peaceful means, and the constant assumption that they were trying to overthrow the government, indicated that they were in growing danger from the oligarchy.

The motives that actuated Cicero in leading these manœuvres are quite understandable to any observer of modern politics. Fundamentally a conservative, he believed sincerely that any policy for relieving debtors from meeting their full obligations was immoral. Catiline he knew was a reckless man who no doubt would resort to violence on slight provocation. The city was full of disquieting rumours of what might happen, of fire and bloodshed — " the wild accusations " that Napoleon recognized. One night early in November Catiline met with some of his friends at a house on Scythemakers Street. There it was decided to send two desperadoes to the home of Cicero to murder him. One of those present blabbed to his mistress, who warned the consul in time for him to foil the plot. Unhappily assassination had become a familiar political weapon in Rome.

Already Crassus had received anonymous letters addressed to himself and several other persons telling of a conspiracy for a general massacre of prominent citizens and warning them to leave the city. Crassus had delivered these letters to Cicero, who had convoked the Senate, distributed the letters, and asked their recipients to read them aloud. All contained the same general information and the Senate then or a little later had declared martial law.

After Cicero had learned of the plot for his own assassination he summoned another meeting of the Senate, at which Catiline himself was present. It was on this occasion that he delivered the first of the four orations against Catiline which are staple fare for American students of Latin. In the circumstances Cicero naturally was nervous and wrought up. He was familiar with the reports that a general massacre had been planned and he had just frustrated an attempt upon his own life. In a fiery, even hysterical address the orator laid bare the details of a terrible conspiracy. To some extent he was bluffing. He did not have convincing evidence to back up his statements; so he failed to order Catiline's arrest, which he might have done under the martial law already declared. Many persons, he admitted, would not believe him and would disapprove of extreme measures. Therefore he urged Catiline to leave the city; either to go into exile, which might be taken as proof of his innocence, or to join the forces of Manlius, which would be a confession of guilt.

From Cicero's standpoint the speech was pretty much a failure. Reading it, one would suppose it would end with an order for the immediate arrest of Catiline. Apparently Cicero observed that he was not making the impression on his hearers that he had expected. So he finished with the anticlimax of the tame request to the arch-criminal to go away.

To this attack Catiline replied that the charges were unfounded; that he came of an old family that had done great service to the state; that the senators should refuse to believe that a man of such ancestry would be a party to the overthrow of the government and that its saviour would be a resident alien, a mere lodger in the city of Rome — a sneer at Cicero's country birth. But he was shouted down and left the Senate house.

That night he concluded that all hope for peace was gone, that he and his followers must be prepared to defend themselves or possibly even to get the jump on their enemies by marching on Rome. Accordingly he left the city to join Manlius at Fiesole. Before his departure he sent a confidential letter to an old friend and Senate leader to explain his position. An exceedingly human document. He has resolved, he says, to make no defence of his course. But he desires to explain it to his friend, who will know the explanation is made with no sense of guilt. "Maddened by wrongs and slights," he continues, "since I have been robbed of the fruits of my toil and energy and was unable to attain to a position of honour, I followed my usual custom and took up the general cause of the unfortunate. . . . I saw the unworthy elevated to honours and realized that I was an outcast because of baseless suspicion. It is for this reason that, in order to preserve what prestige I have left, I have adopted measures which are honourable considering my situation. When I would write more, word comes that I am threatened with violence." He ends by commending his wife to his friend's care.

The letter is the outpouring of an angry man who resents his failure to win high office and is driven partly by that resentment, partly by sympathy for the oppressed, to undertake their cause. Mixed motives are an almost universal phenomenon in politics. Many an American senator has turned champion of some anti-administration measure because of so small a grievance as the failure of the president to consult him on appointments. Senators have been known to reverse their position on a fundamental policy under the promises of large federal expenditures in their states.

My point is that this letter shows Catiline not as a monster of insincerity, but as an ordinary politician running true to form.

For the next few weeks Catiline devoted himself to encouraging the recruiting of the disaffected farmers about Fiesole and arming them against eventualities. He gathered some ten or twelve thousand, of whom only a quarter were equipped with arms.

A group of his friends remained in Rome. They planned that if things should come to a pass where they were attacked as traitors, an appeal should be made to the people and a friendly magistrate should explain to the Assembly that Cicero had forced them to fight for their lives. Meanwhile Cicero kept getting alarming reports of a proposed uprising in which conflagrations would be started in various quarters of the capital, leading citizens assassinated in the confusion, and the government overthrown. Still rumours were not evidence. Fortune and the stupidity of his opponents played into his hands. Early in December they opened negotiations with some Gallic envoys who had gone to Rome to protest against the tyranny of their Roman governor and the extortion of Roman money-lenders. The envoys revealed the overtures made to them and were encouraged to obtain further evidence. As they were leaving by night with one of the supposed conspirators, they were stopped by prearrangement at the Mulvian Bridge on the Flaminian Way just outside Rome and were brought back to the city as witnesses. Precisely what the negotiations involved we cannot be sure. One story was that the Gauls were to stir up revolt at home; another that they were to send cavalry to Catiline. By this time the protesters in Rome may have given up hope of any peaceful solution. In that event they may have been casting about for all the help possible.

Certain correspondence entrusted to the envoys, including a letter to Catiline, was delivered to Cicero, which he took as confirming his suspicions. The Senate was convoked. Shorthand writers were present to take down the testimony.

THE MULVIAN BRIDGE OVER THE TIBER NEAR ROME

It was here that Cicero's guards stopped the Gallic envoys as they were leaving Rome by night. They had been in communication with Roman leaders suspected of taking part in a conspiracy headed by Catiline. The present bridge, the Ponte Molle, was constructed early in the last century on the remains of the original stone bridge of 109 B.C. *The four central arches are ancient. (Photograph by the author)*

A go-between who had turned state's evidence was introduced and gave details of a plot for incendiarism and massacre. The story of the Gallic envoys was heard. It seems to have centred largely on the tall talk of a member of the group concerning the fortune-teller who had predicted that one day this man should rule Rome. Then Cicero played his trump card by producing letters from the men under suspicion. On their face they contained nothing treasonable, Cicero's statements to the contrary notwithstanding. They spoke of fulfilling engagements, but they did not tell what the engagements were. They might have been engagements to unite in an impressive demonstration of the wrongs of debtors. They might have gone beyond a peaceful demonstration. The excited Senate assumed treason and ordered the arrest of the Roman citizens involved.

Afterward Cicero reported the proceedings of the Senate in an extravagant speech to the people. He had been seeking evidence, he said. At last he had found it — the letters, the handwriting, and what he called the confessions. And most certain proof of all, he continued, was the appearance and conduct of the accused — "their pallor, their eyes, their looks, their silence," and the way in which "they cast furtive glances at each other." Of course pallor and furtive glances were not proof. They belong with the tricks of an advocate trying to impress a popular audience. Cicero was seeking to prepare his hearers to accept his statement that a frightful conspirary had been frustrated not by the consul, but by Heaven itself and they had been "rescued from a most cruel and wretched death." Two days later in an address to the Senate he once more unfolded the diabolical plan of the conspirators — "that when all have been killed no one may be left even to mourn the name of the Roman people and to lament the destruction of so great a government." And why did they plan to do this? So that they might set up a Gallic tribe "amid the ruins of the city and on the ashes of the government overthrown."

Such extravagance of statement perhaps was effective at

the moment. Today it helps to confuse the whole affair. We simply cannot know what Cicero actually believed as to a plot and what he invented to help make his case. In Rome when sentiment had cooled, Cicero's violence reacted against him. People came to suspect that he had greatly exaggerated the danger.

The question now arose as to what should be done with the five men under arrest. In ordinary circumstances no Roman citizen might be condemned to death without trial. But the martial law already decreed by the Senate had put the power of life and death in the hands of the consul. Still no consul had undertaken to impose the death penalty except in times of actual rioting. These men were merely accused of conspiracy. There had been as yet no overt act. It might be held unconstitutional to execute them summarily. Cicero rightly desired the advice and consent of the Senate although the responsibility was his alone and the Senate had no legal authority to sit in the case.

The great council was convoked for the momentous session. Standing at the northwest corner of the Forum today, we can reconstruct the setting. Even two thousand years ago before the erection of the magnificent public buildings of the Empire it was the centre of historic memories. Before us rises the long rostra or speaker's platform of the Augustan period. It replaces the earlier rostra from which Cicero addressed the people. Beyond the rostra we see the lower storeys of Sulla's Record Office against the slope of the Capitoline Hill. It is now surmounted by a mediæval senatorial palace which houses municipal offices of modern Rome. As a seat of government the Capitoline has a long history.

In front of the Record Office rose the Temple of Concord, of which only the massive concrete foundation remains. It was in this temple that the Senate met to decide the fate of the prisoners on December 5. A Temple of Concord had stood on this site for three hundred years. This was one of the buildings where meetings of the Senate were occasionally held when they were not held in the Senate hall. It had been to the Temple of Concord that the accused men were first brought to confront the Senate two days earlier and Cicero later had described to the people the solemn procession of conspirators and witnesses passing through the Forum on their way to the hearing.

On the morning of December 5 Cicero had feared friends of the prisoners might attempt to rescue them from the homes of the officials where they had been confined. He had filled the Forum and the adjacent buildings with armed volunteers, men of means who believed the accused had been plotting against their lives and property. Wealthy business men with swords thronged the slope of the Capitoline under the leadership of Atticus. When that keen banker, with his settled policy of taking no part in politics, was ready to head a posse, there can be no question of the intense feeling in the business crowd.

At the opening of the session the appropriate rites were celebrated, just as the sessions of the American Senate and House are opened by prayer for divine guidance. Then in the tense atmosphere of the temple, from which the public was rigorously excluded, Cicero as presiding officer called upon the most distinguished senators for their views as to the proper punishment of the men under arrest. First the consuls-elect and then the ex-consuls were invited to speak. All favoured the death penalty. Crassus was conspicuously absent, but his young lieutenant was on hand and, as judge-elect, was next in turn.

A thrill of excitement must have swept over the assembly as Cæsar rose. His great career was still shrouded in the mists of the future. At this time he was relatively undistinguished. He was regarded as an extravagant fellow, a leader of the smart set, a clever politician, but with no more serious purposes than a hundred others of the *jeunesse dorée*. At the same time he was so close to the big political boss of the People's Party, he had been so active in recent months, and his position was so ambiguous that his audience was deeply concerned in what he might have to say. He must have sensed its hostility. As former supporters of Catiline both Crassus and Cæsar were under suspicion. Already two of the aristocrats had urged Cicero to denounce both of the People's Party leaders as conspirators. The consul had refused. Crassus had furnished him the anonymous letters warning against the violence that was said to have been planned and Cæsar, too, had given him useful information, as he was to admit publicly the next year. In spite of Cicero's attitude an obscure informer had come forward the day before and accused Crassus to the Senate. By a formal vote it had repudiated the accusation. Most senators naturally held it did not make sense to suppose that the richest man in Rome and the largest creditor would be involved in a plot to cancel debts. They were not so sure of the lavish Cæsar.

It was a dramatic moment. Although no one present knew it, the old order and the new were now face to face. On the one side was the head of the state, an accomplished orator and leader of the Roman bar, impressive in appearance, an undoubted patriot, devoted to the Republic as it had been handed down from past generations, with all the glowing prestige that had come to him as the saviour of the country from what the assembled senators believed was deadly peril. What the senators and what Cicero himself did not perceive, was that he was the champion of a vanishing era, of a cause that had been lost through the selfish incapacity of leaders who had failed through a hundred years to deal with the problems that had been forced upon them by a changing world. Whatever the facts of Catiline's movement, it was a significant symbol, a by-product of this failure.

On the other side was the man who was only beginning to find himself; tall, slender, graceful, with a fair complexion and keen black eyes. Always carefully groomed, rather extreme in his dress, he was looked upon as something of a fop. His premature baldness bothered him. His friends smiled

TEMPLE OF CONCORD

Meeting-place of the Senate to consider the fate of the followers of Catiline. Here Cæsar and Cicero were antagonists in the great debate on executing the accused without due process of law. The Record Office of Sulla is in the background. The original Temple of Concord was built on this site in the fourth century B.C. *The building was elaborated and remodelled as shown in the illustration in the early imperial period.* (*Restoration by H. G. Marceau and H. B. Rebert. By permission*)

at his nervous care to comb his scanty locks over the bald spot. Courteous, considerate, and tolerant, as he grew older he was to become a great world citizen. Cæsar was no radical. He had no considered program for reform. But from boyhood he had shown unusual independence, contempt for danger, and an impatience with tradition that was distinctly un-Roman. With a clear head he surveyed a disintegrating society which he found full of fascinating opportunities beckoning to ruthless ambition. In short he was a well of possibilities, good and bad. There is no reason to suppose that at this time he had the faintest idea that he was destined to destroy the old order and open the way to a new which in its turn was to fail to solve fundamental problems and so was destined to go down in anarchy. So hard it has proved to develop a form of government that combines liberty, justice, and order for a large and scattered population!

Now when he stood at the consul's invitation to give his views Cæsar knew he had come to the most critical point in his career. It was a situation loaded with dynamite. Outside the Temple of Concord he could hear the murmurs of angry armed men who already in their own minds had passed the death sentence on the prisoners and who would regard leniency as treason.

This is the first speech of Cæsar's of which we have a record. In its calm and dispassionate lucidity, its statesmanlike outlook, we catch a glimpse of the quality of the speaker.

"Men who deliberate on difficult questions," he began, "ought to be free from hatred and friendship, anger and pity. When these feelings stand in the way the mind cannot easily discern the truth and no mortal man has ever yet served his passions and his best interests. When you apply your intellect, it prevails. If passion possesses you, it holds sway and the mind is impotent."

Here, it may be observed, he outlined what were to prove the guiding principles of his life as statesman and soldier. The application of these principles he proceeded to illustrate from history. Then he turned to the case of the men accused of conspiracy. Their guilt he assumed had been established. In view of the temper of the Senate and of the armed men outside the hall it would have been physically unsafe for him to do otherwise. Still Cæsar never shrank from danger. But there was a further consideration that probably for him was decisive. If he had asserted their innocence he would at once have been shouted down and the result he hoped to achieve would have been made impossible. So assuming their guilt he pleaded that legal procedure be followed. There was no emergency that warranted depriving the prisoners of their constitutional rights. To disregard the law in this case might have far-reaching evil effects.

"All bad precedents," he argued, "have originated in cases which were good. But when the control of the government falls into the hands of incompetent or bad men your precedent may be wrongly applied and the undeserving and blameless may suffer. I have no fear of Cicero, but with this precedent established what might happen to innocent men at the hands of another less scrupulous consul?"

Therefore he urged that the property of the conspirators be confiscated and that they be imprisoned in various towns throughout Italy. On further details the ancient authorities are at variance. Sallust and Dio report that the imprisonment proposed by Cæsar was to be for life. Plutarch and Appian say it was to be for the period of the emergency, after which the Senate might determine what was best to be done; in other words, it might grant the accused men a trial in accordance with law. This second account seems more in accordance with the spirit of the entire plea. It was the sort of speech that an American citizen might make to a mob determined on a lynching—"Doubtless the man is guilty, but let the law take its course."

In any event the proposal was a practical concession to the emergency. The Senate had no more legal right to advise imprisonment than it had to advise the death sentence.

But death would close the chapter. Whatever sort of imprisonment Cæsar may have urged, he was deliberately playing for time for passions to cool. Reading the address today we are impressed with what Cicero later was to call the " noble and high-bred quality " of Cæsar's eloquence.

The plea had a great effect. Many senators were convinced by Cæsar's argument and it seemed likely to prevail. Thereupon Cicero intervened to sum up the issues in a speech which he afterward published as the *Fourth Oration against Catiline.* He was courteous to Cæsar. The punishment of imprisonment, he said, would involve less danger to the consul and less popular disfavour — and here is the evident implication that Catiline had a large popular following. Cicero is willing to take the advice of the Senate whatever it may be. But he reminds the senators that sternness may be mercy in the long run and urges that criminals should be so dealt with that in future no one should ever dream of repeating the crime. The legal argument of Cæsar he answers only sketchily. The prisoners, he asserts dogmatically, have forfeited their Roman citizenship and so cannot claim the protection of the law.

Then he launches into an analysis of the case that becomes increasingly impassioned as he proceeds. He describes the murder and devastation that had been plotted, the " universal massacre," the " heaps of the dead." He seems to see the city, he says, " the light of the whole world, the fortress of all nations, involved in one general conflagration." He shudders at the outcries of the mothers over the slaughter of their children. He impresses upon his hearers that on their decision " hang the lives of your wives and children, the fortunes of all, your homes and firesides." He speaks of his own narrow escape from death and ends by commending to their protection himself and his little son. There was no mistaking his implications. He was for the death penalty.

In its passion and appeal to the emotions the address was at the opposite pole from Cæsar's unemotional plea that reason and dispassionate judgment prevail. The contrast clearly reveals a fundamental difference in the characters of the two men.

His speech did not have quite the effect Cicero intended. Some of his friends thought he should be spared the danger of a popular reaction against the execution of the prisoners and turned to Cæsar's proposal. Thereupon a hard-boiled reactionary got the floor and turned the tide of feeling away from leniency. Marcus Cato, tribune-elect, a conservative zealot, unpopular for his intolerance and lack of tact, but respected for his honesty and courage, would stand for no sentimental nonsense. Cæsar's wishy-washy position, he intimated, might have been due to the fact that Cæsar himself was involved. The conspirators, he said, had threatened property rights. He went on with a brutally frank appeal that unconsciously characterized the sort of audience he was addressing: "You who always have valued your houses, villas, statues, and paintings more highly than your country, if you wish to retain the treasures to which you cling, arouse yourselves to take charge of the state!"

These wicked plotters, he urged, should suffer the extreme penalty. They should be treated as if they had been caught red-handed in a capital crime. "Besides," he shouted, "Catiline with his army is at our throats. Other foes are in the very heart of Rome!" There was no time to waste. Summary punishment should be dealt forthwith. He moved immediate execution.

The appeal evoked an instant response from his wealthy hearers. Cicero put the motion and it was carried. In the excitement as Cæsar left the temple the young men who had volunteered as Cicero's guard — wealthy young nobles, no doubt — rushed at him with their swords. But Cicero called them off, "either for fear of the people," Plutarch says, "or because he thought the murder would be unjust and illegal." A friend threw his cloak about the unpopular advocate of leniency and got him away through the crowd in safety.

The consul acted promptly in accordance with the moral support he had received from the Senate. The five prisoners were at once taken to the state prison near by and strangled. Almost before the crowd in the Forum knew what had happened Cicero appeared and dramatically announced their fate in the one word: " *Vixerunt*," " They have lived." " In this manner," says Plutarch, " the Romans, who choose to avoid all inauspicious words, express death."

The executions had the effect on the followers of Catiline outside the city that Cicero and Cato had expected. The protesters at Fiesole were either frightened or convinced that their cause was hopeless and began to desert their leaders. A few weeks later government forces cut off Catiline with his ragged followers now reduced to only three thousand men as they were trying to escape into Gaul.

In a last impassioned speech the leader had encouraged his little band to resist. " We are battling," he said, " for country, for freedom, for life. Our opponents are in a futile struggle to uphold the power of a few men " — for thus he characterized the Roman oligarchy. Brave words did not prevail against the troops of Rome. In the battle that followed, every one of the insurgents was killed. It was observed that " all the wounds were in front." Catiline was found " far in advance of his men amid a heap of slain foemen, still breathing slightly and showing in his face the indomitable spirit that had animated him in life."

Reviewing the writings available to us, I must say that virtually all historians of the period, ancient and modern, are convinced that Cicero was right and that Catiline had organized a conspiracy of cutthroats to burn Rome, murder its leading citizens, and overthrow the government. In the biographies of Cicero the same story is told with monotonous regularity. The authors depend chiefly on the speeches and writings of Cicero and Sallust, the two contemporary authorities, on Suetonius, who wrote nearly two centuries later, and on later Greco-Roman historians who used various contemporary sources. For confirmatory testimony they point to Cæsar's admission of the guilt of the conspirators when he was pleading against the death penalty, and to a speech of Crassus in the Senate a little more than a year later in which he gave Cicero credit for having preserved his life. The testimony of both witnesses is discredited by the fact that both were in an embarrassing position because of their early support of Catiline. While Crassus had been formally cleared of any complicity in the supposed plot, suspicion still lingered and he doubtless believed his political future required him to come out wholeheartedly on Cicero's side.

In arriving at a judgment we must bear in mind that our accounts of the Catilinarian conspiracy were all written from the standpoint of the business men and nobles who believed their property interests and lives were threatened. In the twentieth century these one-sided reports could be checked by newspaper accounts and interviews presenting the other side. Such material in Ciceronian Rome is entirely lacking. We have only the scraps of evidence quoted in hostile sources, to which I have referred.

There is no question, I think, that the leading citizens of Rome were sincere in their belief that they had saved the city from a conspiracy of desperate men. But we have only to recall the hysterical public sentiment that swept Boston at times during the long-drawn-out Sacco-Vanzetti affair in the 1920's to understand how judgments may have been distorted in Rome in the time of Catiline. We are still uncertain as to the guilt of the two Italians who were convicted of murdering a paymaster and his guard at South Braintree, Massachusetts, in 1920. But we do know they were tried for radicalism rather than for murder, and that inflamed public sentiment made it almost impossible for them to obtain a reasonably fair trial. In Rome of the first century B.C. the hysteria was even greater than it was in Massachusetts in the twentieth century of our era. In times of excitement people believe the wildest rumours that happen to fall into the pattern to which they are emotionally committed.

There was a further consideration that made it easy for Cicero to take an extreme position regarding the motives behind the movement. He had come to believe it was essential to the state to achieve "the union of the orders," to unite the business men and the aristocrats in a firm bloc which experience had shown could control the government. The affair of Catiline provided him with a heaven-sent opportunity. Political expediency marched with his belief that the state was threatened. For every reason he was impelled to make the most of the conspiracy and to magnify the danger. It was a vast satisfaction to him that under pressure of what both orders considered a common peril they had united against a common foe. He was not sufficiently far-sighted to perceive that as soon as the pressure was relieved they would fall apart again. When this happened we find him lamenting to Atticus on the frustration of his plans for a permanent party of the Good, to include both business and birth.

The question is still debated whether Cicero was justified in his summary execution of the five men arrested in Rome. He seems not to have relied on the general power of the consul under martial law. That might be challenged. As a lawyer he recognized that a Roman citizen charged with a capital offence was entitled to a trial by jury. So he fell back upon the technical point that the accused men by their plotting had lost their citizenship and the protection of the law. The argument does not stand up. The purpose of the law was to protect citizens against precisely such arbitrary action by any magistrate.

Was the execution justified on broader grounds? Cicero and the overwhelming majority of the senators professed to believe that the state was in grave danger from armed revolt and that the execution of the men under arrest would prove the most effective means to check the insurgents, prevent further trouble in Rome, and keep the revolt from spreading.

But with the arrest of the five men under suspicion the situation in Rome was in hand. The consul should have known the weakness of the forces with Catiline in the field. He had grossly exaggerated the peril in the statements which I have just quoted from the speeches and in doing this had confirmed Cæsar's warning of the danger of allowing any magistrate to set himself above the law. Perhaps under stress of emotion Cicero had convinced himself that his extravagant statements were true. I think we may be sure that consul and Senate believed the summary execution would be a salutary lesson for the Roman people without regard to the immediate emergency. Indeed, there may have been just a flicker of doubt as to whether the prisoners could be convicted in a fair trial before an unprejudiced jury. That, in the opinion of the well-to-do, would be a great pity, for in the unsound state of the public mind on the sacredness of private property the people needed a lesson. Rome had become accustomed to wholesale purges. We may agree that by the standards of the times Cicero was restrained and humane in putting to death only the five men who were charged with conspiracy. For a man of his bookish temperament he had shown surprising vigour and decisiveness in action. The situation had not got out of hand and degenerated into futile rioting.

The outcome was a triumph for the wealthy, both business men and aristocrats, and they saluted Cicero as the father of his country. The mass of the people took a different view. They came to feel that the fundamental right of a citizen to a trial by his peers had been violated. The dead Catiline became increasingly a popular hero. Four years later the commons scattered flowers upon his grave.

CHAPTER XVI

DEFLATION

THE NIGHT of the execution of the five Catilinarians was the high point of Cicero's political career. Plutarch gives a vivid description of the illumination of the streets with lamps and torches placed by the doors. Women held out lights from the roofs of houses to see and honour the consul who on his way home was attended by a throng of the most illustrious citizens of Rome. All the conversation of these wealthy men was of the danger from which they and their property had been saved and they marvelled at the vigour and enterprise of the consul who had been able to suppress the conspiracy without riots and bloodshed.

This adulation went to Cicero's head. He never was the same afterward. The older generation of Americans remember veterans of the Civil War who bored their friends by always talking about their war experiences. These were so much the most vivid events of their lives that nothing else seemed to matter. His belief that he had saved the country had a similar effect upon Cicero. His miraculous consulship became a monomania with him. His boasting was the talk of Rome for generations. " That consulship," wrote Seneca, " which he praised not without reason but without end." " His writings," says Plutarch, " were so interlarded with encomiums on himself that though his style was elegant and delightful his discourses were disgusting and nauseating to the reader; for the blemish stuck to him like an incurable disease." His vanity proved a heavy handicap. " Because," says Dio, " he was the greatest boaster alive and regarded no one as equal to himself he was wearisome and burdensome and was consequently disliked and hated by those persons he otherwise pleased." That his deeds should not be forgotten Cicero wrote a memoir of his consulship in Latin and another in Greek and also a poem in which occur those unfortunate lines I have already mentioned: " Oh happy fate of Rome to date Her birthday from my consulate." He wrote to a historian urging him to get speedily to the consulship and to lay it on a trifle thick in describing the consul's achievements. Reading his own references to " that glorious December day," its " glorious deed," its " eternal fame," we are reminded of the tiresome boasts of certain contemporary politicians.

Cicero, it must be remembered, recognized that he was a New Man, looked down upon by members of the old families. He never was quite comfortable in their presence. If he had had an assured social position perhaps he would have been more modest about his exploits. But with his feeling of inferiority he was constantly impelled to remind the aristocrats that he had saved the state. A man with Cæsar's aristocratic background would have felt no such compulsion. Undoubtedly Cicero hurt his influence by his obtrusive vanity, as the ancient authorities suggest.

In accordance with his assumption that he was now the nation's most distinguished citizen he bought from Crassus the magnificent mansion on the Palatine, overlooking the Forum, to which I have already referred. " The fairest spot in Rome," he called it. Of the purchase price of $175,000 he had to borrow $100,000 from a wealthy client, and he wrote to a friend that he was so deeply in debt that he would be glad to join a conspiracy if anybody would take him in. There was annoying gossip at this time, perhaps based on his obvious need for money, that he had made a deal with his colleague in the consulship, Antonius, by which Cicero was to be paid for surrendering his claim to the governorship of Macedonia. The provincial administration of Antonius

THE FASHIONABLE PALATINE SITE OF CICERO'S TOWN HOUSE

In the later Republican period this was the most fashionable residence district in Rome. Later it was covered by the elaborate palaces of the emperors. In the photograph we are looking across the Forum to the remains of the palace of Caligula, which occupied the ground where Cicero's mansion once stood. (Photograph by George R. Swain, courtesy of the University of Michigan Near East Research)

had been a scandal and the governor was to be tried for corruption on his return. Cicero had been defending him in the Senate. But he writes to Atticus that in view of public opinion he cannot undertake the case, and besides he has no wish to do so. He has learned that a former slave of his, an accountant, has been with Antonius, and that the governor has been saying that Cicero had sent the fellow to collect a share of the graft that the governor was exacting. Cicero tells Atticus he has been exceedingly disturbed over the gossip, which he cannot believe. He asks his friend to look into the matter and "get the empty-headed idiot out of the country." In this and subsequent letters Cicero complains of the delay of some agent in paying him money that was due, and the reference seems to be to Antonius.

The entire affair looks suspicious, especially the failure of Cicero in his letter to Atticus to show indignation over the reports involving his freedman. Still, we may give him the benefit of the doubt. Cicero was not rapacious. He speaks somewhere of the surprise of people that he came out of his consulship a poor man when he might have collected from the financiers whose cause he was defending. But he is regarded as a good security, he adds, and there is plenty of money to be had at 6 per cent. It may be that the money he expected from Antonius was the fee he was to get for defending him in court, and he actually did defend him later in spite of his protests to Atticus.

Cicero's day of unalloyed glory was short. He had represented the conspiracy as such an immense menace that its abrupt collapse produced a reaction. Dio was doubtless reflecting contemporary opinion when he wrote that Catiline "gained a greater name than his deeds deserved, owing to the reputation of Cicero and the speeches he delivered against him." The people, relieved of their vague fears about the burning of the city, began to consider the implications of the suspension of the Bill of Rights and the execution of the five citizens without trial. The procedure seemed to put a powerful weapon in the hands of the senators and business men, whom they distrusted. The newly elected tribunes were installed a week after the executions, and one of them, Metellus Nepos, the emissary of Pompey, began to make speeches denouncing the Senate for sanctioning the violation of the law. So much feeling was stirred up that Cato felt it wise to propose an extension of the cheap-wheat relief system in order to allay the bitterness of the people.

Cicero must have known he was in a vulnerable position. He appealed to the sister and sister-in-law of Nepos to call off their relative. It was no use. On the last day of December, the last day of his term, in accordance with precedent Cicero attempted to address the people, doubtless to justify his course. Nepos insisted that he confine his remarks to the customary oath that he had faithfully discharged his duty; a terrible indignity, Cicero afterward observed. The born orator was not to be so easily muzzled. He ascended the platform and exclaimed in a loud voice that he alone had saved the state and the city. "The entire Roman people," he said later, "gave me immortality and eternal glory when they with one voice and consent approved of my oath." On his return to his home "there did not seem to be a single citizen," he added, "who was not in my train." Cicero's complacent reports of his own popularity were notoriously inaccurate. He was able to kid himself so successfully that on occasions he seemed quite honestly surprised to find the mass of the people hostile. Presumably the cheering throng on that December day was made up largely of the same aristocrats and business men who had supported him so enthusiastically when he was conducting the proceedings that led to the execution of the five Roman citizens without trial.

In spite of his assumption that all the people were for him Cicero was still so uneasy that he tried to patch up an understanding with the hostile Nepos. But the tribune replied to his emissaries that a man who had punished others without a hearing ought himself to be denied the privilege of being heard. Three days later Nepos made another violent public attack upon Cicero, evidently threatening impeachment. The Senate came to his rescue with a decree granting immunity to all those who had taken part in the condemnation of the conspirators.

Another minor complication for Cicero now arose. It had to do with the attitude of his friend Pompey, still absent on his eastern command. The great general, keeping in touch with affairs at Rome through Nepos, had hoped to be recalled to add to his prestige by dealing with Catiline. Although any danger from the debtors' protest had disappeared and Catiline and his followers were about to be overwhelmed by Roman troops, the faithful tribune hastened to propose a bill summoning Pompey to return with his army and restore order. If Plutarch is right there was a fling at the ex-consul in a line on the need of suppressing "the despotic power of Cicero." In this move Nepos had the support of Cæsar, who had been consistently playing up to Pompey since the middle of the previous year. Cato exercised his prerogative as one of the tribunes to block the measure, and there was rioting, in the course of which the people demonstrated their loyalty to both Pompey and Cæsar.

Meanwhile Cicero had assumed Pompey would be delighted to learn that he had suppressed the conspiracy of Catiline, and had written him a long letter on the subject. He failed to understand that his distinguished friend had marked out that job for himself and would be keenly disappointed to learn that it had been done without him. Also it probably never occurred to Cicero that Pompey might have learned of the rising feeling against the magistrate who had executed men as conspirators without a trial as provided by law. As a politician as well as soldier the victorious general might well have felt it would be prudent to learn the lie of the land at home before identifying himself with a friend who might prove a political liability. Besides, we learn from an ancient commentator that the letter gave an impression of arrogance which did not sit well with the conqueror of the East. Pompey's reply has not been preserved but we may infer something of its tenor from Cicero's answer. He admits that he was deeply disappointed by the slight expression of affection in Pompey's letter. "In all candour," he says, "I did expect some congratulation on my achievements." Nevertheless he feels sure that when Pompey comes home he will recognize Cicero's service to the state and will be willing to be associated with him in politics.

The devotion of Cicero to Pompey is one of the curious infatuations of history. Cicero was keen enough to see his friend's weaknesses. Soon after Pompey's return from the East Cicero writes to Atticus that Pompey is jealous of him. "No good breeding, no straightforwardness, no political morality, no distinction, no courage, no liberality." While Cicero is cultivating close intimacy he knows it is only wise to be on his guard. A little later he bursts out again to Atticus: "He has nothing large-minded about him, nothing lofty, nothing which is not abject and time-serving." Cicero was apt to regard anyone who did not support him politically as rather depraved. It is noticeable that when he differs with Pompey he mentions him scornfully as "the great Pasha" — a sneering reference to Pompey's victories in the East. But these were passing interludes. Four years later it was to Pompey's advantage to double-cross Cicero in a vital matter and he did so without compunction. But nothing that he did, no matter how contemptible, could destroy his friend's devotion. His "old love," as Cicero once said, would break forth. In his final struggle with Cæsar, Cicero long hesitated and then determined to cross the Adriatic to be with his old friend who had set up his standard at the military base of Durazzo on the Macedonian coast.

"I cannot endure," he wrote to Atticus, "the longing desire I have to be with him. Books, studies, philosophy, cease to interest me. Like the bird of Plato I gaze day and night on the sea and long to fly over it. . . . As they say the sick man has hopes while he has breath, so I refused to

POMPEY

A competent soldier but politically a stuffed shirt. The fuzzy bewilderment caught by the sculptor gives a clue to the man who was taken into camp by the Roman oligarchy and became its leader against Cæsar. (Drawn from the Copenhagen bust by Richard F. Hunter)

abandon myself to despair as long as Pompey remained in Italy. But now the sun seems to have disappeared from the horizon." Cicero was faithful to the last.

While Pompey was a competent soldier, politically he was to prove pretty much a stuffed shirt. Apparently he had in mind a pre-eminent position in the state which he hoped to maintain by constitutional means through his great prestige. As he stumbled uncertainly on his way after his return to Rome he showed himself to be, as was once said of an American statesman, a large body entirely surrounded by men who knew precisely what they wanted.

In his relations with individuals Pompey must have had a magnetic personality. He was unsuccessful in dealing with men in the mass. Plutarch tells of his engaging countenance as a young man, of his dignity, his princely air, the quick glance of his eye. To women he was fascinating. The story of one of his affairs as related by his biographer gives a glimpse of this side of his character. Flora, a demi-mondaine, used to tell of the ecstatic passion he inspired. When he discarded her she was "long sick through sorrow and regret." In his later years his devotion to his young wife, Julia, the daughter of Cæsar, was the talk of Italy. "He spent entire days with her in his villas and gardens to the complete neglect of public affairs," and it was only after her death that he broke with her father. At times he showed great magnanimity. When he cleared the seas of pirates and took twenty thousand prisoners, instead of putting them to death in accordance with custom he made good citizens of them by settling them in inland towns and providing them with land to cultivate. After his victories in the East he celebrated spectacular triumphs and again ignored precedent by sending the prisoners home instead of killing them.

In writing to Atticus, Cicero ascribes his attitude toward Pompey to reasons of state, and there is truth in what he says. At the same time there was a background of personal affection which Cæsar, a far greater man than Pompey, never was able to win.

What Cicero had vaguely in mind in regard to Pompey was to develop more sharply in his thought in the years ahead. He believed he had achieved the essential coalition for which he had laboured, the union of the aristocrats and business men. But he was beginning to perceive that this was not enough. He may have missed the significance of the military pressure on the state exercised by the professional armies first under Marius and Sulla, and later under Pompey and Crassus. He could not have failed to observe the apprehension over what Pompey might do with his troops on his return from the East. Himself, he did not share this apprehension. While less than a decade earlier Pompey and Crassus had obtained the consulship through the presence of their troops outside the capital, there had been no fighting and both had retired to private life at the end of their term. Since then, to be sure, Pompey had been given two great commands with such authority as had been bestowed on no other Roman. Cicero, however, was convinced that Pompey was at heart a conservative and could be depended on not to use his military power against the peace and dignity of the state. But upon his return to Rome his prestige could be turned to account, especially with Cicero as his political mentor. Together they could restrain the arrogance of the dominant political coalition and suppress the agitators who might try to stir up trouble among the common people whom Cicero referred to as "the scum and dregs of the town," "the public that like a leech sucks the blood of the treasury, the miserable starveling rabble." The Republic would be safe if the oligarchy could be induced to make reasonable political concessions and provide amusement for the town loafers, and at the same time remain united in the policy of keeping the people in their place. There was no reason for fundamental changes in an economic and social system under which the boy from the country had risen to eminence.

During his consulship Cicero had been gradually driven to identify himself with the Tories, and while he had vast admiration for the successful business men his confidence in the aristocracy had been shaken. He had found the nobles an inconsequential lot of playboys. "Our leading men," he wrote to Atticus, "think themselves in the seventh heaven if there are bearded mullets in their fishponds that will eat out of their hands." And again he wrote of them as "such fools as to think if the state is overthrown they can keep their fishponds." Men of this sort, he was satisfied, needed such wise direction as his own wisdom could supply. They might refuse to accept it from him, a New Man. They would take it at second hand through the foremost commander of Rome, who might call his former troops to his standard if an emergency should arise.

This general idea Cicero elaborated some ten years later in his treatise *On the Commonwealth*. By that time he had seen that the refusal of the nobles to make any concessions to the people had got them precisely nowhere. The intransigent attitude simply wouldn't work. The Assemblies had final power and under competent leadership would exercise it. He was forced to the conclusion that repression inevitably would lead to revolt and that liberty was a natural right of mankind. The problem then arose of how the Assemblies could be made to act intelligently. The solution he proposed was this: Public opinion, selfish, shortsighted, uninformed, must be educated and directed by a high-minded man, for whom he had various names — guide, manager, pilot, overseer, and finally simply first citizen. This leader must be of such recognized pre-eminence that the magistrates, Senate, and Assemblies, would acquiesce in his counsels. *Noblesse oblige* must be this Elder Statesman's motto. Power must involve obligation. To the idealistic Cicero the plan seemed within the realm of possibilities if only the right man could be found — Pompey, Cæsar. . . . At times he thought that first one and then the other might prove the unselfish George Washington for whom he yearned. Perhaps if one of them had measured up to his dream the Republic might have survived for another generation. But the Rome of his day was not producing George Washingtons. In drawing his lessons from the past Cicero overlooked the changes that had come. He failed to take into the account the moral deterioration of the aristocracy, the weakening of the middle class, the bitterness of the dispossessed farmers and the impoverished people of the capital, and finally the power of the commander of a professional army.

In the circumstances the system could have worked only as a veiled dictatorship resting on the known ability of the First Citizen to call demobilized veterans to his support. Even then it would have been subject to challenge by any ambitious commander of troops commissioned to defend and extend the frontiers of the lands ruled by Rome. Cicero was right in believing Pompey was temperamentally disposed to fall into such a plan. He was wrong in believing the Senate would agree to it without a prolonged struggle and he overestimated the ability of Pompey to handle the supreme position to which he aspired.

It was only after a devastating civil war that Rome was ready to be rescued from chaos by the organizing ability of Augustus, who became First Citizen, Princeps, in a system somewhat similar to that outlined by Cicero. But in the background were his soldiers, and the Republic gradually faded as the Princeps gathered the powers of government into his own hands.

With the return of Pompey late in the year 62 came the opportunity for the first test of Cicero's program. When the conquering hero landed with his army at Brindisi, the road to Rome lay open. The state had no comparable force at its disposal. He could have marched on the capital at the head of his victorious legions and installed himself there as dictator. The financiers and business men were under no apprehensions. Pompey had been their representative in his eastern command and his newly acquired wealth would give him an additional common interest with them. Only Crassus, who had been at outs with Pompey during their consulship, thought it prudent to get out of the way with his family and property. But the old families who had been running things with a high hand were nervous, and with reason. While Pompey belonged to the nobility, with baronial estates in Italy, his hundred-year old family was comparatively new by Roman standards. The aristocrats had opposed granting him the authority for his great commands. They feared the measures he might take against them if he should establish his supremacy in Rome. It was therefore with almost incredulous surprise that they learned of the events in Brindisi. Pompey assembled his troops on parade, bade them farewell, and dismissed them to their homes with an invitation to assemble in Rome for his formal triumph. With a few friends he set out for the capital, greeted by admiring throngs along the way.

His renunciation of a military dictatorship that lay within his grasp was in accordance with the fine old Roman tradition that had been violated by his immediate predecessors. The action was patriotic, but whether consciously and nobly patriotic we may doubt. Pompey had prospered under the established order. Why challenge it? He was quite devoid of political ideas, blind to the grave evils that were threatening the Republic. He had no passion for reforms that would be resisted by the constitutional authorities. Two immediate objectives he desired to realize, and only two. He needed ratification by the Senate of the political arrangements he had made in the East, and the grant of an additional soldiers' bonus in the shape of farm lands he had promised to the men who had served under him. Both requests he had no doubt would be immediately granted to a man of his standing and prestige. For the rest he seems to have wished merely to bask in the sunlight of public approbation as the foremost citizen of Rome. He had no taste for a *coup d'état.* Indeed, there was no reason for one. Who was there in Italy to challenge his position? On his way home he had divorced his wife. Gossip involved her in numerous affairs during his long absence — one with Cæsar. Such things happened in high society in the capital and were not taken too seriously. The divorce could be turned to account by giving him the opportunity to make an alliance with the family connections of the powerful Cato. This would strengthen his position if strengthening were needed. But that hard-drinking Tory refused his request for two nieces, one for himself, the other for his son. He disapproved of the general who had represented the financial interests. "Tell Pompey," Cato said to the emissary, " that Cato is not to be caught in a female snare. I will never give hostages, against my country, to the glory of Pompey."

While he was awaiting the spectacular triumph that was always accorded a victorious commander, Pompey surveyed the political scene as it had developed while he was in the East. It was extremely confusing to the slow-thinking soldier, the inept politician. His reputation was that of the strong silent man. Gradually it became evident that he was silent because he had nothing to say. In one matter his native caution came to his aid. He was ready to fall in with only part of Cicero's plan. It would be pleasant to be First Citizen, but he did not care to accept Cicero as his chief political adviser. Doubtless his friends had warned him of the unpopularity of the former consul with the mass of the people. He was not disposed to identify himself with a man who had evoked widespread antagonism. Cicero had hoped Pompey would come out with a ringing approval of the consul's course in saving the state. That he failed to do so was a crushing disappointment to his eager friend. Pompey's one purpose, in accordance with the conventional technique of mediocre politicians of all ages, was to give no offence in any quarter. When he could not avoid speaking he cautiously took refuge in platitudes.

His first speech after his return, according to the prejudiced testimony of Cicero, " did not please the poor, or satisfy the disloyal [that is, Cicero's enemies], or find favour with the wealthy, or appear sound to the loyalists." On another occasion, when an attempt was made to pin Pompey down on a matter of public policy, he made a long speech evading the issue and vaguely commending the decrees of the Senate. When he sat down he remarked to Cicero: "I think my answer covers your case also." The inference was that in commending the Senate he had given indirect approval to the course of the Senate and the consul in causing the execution of the associates of Catiline without trial. This was a terrible let-down for Cicero. But he got what consolation he could out of Crassus, who had recovered his courage sufficiently to return to Rome and now took advantage of a double opportunity that presented itself. He went out of his way to address the Senate in extravagant praise of Cicero's course and thus to clear himself of any lingering suspicion that he had been identified with left-wing activities. At the same time he was able with apparent innocence to throw the harpoon into his old enemy by extolling Cicero instead of Pompey as the saviour of Rome. Cicero commented to Atticus on Pompey's agitation during the speech, though he quite missed the reason for it by accepting Crassus' compliments to himself at face value and not perceiving the intention to embarrass Pompey.

Still in his vulnerable position, with the people hostile and the aristocrats lukewarm toward the aggressive New Man, Cicero desperately needed Pompey's help. In spite of his private grumbling to Atticus he did not abandon hope of winning the powerful support of the great soldier and of eventually seeing him accepted as the supreme Elder Statesman, with Cicero as the unofficial adviser behind the scenes, the *Eminence Grise,* the Father Joseph, who was Richelieu's confidant. Meanwhile, shortly before Pompey's return Rome had been rocked by a minor scandal that gradually developed major proportions and was destined to have an immense influence on Cicero's career.

CHAPTER XVII

THE BIG THREE

IN A letter covering a variety of topics which Cicero wrote to Atticus on January 1, 61, he mentions incidentally a bit of gossip. " I suppose you have heard," he says, " that P. Clodius, son of Appius, was caught in woman's clothes at Gaius Cæsar's house while the state function was going on, that he was saved and got out by a maidservant, and that the affair is causing immense scandal. I feel sure you will be sorry for it." Then he goes on to tell of his distress at the death of a favourite slave, a young man who used to read aloud to him. The death, he adds, has affected him more than the death of a slave should. Cicero was really a warm-hearted man. A month later he mentions the Clodius matter again. A rather inconspicuous senator had brought it before the Senate, it had been referred to the proper religious bodies, which had decreed that a sacrilege had been committed, and the Senate thereupon had instituted proper proceedings. Also as an incident Cæsar had divorced his wife, the aristocratic Pompeia, granddaughter of the dictator Sulla. Evidently the scandal was growing.

It had to do with the escapade of a young fellow who was a member of one of the oldest and greatest families in Rome. The Claudii had left their marks on Roman history from the earliest times. Arrogant patricians, members of the Claudian house had gone their haughty way, soldiers and statesmen of distinguished ability. The Appian aqueduct, the first of the aqueducts that supplied the capital, and the

Appian Way, the Great South Road, stood as monuments to the capacity that was handed down from father to son. Publius Clodius Pulcher — he preferred "Clodius" rather than the conventional "Claudius" — was one of a family of six. A younger sister was the spectacular Clodia. The brother and sister were two of the smartest, wildest, most dashing figures in Roman society.

Early each December the sacred rites for the Good Goddess, the protective deity for women, were celebrated in Rome in the house of one of the high magistrates. Only women were allowed to take part. Every male creature was barred from the premises. In December 62 the rites took place in the pontifical residence of Cæsar on the Sacred Way; not because Cæsar was chief pontiff, but because he was a judge. His mother Aurelia and his wife Pompeia presided. Clodius was having an affair with Pompeia which was made difficult to prosecute by the strictness of her mother-in-law. Apparently Clodius decided it would be a triumph of gallantry for him to meet the lady in her husband's house during the celebration of the rites. He was probably about thirty years old and he went to the house disguised as a girl. A maid of Pompeia's who was in the intrigue ran to tell her mistress. Clodius became impatient while waiting and wandered about in the dark rooms until he happened to meet one of Aurelia's attendants who, Plutarch says, "invited him to play with her as the women did among themselves." His voice betrayed him and the woman ran shrieking to her companions, crying that there was a man in the house. The correct Aurelia stopped the ceremonies and led a searching party. The women discovered the intruder and put him out. He was recognized. They went home and told their husbands and by morning the news was all over town.

Clodius had influential family friends who would have liked to hush up the matter. It is hardly to be supposed that the skeptical aristocrats were greatly shocked over the profanation of a religious rite by a young fellow of the smart set. Why make a disturbance about such an affair? Cicero, usually a stickler for the proprieties, wrote to Atticus that he was not keen about doing anything. But the zealous Cato, he said, was " hot and eager." None of the influential group of ex-consuls was ready to move, but when the question was raised by a senator with Cato's backing, the House was compelled to acquiesce.

The publicity made it impossible for the reluctant nobles to do otherwise. The state religion was one of the instruments of government, used to keep the popular Assembly and the people generally in order. It would never do for the people to get the idea that the aristocracy considered the profanation of sacred rites of no importance. Having started out to make an impressive demonstration of religious devotion for political reasons, the senators were bound to see the case through.

Up to this time there is no evidence that Clodius had been regarded as a leader of the People's Party, or of the left-wing group that Catiline had attempted to organize. He had figured as a prosecutor of Catiline after Catiline's return from his African governorship, and at the execution of the Catiline group in Rome he had been in Cicero's bodyguard. But with the threat of prosecution in the Good Goddess affair Clodius suddenly became a popular favourite. This change in public attitude probably grew out of reasons having nothing to do with the case. In the bitterness that had developed between the underprivileged masses and the hardbitten oligarchy that controlled the government, it was quite possible for a good mob orator like Clodius to convince the people that he was being railroaded by their aristocratic enemies, and so to arouse wide public sympathy. The governing class played into his hands by the methods proposed for the trial. As there was no permanent court with jurisdiction in questions of sacrilege, a special tribunal had to be set up. In order to assure conviction the senatorial crowd proposed to allow the presiding judge to select the jury from the jury wheel. In this way a packed jury could be obtained. The proposal was so unfair that it was resented even by some aristocrats. It infuriated the masses, who were especially sensitive in the matter of senatorial encroachments on the judiciary, in view of what they regarded as the illegal executions in Cicero's consulship. So violent was the opposition that the Senate finally agreed that in the special court the jurors should be selected in the usual way from the jury wheel by lot.

By this time Cicero had become involved. As usual he thought it advisable to go along with his crowd. In a letter to Atticus he gives a vivid if prejudiced account of the trial. In the customary challenges by both sides, he says, the prosecution rejected the most worthless, the defence all the best men. "There was never," he writes, " a seedier lot around a table in a gambling den. Senators under a cloud, business men out at the elbows, known grafters. A few honest men got by who were evidently disgusted at having to rub elbows with such rascals."

Clodius pleaded not guilty and offered an alibi as his defence. He produced a witness who swore that on the night of the festival Clodius had been staying with him at a town ninety miles from Rome. Cæsar was called as a witness for the prosecution. Not caring to antagonize Clodius and his popular support, he testified that he knew nothing about the case.

" Why then," asked the prosecutor, " did you divorce your wife? "

" My wife," he replied in a phrase that has become proverbial, " must be above suspicion."

In modern times a man with Cæsar's reputation for gallantry could hardly have made such an answer without bringing down the house. In Rome, however, a higher standard of conduct may have been expected of the wife of the chief pontiff than of that dignitary himself.

The most important witness for the prosecution was Cicero, who blew up the alibi by deposing that he had seen Clodius in Rome three hours before the ceremonial for the Good Goddess. He was not particularly happy at his prominence. He tells Atticus that he gave no testimony beyond what was so notorious and well attested that he could not evade it. Perhaps, as Plutarch says, he was pushed into the case by his wife, who hated Clodia, whom she suspected, quite unjustly from everything we know, of having designs upon her husband.

In spite of the evidence, to the intense disgust of Cicero and most of his respectable friends, Clodius was acquitted by a vote of 31 to 25. They assumed the jury had been bribed by Crassus, of whom Cicero speaks to Atticus as "Bald Head, the millionaire." At one stage in the proceedings the jury had asked for a guard. After the verdict an old aristocrat met a juror who had voted for acquittal. "Why did you ask for a guard?" he inquired. "Were you afraid of being robbed of the money?"

The verdict plunged Cicero into gloom. When such scum as this jury, he wrote, could find that something had not happened that everybody knew had happened, the foundations of law and justice were undermined and the Republic had gone to pot. There is another possible view. The trial had developed into a political affair and under such circumstances political considerations always weighed with a Roman jury. In an earlier chapter I have cited instances of this sort involving Cicero himself. Appeals to political prejudice are not unknown today. Early in this century a Missouri newspaper was tried on the charge of libelling a Democratic politician and was fined $50,000. "It was convicted," one of the lawyers confided to a correspondent, "not for libel but for treason to the Democratic Party." Clodius may well have been acquitted because the jury disliked the crowd that was prosecuting him. Whether the charges of bribery are true we cannot be sure.

The trial had unhappy consequences for Cicero in his resulting feud with Clodius. There is no evidence that Clodius took Cicero's mild testimony particularly to heart. But Cicero, once his feelings were involved, could not let the matter drop. He was always prodding Clodius about it publicly, " smashing " him, he boasts to Atticus. He was proud of his powers of repartee. Of one such interchange he writes at some length to his friend. In a speech in the Senate he predicted that Clodius would end his career in prison.

" Up gets our dandified young gentleman," Cicero says, " and throws in my teeth my having been at Baiæ " — the fashionable watering-place. " ' What business,' quoth he, ' has an Arpinate with hot baths? ' " That is, why should a country fellow try to crash the gates of high society? Cicero made a stinging retort, and the debate ended on this level: " ' The jurors didn't trust you on your oath,' said he. ' Yes,' said I, ' twenty-five jurors did trust me, thirty-one didn't trust you, for they took care to get their money in advance.' " Here, according to Cicero, there was a burst of applause and his opponent had no comeback.

Three months later we find Cicero writing to Atticus of another return to the attack. In a brutal jest he revived in the Senate an old piece of scandal about Clodius' supposed incest with his sister. " A jest, you will say, unbecoming to a former consul. I confess it, but I detest that woman " — a remark that suggests possible resentment over trouble occasioned by Terentia's jealousy. In the light of these incidents we cannot be surprised that Clodius later seized an opportunity to get even with his tormentor.

Meanwhile Pompey was impatiently waiting for the legal confirmation of his eastern settlements and for legislation providing the farms he had promised to his soldiers. He encountered unexpected opposition from the senatorial machine, which had not forgiven him for his part in overthrowing the Sullan Constitution and for his subsequent course in obtaining the great commands. Cicero, he found, could do little for him against the stubborn and shortsighted oligarchy, and his practical political friend Cæsar had departed for his governorship of Farther Spain, where he was to obtain his first military experience. As usual Cæsar was heavily in debt. He is reported to have remarked jokingly that he needed something over a million dollars to be worth just nothing at all. His creditors prevented his departure until he had obtained a loan from Crassus by which he was able to satisfy the most importunate. It was on his journey to Spain that he is said to have made the famous remark quoted by Longfellow in *The Courtship of Miles Standish* that he would rather be first in a little Iberian village than second in Rome. Whether he said it or not the remark was in character.

From Cicero's standpoint, throughout the year the political situation was steadily deteriorating. Made arrogant by its successes, the governing clique managed things with a high hand. Not only did it stupidly refuse to make the important alliance with Pompey by meeting his just demands; under the leadership of extremists like Cato it alienated the wealthy business class, whose support was essential to its control of the government. While Cicero was absent from the Senate a resolution had been adopted calling for the prosecution of all jurymen who had accepted bribes. The members of the business order always had claimed immunity from such prosecution and were incensed by the move, morally justified though it was. Another difficulty had arisen in connection with Asiatic taxes. The business syndicate had bid too high for its contract to collect the taxes and had applied to the Senate for relief. In both cases Cicero believed the financiers were in the wrong. Yet he thought the harmony of the orders was so necessary to the state that he went to the front for his business friends. He remonstrated with the Senate for its bribery action and made two speeches in favour of reducing the tax contract. But he got nowhere. The influential Cato was inflexible. "Cato," Cicero complained to Atticus, "has been worrying the unhappy business men, who once were devoted to him, for the last three months." As an experienced if ineffective politician Cicero believed in the wisdom of compromise. Cato did not. It was left to the practical Cæsar upon his return to get the necessary relief measure through and so to win the devotion of the business class.

Cicero could only mourn the intractability of the Senate in smashing the coalition for which he had been working. "Politics," he wrote to Atticus, "is in a shaky condition. The business men are all but alienated from the Senate." But he still pinned his hope on Pompey. "Since things are in such crazy shape," he continued, "I am building what I may call a road toward the maintenance of our power. I cultivate close intimacy with Pompey."

That dignitary, finding to his surprise that his prestige was not equal to the task he had laid out, now determined to be practical himself and have one of his own men elected a consul for the next year. He succeeded, but his magistrate proved a poor politician and got nowhere. The return of the resourceful Cæsar from his Spanish command transformed the situation. By this time Cicero was at his wits' end. He wrote Atticus that he hoped to convert Cæsar to the good cause — Cæsar who had made a fine record in Spain and was "now sailing triumphantly before the wind." The nobles were worthless. Even Cato, "with the best intentions and the most sterling honesty, sometimes does positive injury to the country. He talks as if he were in the Republic of Plato instead of in the sink of Romulus." All Cicero could do was to put his trust in Pompey and hope for the best from Cæsar. If the Senate had only been ready to face the facts and come to terms with Pompey as proposed by Cicero, the union of the orders might have been restored and the Republic given a new lease of life. But such statesmanlike action was beyond the oligarchy.

Looking over the situation upon his return, Cæsar discovered that the senatorial opposition to him as well as to Pompey was implacable. The machine was unalterably opposed to his candidacy for the consulship, which he at once had announced. Unlike Cicero he did not resort to eloquent speeches. He turned to more practical measures. If he could reconcile Crassus to Pompey, and obtain the support of Cicero with his influence over the voters in the Italian towns, he believed the combination could carry the election.

So far as Crassus and Pompey were concerned the task was not difficult in spite of their previous enmity. The advantages of the coalition were too obvious. To Pompey he could hold out the expectation of the speedy ratification of the measures upon which he had set his heart — the confirmation of his Asiatic arrangements and the land bill for his soldiers. To Crassus he would promise the tax-contract relief for the business syndicate and perhaps support in other projects. For himself he had far-reaching plans. He was to have not only the consulship but beyond that the governorship of provinces of his choice, with the command of the troops that went with the governorship and perhaps a prolonged term.

Cicero presented a harder problem. Cæsar sent an emissary to the former consul promising to be guided by his advice and Pompey's. Probably he did not disclose all that he had in mind. It was an attractive proposal. The advantages, Cicero wrote to Atticus, would be "a close alliance with Pompey and, if I choose, with Cæsar too, reconciliation with my enemies, peace with the multitude, tranquillity for my old age." But he had been told that Cæsar would expect his help on the land bill that was to be introduced, which it might prove embarrassing for him to support. Besides he could not get over a lingering distrust of the politician who had led the opposition in the Senate to the executions of the 5th of December 63. We may surmise too that he felt the offer did not comport with the dignity of his position. He, a distinguished former consul, was being asked to subordinate himself to a younger man who had not yet attained the consulship. Possibly he may have had an uneasy feeling that the proposed coalition might override the Constitution to which he was devoted, although he did not come to a full realization of this danger until a few months later.

His adherence was not essential to the plan. Even without Cicero three great interests in the state would be represented — Cæsar the popular interest, Pompey the military, and Crassus the financial. So was set up the Committee of Three, the First Triumvirate as it is known in history, which was to control Roman politics for the next decade. Its fundamental principle was that no step should be taken in public affairs over the objection of any one of the three. At first the compact was secret. Only in the development of events did the public learn what had happened.

The Conservative organization was not able to defeat the powerfully supported Cæsar for the consulship. The best it could do was to elect as his colleague a stubborn reactionary, Bibulus, son-in-law of Cato, who contributed to a slush fund for the purpose. Cato had a reputation for integrity, but on this occasion he took the familiar position that the end justified the means.

Cicero had no part in what followed except as an anxious observer. Nevertheless it is necessary to sketch the course of events because of their bearing not only upon Cicero's career, but upon the downfall of the Republic. Cæsar was ready at once with his bill to provide farms for Pompey's veterans. The measure was reasonable. The land was to be bought from the spoils of their conquests. At first he made a conscientious effort to proceed fairly and in accordance with the Constitution. He presented the measure to the Senate, offering to amend any clause that might seem objectionable. The Tories made no criticism but stubbornly opposed any land bill. This was the occasion that led Cæsar to begin publication of senatorial debates for their effect on public opinion. His opponents were too shortsighted to realize that by alienating the demobilized veterans from the government they were destroying the Republic. Ultimate power in Rome now rested with the professional armies. If the soldiers could not obtain what they regarded as just compensation from the Senate, they would be ready to rally behind any generous commander who desired to seize the supreme power.

Cato led a filibuster and Cæsar then submitted the measure to the Assembly without senatorial approval, as he had the constitutional right to do. His opponents resorted to the checks and balances of the Constitution and attempted to obstruct proceedings by setting up the veto of the Tory consul. Cæsar tried to argue with him and asked him to point out any defects in the measure. Bibulus contemptuously refused. He would only say that he would tolerate no innovations during his year of office.

"You shall have the law," Cæsar shouted to the crowd, "if only he wishes it."

"You shall not have this law," Bibulus retorted, "even if you all wish it."

Cæsar was not the man to let such a challenge pass. While the chronology is somewhat uncertain it seems likely that at this time he made one of his surprise manœuvres. In order to keep him harmlessly employed after his term of office, the Senate had assigned to both consuls for the succeeding year the governorship of some inconsequential provinces described as "mere woods and pastures." Overriding the Senate, Cæsar obtained from the Assembly the command of the provinces of northern Italy and of Illyria across the Adriatic (Cisalpine Gaul and Illyricum), with three legions for five years. To these provinces a little later the Senate reluctantly added the province of southern Gaul beyond the Alps, Transalpine Gaul, customarily referred to as the Province, with one legion. This Roman province gave its name to the old Provence of France. With his legions in northern Italy Cæsar could easily descend on the capital if conditions should become acute. But his more immediate purpose was evident. While his term as consul was not to expire until the end of the year, the date of his proconsular commands was set ten months earlier, for February 28, 59. This enabled him to begin recruiting soldiers at once and he had them camped outside of Rome where obstreperous senators could go and look at them. Cicero quotes Pompey as meeting all later obstruction with the terse remark: "I shall coerce you with Cæsar's army."

Thus buttressed with potential force, Cæsar returned

to his interrupted legislative program. At first the Conservatives cherished the strange hope that they might depend on Pompey to mobilize his veterans against Cæsar's recruits. This hope was dispelled when Cæsar appealed to Crassus and Pompey on the first measure brought before the Assembly.

"There is powerful opposition to the bill," the consul said, addressing Pompey. "What will be your attitude?"

"If anyone dares raise a sword," the general replied, "I will snatch up my shield!" Crassus nodded assent.

That settled it. Influential men who were suspicious of Cæsar as a radical were convinced that if the two leading citizens of Rome approved, the measure must be one that all respectable men could support. They had not yet learned of the secret coalition. Events soon demonstrated its existence and power.

There was rioting in the Forum, in the course of which the tribunes who had been persuaded to veto Cæsar's proposal were driven out along with Bibulus. That consul had the legal authority to prevent action on the bill by announcing unfavourable omens. For many years the omens had been used reasonably to prevent the taking of hasty and ill-advised action by an emotional Assembly. Later the oligarchy had resorted to them to block any legislation that it considered objectionable. In spite of the political-religious veto announced by Bibulus, Cæsar proceeded to put the bill through the Assembly. Bibulus appealed to the Senate to declare the law void on the ground that it had been illegally passed. In the prevailing popular temper, with some of Pompey's veterans in the city and with Cæsar's recruits outside, the Senate prudently refused to act. Thereupon Bibulus shut himself up in his house, where he would be safe from the mob, and issued daily bulletins on the omens which technically invalidated all legislative proceedings.

Without regard to the technicalities of the law Cæsar proceeded to put through in rapid succession the various measures to which he was pledged. Because of the course of the other consul, none of them, in the phrase applied to President Theodore Roosevelt's action in obtaining the Panama Canal, was "tainted with legality." Undoubtedly Cæsar was violating the Constitution. He could argue, however, that it was the violation of the spirit of the Constitution by the oligarchy's representative that compelled him to retaliate in kind; that Bibulus was arbitrarily stopping the processes of government on behalf of a small privileged group. The events of the year 59 once more demonstrated that free institutions will work only when their administration is permeated with a spirit of fair play and reasonable compromise.

In addition to the measures agreed upon by the Three, an additional one should be mentioned for the light it throws on Cæsar's gradual development into a statesman with a world view. In his experiences as a provincial administrator he doubtless had been impressed with the defects in Roman provincial administration. He put through a bill intended to remove the more flagrant abuses by provincial governors. Even Cicero pronounced it an "excellent law."

So completely did Cæsar dominate the situation and so impotent was his colleague that humorous citizens began signing legal documents as done "in the consulship of Julius and Cæsar."

Meanwhile Cæsar took steps to strengthen his own position when he should be out of office and to protect his legislation against annulment by a hostile Senate. Cæsar himself married the daughter of one of the men whom he had in mind for one of the consulships (the other was to be one of Pompey's generals) and cemented his friendship with Pompey by giving his daughter Julia to him in marriage. Never permitting personal feeling to interfere with considerations of state, he picked on the energetic and popular Clodius to represent him as a tribune, in spite of Clodius' affair with Cæsar's divorced wife.

This move he decided upon abruptly when Cicero in pleading at the bar had spoken critically of the rule of the

Three. The speech sharply reminded Cæsar that Cicero might be expected later to lead a formidable opposition. Cicero insisted he had been misreported. The keen consul doubtless understood what every newspaper man knows, that the first impulse of a public man is to repudiate any rash statement that threatens to get him into trouble. Clodius, who hated the orator, might be depended upon to keep him in order as a labour of love. The reckless young man belonged to a patrician family and so was ineligible to be a tribune, an office that belonged exclusively to the plebeians. This difficulty would be circumvented if he could be adopted into a plebeian family. With customary swiftness, three hours after he had heard Cicero's speech, Cæsar with Pompey's help had set in motion the necessary formalities for Clodius' adoption.

Throughout the year Cicero withdrew from politics and passed his time in reading and in the practice of law. He was not comfortable in giving in to the Three without a struggle. His timidity he admitted frankly to Atticus. "I have so completely lost my nerve," he writes, "that I prefer the existing despotism with peace to a state of war." And again: "I hold my position with some dignity but with less courage than I should like."

Apparently the series of surprises engineered by the resourceful Cæsar made Cicero as dizzy as he had been made by similar surprise attacks in the first half-year of his consulship. His letters present a picture of a sensitive, vain man, patriotically opposed to what he regarded as a gathering despotism, putting up a front and trying to convince himself that his popularity and service to the state would protect him from threatening danger. His uneasiness on this point constantly crops out in spite of his wishful thinking. While he assumes that he is generally admired — at least by all decent people — he gives himself away by telling of a remarkable ovation he has received at the games, "without a single catcall." Evidently there had been plenty of catcalls on other occasions which he forgot to mention, the memory of which was constantly present in the back of his head.

As soon as the program of the Three got under way Cicero left Rome and for several months wandered among his country villas. From Tusculum he writes in April that he is determined not to think of politics. He has learned of a proposal by the government to send him on a mission to Egypt, doubtless to get him out of the way — a plan that never materialized. From Antium by the shore of the Mediterranean he writes that he wouldn't mind visiting Alexandria and adds in a burst of despondency that the people are tired of him. He would like to bury himself in philosophy. Uneasily he inquires what his enemy Clodius is up to. Again he tells of lazy days at the villa spent with his books or counting the waves. He has just heard of the proposed manœuvre to make Clodius eligible for the tribuneship. But who's afraid? "I am wonderfully anxious to try issues with him." He realizes that he has been thrust off the ship of state and his only wish is "to watch the shipwreck from the shore." In another letter he speaks of "the three unscrupulous men" as "our tyrants." As for Clodius, "if he should attack me, let him attack." Restlessly he moves to his villa at Formiæ, down the coast toward Naples. On the way at Three Taverns he hears that Clodius actually has been made a plebeian and is an avowed candidate for tribune. The news really alarms him and he denounces the move as "tyranny and intolerable." Three Taverns, incidentally, is the place where the brethren met the Apostle Paul on his journey to Rome.

Late in April he writes from Formiæ in criticism of a second land bill that Cæsar had carried to provide farms for men with families living in poverty in Rome. He can't understand what Pompey is thinking of to sanction the illegality of the consul's measures. The great man, he hears, has excused himself by disclaiming responsibility. He approves Cæsar's laws and is not responsible for the methods used in passing them. It is not his business to inquire whether Bibulus is announcing unfavourable omens. A little later Cicero learns of Pompey's marriage to Cæsar's daughter and he fears the worst. "Make no mistake, he is preparing a despotism." At least Cicero has this consolation. He has feared that in the centuries to come the services of Pompey will loom larger than his own. That anxiety at least is now put to rest. Cicero always has the verdict of history in mind. "I am much more afraid," he says, "of the judgment of posterity six hundred years hence than of the petty gossip of today."

In the middle of the year Cicero returned to Rome. He found there an oppressive despotism. "We are tied hand and foot and no longer have spirit enough to object to our slavery, for we fear death and exile as if they were great evils, whereas compared to our abject condition they are relatively of little moment. But nobody dares say a word." Yes, there is one; a young politician named Curio, whom we shall meet later. He speaks out, Cicero says, and is applauded when he appears in the Forum. To that extent people are still allowed to express their sentiments. But it is a hopeless outlook.

In spite of Cicero's opposition, Cæsar, who never got over his respect and admiration for his brilliant opponent, now offered him a chance of escape from the threats of Clodius. He gave him his choice between a mission abroad and a place on Cæsar's staff as deputy in his provincial governorship the next year. Very decent of him, Cicero writes. "But I don't like running away. I am spoiling for a fight." This was tall talk to keep up his courage.

Cicero was a man of moods. At one time he might be up in the clouds, at another down in the depths. In his next letter to Atticus he begins by saying that the threats of Clodius and the conflicts ahead "touch me only slightly." But before he finishes, his mood has changed. Clodius, he repeats, is threatening him and a storm is hanging over his head that should bring Atticus back to Rome at once. Pompey assures him that Clodius will do nothing, but he is sure

Pompey is deceiving himself. Perhaps not. Pompey certainly talks like an angel. Cicero has been offered a place on Cæsar's land-distribution commission — a safe retreat. But his acceptance would alienate the Conservatives and he fears would not placate his opponents — another confession of unpopularity. At any rate he won't leave Rome. He prefers fighting. Then he breaks down. "Why mince matters any longer? All is lost." And he adds the superfluous admission: "By god, I'm rather nervous."

The succeeding letters are in the same vein. He is certain the Three have become intensely unpopular — as indeed they had with the oligarchy. We may doubt their unpopularity with the people in spite of Cicero's gleeful reports to his friend. He speaks of hisses for Cæsar at the games and at the theatre, where the business men from their block of seats just behind that reserved for senators arose and applauded the outspoken Curio. He hears that Cæsar and his colleagues are so outraged that they threaten to deprive the business men of their privileged position in the theatre and to revoke the law for the sale of cheap wheat. In view of the subsequent attitude of these two groups it seems likely that Cicero was exaggerating the hostility shown. It is difficult for even the most unprejudiced observer to appraise the significance of demonstrations at theatres. Modern politicians have discovered the fallacy of judging the popularity of presidential candidates by the comparative applause when their pictures are thrown on the screen at motion-picture shows. Bibulus was so detested that he dared not venture out of his house. Yet Cicero tells Atticus in a subsequent letter that the consul's edicts are so popular that one can hardly get past the place where they are posted because of the crowds reading them. Apparently it never occurred to him that the crowds were naturally curious to see what the old dodo was raving about now.

He writes that he is so managing things that his popularity and the strength of his position are increasing daily. While he doesn't touch politics he is busy in the courts and is " winning extraordinary favour with the people." In the one of his court pleas that has been preserved and in others to which he refers, his technique is revealed. He reminds his audiences again and again of how he had saved Rome from fire and sword by his summary execution of the followers of Catiline, for which he feared Clodius was going to attack him. " Oh, that 5th of December in my consulship! That day I can truly call the birthday of the city, or at least the day of its salvation." In this trial his client Flaccus was charged with malfeasance in office in his governorship of the province of Asia. He probably was guilty although he was acquitted. One of the charges against him was somewhat embarrassing to the attorney for the defence, who was trying to rally all groups of the population to his support in the approaching conflict. It was the custom of Jewish business men scattered over the Mediterranean region to send gold each year to Jerusalem as a temple tax. In order to prevent a financial stringency Flaccus had refused to permit this export of gold. But his action was regarded by the Jews in his province as an unwarranted interference with a religious practice.

There was a considerable bloc of Jewish business men in Rome and Cicero recognized their political power. He taxes the prosecutor with having seen to it that these men were well represented in the audience at the trial. "You know," he says to the prosecutor, " what a big crowd it is, how they stick together, how influential they are in the Assemblies. So I will speak in a low voice so that only the jurors may hear; for there are those who would incite the Jews against me." Then with a frank appeal to religious prejudice he confides to the jury that he looks on the Jewish religion as involving " barbaric superstition."

In other letters he constantly refers to the threats of Clodius but as constantly tries to reassure himself of his safety " behind a rampart of goodwill." " My hopes," he writes, " are so raised that I often think there is no reason for me to shrink from the conflict that threatens." But he wishes Atticus were on the ground and urges him to fly to Rome. He would like to be certain of the attitude of the Three and he suggests that his friend could "find out through Juno [by whom he means Clodia] just how far the great men are to be trusted." Then he no longer would be in a fog. The last letter of the year that has been saved was written in October to his brother Quintus, then serving as governor in Asia Minor. "Should Clodius give notice of action against me," he tells Quintus with feigned confidence, "the whole of Italy will rush to my support." Italy failed him.

The next letter we have was written to Atticus in April of the next year, when Cicero was on his way into exile. Clodius had had his revenge.

CHAPTER XVIII

A POLITICAL GANGSTER IN ACTION

THE YOUNG aristocrat who had become tribune in December of 59 at the end of Cæsar's consulship was an unscrupulous politician with a gift for mob leadership. Clodius was a ruthless demagogue, a political gangster, who took the side of the underprivileged, whom he understood how to manage. The proletariat that had developed in Rome lived in wretchedness. It had begun to settle down into what modern Marxist writers call the "*Lumpenproletariat*," a technical term defined as "that portion of the proletariat whose income, although of proletarian dimensions, is not the result of actual labour but of charity and extortion." But it was still close enough to its middle-class farm origins to look wistfully back to the days when its forefathers were independent farmers. It was ready to follow leaders who professed sympathy for its misery and promised to improve its lot. It loathed the oligarchy, which Cicero with unconscious irony called the party of the Good, although he was coming to admit that he feared they were "an extinct race." He called it the party of the Good because, however unworthily and selfishly, it upheld the Constitution of the aristocratic Republic which he cherished but to which the mass of the people were indifferent. The proletariat had lost confidence in Cicero because in his devotion to political liberty he had identified himself with those whom the poor regarded as their oppressors and exploiters. Political liberty under the Constitution had given the talented boy from the country the opportunity to develop his natural abilities in a way to achieve distinction. He did not perceive that this political liberty was doing nothing for the submerged dwellers in the capital, who could not expect to rise to eminence or even to the level of decent living. The day had passed in Rome when any boy, though born in a log cabin, could hope to be president.

The financial stringency of the year 63 was doubtless relieved to an extent for the big borrowers by the gold acquired by Pompey in his eastern campaigns, which ultimately came to Rome. Before embarking his troops, some 32,000 men, the commander had distributed the loot, $300 to each soldier, and much larger sums to the officers — as much, perhaps, as $160,000 to each of the most important. He reserved what he thought proper for himself, and eventually turned over to the state the generous amount of $10,000,000. At least these are the figures collected from the official records by the ancient historians. The accounts were never audited. In addition the annual revenue from tributes he had imposed amounted to $7,000,000. This, however, did not help the mass of the people. The expenditure of the bonus by officers and soldiers may have produced a temporary flurry. It no more brought general prosperity than did the expenditure of the soldier bonus paid to United States veterans in the great depression. The debtors whose protest was led by Catiline were no better off than they were before. The poor were not vocal. They left no record of their misery except that which can be read in the slums of Rome. But Florus, a historian of the early part of the second century of our era, remarks that the extravagance of the rich produced domestic strife. "People demanded land and food because of the want that luxury produced."

To this situation, which gave to men like Clodius their opportunity and proved a fundamental factor in destroying the Republic, Cicero was blind. He knew that the Roman proletariat was violent and corrupt. He had no suspicion of the economic causes that had produced the proletariat.

If Plutarch is right the great statesman of Greece had undertaken to deal with a similar problem some four centuries earlier with an extensive public-works program. Pericles believed there was unfair discrimination in the distribution of state funds to soldiers but not to working men. "Therefore," he said, "I carried out in the interest of the people great building schemes, work which should keep various industries busy a long time. In this way the stay-at-home population as well as the fighters have their share in the public funds. Thus the public service spreads and distributes prosperity among all ages and conditions of men." Thus was the New Deal Public Works Administration anticipated in ancient Athens. Possibly Gaius Gracchus had something of the same sort in mind in his road-building program, although most of the work must have gone to slaves. In the latter part of the first century of our era the Emperor Vespasian, with a background of poverty and sympathy with the common man, frankly used public works to provide employment. "To a mechanical engineer," Suetonius tells us, "who promised to transport some heavy columns to the Capitoline at small expense [presumably by mechanical means] the Emperor gave no small reward for his invention but refused to make use of it, saying: 'You must let me feed my poor commons.'" He preferred hand labour to machines in order to spread the work.

Cicero seems to have been familiar with this public-works program in Athens, but its economic significance escaped him. In his treatise *On Moral Duties* he discusses the duty of generosity "to the worthy poor." Public games are an allied subject, and while he deplores their extravagance he recognizes that they have become such an accepted part of public life that they must be continued. "The expenditure of money," he adds, "is better justified when it is made for walls, docks, harbours, aqueducts and all those works which are of service to the community" — in other words, a public-works program. But without developing the theme he passes on to deprecate large expenditures for luxury buildings like theatres and colonnades and quotes with approval a Greek writer who criticized Pericles " for throwing away so much money on the magnificent, far-famed Propylæa," the great portal at the western end of the Acropolis.

Returning to the general subject of charity, Cicero admits there are individual cases of men who are overwhelmed with misfortune through no fault of their own and who deserve help. He thinks it incumbent on a man of high station to relieve cases of distress because such action evokes gratitude and binds people to him. The pleasant reaction of the recipients may prove of service to the state in allaying class bitterness. And looking back to the good old days of the Republic he seems to find a partial explanation for them in the fact that " such beneficence used to be the common practice of our order." England long felt that the Lord of the Manor and his Lady Bountiful by their private charities were doing all that could be expected for the poor, and we can hardly blame Cicero for failure to see that masses of people may be victims of general economic conditions for which they are not responsible and which require correcting. Such blindness was common in the nineteenth century. It has not entirely disappeared in the twentieth.

Clodius was as ignorant of economics as Cicero. At least with Cæsar's prompting he knew how to solidify his popular support. In January 58, within a month after his accession to office, he proposed four important bills on one day. Since the tribuneship of Gaius Gracchus, except for a brief period, wheat had been sold at a moderate price to all who applied. Clodius now proposed that it should be distributed free, thus making it an outright dole. Grinding poverty may have justified this measure. It had the political effect of binding the mass of the people to him. The second bill was to end the abuse that had been glaringly practised by Bibulus the preceding year by which a magistrate was permitted to block business by anouncing that he was "watching the sky" for omens. His third bill was to legalize the popular workers' clubs that had been suppressed by the oligarchy six years previously because they could so easily be turned into political organizations — the equivalent of the ward clubs of American cities. The fourth was to remove from the censors their arbitrary power to expel members from the Senate without trial. This power had made it possible for the governing clique to oust senators with liberal leanings. The last three measures were all directed toward weakening the authority of the Senate and were naturally popular with the common people. The second measure, against obstructive omens, soon became a dead letter, or else was full of loopholes. The next year the Senate was forced to adopt a resolution to prevent Clodius from having the omens used in his quarrel with Cicero.

Having thus strengthened his position at the base, Clodius turned to the completion of the program of the Committee of Three. Cicero and Cato, recognized by Cæsar as the two most important leaders of the opposition, were to be removed from Rome. First he dealt with Cicero, then with Cato, who was politely kicked upstairs with the offer of a foreign mission which he could not refuse. The ironical courtesy of this move suggests that it was inspired by Cæsar. Cicero had rejected all of Cæsar's similarly urbane suggestions. A brusquer treatment was required. Clodius proposed a bill under which anyone who had put to death a Roman citizen without due process of law or anyone who thereafter might do so should be "interdicted from fire and water." This was the legal form for the death penalty. As we have seen, exile took the place of capital punishment. The measure brought in by Clodius was another blow at the Senate, which had advised the summary execution of the five adherents of Catiline who had remained in Rome. Primarily it was directed against Cicero, although it did not mention him by name.

In spite of all the warnings the vain and sensitive oratorical statesman was paralysed by the attack. He discarded his senatorial dress and rushed about in a panic, buttonholing everyone he knew and begging for help. Unfortunately for him his sharp tongue and his egotism had alienated many who otherwise might have come to his aid. They were outwardly sympathetic, but inwardly pleased. The people were hostile for reasons already mentioned. The business crowd to which he belonged by birth and training rallied to him — rather timidly, it seemed to him later — and some of his younger admirers accompanied him through the streets as evidence of their support. Plutarch says there were twenty thousand — a rather uncritical estimate. Twenty thousand men would have made something of a traffic jam in the streets of Rome. Two hundred would have been a large number. Clodius boasted that the Three were behind him. At first Cicero simply could not believe him. Then he was horrified to find them silent. Clodius called a meeting outside the walls of the city, where Cæsar was waiting with his troops to see the matter disposed of before departing for Gaul. In response to an invitation to express his views the proconsul replied ambiguously that he had opposed the executions of the 5th of December but that also he opposed ex-post-facto measures. His real feelings regarding Cicero were well known. Crassus disliked Cicero and of course would do nothing.

The panic-stricken man now turned to his old friend Pompey, who so often had promised him protection against Clodius. But the slippery Pompey gave a perfect exhibition of what is known in modern politics as the runaround. He assured the unhappy Cicero of his devotion, but really he was a private citizen and could do nothing. Let his friend apply to the consuls. Cicero hopefully did so. One of them was short with him. The other gave him some realistic advice. His colleague, he said, was in financial difficulties, quite out at the elbows. Only the governorship of a rich province after his term had expired would save him, and as they both would have to depend on Clodius for provinces, they couldn't afford to offend him. "It's no use your applying to the consuls," he concluded. "Every fellow must look out for himself." Again Cicero turned to Pompey. On one occasion his good friend told him frankly he could not oppose the will of Cæsar. On another, when Cicero called on him, he discreetly slipped out of the back door to avoid an interview. The Senate passed a resolution of sympathy but did nothing.

Later, writing to Atticus from exile, Cicero played with the legalistic idea that the law did not touch him — presumably on his old assumption that the men he had executed had forfeited their citizenship and so had lost their right to a trial. He ought, he says, to have ignored the measure. This of course was absurd. The men who had determined on his exile were in no mood to listen to legalistic arguments. After he was recalled to Rome he advanced the theory that he had left because of high public motives; he would not involve his country in civil war. He was rationalizing his conduct. It is perfectly evident from his letters that he fled because he was thoroughly frightened, as he had ample reason to be. Writing to his brother from Salonika he had given a correct diagnosis of his untenable position — "the defection of Pompey, the hostility of the consuls and judges, the timidity of the business men, the armed bands of Clodius." In spite of his assertions about the general indignation and the readiness of all Italy to rush to his aid, he knew in his heart that his support was insubstantial and that he had no alternative to leaving the capital. On the day of his departure Clodius put through another bill mentioning him by name, outlawing him to four hundred miles from Italy, and providing that his property be confiscated and his fine house on the Palatine be destroyed. Anyone receiving him within these limits was likewise to be outlawed. That such a measure directed against an individual was unconstitutional was of no help to the victim.

In compliance with the decree the broken-hearted man proceeded to Brindisi, crossed to Durazzo, and then accepted the invitation of a loyal friend, finance officer for Macedonia, to make his temporary home in Salonika, the Biblical Thessalonica, where he arrived on May 23. His letters from exile make dismal reading. He completely lost his nerve. No one, he writes, has ever suffered such a misfortune. He is heartily sick of life. He is crushed by the weight of his sorrows and with difficulty prolongs his miserable existence. "Your pleas," he writes to Atticus, "have prevented me from committing suicide. But what is there to live for? Don't blame me for complaining. My afflictions surpass any you ever heard of before." Reverting to the theory that he might safely have stayed and faced things out at home, he tries to exonerate himself from the responsibility for his flight. The fault, he says, was with those who advised him to leave Rome when he might have stayed. Although Atticus had provided him with $12,500 for the expenses of his exile, he reproaches his friend for not giving him better counsel. "You looked on in silence," he protests. "My folly lay in thinking your affection for me was as great as I wished it to be." It is vastly to the credit of Atticus that he made allowances for Cicero's overwrought nerves. The flood of unjust reproaches must have been hard to take philosophically, but Atticus did not permit them to cloud his affection. Instead he worked hard in Rome in conjunction with Terentia to obtain the recall of his friend.

While Cæsar had been the brains and driving force of the Committee of Three, his ability was still not widely appreciated in Rome. The distinguished general, Pompey, was regarded as the dominant figure, and the legend lingered until his death. What happened when Cæsar left to take over his provincial commands revealed how essential his presence had been. As he doubtless had foreseen when he put up the energetic Clodius as tribune to represent his interests, the regime rested on a shaky base once its main objectives had been realized. The two members of the Committee who remained in Rome still had the common purpose of preventing the annulment or repeal of Cæsar's legislation. This proved not enough to hold them together. When Cæsar's hand was removed the coalition began to go to pieces. Clodius had begun his term with an intelligent legislative program. Apparently it had been developed by Cæsar, for with the proconsul's departure Clodius took up his natural role of gangster. Without his prompter he was incapable of planning further important legislation. All he could think of by himself was to carry out thoroughly the decree for the banishment of Cicero. He had the mansion on the Palatine plundered and burned and began the erection of a Temple of Liberty on the site so it never could be recovered by the owner. Cicero's two favourite villas, at Tusculum and Formiæ, likewise were destroyed by his gangs.

With Cicero and Cato out of the way the suppressed antagonism between Pompey and Crassus broke out. Crassus had been the financial backer of Clodius at the time of his trial. The ward clubs he organized after he became tribune, if they were like ward clubs in America, needed to be financed and the millionaire probably put up the money. When friction developed between the two bosses, Clodius used his gangs to drive Pompey off the streets. In this performance he was the agent of Crassus, not of Cæsar.

The friction may have had its immediate origin in the manœuvre by which Clodius promoted the escape of an important prisoner of war who had been held by Pompey. Dio says the prisoner bribed the tribune. This may have been true. But Crassus hovers a shadowy figure in the background and it is a reasonable conjecture that he secretly used Clodius to harass his rival. Indications of this crop up later when Clodius frankly appears as the partisan of Crassus against Pompey and when Pompey reports to Cicero that money is being supplied to Clodius, apparently from the millionaire. It is significant too that later, after Cæsar had brought about a second reconciliation of Pompey and Crassus and neither rich man had anything to gain from financing the gangs, Clodius temporarily disappears from public view. He could not operate without funds to pay his followers. Still later, after Crassus had left Rome with a command in the East, Pompey, according to Cicero, became reconciled to Clodius, whose gangs he now needed in the exigencies of politics. The story of Clodius is an instructive record of political deterioration. He was an aggressive popular leader so long as he was under a great man's guidance. Once that guidance was removed, he slumped into a mere political racketeer.

The feud between Pompey and Crassus that had come into the open through the attacks of Clodius proved to the advantage of Cicero and finally resulted in his recall from exile. In order to strengthen himself against Clodius and his silent partner Crassus, Pompey needed the help of Cicero. Only two months after the exile's departure the general had a resolution for his recall introduced into the Senate. A hostile tribune interposed his veto. Before proceeding further Pompey thought it advisable to get the consent of Cæsar, and an emissary was sent to him. Apparently the proconsul thought Cicero had not yet had a sufficient lesson. Later he consented to his recall, but with the proviso that the exile refrain from active hostility to the Three if he should be allowed to return. The efforts of Pompey dragged along, with Cicero eating his heart out from anxiety and Clodius, as the agent of Crassus, obstructing at every turn and resorting to rioting when necessary to block the proceedings. In midsummer of the next year, 57, the Senate adopted a resolution inviting citizens throughout Italy to come to Rome to vote in the Assembly for Cicero's recall. Pompey campaigned for the proposal in the Forum and in the Italian towns.

Perhaps even then the effort would have failed had not another gangster named Milo already been in the field against Clodius. Cicero says Milo had bought a band of gladiators for his laudable enterprise. Gladiators were expensive and we may conjecture that Milo was financed by Pompey, as Clodius probably was financed by Crassus. On the day on which the Assembly was to vote, the out-of-town supporters of Cicero poured into the Campus Martius to cast their ballots. Clodius made no demonstration, either because Milo had the larger gang, as an ancient historian implies, or because Crassus had called him off. Thereafter Milo was one of Cicero's heroes, on the modern political principle that no matter if the fellow on our side is a scoundrel, at least he is "our scoundrel."

The recall measure was passed on August 4. The eager Cicero had been awaiting the news at Durazzo and, unable to contain himself longer, he crossed the Adriatic and arrived at Brindisi on August 5, where three days later he learned from Quintus that the bill had become a law. Once more Cicero was in the clouds. In a letter to Atticus he describes his return to Rome as a triumphal procession. At every town he was met by delegations congratulating him. At Rome, according to his account, his reception was almost a riot. In Cicero's view this was quite natural on public as well as private grounds. "The preservation of the country," he wrote later, "depended upon my recall from exile."

But once again, as after the glorious 5th of December, he found there were those who surprisingly did not take his view of his importance to the state. "Already," he tells Atticus, "those who defended me while I was in exile are beginning to feel annoyance at my presence, though they disguise it, and to envy me without even taking the trouble to disguise that." It was more than two months before the college of pontiffs was ready to decide that the act by which Clodius had consecrated the site of Cicero's Palatine mansion was illegal. The Senate then passed a resolution restoring to Cicero his property and ordering compensation for its destruction. Appraisers valued the house at $100,000, the Tusculan villa at $25,000 and the villa at Formiæ at $12,500. "Very stingy," Cicero writes his friend regarding the appraisal of the villas. Even the common people, he says, expostulated. The reason for the stinginess? Why the very same men who had clipped his wings were unwilling that they should grow again to their old size. Only gradually and painfully did he come to realize that those whose property and lives he believed he had saved from a dreadful conspiracy had little use for him. To the old families he was still the bumptious parvenu. To others who might have been well disposed his vanity and boasting must have made him a difficult person to live with. Reading the speeches he made after his return we can imagine men in the audiences groaning: "My god, why did we bring him home to have him bore us to death all over again about the 5th of December?"

In spite of some lack of warmth which he detected in various quarters after he reached Rome, Cicero could write to Atticus that he had resumed at once the position which he had feared it might take some time to recover — brilliant standing at the bar, influence in the Senate, and a popularity with all loyal men even greater than he had hoped for. "I am on the threshold," he added, "of a second life." An opportunity was offered him at once to speak on behalf of Pompey, whose efforts to secure his recall had atoned to Cicero for acquiescence in his banishment.

On the day of the exile's return the price of wheat suddenly advanced. Consumption had increased under the free distribution that had been provided the previous year by Clodius. The imports had not yet been regularized and Cicero thought speculators were taking advantage of the situation to corner the supply. With his keen political instincts Clodius did not overlook the chance to arouse the people against his hated antagonist. He passed the word among his ward clubs that Cicero was responsible for the scarcity, and crowds flocked about the Senate chamber shouting against the returned exile, but in vain.

Pompey had proved a good organizer in his eastern campaigns and he seemed the natural man to take charge. Cicero moved a resolution in the Senate to give Pompey control of the grain supply throughout the Roman world for five years. Apparently Pompey had hoped for a military and naval command to back up his authority and put him more nearly on an equal footing with Cæsar, who had been developing a finely disciplined army in his campaigns in Gaul. Another bill granting him armed forces was proposed by a tribune. Pompey protested he did not wish this — when he saw it could not be carried — but, according to Cicero, "his friends think he wants it." In any event, in supporting the grain bill Cicero was repaying his debt to the man who had led the fight for his restoration and he was returning to his old plan of strengthening the Senate and allying it with Pompey, whom he hoped to be able to detach from his coalition with Cæsar. While the Senate adopted the resolution it did so grudgingly. With strange blindness it was still unwilling to forgive Pompey's past and to come to an understanding with him.

Meanwhile Clodius continued his riotous disturbances whenever the opportunity offered to embarrass Pompey, who finally confided to Cicero that plots were being formed against his life. A hostile tribune, he said, was being supported by Crassus, and money was being supplied to Clodius by Crassus and other rich men — presumably anxious to finish breaking up the Committee of Three.

While Cicero had tried to do what he could for Pompey he had been disappointed by his friend's lack of energy. "He is not the man he was," he wrote to Quintus. At least the obvious disintegration of the Committee offered a chance to restore the Senate to the dignity which Cicero coveted for it, and perhaps then he could make a combination with Pompey to give the government the guidance it so badly needed. Himself, he was encouraged by his success at the bar. "My position," he told his brother, "is what you used to assure me that it would be, although I could hardly believe it — one of dignity and honour." He had just "made mincemeat" of one of his antagonists, "with the applause of gods and men. . . . In the courts I am as strong as ever. Never was my house more crowded."

All this pumped up his courage to a point where he believed he could give the *coup de grâce* to the weakened Committee by striking out boldly at its absent head. He determined, as he wrote to one of his friends, to "assault the citadel of Cæsar's policy." On April 5, 56, he moved in the Senate that the validity of one of Cæsar's land bills be considered at a full meeting of the House on May 15. It was an audacious proposal. Pompey, as well as Cæsar, was concerned in upholding the legislation of Cæsar's consulship by which farms were distributed to the veterans of the eastern wars.

Just how Cicero figured that Pompey would acquiesce in this attack we do not know. Perhaps he thought the great man's position had become so unhappy that he would welcome the opportunity to prove to the Tories of the Senate that they no longer need distrust him. At any rate Pompey gave no sign of displeasure — or Cicero thought he gave no sign; he was often obtuse at reading what people really thought. Two days later he went in his sedan chair to call on Pompey at his suburban villa after dinner. In a letter to Quintus the next day describing the visit he mentions only Pompey's cordiality. His host told him he was about to sail for Sardinia shortly to look after the grain supply. He would embark, he said, at Leghorn or Pisa. Apparently it did not occur to Cicero that these towns were far to the north of Rome, while Sardinia was to the south. The coincidence also escaped him that both towns were just outside of Cæsar's province of northern Italy. A roundabout way, certainly, for Pompey to take to reach Sardinia. What was in the wind soon became evident. Crassus had been visiting Cæsar at his winter quarters in Ravenna and had reported how badly things were going in Rome. The Senate was getting out of hand. Cicero was threatening the land legislation. One of the candidates for consul the next year was running on a platform pledging the recall of Cæsar from his provinces. As usual the proconsul acted with lightning speed. With Crassus he crossed the Apennines to the little town of Lucca (in Roman times, Luca), a few miles northeast of Pisa, where Pompey joined them shortly after his pleasant talk with Cicero. Lesser politicians including more than two hundred senators flocked in to make terms with the Big Boys and pledge support.

There was a brief conference of the Three about April 15. Then Cæsar hurried back to Gaul. His dominating personality once more had brought Pompey and Crassus together and the Committee of Three emerged again as the rulers of Rome. No public announcement was made of the terms of the deal. Events gradually disclosed them. Cæsar needed additional time to complete his work in Gaul. In exchange for a five-year extension of his proconsular command he allotted to his two associates prizes which without his help they would have sought in vain. They were awarded the consulships for the next year. After their term each was to have a five-year proconsular command, Crassus in Syria, Pompey in the two Spanish provinces.

The news was broken gently to Cicero. From Sardinia came a message politely suggesting that he do nothing about the land law for the present. Pompey talked more bluntly to Quintus Cicero, whom he met on the island. Marcus reports the conversation in a letter to a friend. "You are the very man I want to see," said Pompey. "Unless you speak very strongly to your brother Marcus you will have to pay up what you guaranteed on his behalf." This was a whimsical remark, assuming that Quintus had gone bail for his brother's good conduct if he should be allowed to return from exile. There was no mistaking its meaning and Cicero was compelled, as he tells his friend, to reconsider his position and to drop the attack on the land law.

At last Cicero was thoroughly whipped. He recognized that he was helpless and that he could get no effective support from the decadent Senate. The old American political maxim: "If you can't beat 'em, jine 'em," was brought grimly home to him. He found he was expected not only to cease his opposition to the Three, but to jump through the hoop at their command and publicly defend men he previously had attacked. He tried to make the best of the situation although he was humiliated by being compelled to deliver some of the speeches required of him.

He was not happy. "What is more degraded," he wrote to Atticus, "than the life we are living — I especially? If I speak as I ought I am regarded as a madman; if as I must, as a slave; if I hold my peace I am accounted as crushed and baffled. Well, then I must submit to be a servant — I who refused to be one of the masters" — the last reference being to his original refusal to join the Committee of Three. To another of his friends, absent from Rome as governor of Cilicia, he makes a more guarded and laboured defence of his course. The Senate, he says, has been manœuvred into an untenable position and has provided its opponents with good arguments. "I tell my story briefly," he adds, "for I take no pleasure in the present state of things."

In a letter to Atticus he refers to something he had written and had sent perhaps to Pompey or Cæsar as his "recantation," for it had acknowledged his submission to the Three. But he blames the senatorial crowd for deserting him. His resentment against the nobles for their contemptuous treatment after his return from exile flares out. Since these fellows, he says, who have no power have shown their indifference to him, he will take care to obtain the affection of those who have power. "You will say," he continues, "'I could have wished you had done so before.' I know you did wish it and that I have made a real ass of myself." At last Cicero was getting practical.

Meanwhile political affairs in Rome moved rather haltingly according to the agreement at Lucca. Pompey and Crassus secured the consulships for the year 55 with some help from Cæsar's veterans, who were sent to Rome for the election. The next year Crassus set out for his eastern province. Pompey thought it advisable to remain on the ground to look after things and governed his Spanish provinces by deputies. Two events now occurred that proved heavy blows to Cæsar's plans. The death of Pompey's wife Julia, Cæsar's daughter, in 54, severed a strong personal tie between the two men, and the next year Crassus was defeated and killed in a war he had undertaken against the Parthians. With the Three thus reduced to a Committee of Two, Pompey was attracted to the idea of becoming the dominant figure in Rome by allying himself with the Senate. This plan was threatened by the emergence of his former gang leader Milo as a candidate for the consulship with the support of the senatorial machine. If Milo should win, the senators might not need Pompey. In order to stall off the election Pompey was forced to resort to his old enemy Clodius, who now revived his gang. Early in the year 52 the rival gangsters happened to meet on the Appian Way outside of Rome and Clodius was killed. Something had to be done to end the constant disorders. Even Cato remarked that any government was better than anarchy. The Senate reluctantly passed a decree naming Pompey as sole consul, with power to take a colleague when he chose. The consul at once had Milo brought to trial for murder. Cicero appeared as counsel for his old friend. The armed guards stationed in the Forum to preserve order dismayed Cicero. Always nervous on beginning his speeches, on this occasion he was completely rattled. He trembled, and the chronicler says the words died on his lips and he had to sit down. Milo was convicted and withdrew into exile at Marseille. Later Cicero wrote out and published the speech he should have delivered. A copy was sent to Milo, who is reported to have remarked: "It is just as well that Cicero did not succeed in delivering this speech or I never should have known the taste of these excellent mullets" — perhaps the forerunners of the bouillabaisse for which Marseille is now celebrated.

With a virtual dictatorship thus established once more in Rome, it was evident that constitutional government was approaching the end. Cicero and Cato, its sincere defenders, were reduced to the role of impotent spectators on the sidelines.

In the next century a young poet, Lucan, wrote that the whole imperial domain of Rome was not enough for two such men as Cæsar and Pompey. " Rivalry spurred them on. Pompey feared that fresher exploits might dim his past triumphs, while his opponent was urged on by fortune that brooked no second place. Cæsar could no longer endure a superior nor Pompey an equal."

This judgment was more smart than just. Certainly at this time Cæsar would have been content with equality, perhaps counting on his superior ability for the future. Pompey instinctively felt that equality eventually would mean subordination with unhappy consequences for the Conservative cause, so his manœuvres were directed toward inclining the balance in his favour. In these manœuvres he had the active sympathy of the conservative senatorial crowd, which shared his distrust of the radicalism of Cæsar.

CHAPTER XIX

EXPONENT OF BLITZKRIEG

WHILE ROME was engrossed in the struggle of the oligarchy to maintain its privileged position, while rival politicians were striving for personal supremacy with the help of paid mobs, we may turn from the sordid intrigues of the capital to events of immense significance that were taking place in western Europe. Under the commanding genius of Julius Cæsar the gifted but divided French people were united, organized, and brought into the orbit of the Mediterranean civilization of Rome. At the same time the frontier of the Rhine was established to block German invasion.

Of these events Cicero was an interested but anxious spectator. As a patriotic Roman he could not help thrilling at the brilliant military successes of Roman arms. But he was torn by the apprehension that the commander who was winning these splendid victories was becoming so powerful as to threaten the ancient freedom of the Republic. When it was proposed to extend Cæsar's five-year command in Gaul for another five years, Cicero privately advised Pompey against it. He probably did not know that his friend already was committed to the extension under the Lucca agreement. His position was quite understandable. He had only a hazy knowledge of the situation beyond the Alps. The country, he supposed, already had been brought under the eagles. Why should it be necessary to prolong the proconsul's command? He did not comprehend the job that still had to be done of repelling German invasions and subduing rebellious elements. Pompey, however, was able to overcome his reluctance and to persuade him to support the extension. In the great speech *On the Consular Provinces* delivered to the Senate soon after the conference at Lucca, Cicero concealed his misgivings. He spoke with pride of the ending of the Gallic menace. He did not know it was really the German menace against which the far-sighted Cæsar was deliberately building a barrier. " Nature," he said, " piled the Alps to be a rampart to Italy. . . . Now let them sink into the earth, for beyond those mountain peaks as far as the extremest verge of ocean there is nothing left for Italy to fear."

The problems with which Cæsar had to deal were so remote that Cicero did not understand their importance. The danger to the Roman Constitution was much more vivid in his mind. To Atticus he apologized for making the speech because it involved an abandonment of principles for which he had always stood. But he felt helpless before the march of events. " Peace," he wrote the next year, " is the best we can hope for now, and this the present rulers seem likely to secure us if men will submit patiently to their domination." He doubted " whether this generation will see any change in the situation."

To Cicero the problem presented by Cæsar involved irreconcilable contradictions. By giving him the power to protect it abroad, the Republic was taking the risk that this power might be used against it at home. Yet the risk had to be taken.

It is necessary to glance briefly at the Gallic campaigns because of their eventual impact on Cicero's career. They developed a man whom he had once regarded as his chief political opponent from a shrewd local Roman politician into a world statesman and one of the great captains of history. In their consequences they completely frustrated Cicero's hope of maintaining the aristocratic Republic. Incidentally they were crowded with aspects of importance to

JULIUS CÆSAR

Hard incisive intelligence and supreme self-confidence characterize the face of the greatest of the Romans. The artistic feeling and charm of the man escaped the sculptor. (Drawn by Richard F. Hunter from the statue in the Palazzo dei Conservatori, Rome)

The ROMAN WORLD of *Cicero and Caesar*

At Caesar's Death in 44

Domain of Rome and Its Protectorates in White
Non-Roman and Barbarian Territory Shaded
(Eastern boundaries of Roman domain in Asia Minor are uncertain, as are the boundaries of Armenia and Parthia.)

All Dates are B.C.

the modern world. In his campaigns Cæsar discovered that he had to deal with nationalistic traits of the French and Germans that have persisted into the twentieth century. In his military operations he developed in spectacular fashion the principles of the modern Blitzkrieg.

Unhappily the notes on his campaigns written by Cæsar are usually studied by American beginners in Latin as exercises in indirect discourse and the subjunctive mood. Read rapidly in English translation, with some knowledge of the background, they constitute an impressive political and military history. They were published near the end of Cæsar's service in Gaul and perhaps were an expansion of his official reports to the Senate. Cicero, a competent critic, wrote of the *Commentaries:* " They are like nude figures, straight and beautiful; stripped of all ornaments of style as if they had laid aside a garment. His aim was to furnish others with the material for writing history. Perhaps he has succeeded in gratifying the inept who may wish to apply their curling-irons to his material. But men of sound judgment he has deterred from writing, since in history there is nothing more pleasing than brevity, clear and correct." Written in the third person, the story is so objective and dispassionate that the reader has to stop from time to time to remind himself of the organizing ability, energy, audacity, and clarity of vision that must have been required to produce the results so concisely and calmly recorded.

When Cæsar in organizing the Committee of Three bargained for the governorship of the two provinces of northern Italy and the Illyrian coast at the end of his consulship, there is no reason to suppose that he had anything further in mind than to strengthen his position in Rome by the command of the troops that went with these provinces. Later, rumbles of trouble in Gaul induced him to obtain the governorship of the Roman province of southeastern Gaul beyond the Alps, which had been left vacant by the death of the governor. At one time the Romans had called this province *Gallia Bracata,* " Trousered Gaul," because of the predilection of its men for wearing trousers instead of togas. Included with the Gallic province went a commission to act beyond its boundaries within the Roman sphere of influence. This was necessary because reports from Roman agents indicated that there was unrest in Switzerland, adjoining Provence on the north. There had been a minor German invasion shortly before and the Senate had thought it well to come to terms with the invaders so as to assure their neutrality in case of trouble with the Swiss. Even in the case of the third province Cæsar may have had chiefly in view the prevention of its assignment to a rival who might prove embarrassing to him.

It would be a mistake to think of Gaul at this time as a country of savages. Roman civilization was already penetrating the land. Gallic society was on an aristocratic basis like that of Rome. The more advanced states had developed constitutional republican governments with elective magistrates, senates, and codes of civil law. They had their own coined money and a thriving trade. Nationalistic feeling, however, was weak and was tempered by a growing pro-Roman sentiment. In short, in both culture and politics a good share of Gaul was in process of Romanization.

At the expiration of his consulship, while Cæsar was waiting outside of Rome for the disposal of his two chief potential opponents, Cicero and Cato, disquieting reports came of the Swiss situation. A warlike people, Cæsar writes, the Swiss resented the fact that in proportion to the size of their population and their reputation for bravery, " they had too small a territory." In other words, they were actuated by the modern German desire for *Lebensraum*. Accordingly they were planning a mass migration to western Gaul. Their route would take them through Provence, and they would become uneasy and undesirable neighbours to the Roman province. This news sent Cæsar hurrying to Geneva. After he had defeated the Swiss and herded them back into their own country came an event that probably for the first time gave the proconsul a real insight into the fundamental problem that confronted him. The heads of the Gallic states asked for a conference. In an executive session they informed him of the great German threat. There had been two rival groups of Gallic states. In their conflict one group had employed mercenary troops from Germany. To their dismay other Germans had followed the troops across the Rhine until one hundred and twenty thousand had come, attracted by the civilization and resources they had found in the pleasant land of France. Ariovistus, the German Führer, had driven out the Gallic inhabitants from the fertile plain of Alsace to make room for the Germans and was planning further encroachments. The significance and possibilities of this German invasion did not escape Cæsar. In the year of his birth the Germans had swept down on Provence on their way to Italy and had been turned back by Marius in the great battle of Aix-en-Provence. The next year another invading army had poured through the Brenner and was within a few days' march of Rome when it was stopped by Marius in another great battle in the valley of the Po. With this background the thoughts that went through Cæsar's mind at the conference are concisely set forth in the first book of his *Commentaries.* "If the Germans," he wrote, "should gradually become accustomed to crossing the Rhine and if a great body of them should come into Gaul, he saw a potential danger to the Roman people. He felt that wild and savage men would not be likely to restrain themselves. After they had seized all of Gaul they would pass into Provence and thence march into Italy as their predecessors had done, and he was convinced that he must face these difficulties as soon as possible." Evidently for the protection primarily of Rome and only secondarily of Gaul the Rhine boundary must be maintained. The Germans, not the Gauls, were the real menace.

Accordingly Cæsar invited Ariovistus to a conference. The Führer sent back an arrogant refusal in which he inquired what business Cæsar had in a country which the Germans had won by their swords. Thereupon Cæsar sent a brusquer message setting forth his terms. No more Germans should cross the Rhine, Gallic hostages must be returned, there must be no further oppression of the people in the conquered territory. Ariovistus replied that as a conqueror he had the right to treat his subjects as he pleased and the Romans had no business to interfere. If Cæsar should start something he would be taught a lesson by the invincible soldiers of Germany.

All this sounds extremely modern and in character. It is modern too that many Roman politicians failed to recognize the problem and objected strongly to Cæsar's anti-German policy. Indeed, at a conference to which Ariovistus finally consented the Führer had assured the proconsul that messengers had come from Rome informing him that numerous Roman nobles would be delighted to hear of Cæsar's death. Conservative senators believed he was needlessly aggressive and was inviting trouble by his attacks on the Germans. After his campaigns were well under way the Senate sent an investigating committee to Gaul to inquire into his conduct. On one occasion Cæsar had retaliated for a treacherous German attack with terrible reprisals. His ruthlessness stirred the conscience as well as the political animosity of some of his domestic opponents to a point where Cato actually proposed that the governor be handed over to the Germans for punishment.

It was not an easy situation for Cæsar. He has given us keen and illuminating observations on the traits of the Germans and the Gauls. The Germans, he reported, were a vigorous and warlike people, inured to hardship. "It is the greatest glory of the German states to have the territory surrounding their borders unoccupied, for they consider it a mark of courage to have expelled their neighbours and to have struck such terror into them that they dare not return to their territories. . . . They consider it not wrong to steal beyond their own boundaries but rather an exercise that preserves their youths from idleness."

As for the Gauls, there had been a time when they were

superior to the Germans in arms. But they had been softened by " refinements and comforts." Their decisions were " sudden and hasty." Though their temper was " impetuous and ready to undertake war," their spirit was " weak and not resolute in enduring misfortunes." On one occasion when the Germans had started an invasion Cæsar felt it necessary to take charge in person, " fearing the fickle disposition of the Gauls, who are irresponsible in their decisions and addicted to change; so nothing could be entrusted to them." The difficulty of maintaining unity among them impressed him. " The Gauls are so addicted to faction," he wrote, " that they have divisions not only among their several provinces, cantons, and districts, but even in every family."

Under these circumstances Cæsar's work was laid out for him. His enemies at Rome, and they were many and bitter, saw in him only a ruthless man of boundless ambition obsessed with the desire to build himself into a position from which he could dominate the government. This diagnosis of motives may have been partly correct, but only partly so. Cæsar was one of those men of genius who are not satisfied with using power for mere personal aggrandizement. His personality was so sweepingly inclusive that it identified itself with the broader interests of humanity. In serving these interests he was satisfying his deepest personal ambitions. He had gone into Gaul with the limited objectives of protecting his position at home and of defending Provence from the Swiss threat. He had discovered that in the long view the defence of the province and of Italy itself required the unification of Gaul behind the Rhine boundary. Here was a task that appealed to all his capacities and he methodically set himself to accomplish it during the nine years of his governorship.

Year by year he spread the Roman influence, by force of arms where necessary, by shrewd diplomacy where diplomacy would serve. He cultivated the existing pro-Roman parties in the various states, suppressed revolts, drove back invading Germans. Twice he invaded Britain, the first time for reconnaissance, the second for conquest. While this second aim failed, he succeeded in stopping the flow of supplies from Britain to hostile forces in Gaul. In the year 52 his whole work was threatened when the rioting in Rome and the murder of Clodius gave encouragement to the anti-Roman elements in Gaul. It was widely assumed that Cæsar would be detained in Italy by the disturbances in the capital. An able leader of Gallic independence, Vercingetorix, succeeded in fanning smouldering resentment into a flame and stirring a general revolt, which after desperate fighting Cæsar finally suppressed. In the next two years the entire country was pacified. With a large measure of home rule which the proconsul organized, the whole of France, most of Switzerland and the Rhenish provinces, and the Low Countries to the Rhine became a loyal and prosperous part of the Roman domain, prepared to make its immense contribution to the civilization of Europe.

Thereafter there was little trouble in the West. It accepted Roman culture so thoroughly that within a comparatively few years it was possible to withdraw the garrisons, leaving a detachment at Lyon to protect the mint. Only on the border the legions kept the watch on the Rhine and for centuries protected the Empire against German aggression.

Although Cæsar's Gallic campaigns have been intensively studied, I do not know of any civilian writer who has appraised his military qualities so adequately as has Donald Armstrong, Lieutenant Colonel, U.S.A. In service in France and on leave in Italy, Colonel Armstrong went over the ground covered by Cæsar and has interpreted his findings in the light of modern military developments. It is hardly enough to say with Professor F. E. Adcock in *The Cambridge Ancient History* that Cæsar fashioned his troops into an instrument of war that fitted his own personality; that faith in his own genius was his " most striking quality "; that he understood the importance of supply. Or with the German military authority, G. Veith, that Cæsar made no innovations but handled the traditional Roman art of war with a virtuosity and drastic application which marked his genius. Cæsar had had a brief military experience in Spain before he went to Gaul. He was a man of middle age, forty-three, before he began his great campaigns. It is perhaps natural for military authorities to regard him as a distinguished amateur. "Tactically," an instructor in the Command and General Staff School at Fort Leavenworth says in a letter, "Cæsar was not great. He was not a trained soldier, not a professional. He contributed nothing but thoroughness to his campaigns. He was not a great military thinker. He was an indifferent but energetic tactician. But he was a leader of men. Even if he did not contribute much to the art of war, men fought, bled and died for him. And that makes greatness." He goes on with the interesting observation that Cæsar certainly lags behind Alexander, Hannibal, Napoleon, and Moltke; that he cannot be classed with Marshal Saxe, Marlborough, or Eugène, or with the moderns Schlieffen or Ludendorff. "On the other hand," he says, "he had the thoroughness of a McClellan, the leadership of a Lee, and the mobility of a Jackson."

These three factors were essential elements in Cæsar's success. It is the mobility that especially impressed ancient writers: Cicero in writing of "Cæsarian velocity" (*Cæsarina celeritas*) and stressing his "incredible rapidity"; and especially Dio in describing his campaign in the Civil War in North Africa a few years later. Cæsar's winter operations, Dio says, took his enemies by surprise, and the historian adds this keen appraisal of Cæsarian strategy: "He met with no little success from this very circumstance, by attacking his opponents unexpectedly. On all occasions, indeed, he accomplished a great deal by the rapidity and unexpectedness of his movements. If one should attempt to discover what it was that made him so superior in the art of war to his contemporaries, he would find by careful comparison that there was nothing more striking than this very characteristic." This appraisal has been adopted by modern historians, but by none, I think, with the real understanding of Colonel Armstrong.

Rapidity and unexpectedness of movement, with co-ordination, timing, and other related factors, were developed in the modern Blitzkrieg with a mastery which gave them a new significance in the art of war. According to Armstrong, whom I follow here, Cæsar was pre-eminently the ancient exemplar of Blitzkrieg. Its essence always has been an extremely rapid and violent offensive in which surprise plays a major role. This strategy, I have pointed out, characterized Cæsar's political movements. He applied them in war with astonishing results. Any attentive reader of Cæsar's *Commentaries* will observe the number of times in which he speaks of forced marches, marching day and night, and reaching his own forces "when even his own soldiers did not expect him."

Let us consider a few instances. When Cæsar left Rome for Geneva to deal with the Swiss at the outset of his campaigns, he made the record to which I have previously referred, travelling more than seven hundred miles in eight days, driving in a carriage with relays of fresh horses day and night at the unheard-of speed of ninety miles a day. With only the protection of the river Rhone, he was facing ninety thousand Swiss soldiers with his one legion that was stationed in Provence, reinforced by a body of raw recruits. The Roman legion of Cæsar's time numbered usually about five thousand men. It was a self-contained unit like an American division, including scouts, engineers, and field artillery in addition to the infantry. Cavalry were attached to the army, not to individual legions.

Holding the Swiss by negotiations, Cæsar destroyed the bridge across the Rhone while he established a Maginot Line seventeen and a half miles long south of the river to defend the fords. When the Swiss were ready to move they tested the line in several places, found it too strong for them, and so were forced to leave their country by the narrow road between the Jura Mountains and the Rhone. Leaving his second in command, Labienus, in charge, Cæsar hurried back across the Alps to mobilize the rest of his army. He returned at once with five legions, marching them fifteen miles a day through the mountains in the face of desultory resistance — an amazing speed. When he overtook the Swiss three fourths of them had crossed the Saône. They had no idea that he was in the neighbourhood. His surprise attack on the force that had not crossed the river resulted in a rout. His engineers then threw a pontoon bridge over the Saône and in a day the Roman army was on the other side. The Swiss had taken twenty days for the crossing. They were demoralized — "alarmed," he says, "by his sudden approach" — and were overwhelmed.

Three years later when he determined to carry the war into Germany he decided that a pontoon bridge would not answer and set his engineers to construct the substantial wooden bridge with which students wrestle in the fourth book of the *Commentaries*. The work was done in ten days and the speed probably surprised the Germans as much as the French were surprised by the bridges the Germans threw across the Meuse in 1940.

In the year 52 it was midwinter when Cæsar, holding court at Ravenna as governor of northern Italy, heard of the insurrection of Vercingetorix. At once he rushed to Narbonne in Provence, organized the defence of the province, and then set out with a handful of troops to join his forces that were wintering in Gaul. Snows blocked the roads through the Cévennes Mountains and the Gallic leader believed he would not have Cæsar on his hands until spring. In the *Commentaries* Caesar merely says that the insurgents considered themselves defended by the Cévennes as though by a wall. "Yet having cleared away the snow to a depth of six feet and having opened the highways, he reached the country of the insurgents with infinite difficulty to his troops." It was in his campaign against Vercingetorix that with four legions, some twenty thousand men, he marched forty-six miles in twenty-four hours, with only three hours' rest. It would be difficult to match this feat in military history.

Cæsar's objective was the destruction of the Gallic army. " He saw," Colonel Armstrong writes, " that this could be accomplished not only by fighting a decisive battle but also by manœuvre and even by counter offensive from a defensive position. He realized for the first time in warfare the importance of a reserve, and on occasion the use of his reserves meant decisive victory. He constantly sought to obtain surprise by manœuvre . . . and his subtile artifices left the enemy puzzled and beaten."

Of course, as military critics point out, Cæsar was not a trained soldier and he made mistakes that a professional might have avoided. He had a competent secret service by which he was kept informed of enemy plans. Curiously his scouting service was poor. Its failure on three conspicuous occasions subjected him to surprise attacks. He never was at home in handling cavalry. But his flaming intelligence overcame his lack of military training.

Plutarch says Cæsar attributed his success to luck. Certainly like Napoleon and some other great commanders he had faith in his star. But with Cæsar luck was carefully planned audacity. His development of Blitzkrieg seems to have been a real if unrecognized contribution to the art of war. Colonel Armstrong quotes Napoleon as saying that strategy was the art of making use of time and space. Space may be recovered, but lost time, never. Here Cæsar shone.

One principle animated him throughout his campaigns and helps explain the devotion of his soldiers. He held, he says in the *Commentaries,* the lives of his soldiers dearer to him than his personal safety. This principle he elaborates in his later account of the Civil War. " Cæsar," he says, writing as usual in the third person, " hoped that by cutting off his enemy from their food supply he would be able to finish the business without battle and without risk of loss of life and limb to his own men. Why should he lose any of his own men in a successful battle? Why should he allow soldiers to be wounded who had deserved so well of him — especially when it was no less a general's duty to win by strategy than by the sword? "

Still he could be a strict disciplinarian. "Although he was the kindliest of men," Dio writes, "and showed many favours not only to the citizens in general but particularly to his soldiers, he bitterly hated those who were mutinous and punished them with extreme severity."

In connection with Cæsar's care for his soldiers should be mentioned his success in keeping his supply lines open. Vercingetorix had adopted the "scorched earth" policy. On one occasion this led to an incident that throws light on Roman dietary habits. Wheat was the staple food. It has been said that Roman soldiers conquered the world on a diet of porridge. Supplies were temporarily interrupted. The soldiers were forced to satisfy their hunger with meat from cattle driven from remote villages. Cæsar remarks that even under this hardship of having to live on meat, not a word of complaint was heard.

By the standards of his time Cæsar was a humane man. In dealing with his countrymen in the Civil War he showed unexampled magnanimity. But he was perfectly hard and ruthless in his campaigns, especially in punishing Gallic rebels, on the theory that frightfulness would tend to prevent treacherous uprisings against the rule of Rome. In particular his treatment of Vercingetorix has left a stain upon his name. After the rebel chief surrendered, he was sent to a Roman prison for six years, displayed in Cæsar's formal triumph, and then put to death. This was delayed and cold-blooded cruelty. Human nature has its depths of savagery. More than thirteen hundred years later the English treated with greater cruelty the gallant Scottish chieftain Sir William Wallace.

In the years immediately following the conference at Lucca Cicero bowed to the inevitable, although with mental reservations. For Crassus, in spite of a formal reconciliation, he had no use. His real allegiance continued to be to Pompey, who remained for him the outstanding member of the Committee of Three. "So powerfully is my mind attracted to Pompey," he writes to a friend, "so strong may I say is my passion for him, that all that is profitable to him and agreeable to his wishes appears just and right in my eyes." In compliance with Pompey's wishes, however, he had come to terms with Cæsar, who at once turned on him his well-known charm. No one could be more courteous, gracious, and considerate than this hard-boiled commander. Recognizing Cicero's influence, he went out of his way to win the brilliant orator to him. "Never does the slightest word of mine pass in Cæsar's cause," Cicero writes, "to say nothing of acts, without his acknowledging it with such distinguished courtesy that I cannot but feel myself bound to him."

When Clodius wrote to the proconsul a letter smearing Cicero, Cæsar did not answer it. The orator was flattered to be pressed by the governor to send him any friends who desired to find an opening in Gaul. Enriched by the perquisites of his Gallic campaigns, Cæsar lent him money for his building operations. The absent proconsul desired to keep the Roman people reminded of his existence and he constituted Cicero and another friend his agents to erect public buildings and to enlarge the Forum at a cost of three million dollars. The restless Quintus now wished to make a name for himself as a soldier. Cicero had only to send an intimation to Cæsar to receive a cordial reply. The mail had got soaked on the road and the letter was illegible. But a friend had written to the same effect and his letter had not suffered so badly. "I see," Cæsar replied, "that you have written something about Cicero. I could not make it all out but so far as I can decipher the meaning it was something so good that I could wish for it but hardly hope for it." It was characteristic of the gentleman that Cæsar was to make it appear that Cicero was doing him a favour to offer his brother's services, as he was to an extent, for the proconsul was anxious to do everything possible to gain support in

Rome that he might possibly need eventually against his ally Pompey.

Temporarily he was successful. Cicero was an impulsive and responsive fellow. He was impressed by Cæsar's military successes and deeply moved by these evidences of friendship. Quintus became one of the commander's foremost lieutenants. "I have taken Cæsar to my bosom," Marcus wrote to his brother, "and will never let him slip." "I can have no reserve when I deal with Cæsar. He comes next to you and to our children in my affections, and not far behind." These expressions of devotion must not be taken too seriously. When he wrote them he was taking something of a moral holiday. But his deepest devotion was to the Republic. "We have lost, my dear Atticus," he wrote a little later, "not only the blood and substance but the very outward hue and complexion of the state as it used to be. There is no Republic left which can give me any pleasure or on which my eye can rest with any satisfaction. 'And do you take that so easily?' you will say. Well, yes, even that. . . . The place in my heart where resentment used to dwell has grown callous."

There was a certain canniness about Cicero that occasionally broke through. Pompey, he felt, was his main reliance, but on conspicuous occasions Pompey had failed him. He felt the need of an anchor to windward. He reminds Quintus in Gaul of the "object we had in view when you went to join Cæsar. It was no trifling or ordinary gain we sought. . . . We desired to obtain with the friendship of the best and most powerful of men a firm support for our dignity and our very existence in the state." What he had in mind appears in another letter more definitely: "As for Pompey, I cannot depend on him alone, nor is he the man upon whom we can establish our fortunes. In this I agree with you, or rather with my own inclinations. For, as you know, Cæsar has long been the hero of my song. He is seated in my heart and there he will remain."

Cicero could find no pleasure in politics. But there was

a certain relief in the sense of security that he found in the friendship of the Two. "After all," he writes apologetically to a friend, "we should not persist in an opinion when the circumstances have radically changed, but we should move with the times. Persistence in the same view has never been considered a virtue in distinguished men who have steered the ship of state. In sailing in a gale it is folly to stick to your original course if that invites disaster, especially if you can reach port by tacking. So in public affairs we should keep the one object in view that I have so often preached: namely, peace with honour. But it does not follow that we ought always to use the same language, although we ought always to have the same goal."

At least he could turn to the practice of law and to literature. In July 54 he writes to Quintus: "You ask what sort of year is before me. Well, I think that it will be one of complete peace, or at least that I have ample protection. My levée, the Forum, and the expression of feeling in the theatre give daily evidence of this. My friends are free from anxiety, knowing the forces I have at my command in the support of Cæsar and Pompey. All this makes me confident." Again he writes in October: "You must know that not a day passes in which I do not speak for some accused person."

Another incident of this period gave Cicero pleasure. He was named to a vacancy on the important board of augurs. It was a life office of great dignity and was sought by the cultivated agnostics of Rome because of the political power it conferred. Early in the regime of the Committee of Three there was a vacancy on the board toward which Cicero cast longing eyes. He inquired of Atticus, who was likely to get the office from the Three, and added whimsically: "That is the only bait with which they could catch me." At last it was awarded him as a sort of consolation prize.

His practice at the bar gave him leisure to turn to the work which he found most absorbing and through which he was to influence the thought of mankind for centuries. In these years he produced his delightful treatise *On the Character of the Orator* (*De Oratore*); his keen study of government, *On the Commonwealth* (*De Re Publica*); and began his famous treatise *On the Laws* (*De Legibus*), which was not finished until some years later — if, indeed, it ever was finished — and in which he was forced to modify some of his earlier conclusions in the light of events. In letters to Atticus he gives glimpses of the circumstances under which he worked. It was on a holiday at Puteoli that he outlined *On the Character of the Orator*. " Here I am," he writes, " feasting on Faustus Sulla's library." This was the library that the father of Faustus, the dictator Sulla, had brought from Athens. His feasting, he continues, is not on the oysters from the Lucrine Lake, although these are not wanting. " But the truth is that in proportion as my taste for all other studies is spoiled by grief for the commonwealth, I find myself more and more dependent upon literature for support and comfort."

When he came to his works on politics he asked Atticus for the run of his library. There were certain books in it which he desired especially to consult " for the purpose of the work which I have in hand and which I think will give you pleasure."

This comparative leisure and comfortable security were not to last for long. Cæsar was finishing the pacification of Gaul. The second five years of his proconsulship were approaching an end. It was part of the Lucca agreement that then he was to be rewarded with a second consulship, as the ten-year interval required by law between the holding of consulships would have expired. Not only the Tories but Pompey as well had begun to be disturbed over the prospect; the Tories because of their fear of radical legislation, Pompey because he would no longer be supreme in Rome with the conqueror of Gaul as consul. In this situation the Tories came to a realization of their stupidity in failing to come to terms with Pompey, who, as they now recognized, was their natural supporter. To his distress Cicero realized somewhat later that his old dream of an understanding between Pompey and the Senate was about to come true too late, at a time when such an alliance would alienate a man who had grown to such power that he might resort to arms to establish his own supremacy. When at Pompey's urging Cicero had made friends with Cæsar it never had occurred to him that he might be forced to choose between them. "My idea," he wrote to Atticus, "was this: If I were allied with Pompey I should not hereafter be compelled to take any improper steps in politics; nor if I agreed with Cæsar, should I have to fight with Pompey; for their union was so close." Now a rift was developing and his anxiety was revealed in his efforts to raise money to pay off the loan he had obtained from Cæsar, so that he would no longer be under obligations to him.

The rift had been foreshadowed after the death of Pompey's wife Julia, Cæsar's daughter, two years after Lucca. Cæsar suggested that he marry Pompey's daughter and that Pompey marry Cæsar's grand-niece. Pompey refused both proposals. Instead of falling in with Cæsar's plan he allied himself with the Sullan connections by giving his daughter to Faustus Sulla, while he himself married Cornelia, the attractive young widow of Crassus' son. She was a daughter of one of the great nobles, Metellus Scipio. Evidently Pompey was preparing to cut loose from Cæsar and ally himself with the old families.

Throughout the last two years of Cæsar's tenure in Gaul politicians at Rome were busy attempting to block a second consulship without too obviously showing their hand. Briefly, this was the situation: Cæsar's term in Gaul would expire at the end of February 49. He desired to be elected consul in July of that year and take office at the beginning of 48. He could not risk giving up his command and going to Rome as a private citizen to make his canvass, as had been required by law. His enemies, headed by Cato, were waiting for just this procedure to prosecute him for the illegalities of his first consulship. He knew perfectly well that all his subsequent vast services to the state would not protect him from their vindictiveness. With his customary foresight he had guarded against this contingency. If the provincial governors should be assigned to succeed him they could not take office at the normal time, on the first of January 49, since his term would not expire for two months. Therefore they would be given other assignments. In accordance with long-established custom he would continue as governor until the end of the year, and by a law which he had obtained two years earlier he had received a special dispensation to run for consul without appearing in person in Rome. Therefore he could expect to continue in command of troops until he should go to Rome as consul, when he would be safe from prosecution.

Pompey had obtained for himself the proconsular command in the Spanish provinces for some years — there is disagreement as to the exact number — which would give him command of troops after Cæsar had taken leave of his army. But by permission of the Senate he remained in Italy. Also he had obtained the enactment of a law under which consuls could not serve as proconsular governors until five years after the expiration of their terms. This left vacancies which made it necessary to send out former magistrates as proconsuls. These officials could be sent at any time and so could displace Cæsar in his provincial commands as soon as his term had expired at the end of February 49. To show his fairness Pompey agreed that Cæsar might continue to hold his command of troops until November of that year. This concession still would leave Cæsar at the mercy of his enemies. As soon as he gave up his guard they would seek to annul his election on the grounds of bribery and, without regard to his guilt or innocence, he could have no confidence in the outcome of a trial before a packed jury.

It was with this hazardous situation that Cæsar now had to deal, peacefully and constitutionally if possible, if not . . .

CHAPTER XX

THE CRISIS OF THE RUBICON

WITH AFFAIRS at Rome in this uncertainty it came time to dispatch former magistrates to the provinces in accordance with the new law. Cicero was drafted for the province of Cilicia on the southern coast of Asia Minor. The province included the island of Cyprus. Nearly two thousand years later Sir Ronald Storrs while governor of Cyprus compiled a roll of all the governors of the island. His most distinguished predecessor on the list was Marcus Tullius Cicero. It was with great reluctance that Cicero set out in May 51. He regarded the assignment as a "gigantic bore," he wrote to Atticus. It was "entirely unsuited" to his character and habits. They had "put a saddle on an ox." "I can't describe to you," he says, "the warmth of my longing for the city or the difficulty I feel in putting up with this boredom." It is disgusting that he should be required to preside over a court in a wretched provincial town instead of in Rome. "But the fact is that it is not such things as this that I miss. It is the broad daylight of life, the Forum, the city, my town house, *you* that I miss. But I will endure it as best I may for a year. If there is any extension I am lost." Repeatedly in his letters from the province he recurs to this theme. His friends must unite to prevent any extension of his governorship. Only when he is nearing home the next year with civil war in immediate prospect does he express the wish that he might be back in his province and relieved of the necessity of taking sides.

Yet Cicero always had stood for decent government for the provinces and he recognized that "the professions I have been making these many years past are now being put to the test." His letters give a vivid picture of the administration of a Roman province and the difficulties arising from the lack of continuity of provincial government and the laxity of control over the governor from Rome, complicated by the pressure of Roman business men who regarded the provinces as a natural field for exploitation.

His province, he discovered, had been almost ruined by the exactions of his predecessor, Appius Claudius, a brother of his old enemy Clodius. Cicero set earnestly to work to repair the damage and rehabilitate the communities that were hopelessly in debt. Theoretically Rome had adopted an enlightened provincial system with a large measure of autonomy. Each subdivision had its own laws, courts, and local taxation. Superimposed on all this was the imperial administration of defence, public order, justice, and finance. In the absence of a strict central authority such as was provided later under the Empire, everything depended on the character of the governor. After he had been in Cilicia a few months Cicero writes with pride to Atticus of his achievements. "A great number of states have been entirely released from debt, and many very sensibly relieved. All have had their own laws and with attainment of autonomy have quite revived. I have given them the opportunity of freeing themselves from debt or lightening their burdens in two ways: first, in the fact that no expense has been imposed upon them in my government, and when I say 'no expense' I mean *none,* not a penny. It is almost incredible how this has helped them escape from their difficulties. The other way is this: there was an astonishing amount of peculation in the states committed by the Greeks themselves. I mean their own magistrates. I personally questioned those who had been in office in the last ten years. They confessed it, and without being openly punished repaid the money to the communities out of their own pockets. The consequence

is that whereas the communities had paid the tax syndicates nothing for the present five-year period, they have now without any distress paid them the arrears of the last five years also. The rest of my administration of justice has not been without skill." He goes on to relate how accessible he has been to everyone and how popular his conduct has made him.

In the middle of his term he tells his friend that his "exile has been worth while." "I didn't realize what I was capable of in this line," he says. "I may well be puffed up. It's splendid. It isn't so much the reputation I get by it that delights me. It's the feeling that I'm doing the decent thing."

One of his limitations stands out in the correspondence. Apparently he was satisfied merely to make a record for his year of office. He liked sunning himself in the goodwill of the provincials. He was not concerned with the general colonial problem or with going back to the capital to attempt to have the weaknesses of the Roman imperial system corrected. Cicero had nothing of Cæsar's sense of responsibility for the government of the vast congeries of peoples and nations outside of Italy who acknowledged the rule of Rome.

A conspicuous instance of the sort of oppression to which the unfortunate provincials were sometimes subjected appears in the case of the city of Salamis on the island of Cyprus. The city had been heavily in debt and in order to force payment Appius Claudius had allowed its Roman prefect to use a troop of horse to blockade the Senate chamber until five senators had died of starvation. The horsemen were promptly recalled by Cicero, who had learned that the city was being charged forty-eight per cent interest by its creditor in Rome although the legal rate was only twelve per cent. A special and illegal resolution had been slipped through the Senate authorizing the forty-eight per cent. At length Cicero discovered that the creditor was that zealous patriot and puritan Marcus Brutus. His principles of conduct did not cover provincials. They were regarded as fair game. Even Atticus wrote to Cicero in support of Brutus' claims. "If I did anything of the sort," Cicero replied, "how should I ever dare look again on the pages of that book of mine which you commend [*On the Commonwealth*, in which he had pictured the ideal statesman]? No, my dear Atticus, you have shown yourself in this matter too much, far too much a friend to Brutus and too little, I fear, a friend to me."

While the governor gave judgment for the Salaminians,  the story has an unhappy ending. Cicero did not have the nerve to antagonize Brutus and the financial crowd at Rome. When Brutus refused to accept payment under the judgment, Cicero left the case up in the air so it could be reopened by his successor.

Rome undertook the defence of its provinces. There was trouble with the hill tribes on the Cilician frontier and Cicero led an expedition against them. He had the advantage of the presence on his staff of his brother Quintus, an experienced soldier, and the expedition was successful. Writing to Atticus, Cicero does not take his military exploits too seriously. He had camped, he says, on the very spot which Alexander had occupied against Darius at Issus — "a commander just a trifle superior to either you or me." On December 17 the Pindenissitæ had surrendered. "'Who the mischief are your Pindenissitæ?' you will say. 'I never heard of them.' Well, what am I to do? Could I turn Cilicia into an Ætolia or a Macedonia?" Cicero had led one attack and had been greeted by his soldiers as "Imperator." This flattered his vanity. Hereafter according to custom he was entitled to sign formal letters with "Imperator" after his name, and how he loved the distinction! Also he could expect a Thanksgiving to be decreed by the Senate, to be followed by the authorization of a formal triumph. He obtained the Thanksgiving over the protest of the sour Cato, whose attitude irritated him. But he never was granted the triumph, although he dragged his bodyguard all over the country after his return, in the wistful hope that it would be voted before he dismissed his attendants.

As we might expect, Cicero was careful in his financial dealings. At the end of his term he paid into the treasury $50,000, about which his staff " grumbled, thinking that this money ought to have been divided among them." Of his personal savings of $110,000 I have already spoken.

While he was absent from Rome Cicero got what information he could from others, but he had arranged specially to be supplied by his young friend Cælius, a clever and unprincipled politician, once a member of the group of parlour pinks who had frequented the salon of Clodia in the period preceding the debtors' protest under Catiline. In fact it was probably Cælius who had superseded Catullus in Clodia's affections, and he had had an affair with the lady which was ardent while it lasted. When he finally tired of her she was furious and sprang upon him like a tigress with a charge that he had attempted to poison her. Cicero was of counsel for the defence and in his address to the jury laid bare all the scandals of her life that he could find, and they were many. Cælius was acquitted. It has been remarked that ultimately, after a long struggle, the young blade escaped from both Clodia's love and her hatred; but it was doubtful whether he ever forgot her.

Cælius took seriously his assignment to keep Cicero informed, and employed a roving reporter to run down information, which he duly forwarded to Cilicia. We have fourteen of his letters, the first including his cynical comment on Pompey: " He is accustomed to think one thing and say another, and yet is not clever enough to conceal his real aims "; a true bill. Cicero enjoyed hearing of the personal scandals of Rome as well as of its heavy politics — the case, for instance, of the gentleman in whose baggage were found " five small portrait busts of married ladies." " I wanted you to know these historiettes," he writes to Atticus, " for we both have a pretty taste in gossip." Cælius kept him well supplied.

At the earliest possible date, on the expiration of his term, July 31, 50, Cicero left his province, stopping for a time at Athens on his way home. In spite of his correspondence he seems to have lost touch with the situation in Rome. Just before leaving he wrote to Atticus that he was confident everything would be all right so long as Pompey stood firm. The first clear intimation of impending trouble came from Cælius in a letter written from Rome in September. He sees no chance, he says, that peace will last a year. "The point on which the men in power are bound to fight is this: Pompey has made up his mind not to allow Cæsar to become consul except on condition of his first handing over his army and provinces, while Cæsar is convinced that he cannot be safe if he gives up his army. He, however, proposes as a compromise that both give up their armies."

As a practical politician Cælius is frankly puzzled about what to do. "In the case of domestic differences," he writes, "so long as the contest is carried on constitutionally without an appeal to arms, men ought to follow the party most nearly in the right; when it comes to war and the camp, the stronger party." In this quarrel he sees that Pompey has the Senate and the respectable element generally on his side. Cæsar has the discontented; but there is no comparison between their armies. As Cælius recognized, Cæsar's was incomparably the stronger — something of which Pompey and his friends seemed curiously unaware.

All this came as a shock to Cicero. Civil war had never entered into his calculations. During his stay in Athens he received letters from each of the rival leaders counting on his support. "What am I to do?" he despairingly exclaims to Atticus. In the past he has supported both men. If it should come to war, of course it would be "better to be beaten with one than to conquer with the other." But meanwhile what position shall he take? If he should be called upon for his vote in the Senate must he say: "Wait until I have talked with Atticus?"

In the midst of all this mental anguish his essential kindness is displayed. On the journey home his secretary Tiro became ill and had to be left at Patras in Greece, just west of the Gulf of Corinth. Cicero writes to him almost daily for a fortnight, writes to his physician " with the greatest earnestness " about him, and arranges for payment for medical services. A few weeks later he writes to Atticus: " I see you are anxious about Tiro. Though his services are invaluable to me in all my pursuits and occupations when he is in health, yet it is his intrinsic worth and excellence rather than consideration for my own interests that make me long for his recovery."

Cicero's relations with Tiro constitute a most attractive side of his character. Tiro had been a household slave. But his native talents under association with his master had made him a learned man and an accomplished writer. He could discuss philosophy and write a treatise on grammar. He published a life of Cicero and edited his letters, modestly withholding from publication all that he himself had written to Cicero. He was an expert shorthand writer. Cicero says Tiro could " follow whole sentences as dictated," whereas his substitute had to take them " syllable by syllable." Cicero's handwriting was the despair of his publisher. Sometimes, like Horace Greeley, he could not read it himself. On one occasion he writes to Tiro to look after one passage in particular in a manuscript that has gone to the printers (copyists, of course). It has to do with an incident about Cato at the age of four, " and I myself," he says, " always find it difficult to decipher." In the same letter he asks Tiro to see about guests for a dinner party. One lady he is certain won't come if a certain gentleman is invited.

Three or four years before the illness of Tiro at Patras Cicero had given him his freedom. Tiro was beloved by the whole family, and Quintus writes to Cicero that he had jumped for joy at the news that Tiro " was to be our friend rather than a slave." The manumission made no difference in the relations of the two men. Cicero always regarded him with affection and was solicitous about his health. " I have got your letter," he writes when Tiro was convalescing, "though your handwriting is very shaky." Before long Tiro was able to buy a farm to which he retired, where he lived to the age of one hundred.

On November 24 Cicero landed at Brindisi and proceeded to his villa at Formiæ in order to gain time to learn more about the situation before going on to Rome. Cæsar and Pompey by this time were profoundly distrustful of each other — Cæsar perhaps with the more reason, remembering the way in which Pompey had yielded to pressure in twice double-crossing Cicero a few years before. For a year each had been manœuvring to put the other in the role of the aggressor for the influence this situation might be expected to have on public opinion. In these manœuvres Cæsar ran rings around his slower-thinking opponent. By liberal use of Gallic gold he had attached some influential men to his side, especially his former political enemy Curio, to whom Cicero had referred as the one man who dared speak out against the Committee of Three at the beginning of its rule. Curio, now a tribune, was in a position to be of great help to Cæsar because he was supposed to be against him. He vetoed every attempt to appoint a successor to Cæsar in his provinces on the ground that Cæsar was needed as a counterbalance to Pompey and that the authority of the Senate would be secure only if Cæsar and Pompey were both deprived of their armed forces. While upper-class opinion was strongly on the side of Pompey, only a small group of extremists was willing to bring on civil war to assure Pompey's supremacy. This was demonstrated in the Senate on December 1, 50 when Curio moved that both proconsuls lay down their commands simultaneously. The motion was carried, 320 to 22, but it was simply an advisory resolution without practical effect. Cæsar renewed the proposal through Curio on January 1.

Pompey took this as a sign of weakness. He misjudged his opponent. Lucan, who had a better understanding of the man, was to write: "He deserved to be feared for he feared nothing." Under his illusion Pompey assured Cicero that when Cæsar learned of the energetic preparations that were being made against him he would give up his designs on the consulship. If he should be so crazy as to proceed, Pompey had a very low opinion of his power and felt confidence in his own and the state's resources. When Cicero left he was convinced that his friend no longer desired peace. He had only to stamp on the ground, Pompey had said previously, and soldiers would spring up for him everywhere. Presumably he was counting on reports that had reached him of disaffection among Cæsar's soldiers and of the fact that Cæsar's lieutenant general Labienus was ready to desert to the side of the Senate. Pompey had troops outside of Rome, and the senatorial majority yielded to his pressure and to that of the small war party, which shared its leader's confidence that he could easily dispose of his rival. It yielded the more readily because of its fundamental fear that its special privileges would not be safe with Cæsar as consul. The struggle that followed was not primarily between rival generals. It was between Cæsar and the Roman oligarchy.

Accordingly the proposal that Curio conveyed was again refused and the Senate voted that Cæsar must surrender his army and provinces on an undetermined day or be declared a public enemy. To override a veto of the decree by Cæsarian tribunes the Senate then declared martial law and the tribunes fled to join Cæsar. We cannot be sure, but I see little reason to suppose that Cæsar was not sincere in his offer. For his personal safety he could not afford to give up his army so long as his bitter opponents had armed forces at their command. But he would have liked to avoid war and he had every reason to believe he could handle Pompey successfully if they were on even terms. Lack of self-confidence was not one of Cæsar's failings.

In the negotiations that followed, even after hostilities had begun, there is every evidence that Cæsar was anxious for a negotiated peace, while Pompey was obdurate. Cæsar even appealed for a personal interview, which Pompey refused, perhaps fearing to subject himself to his rival's charm. As a result of his implacable attitude Pompey almost at once lost the sympathy of Italy. The people, Cicero reported later, loathed the idea of civil war. From the outset they were impressed by the fact that to avoid a resort to arms Cæsar was willing to make concessions which Pompey rejected. Sentiment veered sharply toward the conciliator.

The conqueror of Gaul was not the man to overlook the opening that the blunders of his opponents had given him. He addressed his legion at Ravenna, stressing on the public side the illegal treatment of the tribunes; on the private, the threat to their general's honour and safety. The affair of the tribunes served him in another speech made a little later when he said he was defending the dignity of the tribunes and the liberty of himself and of the Roman people, "who were oppressed by a few factious men." Incidentally he admitted that he was protecting himself "from the injuries of his enemies." We may assume that his own interests came first. The tribunes constituted a useful talking point.

Once more the Blitzkrieg surprise tactics that had served Cæsar so well in Gaul were employed against his opponents in Rome. It was the beginning of winter, a season when military operations were customarily suspended. Pompey assumed he would have plenty of time before spring to conduct negotiations while raising troops in Italy. But the Italian winter meant nothing to the soldier who had crossed the Cévennes through snowdrifts. Within a few weeks Cicero was to write in alarm to Atticus: "Cæsar moves so rapidly!" And again: he is "a man of frightful vigilance, rapidity, and energy."

Sending word to his scattered legions in Gaul to join him, Cæsar at once started down the Adriatic coast. The Rubicon, a little stream, hardly more than a creek, marked the boundary of his northern Italian province. When he had crossed it into Italy he would have violated the law and put himself in open rebellion against the government. We have slightly varying stories from Plutarch and Suetonius of how he hesitated at the brink of the stream, reviewed the situation in his own mind, and then, exclaiming: "Let the die be cast," plunged across, followed by his men. This was somewhere between November 20 and November 23 by the solar calendar, January 10 and January 13 by the distorted calendar then in use, which Cæsar afterward corrected. In his memoirs he says nothing of this incident, but the tradition may well be authentic. His secret service had informed him that the towns were on his side and within a short time he was far down the coast. Pompey had gone to the south of Italy to supervise the recruiting, leaving the consuls to take measures for the protection of the capital. But they and the Senate became panic-stricken over the unexpected rapidity and success of Cæsar's movements and on January 18 fled from the city to join their leader.

This is not the place to recount events in detail. Pompey became convinced that he could not make a successful stand in Italy and gathered his forces at Brindisi to transport them across the Adriatic to Durazzo, at that time an important seaport. From Durazzo ran the great Roman road to the East through Salonika to Constantinople and Jerusalem. Pompey had reason to believe his prestige from his eastern campaigns would bring men flocking to his standard. Events justified his hopes and he was able to train recruits near Salonika.

Cæsar raced to blockade him at Brindisi, but the Pompeian forces broke through successfully to Durazzo. Meanwhile the generosity with which Cæsar had treated his opponents had made a profound impression. They had made a stand in the town of Corfinium under one of Pompey's chief lieutenants. When the garrison insisted on surrendering, Cæsar enlisted the soldiers in his own army and freed the commander and the Pompeian senators with him. Cicero wrote in appreciation of his clemency and Cæsar replied: "You judge me quite accurately — for my character is well known to you — when you say that nothing is more remote from my disposition than cruelty. For myself, as I take great delight in this policy for its own sake, so your approval of my action gives me pleasure. I am quite indifferent to the fact that those whom I released are said to have gone to make war against me again. All I wish is that I should act like myself, they like what they are." The expression of a great spirit. These words, the exuberant Macaulay used to say, contained the finest sentence ever written. On the margin of the volume beside Cæsar's letter the English historian wrote: "Noble fellow!"

As Cæsar had no transports, he could not follow his enemy. He was threatened on the flank by forces in Spain loyal to Pompey and he determined to dispose of these before returning to his major attack. Hurrying to the peninsula he subdued the armies there by a lightning campaign, in which, however, he took risks that for a brief period threatened disaster. His work was ended in August. Then he returned to Rome and supervised the elections in which he was chosen consul. In the eleven days he remained in the capital he showed his practical genius in statesmanship. The war had brought on a financial crisis. It was impossible for borrowers to meet their obligations. The panic was accentuated by fear that pressure from some of his bankrupt followers would induce Cæsar to enforce a general cancellation of debts. Instead he devised a bankruptcy procedure for the emergency which was so reasonable that it afterward was revived by Augustus. Debtors were permitted to discharge their obligations by turning in their property at pre-war value instead of at the distress value that attended the panic. Interest paid was to be deducted from the principal. The result was to scale down obligations by about twenty-five per cent. This wise measure alienated some of his radical entourage, including Cælius, who the next year went recklessly into open rebellion, in which he lost his life. But it won the business crowd to Cæsar's cause.

In addition Cæsar recalled many of those who had been driven into exile under Pompey. Other necessary arrangements were made and then he proceeded to Brindisi, where he pushed the preparations for crossing the sea for the final struggle.

Cicero had reached Rome early in January 49, a few days before final action was taken by the Senate. Essentially a man of peace, he had protested in vain against a policy that seemed to him inevitably to mean a war that would end the Republic. With unusual insight he had written to Atticus in December: "What we want is peace. From a victory, among many evil results one at any rate will be the rise of a tyrant." To Tiro he wrote: "A strange madness has possessed not only bad men but even those who are esteemed good, so that all desire to fight, while I cry out in vain that nothing is more wretched than civil war." By January 12 he had realized that his leader had been overconfident and was not prepared. Preparations, he said, were being pushed with great energy by Pompey, who "now that it is too late begins to fear Cæsar." Cicero had been clinging to the hope, however, that Cæsar would not make the final move of defying the government by advancing from his province. The news of the invasion of Italy filled him with dismay. On the 19th he wrote a hysterical letter to Atticus denouncing Cæsar as a "madman," a "wretch."

His letters for the next few months reveal the hesitations and vacillations of a sensitive soul, not a man of action, utterly unprepared to ride the storm that raged about him. To Atticus, referring to his frequent changes of opinion (in one letter he had completely reversed the position with which he started), he writes: "'Do you change your opinion as often as that, then?' I speak to you as to myself; and who in a matter of such importance does not argue with himself in a variety of ways?"

One difficulty was his conscience. It is impossible to read his letters in this trying period without concluding that the man was honestly trying to make up his mind which course was better for the welfare of the state. He was plagued with an intelligence that enabled him to see so clearly the weaknesses on both sides! He feared that no matter which leader won, the old Republic was gone. Yet might there not be a chance to save something from the wreckage? And reasons of state were complicated by personal considerations. There is a measure of truth in the statement attributed to Cicero by Quintilian in the next century. "I am not timid," he said, "in facing dangers, but in attempting to guard against them."

Anyone who has observed politicians behind the scenes, when they are not on dress parade, will recognize Cicero's uncertainties as quite normal. Every American national convention when the outcome is not set in advance is full of bewildered delegates trying to figure what is best for the country, the party — and themselves. Shall they support this man who would be an attractive candidate but probably a poor president, or his rival who is better fitted for the place but has a way of antagonizing voters by his forthrightness? Shall they make an early jump for what seems the bandwagon, or shall they hold back for developments? They have not only the welfare of the country but their own political future to consider. In the great Republican political split of 1912 the party was full of perplexed Ciceros. The case of a distinguished senator was typical. In his first speech in the Bull Moose campaign he told how eagerly and enthusiastically he and his friends had responded to the call of their great leader. His professions sounded rather hollow to those who had known of his vacillations and of the pressure that finally had brought him reluctantly into the Progressive camp.

Cicero was in a more difficult position than any of these American politicians. So far as he knew, his life as well as his political future might be at stake. He had been sent by Pompey to supervise the raising of troops in southwestern Italy. If Cæsar should win, what would happen to Cicero? For once in his life he abandons wishful thinking and frankly recognizes his unpopularity with the mass of the people. "What kind of attack," he writes to Atticus, " will

Cæsar employ against us and our property in our absence? Something more violent than in the case of others, for he will perhaps think that he has a chance of winning popularity by damaging us." No wonder he was worried.

After he had recovered from his first outburst of indignation against Cæsar and had had time for reflection, he came to a juster view. Late in February he wrote to Atticus that there was no difference between the motives of the two leaders. "Supremacy," he says, "has been the object of both; there has been no notion of securing the happiness and virtue of the citizens. . . . The object of neither is our happiness. Both want to be kings." Prejudice kept him from realizing that if there was to be a monarch Cæsar was incomparably the abler man and his rule might be expected to be far better for Rome and her dominions.

Until Pompey left Italy, Cæsar did not abandon hope of a peaceful settlement. After his display of clemency at Corfinium he wrote to friends in Rome that he had resolved on a policy of generous treatment to his enemies and would do his best to effect a reconciliation with them. "Let us try in this way," he said, "if we can recover the affections of all parties and enjoy a lasting victory. . . . Let this be our new method of conquering, to fortify ourselves by mercy and generosity." Cicero was greatly impressed by this attitude. On March 1 he wrote to Atticus that if Cæsar should overtake Pompey at Brindisi, there would be a faint hope of peace, although two days later he was certain Pompey would reject any overtures. "Do you realize," he adds, "the sort of man upon whom the Republic has fallen? How clear-sighted, how alert, how well prepared? By heaven, if he puts no one to death nor despoils anyone of anything, he will be most adored by those who have feared him most. The residents of the towns and the farmers too talk a great deal to me. They don't care a cent for anything but their lands, their poor houses, their paltry finances. And observe the reaction. The man in whom they once trusted they now dread; the man they dreaded they worship." His reference here was to threats of proscription that had come from the bitter-enders with Pompey. These greatly distressed him. "A good cause," he wrote to Atticus, "but it will be conducted in a most criminal way by devastating Italy. If Pompey wins he will not leave a tile roof in the country."

Throughout these weeks, as an amateur strategist, he was bitterly critical of Pompey's abandonment of Rome, although the city could not have been defended, and of his withdrawal across the Adriatic, which obviously was required by the deficiency of Pompey's forces in Italy. He declares that his leader is not only a poor statesman but a rotten soldier. Late in February Cælius had written him summing up his estimate of the two leaders: "Did you ever see a more futile person than your friend Pompey, or ever read of anyone prompter in action than our friend Cæsar, or more moderate in victory?"

It was all very perplexing to Cicero and he bombards Atticus with questions as to what he should do. His misgivings torment him. "I would die for Pompey," he writes, "but for all that, I don't think all hope for the Republic is centred in him." And six days later: "Yes, I said I preferred defeat with Pompey to victory with the others. I do prefer it, but it is with the Pompey as he was then, or as I thought him. But he has betrayed our party and is about to abandon it." And again with a wave of prudence: "Although my standard is always duty . . . I now want to follow a course that will not simply aim at duty but will conduce somewhat more to my safety as well." He remembered that he had stuck to what he regarded as duty in the case of the Catilinarians and had ended in exile. For a time he took refuge in the hope that he might be able to preserve his neutrality and serve the state by promoting a reconciliation between the chief contenders. After all, he had not taken "any part whatever in the war," as he wrote to Cæsar, and always had preferred peace at any price to an armed conflict. With his usual insight and sagacity Cæsar undertook to play on this frame of mind in order to keep him neutral if he failed to win him over. He sent word to Cicero through friends that he understood the obligations Cicero was under to Pompey and did not blame him for what he had done, but that now he had a great opportunity to bring about a reconciliation. Early in March the commander took the time to write to Cicero personally, asking to see him at Rome, "to enable me to avail myself of your advice, influence, position, and support of every kind." In reply Cicero expressed the hope that Cæsar wished to consult him "for the tranquillity, peace, and harmony of our fellow citizens. . . . In this case, and if you are at all anxious to preserve our common friend Pompey, and to reconcile him to yourself and to the Republic, you will assuredly find no one better calculated than myself for supporting such measures. . . . It is now a good number of years ago since I picked out you two as the especial objects of my political devotion and, as you still are, of my warm personal affection."

Cicero finally made up his mind not to go to Rome; he might run into too many embarrassments. So Cæsar visited him at Formiæ. We are fortunate to have in a letter to Atticus a report — perhaps a naturally distorted report — of the conversation of these two famous leaders of the ancient world, sparring for advantage at a time of crisis. "I found myself mistaken in one respect," Cicero writes, "in thinking that he would be easily satisfied. I never saw anyone less so. He kept remarking that he was condemned by my decision not to come to Rome; that the rest would be slower in coming if I did not. I remarked that their case was quite unlike mine. After much discussion he said: 'Come then and discuss the question of peace.' 'At my own discretion?' said I. 'Am I to prescribe to you?' said he. 'My motion will be this,' said I, 'that the Senate disapprove of any going to Spain or taking armies across to Greece and,' I added, 'I shall make many regretful remarks as to Pompey.' Thereupon he said: 'Of course I don't wish such things said.' 'So I supposed,' said I; 'then I must decline to go to Rome, because I must either speak in this sense and say many things which I could not possibly pass over, if present, or I must not go at all.' The upshot was that by way of ending the discussion he requested that I think it over. I couldn't say no to that. So we parted. I feel certain therefore that he has no love for me. But I felt warm satisfaction with myself, which hasn't been the case for some time past. . . . His closing remark in our interview, which I had almost forgotten to mention, was very offensive, that 'if he was not allowed to avail himself of my counsel, he would avail himself of such as he could and would stick at nothing.'"

If Cicero really talked up to Cæsar as he says he did, he showed more nerve than he had shown previously when he had obviously tried to ingratiate himself with the great man. In twentieth-century America men have been known to come away from a conference with the President at the White House and tell their friends how sternly they had reproved the Chief Executive for his mistakes. Their friends know better. It is likely that Cicero reported to Atticus what he would have liked to say rather than what he actually did say. But undoubtedly his attitude was beginning to stiffen at this time as the result of immense travail of soul. Looking over Cæsar's entourage with a rather jaundiced eye, Cicero was confirmed in his opinion that their cause was bad. Presumably in the company were men who were down and out, hopeless failures, radical left-wingers. "By god," he adds in the letter to Atticus, "they weren't human beings; they were a troop of shadows from the kingdom of the dead."

At this time he had not seen Pompey's followers. When he finally went to Durazzo and met the men around his hero in the camp, he felt there was little to choose between the parties. Undoubtedly the Pompeians included the abler men of the country. But they showed the same deficiency in character that had long made the Senate the mere mouthpiece of a reactionary and ineffective oligarchy. Except for the general and a few others, Cicero wrote to a friend, "I found them a bankrupt outfit, greedy for war loot, and so bloodthirsty in their talk that I shuddered at the idea of their victory. In short, there was nothing good except the cause."

At the time of his conference with Cæsar he was coming to the conclusion that, in spite of everything, Pompey represented, however imperfectly, the cause of constitutional government to which he was devoted. The senatorial crowd had become Cicero's crowd. He admitted quite frankly that he was obeying the herd instinct. "I shall do what the cattle do when they are scattered," he writes to Atticus. "They follow their own kind. As an ox follows the herd, so shall I follow the party of the Good, or those who are called the Good, even if they rush to destruction." He had previously expressed the opinion that "we can never have our Constitution while these two men are both alive." Yet he recognized that the restless Cæsar was by nature an innovator, while the phlegmatic Pompey would at least try to maintain the outward semblance of the Republic. Besides, personal affection was involved and he could not forget that Pompey had been the prime mover in his recall from exile. He had a horror, he said, of seeming ungrateful and he would not be able to stand the gossip among his friends if he should abandon Pompey. All these considerations combined to produce a decision.

Cicero made up his mind that at all costs he must join Pompey at Durazzo. Early in May he tells Atticus that Tullia keeps urging him to wait for the outcome in Spain. But in his present mood he can't abide the thought. "I think myself," he writes, "more bound to abandon Cæsar when he is victorious than when he is beaten." Then he draws a distressing picture of what will happen if Cæsar conquers — a picture wholly unjustified in the light of what had already happened. He foresees "massacre, an attack on private wealth, a recall of exiles, repudiation of debts, promotion to office of the lowest dregs, and a despotism intolerable."

There were obstacles to be overcome. Mark Antony had

been put in charge of Italy by Cæsar and it was necessary to get his permission to leave. Cicero proposed withdrawal to Malta, whence he might make a dash later to the Macedonian coast. But Antony replied that he must consult Cæsar. So Cicero wrote to Atticus that he would assure Antony he was in no hurry and would communicate with Cæsar in Spain. Meanwhile he would lie low and take advantage of any opportunity that offered to get away.

The opportunity came early in June and he sailed for Durazzo. A few weeks later Cæsar's temporary reverses in Spain sent a number of fence-sitters in Rome to join Pompey. At least Cicero had the satisfaction of knowing that he had not waited to go with these men. At the same time he could not really have believed, as he had hinted, that he was joining a lost cause. Pompey had been extremely energetic in raising and training troops in Macedonia and the East and in assembling ships. He had obtained some three hundred. While he had been unprepared for the war and had been taken by surprise by Cæsar's demoniacal energy, he had shown himself a master strategist in making his stand at the great naval and military base of Durazzo. Unlike many soldiers he recognized the importance of sea power two thousand years before Captain Mahan wrote his classic, *The Influence of Sea Power upon History*. He had told Cicero that in his view "the master of the sea must inevitably be the master of the empire. The equipment of a fleet has always been his first care." He expected to starve Italy out by a rigid blockade and then finish the war by an overwhelming invasion. Modern strategy.

But only disappointment awaited Cicero when he reached the camp. The blunt Cato at once took him aside and told him his coming had been a big mistake. He ought to have stayed at home and played the part of the great conciliator. Pompey had nothing for him to do, for Cicero was not a military man. So he wandered moodily about, making cutting remarks — and Plutarch says he did not smile when he made them. Another émigré had come in such a hurry that he had left his horse behind him. " His horse must be much obliged to him," commented Cicero. " You're late in coming," an officer remarked. " Late, but soon enough to find nothing ready." Pompey found him trying — for he had had to borrow money from Cicero — and they had a little interchange about relatives. Cicero's son-in-law, Dolabella, was a Cæsarian and Pompey had once been Cæsar's son-in-law. " Where's your son-in-law? " Pompey acidly inquired. " With your father-in-law," was Cicero's comeback.

Early in the year 48 Cæsar crossed the Adriatic with his troops and undertook to besiege Pompey in Durazzo. His men were inferior in numbers but superior in training to those of the enemy. For the first time Cæsar now encountered a professional soldier and he perhaps underestimated his opponent. He extended his lines until they were too thin. Pompey broke through with a surprise attack and Cæsar was forced to retreat with Pompey in pursuit. But Pompey did not know how to use his victory, his adversary commented later. Cæsar withdrew southeastward into Thessaly, and the two armies faced each other near the town of Pharsalus.

At first Pompey stood on the defensive, but at length pressure from his followers persuaded him that with his superiority in numbers he could defeat the enemy. " His army," Cæsar writes, " was so eager to divide the spoils of victory that they failed to consider how the victory was to be won." In the battle that Pompey invited, the genius of Cæsar again shone. He won an overwhelming victory and Pompey fled to Egypt, where he was murdered by an Egyptian officer.

Because of illness Cicero had stayed behind at Durazzo. Some weeks later at Brindisi he learned of Pompey's death. In the shock of this tragic news he forgot his bitter criticisms of his leader. But he had been too thoroughly disillusioned to think of him as a real statesman. Four years later in a pamphlet attacking Mark Antony he referred to Pompey as " illustrious at home and admirable abroad "; as a " great and pre-eminent man "; and as the " glory and light of the empire of the Roman people." These were statements of an advocate making a political case. His considered judgment is given in a letter to Atticus. It is moderate and fair, significant for what it does not say: " I never doubted," he writes, " that such would be his end. . . . But I cannot but lament his death for I knew him to be a man of virtue, sobriety, and integrity."

As for Cæsar, his stern heart was moved as he saw the carnage at Pharsalus. One of his officers reports his saying bitterly: " They would have it so. Even I, Gaius Cæsar, after so many great deeds, would have been condemned if I had not appealed to arms."

CHAPTER XXI

SORROW INTERVENES

THE OUTCOME at Pharsalus had settled the conflict for Cicero. He was through. Before he left for Italy the Pompeian fleet had a rendezvous at Corfu. At a conference there, headed by Cato and Pompey's impetuous son Sextus, it was decided to continue the struggle. Cato urged Cicero as the senior ex-magistrate present to take over the command. He refused on the ground that the war was over. The angry Sextus called him a traitor and threatened him with his sword, but Cato intervened. It was the plan of the die-hards to retire to North Africa and there collect and organize their forces. This the absence of Cæsar, who had followed Pompey to Egypt, gave them an opportunity to do.

Cæsar's eastern journey, including his wars in Egypt and Pontus, is remembered today chiefly for two incidents, his love affair with Cleopatra and the brief note: "*Veni, vidi, vici*" ("I came, I saw, I conquered"), with which he reported to a friend his victory at Zela, Asia Minor, on August 2, 47. Evidently Cæsar thought he had happened on a swell phrase and later he had it displayed in a triumphal procession in Rome. His antagonist was the son of Rome's old enemy Mithridates. Once more a Blitzkrieg. The Asiatic commander, according to an ancient historian, "feared Cæsar's rapidity more than his army."

Returning to Rome in September, Cæsar suppressed disorders in the capital, put through needed legislation, and then turned to Africa, where he defeated the Pompeians early the next year in the battle of Thapsus. Soon afterward

Cato committed suicide. As a Stoic he preferred death to what he regarded as tyranny combined with clemency from the conqueror he despised. It was a real misfortune to Rome that during these critical years the tremendous courage, persistence, and will-power of Cato were uncompromisingly on the reactionary side. Although he was a doctrinaire — he has been called the Don Quixote of the aristocracy — his qualities and the impression he made on his contemporaries entitle him to a conspicuous place among the public men of his age.

But not yet was Cæsar permitted to settle down to the work of administration. Pompey's two sons, Gnæus and Sextus, had taken refuge in Spain with Labienus, the deserting marshal. They raised the standard of revolt and late in the year 46 Cæsar went to Spain for his final conflict. We gather from Cicero that by this time the people were sick of war. "At least we know what Cæsar will do," he observed. "But Gnæus Pompey is so wild that everybody is frightened at the thought of his victory."

Cassius, a follower of Pompey whom Cæsar had pardoned and who later was to lead the assassination plot, was all for Cæsar as against Pompey's son. "Hang me," he wrote to Cicero, "if I don't prefer our old and merciful master Cæsar to such a new and cruel one as Gnæus. You know what a fool the fellow is. You know how he thinks that cruelty is courage. You know how he always thinks we are laughing at him. I'm afraid he'll want to get back at our jokes with the sword." The victory of Munda, March 17, 45, virtually ended the war. Labienus was killed and later Gnæus Pompey. Sextus escaped to become, as someone has said, a gentleman pirate.

As for Cicero, in the years of stress following Pompey's defeat in 48 his world had gone out from under him. Troubles piled up, domestic, financial, political. His relations with Quintus had always been unusually close and affectionate. But the brother had a violent temper. He had sided with Pompey and very likely blamed Marcus for inducing him to put his money on the wrong horse. After Pharsalus the brothers went to Patras, where a quarrel took place. Both were nervously on edge and probably out of funds, a situation conducive to sharp tempers. The trouble began, Marcus reports, when Quintus reproached him for not sharing the proceeds of his Cilician governorship which had been lent to Pompey. "He never asked me for anything at the time!" Marcus exclaims. They separated at Patras. Marcus went to Brindisi, where he spent eleven wretched months waiting for Cæsar's return, while Quintus and his son, Quintus junior, departed for the East to make their peace with the victor. Both father and son behaved badly. In December Marcus writes to Atticus that the elder Quintus has sent his son to Cæsar, "not only to plead on his own behalf, but also to accuse me. He never stops, wherever he is, heaping every kind of abuse upon me. Nothing in these troubles has given me so much pain. You know his style. You may have had some personal experience with it." Quintus junior was living up to his uncle's expectations. A friend told Marcus of meeting the youngster at Ephesus. "Quintus told him I was his deadliest enemy," Marcus writes, "and showed him the notes of a speech which he said he was going to make to Cæsar against me."

As to the senior Quintus, two other friends came to Marcus "boiling with indignation." They had just received letters from Quintus abusing his brother. One of them, a friend of Cæsar's, remarked that he knew Cæsar disliked Quintus and had favoured him only because of Marcus. The disconsolate older brother concludes a report to Atticus with the wish that he had never been born, or at least that his brother had never followed him into the world.

In these trying circumstances Marcus' conduct showed generosity and devotion. Cæsar understood the brothers and appraised them justly. He paid no attention to the malicious charges of Quintus, and indeed pardoned both Quintus and his son on Marcus' account. Marcus heard from a friend in Cæsar's entourage that the dictator blamed Quintus for inducing Marcus to join Pompey — that Quintus had "sounded the trumpet" for Marcus' retreat. Whereupon Marcus wrote to Cæsar exonerating his brother — "He was the companion not the leader of my journey" — and begging Cæsar "not to let me stand in his light with you." It was a considerable time however before the brothers were reconciled.

Nevertheless, in spite of favourable but indirect reports, Cicero could not fail to be anxious as to Cæsar's attitude. He had definitely broken with Pompey's party and he began to be greatly disturbed when he heard reports of Cæsar's difficulties in the East and of the growing strength of the Pompeians in North Africa. Suppose after all they should win and he should prove again to have chosen the wrong side. How would the victorious and vindictive Sextus Pompey treat him? He was plunged in gloom. "I can discover nowhere any ground for hope," he writes Atticus in one of his disconsolate moods. And again: "My own error has been my ruin. I cannot attribute my misfortunes to accident. I have brought them all upon myself."

Cicero once more had misjudged Cæsar, the most magnanimous of the Romans. After Pharsalus he had had Pompey's letter files burned without reading the correspondence, "in order," Dio says, "not to be forced by what was in the letters to take severe measures." His was to be a policy of reconciliation. Later Cicero was impelled to exclaim to the dictator: "You never forget anything except injuries!" This magnanimity was not only in harmony with Cæsar's character. It was part of his long-sighted policy. His own followers included a rather motley crew. Most of the administrative experience of the government had been in the senatorial party, which had sided with Pompey. While Cæsar was anxious to recognize and reward merit in any walk of life, he knew he must draw on men of experience and ability for the administration of the imperial system, and his policy of conciliation was directed to this end.

Cicero he always had liked. He realized that the former

consul had influence and respectability. In addition as a man of broad culture and wide interests Cæsar was drawn to the greatest literary genius of the age. Cicero probably was the one Roman with whom Cæsar could engage in stimulating conversation on a wide variety of subjects. He knew Cicero's weaknesses but was tolerant of them. For some time, however, Cæsar was too busy in his eastern campaigns to write, and Cicero continued to stew. It was not until he had spent eight uneasy months in Brindisi that Cicero received a kindly letter from the victor. It did not wholly reassure him. "What a master gives," he wrote to Atticus, "a master can take away." A minor incident of the period shows that Cæsar overlooked nothing. In spite of all his troubles Cicero still held to his bodyguard carrying the bundle of rods, the *fasces*, crowned with laurel, which he had won in Cilicia, and with which he hoped to enter Rome in celebration of a formal triumph. Cæsar stole up on his blind side with a flattering message from Egypt which he must have sent with vast amusement, recognizing Cicero as Imperator and authorizing him to keep the laurelled fasces as long as he wanted. Apparently Cicero was sufficiently comforted by this recognition to dismiss his attendants, for we hear nothing more about them except a reference to the incident in a speech the next year.

At length in September 47 Cæsar landed at Tarentum in southern Italy and came by land to Brindisi to take the Great South Road, the Appian Way, to Rome. Cicero believed he must go to greet the conqueror. Plutarch tells the story. When Cæsar saw him coming, he dismounted from his horse and went forward to meet him. They embraced and then walked for some distance without attendants, in friendly conversation.

With his anxiety finally relieved, Cicero now set out for his favourite country place at Tusculum. His worries were not yet over. Domestic trials awaited him. The next year he divorced Terentia. He was in financial straits and was pressed for repayment of her dowry. His solicitous friends encouraged him to find another wife with enough money to relieve his embarrassment. At least this is Tiro's report, relayed through Plutarch, and it was in accordance with custom. A man of his distinction of course was a desirable catch. Cicero confides to Atticus that he isn't considering Pompey's daughter, who has been suggested. Under the circumstances such an alliance would not have been tactful. As to another lady whom his friend has mentioned, well, he never had seen such a fright. Finally a marriage was arranged with a young, beautiful, and wealthy girl named Publilia, who was his ward.

Cicero was now sixty-one years old and the marriage of May and December had an unhappy ending. Within a few weeks after the wedding his daughter Tullia died. Publilia had been jealous of her and was so unsympathetic over her death that Cicero sent her home to her mother and divorced her. The family were reluctant to give up the distinguished connection. Cicero's old friend Cærellia called on him to urge a reconciliation. But he convinced her this was not desirable. Then he reports to Atticus a letter from Publilia which he thinks someone else wrote, telling him that she and her mother and brother want to come to see him. He had immediately written asking her not to come. But he fears the family will descend on him anyway and he asks Atticus to find out when they are coming so he can leave his villa at Astura, where he is staying, and avoid them.

The death of Tullia was a terrible blow — his darling Tulliola, his companion from her earliest years, the one human being for whom he never had a word of criticism. He had done his best to keep her from marrying the irresponsible but clever young Dolabella. Later when Dolabella was breaking her heart he blamed himself, not his daughter, for the marriage. Finally she got her divorce and in January 45 her son was born while she was staying with her father in Rome. When she was able to travel they went to Tusculum. Her strength suddenly failed and she died in the middle of February.

Cicero was stunned. "I have lost the one thing that bound me to life," he wrote to Atticus. His old friend insisted on a visit from him. A few days later he decided he must be alone and went to his villa at Astura, a small island forty miles southeast of Rome on the edge of the desolate Pontine Marshes. To reach the place one crosses a wide moor covered with coarse ferns, brambles, and scrub evergreens. At the time the island must have been a wilderness. Cicero calls it "a lovely spot right in the sea." The sea has filled in behind until today the former island is a narrow promontory from which one may look out on Roman ruins. On either side is a long sandy beach where the waves roll gently in. From the blue waters of the Mediterranean the moor rises to a spur of the Apennines against the horizon. At Astura a "passionate unrest" haunted Cicero. "In this lonely place," he tells Atticus, "I have no one to talk to. I plunge into a dense wild wood early in the day and stay there until evening."

His friends understood his grief and did their best to help him. Even Cæsar took the time to write him a letter of condolence from Seville in Spain. A letter from Brutus, he says, contained "a great deal of good sense but nothing to give me any comfort." The most elaborate and most Roman of the letters is one from an old friend, Servius Sulpicius, then governor of Greece. It has been made famous in Byron's verses in *Childe Harold* in which he refers to Servius as "the Roman friend of Rome's least mortal mind." The lines paraphrase part of the letter:

Wandering in youth, I traced the path of him,
The Roman friend of Rome's least mortal mind,
The friend of Tully: as my bark did skim
The bright blue waters with a fanning wind,
Came Megara before me and behind
Ægina lay, Piræus on the right,
And Corinth on the left; I lay reclined
Along the prow, and saw all these unite
In ruin, even as he had seen the desolate sight.

THE TOURING CAR OF THE ROMAN ROADS

In a springless two-horse vehicle like this, forerunner of the American covered wagon, Cicero probably travelled to his villas. Roman carriages usually were drawn by mules. (From an ancient bas-relief)

Servius writes to Cicero that he recently sailed by these cities, Ægina, Megara, Piræus, Corinth — "cities at one time most flourishing but now prostrate and decayed." And the thought came to him: "Why do we insignificant mortals feel rebellious if one of us dies or is killed, we whose life must be brief, when in one place the remains of so many cities lie prostrate before us?" Why should Cicero be so distressed by the loss of "the frail spirit of one poor girl, who if she had not died now would have had to die a few years hence, for she was mortal born"? Servius tells him to remember he is Cicero, accustomed to instruct others, and urges him to take to heart the admonitions he so often has commended to his friends. Then he draws on the age-old experience of the race for one of the universal medicines for grief: "There is no sorrow," he adds, "beyond the power of time at length to diminish and soften." Another medicine, absorbing work, Cicero discovered for himself.

From Astura he writes to Atticus that he has read everything he can find on the subject of assuaging grief, but his sorrow has been too deep for help. So he has tried to console himself by writing a book of his own. "I assure you," he says, "there is no more effective consolation. I write all day long, not that it does any good, but for a while I experience a kind of relief, or if not quite that — for the violence of my grief is overpowering — yet I get some relaxation, and I try with all my might to recover composure." This book, or pamphlet, was a *Consolatio* (Consolation). *Consolatio* was the name used for a literary form prevalent in Roman antiquity. Usually it was intended as a consolatory message for others. Cicero wrote his *Consolatio* to console himself. Unfortunately only fragments survive. The poignancy of one paragraph is eternal. "I have always fought against Fortune," he cries, "and beaten her. Even in exile I played the man. But now I yield and throw up my hand!"

The death of Tullia brought to Cicero his second great religious experience. The first came while he was a student in

Athens in connection with the Eleusinian Mysteries. The second was far more profound while it lasted, although its effects, too, were temporary. Sir Oliver Lodge and Sir A. Conan Doyle furnish two conspicuous instances of the same sort of experience of immortality. Each lost a son prematurely. Under emotional stress each was convinced that something so precious as his son's spirit could not possibly go out into nothingness. Each believed he could communicate with his son in the other world. Cicero came to a very similar conclusion. He sought out the books of the Greek mystics and found in them the hope for which he yearned. The basis of the argument in the *Consolatio*, taken from Plato, is that the soul reveals capacities that imply eternal existence. He concluded therefore that Tullia would live eternally as a divine being and that he should recognize her divinity by erecting for her not a tomb but a shrine. In this mood of mysticism he ended the *Consolatio* with the pledge: "I shall consecrate you before all the world . . . as one of the immortals."

The matter absorbs him in his letters to Atticus. He knew his friend was a man of the world and would regard his plans as fantastic. "You must bear with me," he writes, "and with these silly wishes of mine." For the next three months his letters are full of the subject — the proper design, and the appropriate site where people will see it. Then the subject disappears from the correspondence. Almost unconsciously he reverts to his ingrained agnosticism even when writing about the continued existence of Tullia. Educated Romans held to the idea of the immortality of fame. "Brief is the life given us by Nature," is the way Cicero puts it in one of his addresses, "but the memory of a life nobly resigned is everlasting." It is the conception expressed by George Eliot:

Oh may I join the choir invisible
Of those immortal dead who live again
In minds made better by their presence.

And George Eliot heads the poem with the Latin line from Cicero's letter to Atticus: "*Longum illud tempus, quum non ero*" – "that long time when I shall not be." "I am more concerned," the passage runs, "about that long time when I shall not be than about my short day, which, short though it is, seems all too long for me."

But while his immediate interest in Tullia's immortality faded, the religious experience which had come to him was continued in his reawakened interest in the problems of religion and philosophy. He had gone to the Greek writers for comfort and they had brought back to him his studies in his college days at Athens. As there was no place for him in politics under the Cæsarian dictatorship, Cicero had plenty of time to read and write. In the next few months he produced an amazing series of books, including such familiar titles as the *Tusculan Disputations* (*Tusculanæ Disputationes*), *On Old Age* (*De Senectute*), *On Friendship* (*De Amicitia*), and *On Moral Duties* (*De Officiis*). These were based on Greek literature, but he was over-modest when he wrote to Atticus: "They are translations. They don't cause me so much trouble. I contribute only the language, with which I am well supplied." Cicero was much more than a translator and a popularizer. His writings reflect the impact of Greek thought upon a ripe experience and a brilliant intellect.

Reading his books on political science, the *Commonwealth* and *Laws*, we feel we are in the presence of a man who speaks our political language, who is familiar with problems very like our own. His feet are firmly on the ground. He refers to Plato as "that divine philosopher." But he never soars away with the Greek into any cloudland. Always it is the Roman statesman who addresses us.

The same Roman practicality infuses his philosophical works, in which he was heavily indebted to his Greek predecessors. In contrast to them Cicero has been criticized as heavy and stodgy. Perhaps he is. Nevertheless he brings abstract speculation into contact with human needs. Through the centuries men have been uplifted by his exposition of the eternal values in the noble epilogue to the *Tusculan Disputations.* They have found inspiration in the broad humanism of the *Moral Duties* with its recognition of " the universal bond of our common humanity." However lacking in originality he may have been, he was the channel through which the fresh wisdom of the Greeks reached the Western world.

With his varying moods, his intellectual curiosity, his sensitive response to the particular audience he happens to be addressing, Cicero presents stimulating views but no well-ordered system. It is difficult to determine his opinions from his writings. In his public addresses he falls as naturally into the phraseology of the popular religious beliefs as an American congressman at a camp meeting. These fundamentalist ideas are obviously not his own. In his letters are occasional religious references. They are generally casual — " With heaven's help," " I call the gods to witness," " Unless some god intervenes." The same sort of casual references were used by the older generation in America — " I hope to leave tomorrow, *deo volente.*" In two letters to his wife cited in an earlier chapter he implies that religion is her affair, not his. His letters to Atticus during his religious experience after Tullia's death reflect only a passing emotion, which is broken by the sentence quoted denying his own immortality. Passages in letters to two other friends carry the same skepticism. " If I cease to live," he writes, " I cease to have any sensation." And again: " We should bear with resignation whatever occurs, especially as death ends all."

His formal treatises do not help greatly to clarify his own creed. Indeed, he seems to have had in mind chiefly the patriotic desire to enlarge the boundaries of the narrow Roman mind by bringing it in contact with the liberating thoughts of the Greeks. Cicero was essentially an artist, and as an artist he plays with various philosophical ideas and develops them. They were for public consumption and do not seem to have meant a great deal in his own life. One exception perhaps should be made. His devotion to duty, however imperfectly realized, was far in advance of the level of his time.

The arguments for and against immortality are judicially set forth in his writings. On several occasions he affirms his faith. But in the light of the letters just mentioned it is a fair assumption that he was speaking for himself in a passage in the *Tusculans* where one of the characters is urged to read Plato on the soul. "I have done so many times," the man replies, "and I agree while I am reading. But somehow, I am sorry to say, when I lay the book down and begin to reflect on immortality all my previous agreement with Plato slips away." Cicero had a similar difficulty in keeping his faith alive.

In general he was a rationalist and the current superstitions did not appeal to him. Although he was an augur he had no patience with the art of divination except as a useful political instrument to check the radicalism of the Assemblies. As to the existence of a supreme being he gives the familiar argument from design. "The celestial order and beauty of the universe," he says, "compel me to confess there is a surpassing and eternal Nature which deserves the respect and homage of man." This passage occurs in an essay *On Divination.* Previously he had elaborated the argument in a volume *On the Nature of the Gods* in which the views of three schools of Greek philosophy are presented. The second book of the treatise argues for the existence of a divine providence, but the skeptical speaker of the third book demolishes the argument. In conclusion Cicero expresses the cautious opinion that the deistic contention "approximates more nearly to a semblance of the truth." But even this was hardly a firm conviction. In a treatise, the *Academics,* mostly borrowed from the Greeks, in which he reviews the foundations of knowledge, he comes back to the agnostic position of the Greek school of philosophy with which he identified himself. His final word addressed to his son in his last book, the *Moral Duties,* written just a year before his death, is curiously modern. "We maintain," he says, "that nothing is known for certain. But probability furnishes a sufficient guide for life." This sentence recalls the unpublished reply of Justice Oliver Wendell Holmes to a young friend in the last year of his life. She had urged him to write a book summing up the conclusions of his long career. "My dear," he answered, "I could set them all down in a single paragraph, and it would end, 'And of these I am not sure.'"

Cicero's religious and philosophical studies, inconclusive as they were, proved immensely suggestive to those who came after him. The early Christian fathers felt his influence. St. Jerome believed that he sinned by reading Cicero on fast days and in the delirium of illness heard a voice reproaching him for being "not a Christian but a Ciceronian." His writings opened a new world to Petrarch, the father of humanism. Erasmus wrote: "He inspired my soul and made me feel myself a better man." Copernicus found a quotation from a Greek writer in Cicero that suggested to him the movement of the earth. The skeptical Voltaire spoke of the *Tusculan Disputations* and the treatise *On the Nature of the Gods* as "two of the noblest works that ever were written by mere human wisdom," and of the volume *On Moral Duties* as "the most useful book that we possess on morals." In another place he says: "We hiss them off the stage, then, those rude scholastics who ruled over us so long. We honour Cicero, who taught us how to think." Something more than a century after Cicero's death the elder Pliny quoted a generous appreciation from Cæsar: "How far greater and more glorious to have enlarged so immeasurably the limits of the Roman mind than the boundaries of their empire!" It was a deserved tribute that was paid by a Russian scholar, Thaddeus Zielinski: "The history of civilization knows few moments equal in importance to the sojourn of Cicero in his country seats during the brief period of Cæsar's sole rule."

CHAPTER XXII

THE IRREPRESSIBLE CONFLICT

IN DEVOTING himself to writing, Cicero sought refuge not only from his private sorrow, but from his growing concern over the state of the Republic. Cæsar had invaded Italy in 49 in order to obtain the consulship for the next year. He was elected of course, but the consulship was subject to various inconvenient restrictions. Soon he felt it advisable to add to it the powers of the dictatorship, which were not subject to a tribune's veto. Originally an emergency office with a tenure limited to six months, the dictatorship had fallen into abeyance a century and a half earlier, to be briefly revived under Sulla. Cæsar took first a limited dictatorship, then had the term extended for ten years, and finally shortly before his death was granted an extension for life. At the same time he evaded the law which barred him as a patrician from the tribunate by having what were called tribunician powers conferred upon him, which theoretically guaranteed the inviolability of his person. For good measure he created for himself an office for the supervision of morals that gave him a lesson in the futility of attempting to make men good by decree. By accumulating all these powers in his own hands he made himself supreme in the state, above all laws, with no appeal from his decisions. The forms of constitutional government were still observed, but his endorsement assured the election of magistrates, and the measures he proposed were enacted into law.

Cæsar had fought Pompey and the oligarchy primarily

to save himself from ruin and exile. He had emerged master of the civilized world, with vast responsibilities for its well-being. These responsibilities he accepted. They involved extensive reforms which appealed to his passion for order and achievement. As he had shown in his first consulship, he was impatient with the slow and wrangling parliamentary processes and the peculiar facilities for obstruction offered by the Roman system. The program he now contemplated interfered with the special privileges of the senatorial oligarchy and he could not obtain its co-operation. To achieve his ends he was forced to cut through constitutional procedure.

In the intervals between the wars necessary to establish his position from 49 to 44 he had only a little more than a year in Rome, a few weeks or months at a time. The amount of work accomplished in these broken intervals testifies to his resourcefulness and driving force. His bankruptcy arrangements already have been noted. He found three hundred and twenty thousand persons were receiving free wheat from the government. By a means test he reduced the number to one hundred and fifty thousand — undoubtedly a blow to his popular following. He dealt with the unemployment problem by settling eighty thousand citizens overseas, and by providing that at least one third of the slaves employed on ranches be replaced by freemen. Concerned as he was with imperial problems which had been grossly neglected by the Senate, he extended Roman citizenship. The franchise was granted to northern Italy beyond the Po, and, as a gesture of goodwill, to the city of Cadiz (Gades) in Spain. The men of the Fifth Legion, the Larks, recruited in Provence, were rewarded with citizenship, and the dictator granted it as well to certain notables in Gaul to strengthen their ties with Rome. The tax syndicates were deprived of their extortionate profits in the province of Asia. A fixed sum for taxes was set and the communities were allowed to collect it. A start was made in what was to become the great imperial civil service by replacing the irresponsible senatorial governors with lieutenants nominated by Cæsar and responsible for their conduct to his vigilant supervision. We get a glimpse of the procedure in a letter of a provincial governor to Cicero asking his good offices with the dictator. Because of the severity of the winter the governor had been obliged to abandon a district he had captured and he knew his chief in Rome was displeased. He desired Cicero to intercede for him. Evidently nothing escaped the ruler's eye.

New blood was brought into the decadent Senate and it was given a more representative character by enlargement to nine hundred members. The new senators represented various elements in the population, including Gallic notables, distinguished soldiers, and able men who had risen from the submerged classes. The ruler's wide cultural interests were reflected in his project for the establishment of public libraries under Rome's greatest scholar, Varro, who incidentally had been one of Cæsar's opponents, and in the conferring of citizenship on alien physicians and teachers of the liberal arts living in Rome.

His most spectacular reform was that of the calendar. Nearly two centuries previously Egyptian astronomers had computed very closely the length of the year. The Romans had applied the available information awkwardly. They maintained the old year of 355 days and injected an extra short month occasionally, at the discretion of the pontiffs. For various reasons, some of them political, the necessary corrections had not been made for several years prior to the Civil War and so the calendar year had got two months ahead of the solar year. In consultation with an astronomer from Alexandria, Cæsar worked out the adjustments required. The calendar was brought into harmony with the seasons by prolonging the length of the year 46. Thereafter ten additional days were distributed through the year to bring it to 365 days, and provision was made for an extra day for February every four years. Thus was devised the Julian Calendar, which needed only the slight revision made by Pope Gregory XIII in 1582 to serve indefinitely.

To expedite justice the dictator increased the number of judges and administered the law, Suetonius says, "with the utmost diligence and the most rigid austerity." He worked out a municipal code for Rome with provisions to relieve traffic congestion and to care for street cleaning and maintenance. Laws governing municipalities outside of the capital were revised and codified. An extensive building program was undertaken. Numerous other projects were planned which the dictator did not have the time to carry out — codification of the civil law, improvement of the harbour at Ostia, draining of the Pontine Marshes and the Fucine Lake, a new road across the Apennines, a ship canal through the Isthmus of Corinth.

Of this immense constructive program Cicero was an increasingly uneasy spectator. At first he cherished the hope that after Cæsar had completed the essential parts of his work he would lay down the dictatorship as Sulla had done and restore constitutional government. His personal relations with the dictator were good. Looking back later, he remarked to Atticus, "I don't know why it was, but Cæsar always was surprisingly patient with me." But the threat to freedom was constantly before him. "From the man who has all power," he writes to another friend, "I see no reason for my being alarmed except the fact that, once depart from law, everything is uncertain; and that nothing can be guaranteed as to a future which depends on another man's will, not to say caprice." It was his limitation, perhaps an inevitable limitation in the circumstances, that he envisaged no alternative to autocracy except a return to the old system, which had become obsolete and unworkable. Rome was in the last stages of an irrepressible conflict. The conflict was between the policies required to realize and reconcile two great ideals sincerely held: the ideal of liberty under self-government, which Cicero mistakenly believed could be regained under the old system, and the ideal of order and efficiency that Cæsar finally saw no possibility of attaining except under his benevolent despotism. It was the tragedy of the Roman fate culminating in the murder of the ides of March that the best minds of the ancient world could find no way to compose the conflict.

In the light of modern experience there may be speculation whether a representative system might not have saved the Roman democratic experiment. Representative government was known in the ancient world. It had been tried in Greek federations, proposed for Italy in the course of the second war with Carthage, applied by Roman generals in organizing Thessaly and Macedonia, and adopted by the Italian towns that revolted to obtain Roman citizenship early in the first century B.C. Where tried, it had not been so successful as to commend itself for adoption for Italy or for the Italian dependencies. The Roman domain was too vast, communications too slow, the included populations too varied, too inexperienced in self-government, too uninformed and ignorant, to permit representation on an imperial scale. For Italy it might have worked. But even if the conservative Romans had been willing to adopt the representative system the change would not have remedied the fundamental evils that had wrecked the aristocratic Republic. The shortsighted senators who had forced the soldiers to transfer their loyalty from the state to their commanders had opened the way to military dictatorship. Representative institutions would not have cured this condition or the underlying factors that had produced it. They would not have brought enlightenment to stupid aristocrats and grasping financiers, or public spirit to the masses who loafed at the games. Roman development had reached a point where the selfish incompetence of the old ruling class, combined with the demoralization of the city population, had proved fatal to a free state.

Relieved from apprehensions as to his personal safety, Cicero regained for a time his gaiety of spirit. " I have effected a reconciliation," he writes, " with my old friends, I mean my books." A sociable fellow under normal circumstances, he was welcomed by a group of Cæsar's intellectual friends, including curiously his son-in-law Dolabella, with whom he remained on good terms in spite of the young man's heartless treatment of Tullia. He gave some of the younger men lessons in public speaking and they invited him to elaborate dinner parties. In return he entertained them simply in his own home. "Think of my nerve," he says. "I even gave Hirtius a dinner, but I didn't serve peacock. My cook imitated him in everything but the hot sauce." His house was thronged with morning callers and in the afternoons when he did not dine out he devoted himself to reading or writing.

The retired statesman was celebrated for witty conversation. Cæsar, who enjoyed good stories, directed his friends during his absence from Rome to send him all worth-while remarks of Cicero's, to be included in his volumes of *bons mots*. Perhaps one of these was Cicero's dig after the reform of the calendar. Someone remarked that the constellation Lyra would rise the next morning. "Yes, no doubt," said Cicero, "in obedience to the edict." The dictator was a keen higher critic. Cicero writes that Cæsar was able to detect and reject jokes not of Ciceronian origin. After all he found the situation not intolerable. "To submit to necessity," he tells a friend, "has ever been held the part of a wise man. Things aren't too bad. You may not be able, perhaps, to say what you think; you may certainly hold your tongue."

In his conciliatory mood Cæsar often responded to Cicero's pleas for clemency to exiled followers of Pompey. Two speeches made in the summer of 46 in the interval between Cæsar's campaigns in Africa and Spain are of especial interest in showing the dictator's tolerance and Cicero's hopes for the future. Plutarch tells the story of the defence of one Quintus Ligarius before Cæsar. The dictator is reported to have remarked that he already had made up his mind that Ligarius was a scoundrel as well as a personal enemy. But he was inclined to give himself the pleasure of hearing Cicero speak. " He was much moved when Cicero began; and the speech as it proceeded had such a variety of pathos, so irresistible a charm, that his colour often changed, and his mind was evidently torn by conflicting emotions. At last when the orator touched on the battle of Pharsalus he was so affected that he trembled and let drop some papers from his hand. Thus subdued by eloquence, he acquitted Ligarius."

The other speech, made in the Senate shortly before the one for Ligarius, was significant for its plea for a return to the Constitution. It was delivered in appreciation of the clemency of Cæsar, who at the Senate's request had pardoned an implacable enemy, an arrogant aristocrat and former consul, Marcus Marcellus. Cicero jumped at the conclusion that Cæsar in yielding to the Senate was on the point of restoring constitutional government. " I fancied," he wrote to a friend, " I could see, as it were, some vision of the Republic springing to life again." With his customary extravagance he expressed unbounded gratitude to Cæsar for his greatness of soul. The destiny of the commonwealth was wrapped up in him. "On your sole life," Cicero exclaimed, " hang the lives of us all. I mourn that while the state must be immortal, its existence should turn upon the mortal breath of a single man." This led naturally to his favourite theme and he urged Cæsar to set up the courts and rebuild the Republic. Summoning all his eloquence, he made his appeal: " This chapter still awaits you, this act remains to be played, to this must you summon all your powers — to restore the Republic, and yourself to reap the chiefest fruits thereof in peace and tranquillity." To Cæsar the restorer of ancient liberties the speaker pledged protection — " the shelter of our own breasts and bodies " — against any secret foe.

In this same mood he wrote to a friend that Cæsar had a disposition naturally placable and clement, with a great liking for men of superior ability. " I am always struck with astonishment," he says, " at Cæsar's sobriety, fairness, and wisdom. He never speaks of Pompey except in the most respectful terms."

An episode of the year indicates the relative freedom of speech that still existed under the dictatorship. After the suicide of Cato it was suggested to Cicero that he write a eulogy of his friend. He discussed the matter with Atticus, outlining what he would have to say: "That Cato had seen that the present state of things was to occur, that he had exerted himself to prevent it, and that he had quitted life to avoid seeing what actually had happened." Such a pamphlet he recognized would not please Cæsar's friends; nevertheless, if he was to write anything, he must write his convictions. The publication of Cicero's eulogy prompted Brutus to write one. Cæsar took no offence. Instead he wrote to one of his friends that he had repeatedly read Cicero's *Cato* to increase his command of language, whereas Brutus' *Cato* had made him feel he could do better himself. Accordingly he took time off in his Spanish campaign to write an anti-Cato pamphlet in which he complimented Cicero while criticizing Cato. Presumably he felt it necessary to reply to political pamphlets that were essentially criticisms of his own course. He replied with argument, not with sentence to a concentration camp.

Nevertheless, as Cicero wrote to a friend, events constantly reminded him that Cæsar's kindness could not "make up for violence and the complete upsetting of the established order." And to another friend he wrote: "I have mourned for my country more deeply and longer than any mother for her only son." The benevolent dictator found it difficult to restrain some of his rapacious followers and there were frequent illegal seizures of property. The moderation of the victor, Cicero wrote, could not be surpassed, but as always in a civil war, the victory itself was the trouble. "A conqueror is forced under pressure from those who won him his victory to do many things which he would prefer not to do. . . . Even the leader cannot say what is going to happen. While we are his slaves he is a slave to circumstances."

There were other annoyances. In the press of public affairs Cæsar was obliged to keep some of his visitors waiting. Cicero, always sensitive to slights, remarked that he had not the entree to the great man, but needed someone else to show him in. Cæsar recognized hurt pride. On one occasion after keeping Cicero waiting, he said to one of his friends: "Do you suppose I'm such a fool as to think that this man, good-natured as he is, can like me when he has to sit all this time waiting on my convenience?"

Indeed, Cicero was so egotistical, so self-centred that at times in reading his correspondence one is almost in doubt whether his attitude was not determined as much by wounded vanity as by devotion to the lost Republic. "In that city," he writes, "where once I flourished in honour and renown, I now live in destitution. Born for noble exertion, I now have no motive either for action or for thought." Again: "By some misfortune our age has fallen upon circumstances which, just when we ought to be at the very height of prosperity, make us ashamed even of being alive." He frankly confesses his keen personal disappointment in the turn of events which had deprived him of the influence for which he had striven all his life. "Once," he says, "I sat at the helm and held the rudder. Now there is scarcely a place for me in the hold of the ship. Would one decree the less be passed if I were in Naples instead of in Rome?" And he goes on to tell of the way in which his name has been used without his knowledge or consent. Cæsar was still trying to observe the constitutional forms, but it was only a formal observance. The senatorial decrees, Cicero continues, are prepared in the dictator's home, and Cicero finds himself occasionally set down as backing some resolution of which he knows nothing. "I wouldn't have you think I'm joking. I actually have had letters from kings at the other end of the earth thanking me for having voted to give them the royal title, when I swear I didn't even know of their existence."

For a man who considered himself the saviour of his

country and by right the most distinguished citizen of Rome it was a bitter experience and the iron entered into his soul. In the introduction to one of his books he voices his resentment. "It is a source of deep pain," he says, "that the state feels no need of those weapons of counsel, of insight, and of authority which I had learned to handle and to rely upon — weapons which are the peculiar and proper resources of a leader of a civilized and law-abiding state. . . . It was to me a peculiar sorrow that after a career of conspicuous achievements, at an age when it was my right to take refuge in a harbour, not of indolence and sloth, but of honourable and well-ordered ease, when my oratory too had attained a certain ripeness and maturity of age — it was, I say, a peculiar sorrow that at that moment resort was had to arms."

Undoubtedly Cicero was sincerely convinced that the ancient liberties of the Constitution ought to be upheld. Undoubtedly too his enthusiasm for the Constitution was deepened because it gave him such a wonderful platform upon which to display his powers.

As the months passed, Cicero was the victim of constantly changing moods, as he was in the early months of the Civil War. His letters give a vivid picture of his agony of soul. As we read them we sympathize with Macaulay's comment: "What a picture of a mind that well deserves to be studied! No novel ever interested me more. Often as I have read them, every sentence seems new." At one time, impressed by the dictator's tolerance, Cicero thought he might win him over by argument. As always he exaggerated the power of words. With the approval of Atticus he prepared an essay on government to be sent to Cæsar in Spain. He had the caution to submit it to two of his friends who were close to the dictator. Apparently they believed his appeal to restore the Constitution was too obviously written from the aristocratic standpoint and advised so many alterations that he abandoned his plan. Convinced at last of the futility of anything he might say, he wrote ironically to Atticus that no doubt Cæsar was waiting to hear from him and would not do anything except upon his advice. " Well," he added, " we can dismiss such follies and at least be half free. We can hold our tongues and live in retirement."

The moods of gloom gradually extinguished the flashes of hope as it became increasingly apparent that Cæsar had no notion of letting the government escape from his firm grasp and fall into the hostile and muddling hands of the Senate, with final authority resting in the uninformed Assemblies. In August 45 Cicero first characterizes Cæsar with a word that for centuries had been anathema to all Romans — the word " King." " The King," he writes to Atticus, " knows I have no fight left in me."

Still the personal relations of the two men remained rather painfully cordial. Late in December Cæsar paid a state visit to Cicero at his villa at Puteoli. His guard of two thousand soldiers was with him. " Well," Cicero writes to Atticus, " I have no reason after all to repent my formidable guest. For he made himself exceedingly pleasant. On his arrival at the villa of Philippus [the husband of Cæsar's niece and stepfather of Augustus] on the evening of the 18th, the house was so full of soldiers there was hardly a room left for Cæsar to dine in. Two thousand men, if you please! I was in a dither as to what would happen the next day, but Cassius Barba came to the rescue and gave me guards. A camp was pitched in the open and the house put under guard. On the 19th he stayed with Philippus until one o'clock and admitted no one; busy with his accounts, I suppose, with Balbus. Then he walked alone on the shore. After two he took his bath. . . . It was a very good dinner and well served, and not only that, but

Well-cooked, well-seasoned food, with rare discourse:
A banquet, in a word, to cheer the heart.

" Besides this, the staff were entertained in three rooms in a very liberal style. The freedmen of lower rank and the slaves had everything they could want. The upper sort were entertained in style. In short, it was a civilized occasion. Still he is not the sort of guest to whom one would say: 'My dear fellow, look me up on the way back.' Once is enough. We didn't say a word about politics. There was plenty of literary talk. In short, he was pleased and enjoyed himself. That's the story of the entertainment, or I might call it the billeting on me — trying to the temper, but not seriously inconvenient."

Cicero's final flare of resentment and indignation came at the end of the year. A consul had died on the last day of his term and Cæsar had obtained the election of a successor to be consul for only a day. Writing of the event to a friend, Cicero remarks: "Thus I may inform you no one breakfasted in the consulship of Caninius. However, no mischief was done while he was consul, for he was of such astonishing vigilance that throughout his consulship he never had a wink of sleep. You think this is a joke, for you are not here. If you had been you could not have refrained from tears. There is a great deal more that I might tell you, for there are countless transactions of the same kind. In fact I could not have endured them had I not taken refuge in the harbour of philosophy and had I not had my friend Atticus as a companion in my studies."

In expressing this bitterness we may assume that Cicero was the spokesman for many other members of the old oligarchy who for patriotic or for selfish reasons had felt themselves outraged by the procedure of the dictator. The stage was being set for the ides of March.

CHAPTER XXIII

COLOSSUS OF THE NARROW WORLD

ON HIS way to power Cæsar had shown an uncanny insight into human nature and had played upon it to carry out his plans. In the last months of his life that insight seems to have been dulled. He became irascible and arbitrary in dealing with the traditional governing class, whose influence he underestimated. Apparently he was unable at times to conceal his contempt for the incapacity of the old families, which he understood the more clearly because he belonged to them. He did not suffer fools gladly nor was he tolerant of ancient abuses. His program was bound to arouse bitter opposition from those whose privileges it infringed. His attitude antagonized the moderate Conservatives as well. It was reported he had said that the Republic was a sham and Sulla a fool to lay down his dictatorship. He disregarded both special interests and patriotic susceptibilities in driving toward his goal.

Perhaps one difficulty was his health. He was now in his fifty-eighth year and in the last few years he had done the work of a dozen men. Cicero quotes him as having said that he had lived long enough for nature and for glory — the remark of a very tired man.

The tradition that he suffered from epilepsy rests on quite insufficient evidence. Shakespeare gave it currency in his *Julius Cæsar*. Casca tells Cassius and Brutus that "He fell down in the market-place, and foamed at the mouth, and was speechless." " 'Tis very like," Brutus replies; " he hath the falling sickness " – the ancient term for epilepsy. Shakespeare was depending on Plutarch, who wrote a century and a half after Cæsar's death. It may be observed that the details of falling in the market-place and foaming at the mouth are supplied by the dramatist. They do not appear in any of the ancient writers. But if Cæsar had epilepsy Shakespeare assumed that he would have foamed at the mouth. Plutarch writes merely: " He was distempered in the head and subject to an epilepsy which, it is said, first seized him at Cordova." Appian mentions " epilepsy and convulsions." Suetonius has a similar report. Toward the end, he says, Cæsar was subject to fainting fits and twice was attacked by " the falling sickness " during his campaigns. The picture of Cæsar with his immense physical and mental energy is not one of an epileptic. There were similar reports about Napoleon. They were circulated by his enemies. None of his attendants ever saw him in an epileptic fit. It is significant that Cicero, who carefully reports Cæsar's weaknesses, never mentions epilepsy among them.

Unfounded gossip about conspicuous men who have aroused violent antagonisms is common. Every correspondent knows the stories that often circulate in Washington about the President of the period, especially if he happens to be a storm centre. Convincing details are supplied about the great man's attacks of manic-depressive insanity. These gossip orgies would be incredible if they were not familiar phenomena. In my own experience in running down such slanderous stories I have concluded that the technique is usually something like this: some indignant citizen comes out of a White House conference and explodes: " I believe the President is unbalanced." The remark is heard by one of those fellows who love to make themselves seem important by imparting cryptic and confidential information which must be embroidered to make it appear more striking. This man expands the comment in this fashion: " I hear there is a lot of concern about the President's mental condition.

At times he goes into tantrums and throws himself on the floor." And so the rumours grow and spread. Experience in Washington makes me skeptical of the reports on Cæsar preserved by the ancient historians.

But even if the reports of the illnesses, including fainting spells, are correct they do not necessarily mean epileptic seizures. As every physician knows, there are numerous ailments that produce symptoms that might readily be mistaken for those of epilepsy. Dr. Ralph W. Major, author of *Classic Descriptions of Disease*, writes: "It seems to me quite impossible to determine whether or not Cæsar had epilepsy. Even today when we can examine the patient, we often have considerable difficulty in making the diagnosis. Patients with heart block often have epileptic seizures. One of the earliest cases is described by Morganini and is labeled, 'epilepsy with a slow pulse.' I saw a patient only this week who had sudden attacks due to carotid sinus disease. As you have mentioned, disease of the semicircular canals might have caused giddiness, and we often see it in vasomotor disturbances."

Whatever may have been the trouble, and while he was a prodigious worker to the very last, Cæsar was not well. Suetonius mentions his poor health, which almost prevented his going to the Senate on the ides of March. The matter comes up again in connection with rumours of a conspiracy involving Marcus Brutus. "Is Brutus really so impatient?" Cæsar is said to have remarked. "Do you suppose he won't wait until this feeble body collapses?"

We cannot be sure what kind of government Cæsar really intended to establish. He had decided to undertake a campaign against some wild Danubian tribes and the Parthians to stabilize the eastern frontier, and he may have thought he would wait until he returned before giving permanent form to the new regime. Ancient historians report procedure that might indicate a purpose to adopt the Oriental practice and have himself deified. The evidence is hopelessly confused. The chronicles of the time are full of reports that again remind me of Washington. Stories of Cæsar's refusal of the crown, of his reply when addressed as King, of his slight to the Senate by his failure to rise when it waited upon him, of his intention to transfer the capital to Alexandria — all these, some perhaps unfounded, others exaggerated and their significance distorted, could be matched by analogous gossip about American presidents. Persons who have not happened to spend time in some national capital can hardly realize what a gossip factory such a centre may become.

Soon after his visit to Cicero's villa Cæsar had dismissed his bodyguard on the theory, as he put it, that "it is better to die once than always to be in fear of death." Apparently he desired to avoid a dictatorship based on force. We may guess that at one time he hoped to modify the old Constitution so that it would produce enlightened and efficient government. He ran into a stone wall of sullen opposition. His attempted reform of the Senate by introducing new members of known ability, including leading provincials, did not yield the results hoped for. Upper-class snobbery had been sufficiently powerful to make the new senators a joke and destroy their necessary prestige. A sneering placard was posted calling upon citizens not to show new senators the way to the Senate chamber. A popular song made sport of the trousered Gauls whom Cæsar had led to the Senate, where they took off their breeches and put on the senatorial tunic with its crimson stripes. The best people pulled all the old familiar stuff that showed the well-bred contempt of the cosmopolite for the rubes from the sticks.

The dictator tried another method. The Senate was recruited from the young finance officers who at the expiration of their term became members of the Upper House. He thought he might gradually alter the Senate's personnel by increasing the number of lower magistrates — a necessary procedure designed to meet the growing needs of imperial administration. So he raised the number of finance officers to forty and of judges to sixteen. His plans would have meant two hundred new senators and eighty judges in five years. The family founded by a judge, if he was a commoner, automatically joined the nobility, and this man Cæsar, devoted to using able men in every walk of life, might be expected to select capable commoners for judgeships. Indeed, we know of one who had been an army mule contractor whose capacity had been observed by Cæsar and who was made a judge for the year 43. A mule-dealer's family in the ranks of the nobility! Horrid thought! No wonder the old families were infuriated. Not only was the change calculated to destroy their control of the Senate. It was a blow at the very structure of Roman society. In time it would swamp the ancient nobility with upstarts and lower the prestige of the blue-bloods of Rome.

The great reform program that he constantly pressed had alienated various important groups. The enthusiasm of the people was dampened by the new restrictions on indiscriminate relief; of the business men by the abolition of the abuses of the tax-collecting syndicates; of the nobles by his refusal to give them a free hand as provincial governors and stockholders in syndicates to exploit the provinces with forty-eight per cent interest.

For the moment Cæsar must have realized that he was frustrated. Possibly one reason for his proposed eastern campaign was to give him time. It would provide a valid reason for maintaining a military dictatorship with supreme power in his own hands, and the prestige from his victories might help toward the acceptance of whatever plan he would finally think it wise to propose.

Meanwhile the situation was an invitation to conspiracy. If the old order was to be preserved this reckless innovator, this dangerous remover of ancient landmarks, must be rubbed out. Sympathetic with the aristocrats were some of the dictator's able lieutenants who had failed to receive the recognition that they thought was their due. Napoleon had the same trouble with his marshals: with Bernadotte, Masséna, Murat, Marmont. Bitterness of class feeling and personal jealousies could readily be camouflaged under a veil of patriotism. There were sincere defenders of the *ancien régime* who were outraged by Cæsar's flouting of the Constitution. As a background looms the fact that under Roman moral standards, adopted from the Greek, the murder of a tyrant was regarded not only as quite ethical, but as praiseworthy — a duty laid upon all good citizens. A tyrant was any ruler who had seized illegal power and ruled in defiance of the established Constitution. An echo of the same feeling has come down to modern times. John Wilkes Booth appealed to it in his cry: "*Sic semper tyrannis!*" — the motto of the state of Virginia — after he had shot Lincoln. No religious scruples stood in the way of such a political assassination in Rome.

The malcontents decided that now was their opportunity while the dictator was still going about the city unprotected, before he should be surrounded by troops for his eastern campaign. More than sixty men joined in the conspiracy. It was headed by Cassius, who brought in Marcus Brutus. Both were beneficiaries of Cæsar's clemency after Pharsalus. Another leader was Decimus Brutus, a marshal in the Gallic wars. Cæsar paid scant attention to reports of plotting. His indifference is suggested in his remark about Brutus already quoted. He had only a feeling, a hunch it might be called, that Brutus and Cassius were unreliable. Of them he made the comment recorded by Plutarch, which has come to us through Shakespeare: "What do you think Cassius is aiming at? I don't like him, he looks so pale. I have no apprehensions of the fat and sleek men. I rather fear the pale and lean ones." There is insight into human nature in the famous Shakespearean passage giving the admonition of Cassius to Brutus:

Men at some time are masters of their fates:
The fault, dear Brutus, is not in our stars,
But in ourselves, that we are underlings.
Brutus, and Cæsar: what should be in that Cæsar?
Why should that name be sounded more than yours? . . .

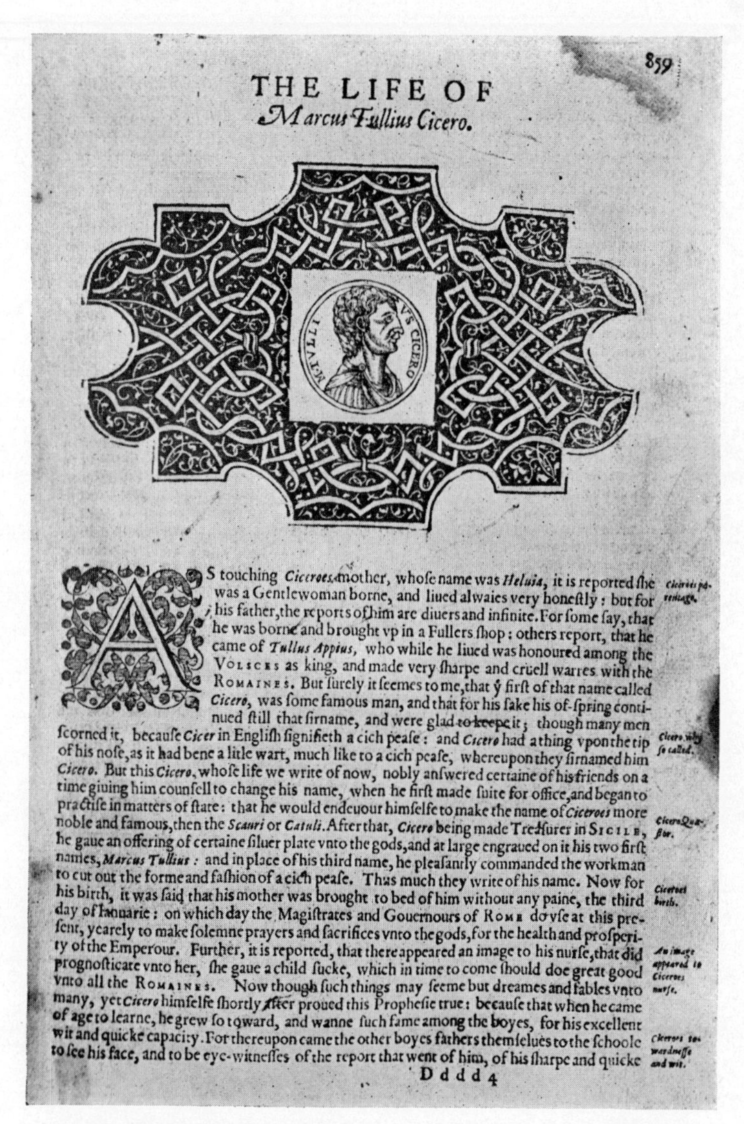

859

THE LIFE OF
Marcus Tullius Cicero.

AS touching *Ciceroes* mother, whose name was *Heluia*, it is reported she was a Gentlewoman borne, and liued alwaies very honestly: but for his father, the reports of him are diuers and infinite. For some say, that he was borne and brought vp in a Fullers shop: others report, that he came of *Tullus Appius*, who while he liued was honoured among the VOLSCES as king, and made very sharpe and cruell warres with the ROMAINES. But surely it seemes to me, that ẏ first of that name called *Cicero*, was some famous man, and that for his sake his of-spring continued still that sirname, and were glad to keepe it; though many men scorned it, because *Cicer* in English signifieth a cich pease: and *Cicero* had a thing vpon the tip of his nose, as it had bene a litle wart, much like to a cich pease, whereupon they sirnamed him *Cicero*. But this *Cicero*, whose life we write of now, nobly answered certaine of his friends on a time giuing him counsell to change his name, when he first made suite for office, and began to practise in matters of state: that he would endeuour himselfe to make the name of *Ciceroes* more noble and famous, then the *Scauri* or *Catuli*. After that, *Cicero* being made Treasurer in SICILE, he gaue an offering of certaine siluer plate vnto the gods, and at large engraued on it his two first names, *Marcus Tullius*: and in place of his third name, he pleasantly commanded the workman to cut out the forme and fashion of a cich pease. Thus much they write of his name. Now for his birth, it was said that his mother was brought to bed of him without any paine, the third day of Ianuarie: on which day the Magistrates and Gouernours of ROME do vse at this present, yearely to make solemne prayers and sacrifices vnto the gods, for the health and prosperity of the Emperour. Further, it is reported, that there appeared an image to his nurse, that did prognosticate vnto her, she gaue a child sucke, which in time to come should doe great good vnto all the ROMAINES. Now though such things may seeme but dreames and fables vnto many, yet *Cicero* himselfe shortly after proued this Prophesie true: because that when he came of age to learne, he grew so toward, and wanne such fame among the boyes, for his excellent wit and quicke capacity. For thereupon came the other boyes fathers themselues to the schoole to see his face, and to be eye-witnesses of the report that went of him, of his sharpe and quicke

Ciceroes parentage.

Cicero why so called.

Cicero Quaestor.

Ciceroes birth.

An image appeared to Ciceroes nurse.

Ciceros towardnesse and wit.

Dddd 4

PAGE FROM AN EARLY EDITION OF NORTH'S PLUTARCH

Plutarch's Lives *were translated from Greek into French by Jacques Amyot, later Bishop of Auxerre, in 1559, and from French into English by Sir Thomas North twenty years later. It was this translation and format that Shakespeare used.*

Upon what meat doth this our Cæsar feed,
That he is grown so great?

Perhaps Cæsar had a premonition in what he said at dinner the night before the assassination. With his customary industry he was signing letters at the table. The question came up as to what sort of death was the most desirable. Cæsar looked up from his letters. "A sudden one," he said.

Cicero had been excluded from the conspiracy. The conspirators were young men and Plutarch suggests they failed to include Cicero "because they feared his natural deficiency in courage as well as his time of life, at which the boldest begin to droop." Whether Cicero actually saw the assassination is uncertain. Possibly he did. Later he wrote to Atticus of "the joy with which I feasted my eyes on the just execution of a tyrant." This may have been a figure of speech. For though Mark Antony later said that "Brutus, lifting high his bloody dagger, shouted for Cicero by name and congratulated him on the recovery of freedom," he was obviously making a political attack. Dio reports that the conspirators rushed into the Forum calling for Cicero. At any rate Cicero approved the murder as tyrannicide. He stated his view of the affair to his son Marcus in his treatise *On Moral Duties*: "If anyone kills a tyrant, be he never so intimate a friend, he has not loaded his soul with guilt. The Roman people, at all events, are of that opinion; for of all glorious deeds they hold such a one the most noble."

Cæsar was struck down on March 15, 44, in a hall adjoining the Theatre of Pompey in the Campus Martius, in which the Senate had convened. The conspirators were so naïve, so lacking in practical understanding, that they assumed the Republic would automatically function in the old way once the dictator was removed. They had made no plans to handle the situation and were taken completely by surprise at the outburst of popular feeling against them, perhaps led by Cæsar's demobilized soldiers who had been waiting in Rome for the bonus in public lands which they had expected from their murdered leader. Nor did the conspirators seem to realize that the civil authority could not function freely in the presence of soldiers under command of Cæsar's officers and the angry veterans. The first man to recover his self-possession was Mark Antony, surviving consul and Cæsar's first lieutenant. With the armed forces at his disposal he was able to maintain order and convoke the Senate. In the general uncertainty his own position was insecure and he had to feel his way.

Under his conciliatory policy, adopted by the Senate with Cicero's support, there was to be no inquiry into the murder and a general amnesty was proclaimed. Enthusiastic Conservatives who desired the murder to be approved as justified tyrannicide were easily suppressed. Such action would have invalidated Cæsar's acts and produced a chaotic condition. Antony was able to point out that many senators, including even some of the assassins, were beneficiaries of Cæsar's edicts — not merely those already issued but others drawn up by the dictator and not yet promulgated. Some of them held offices and provinces and looked for advancement by Cæsar's decrees. On this basis the consul was able to obtain a blanket ratification of Cæsar's plans. This action put a new weapon in his hands, for he had already obtained from the widow her husband's papers and his ample fortune, amounting to $5,000,000. Later he was to supplement his resources by drawing on the public treasury, in which Cæsar had accumulated $35,000,000 — or at least so his enemies charged, and they may have been right. For many years rule in Rome had been profitable to the ruler, who often regarded state funds as his own.

Three days after the assassination, at a public funeral, the will of the dictator was read. It left to the people his gardens beyond the Tiber and to every citizen a legacy of $15, amounting to several weeks' wages for the average man. Then Antony delivered a short and, as Cicero wrote, a "moving" funeral oration. The elaborate speech recorded in Shakespeare's *Julius Cæsar* probably was not actually delivered. It was no part of Antony's policy at this time to stir up mob violence. Doubtless he was taken by surprise at the popular outburst that followed the reading of the will. The shadow of the great dictator still dominated Rome. Its domination was to continue in the months ahead and far into the future. Shakespeare was historically correct when he made Cassius say:

> *Why, man, he doth bestride the narrow world*
> *Like a Colossus, and we petty men*
> *Walk under his huge legs and peep about*
> *To find ourselves dishonourable graves.*

For the first few weeks Antony worked toward a coalition of the divergent elements. He accepted a colleague in the consulship. Two of the assassins were allowed to proceed as governors to the provinces to which they had been assigned by Cæsar. Popular feeling ran so high that Brutus and Cassius thought it advisable to withdraw from the city. They were judges and under the law could not be absent longer than ten days. The consul obtained a special dispensation to permit them to prolong their absence. He wrote a polite letter to Cicero asking his acquiescence in the recall from exile of a hanger-on of Clodius, Cicero's old enemy. Cæsar had promised the recall, he said, but if Cicero objected there would be no clemency. Cicero acquiesced and assured Antony that he had always loved him. But he was deeply offended at the idea of pardoning his enemy's man and wrote to Atticus that the proposal to recall the exile was "unprincipled and improper" — an expression of personal resentment. When Antony under his senatorial authorization began to issue Cæsar's decrees that had been found in his papers, Cicero again was angry. He suspected some of the decrees had been forged. In any event it came home to him that "we now obey the man in his grave whom we could not endure in his lifetime." "We could not endure being his slaves," he wrote; "now we are the humble servants of his memorandum books."

In spite of his indignation Cicero continued for a time to keep on terms with the consul. He was ready to ask favours and late in June he wrote to Tiro that he really wished to maintain his friendship with Antony, "which has now lasted a long time without a quarrel."

In these months while Antony was trying to consolidate his position there is no evidence that he aimed at anything more than a kind of constitutional pre-eminence with enough military support to implement his authority. The fate of Cæsar had been a warning and he had moved to have the office of dictator permanently abolished. The tyranny was no more oppressive than Rome had become accustomed to since the emergence of the Committee of Three sixteen years earlier. Something had to be done to meet the expectations of the demobilized soldiers, and the consul obtained a land allotment for them. Late in April conditions in Rome seemed sufficiently stable for him to leave the city to carry out the land-distribution.

Antony's plans were abruptly upset by the appearance on the scene of a new and incalculable figure. Cæsar's grandnephew Octavius, later known as Octavian and finally as Augustus, was a young man only eighteen years old. He had followed his great-uncle to Spain for the final Spanish campaign and Cæsar evidently had been impressed by the quality of the youth. In his will he had provided for the adoption of Octavius as his son and had made him his chief heir. After his return Octavius had been sent to Apollonia across the Adriatic for study. Among his companions was one who was to become famous as general, admiral, and administrator, Agrippa, the right-hand man of the future Augustus.

At Apollonia Octavius received the news of the assassination. He left at once for the home of his mother and stepfather at Puteoli. On the way he heard the news of the will and received letters from his mother urging him to join her and to avoid the jealousies aroused by his adoption, and from his stepfather prudently advising him to refuse the inheritance and the name and to stay aloof from politics.

This advice he filed for reference and ignored. But he felt his way cautiously. He was driven by an ambition as remorseless as Cæsar's; he had complete self-confidence, no scruples, and curiously he proved to have the ability to make good. For the present he knew he would be contemptuously regarded as an inexperienced boy whose only asset was the name of his towering adoptive father. Naturally he would be expected to seek vengeance on Cæsar's murderers — a pious duty. That would have to be postponed until he should have established himself. Meanwhile he recognized that Antony was the immediate obstacle to his rise to power. His later development under responsibility, his future immense service to the Roman world, and through that world to civilization, need not blind us to the nature of the methods through which he started on his spectacular career.

With the resourcefulness of a mature man and the morals of a gangster he coldly entered upon a game of intrigue that eventually carried him to the top. This involved the difficult task of winning Cæsar's followers and at the same time hiding his feeling toward the assassins and gaining the support of Cicero and the influential senatorial group which disliked and distrusted Antony. If he played his cards well, he might accomplish the miracle of emerging as the champion of the old order while at the same time holding the allegiance of the bulk of the Cæsarians.

How much farther he looked into the future at this time we do not know. In what followed he may simply have been the clever opportunist taking advantage of situations as they arose. But he was a long-headed youngster. It seems more likely that he envisaged the possibility of building himself up to a point where he could challenge Antony on equal terms and then make a deal which would enable him to kick over the senatorial ladder by which he had mounted. This accomplished, he could await a favourable opportunity to get rid of his ally and establish his personal supremacy.

Early in May Octavius reached Rome and a fortnight later Antony returned to see what was doing. At the outset the young man was received disdainfully by his older and far more distinguished rival. But Antony soon realized that he would have to defend himself against an ambitious and resourceful antagonist. He refused to turn over Cæsar's legacy. Presumably it had already been spent. The heir sold the property that had been left him and used the proceeds, with money borrowed from friends, to make a cash distribution to the citizens, as had been provided under his adoptive father's will. He harangued the populace and improved every opportunity to make himself popular with the people and with the veterans of Cæsar. His trump card was his adoption. While this was not legally recognized until the next year, he at once assumed the name of Gaius Julius Cæsar Octavianus, shortened to Octavian in ordinary English usage. In Italy he was now addressed as Cæsar, a form that proved as great an asset to him as the name of Napoleon proved to the third Emperor of the French.

In the face of potential combinations against him Antony was obliged to reconsider his position. He already had obtained for himself from the Senate the governorship of Macedonia for the year following his consulship. This would give him command of troops. But Macedonia was far away. Meanwhile he had thought it advisable to collect a bodyguard of several thousand men from Cæsar's veterans. Now he obtained a law from the Assembly authorizing him to exchange the Macedonian governorship for the governorship of the province of northern Italy — now held by Decimus Brutus — and Provence in Gaul while continuing his command of four of the Macedonian legions that had been assembled by Cæsar for his eastern campaigns. Under this arrangement he would have troops fairly close to Rome which might be handy in the event of trouble. And his commission was extended for five years. Brutus and Cassius he recognized as sources of possible danger. It would be prudent to get them out of the country. He induced the Senate to give them temporary assignments; Brutus to supervise the export of grain from Asia Minor, Cassius from Sicily.

Cicero was outraged over this slight to his " heroes " as he called the assassins, and so were they.

In a letter to Atticus he gives a lively account of a family council at Antium that he attended early in June at which Brutus, Cassius, and three women of the family were present. " I advised Brutus," he writes, " to accept the grain-purchasing office in Asia Minor. I urged that all we could do now was to consult for his safety; that on him depended the defence of the Constitution itself. I had just got well into my speech when Cassius came in. I repeated the remarks. Whereupon Cassius with flashing eyes — you would have said he was breathing war — declared he would not go to Sicily. 'Am I to take an insult as a favour?' 'What are you going to do, then?' said I. He said he would go to Achaia [in Greece]. 'And you, Brutus?' said I. 'To Rome, if you think it is right.' 'I don't think so at all,' said I, 'for you won't be safe.' Then followed a long conversation in which they complained, especially Cassius, of the opportunities that had been let slip." Finally Servilia, Brutus' mother, promised to see that the grain commissionership should be cut out of the senatorial decree, and " Brutus was induced to give up that foolish talk of going to Rome." Cicero was disgusted with the indecision of his two friends. " I found a ship," he says, " with timbers coming loose, the vessel breaking up. No plan, no system, no method! "

Through the summer the jockeying for position between Antony and Octavian continued. They tried to disguise the fact that they were opposing each other, Dio says, although in reality they had become enemies. " To a casual observer Antony, as consul, seemed to be getting the better of his adversary. In reality the support of the mass of the people went to Octavian." Dio's analysis of the situation is acute. The people were for Cæsar's heir, he writes, partly because of sentimental regard for the great name he now bore, partly because of his promises, but most of all because they were always for the outs as against the ins. In other words the government in office never was able to satisfy them and they always hoped to benefit from a change. Consequently the young aspirant for power was becoming a growing menace. The moderates had had enough of civil war and they saw no reason for an armed conflict to gratify a young man's personal ambitions. But a stable government was not what Octavian wanted. It would leave him in a permanently subordinate position with many years to wait before he would come of legal age for the consulship. To prevent any such settlement he was ready to make the country pay in blood.

In these circumstances Antony was forced to attempt to reconstruct the coalition he had organized immediately after the death of Cæsar. He believed he had the Cæsarians. He needed the Conservatives. In August he made a conciliatory speech appealing to the Old Guard and summoned the Senate to meet on September 1. Cicero had been wandering about his villas since shortly after the assassination. He had no stomach to stay in Rome to vindicate his dignity against the forces of the powerful consul. In late summer he decided to make a trip to Athens to see his son. This would keep him out of the country until the new consuls should be installed in January. Driven back by unfavourable winds after his embarkation, he got reports that Antony was listening to reason. Accordingly he determined to return to the capital and take his place in the Senate. Before reaching there, however, he learned that Antony had recovered some of his confidence and his mood was no longer conciliatory. Cicero heard also that he had been criticized for running away from a fight. To live up to his reputation as the most distinguished ex-consul and to sustain his prestige it was imperative that he speak out.

On September 2 he made the first of the series of speeches against Antony which Cicero himself called his *Philippics*, borrowing the name from the speeches of Demosthenes against Philip of Macedon, father of Alexander the Great. He began by telling the Senate that he had been on guard in Rome and had not left the city since the death of Cæsar, although every man present must have known better. Then after commending the consul for his early attitude of conciliation he launched into a criticism of his subsequent course. By Ciceronian standards the speech was moderate in tone. But it was plain notice to Antony that he could not depend on the support of Cicero or the senatorial group for which he spoke. This was a blow to the consul and his coalition plans. Under growing apprehension of the encirclement policy of Octavian, who was winning the support of an increasing number of Cæsar's followers, as well as of the senatorial crowd, Antony fell into a state of nerves. He retired to his country house and according to Cicero went on a protracted drunk, in the course of which he composed a savage reply to the elder statesman's attack, which he later delivered in the Senate. In this he outraged Cicero's feelings by reading the letter previously mentioned in which his opponent had professed his warm regard for the consul. This provoked Cicero into writing the *Second Philippic*, which was greatly admired in antiquity as a perfect example of invective. Juvenal called it "divine." Tastes change. It impresses at least one modern reader as a piece of mendacious scurrility. The author accuses Antony of cowardice and most of the other crimes he can lay his pen to. The man ought to be executed as a criminal. He ought to be assassinated as a tyrant. If Cicero had been in the conspiracy against Cæsar Antony would not have been left alive. In short the *Second Philippic* was a challenge to the death. While it was composed in the form of a speech it never was delivered, but later was circulated as a pamphlet.

A few months earlier Cicero had proclaimed his disinterested patriotism in the Senate. "My likes and dislikes," he had said, "never have been determined by personal considerations, but always by regard for the common welfare." He seems to have been sincerely under this illusion. It never occurred to him that by a curious coincidence his personal feelings and his conception of the public welfare always marched hand in hand. His contemporaries took another view. "What was your private and personal quarrel with

Antony?" Brutus inquired of Cicero later. Dio, depending on earlier authorities, found the explanation for Cicero's turning to Octavian in his "bitter hatred of Antony." Plutarch voices the same opinion. His contemporaries and the later writers perhaps understood Cicero's weaknesses better than he himself understood them. Their judgments are borne out by the evidence.

We note that at about the time Cicero was working on this venomous political document he was writing his charming essay *On Friendship*, which contains such expressions as: "Robbing life of friendship is like robbing the world of the sun"; "the effect of friendship is to make, as it were, one soul out of many"; "in case discord arises among friends our care should be that the friendships appear to have burned out rather than to have been stamped out." Nothing gives a more vivid idea of the difference between Cicero as a public man and as a man of letters than the contrast between the hysterical invective of the *Second Philippic* and the coincident placid treatise *On Friendship*.

It was now borne in on Antony that his proposed coalition was being constructed, but that it was being constructed by his young rival, who was taking both the Conservatives and the Cæsarians away from him. He was forced to make a choice and in October he plumped for Cæsar's adherents. For the first time he denounced the tyrannicides and proclaimed that so long as he was alive there would be no room in the state for them. He was dangerously late. Octavian's agents had been busy with money to hire a private army. Antony hurried to Brindisi to meet the four legions from Macedonia that had been allotted to him, intending to march at their head to his northern Italian province. Its governor, Decimus Brutus, had given notice that he would refuse to recognize the law turning over the province to Antony and would not surrender it. The consul was to find that two of his legions had been bought out from under him by the agents of Octavian. With the other two he started north to dispossess the recalcitrant governor.

The raising of an army by a private citizen was illegal, even treasonable. But questions of legality did not trouble the young man on his road to power. It would be interesting to know where he got the money to overbid the consul for soldiers and to pay them after they were in service. In April at Brindisi he had had access to state funds intended by Cæsar for his eastern campaigns. As a private citizen he would have had no right to dip into these. But any qualms would have been stilled by the reflection that the goodness of the cause — his cause — justified anything he might find it necessary to do. The fact that he was able to outbid his rival, incidentally, makes us wonder about the charges of Antony's looting the treasury. If he had had $35,000,000 at his disposal he should not have been so hard up. Octavian may have obtained additional resources from financiers who hoped to cash in on his success. There were men whom Cæsar had enriched, including some of his freedmen, to whom his heir might confidently turn. To obtain the backing of wealth has been the familiar practice of aspirants for power down to modern times. The great financial interests of Paris threatened by a hostile and incompetent Directory financed Napoleon in the revolution of Brumaire. Italian big business supported Mussolini to stop the spread of anarchy. The German industrialists financed the rise of Hitler. Roman business men could have had little confidence in the hot-tempered, roistering Antony. In Octavian they recognized a man of their own sort, shrewd, thrifty, restrained, from a substantial middle-class family. They got their reward when the young revolutionist Octavian developed into the world-organizer Augustus.

CHAPTER XXIV

LAST CRUSADE

IN FORMING his coalition against Antony Octavian realized the importance of Cicero's influence. Where Antony had failed he hoped by flattery and deference to succeed. It was not easy. Soon after his arrival at the home of his stepfather at Puteoli he had met the elder statesman, who owned the adjoining villa. At once he had set out to make an impression. Cicero wrote to Atticus that the boy was devoted to him. Soon Octavian was calling him "father." Nevertheless the older man was wary. "It is impossible for him to be a good citizen," he told Atticus. "He is surrounded by such a number of people who even threaten our friends [the conspirators] with death. He says the present state of things is unendurable. But what do you think of it when a boy like that goes to Rome, where our liberators cannot be in safety?"

By early autumn, however, Cicero, in spite of his misgivings, was beginning to consider the possibility of playing off Octavian against Antony. Once more we are impressed by the way in which personal feeling affected his judgment. Strict constitutionalist though he thought himself, he was ready to swallow the illegality of Octavian's procedure in raising a private army, while he was outraged that Antony as consul in legal command of troops should pay them in an attempt to hold their loyalty against the bribes of Octavian. He grasped at any rumour that reflected upon the consul, while he was ready to overlook or justify any action by the young man who was deliberately scheming as a private citizen to bring on civil war. A typical instance of his attitude occurs in a speech in which he builds a case against Antony on a rumour that the consul had threatened to enter and leave Rome at will after his term as consul had expired and while he was in command of troops as proconsul — a procedure forbidden by the Constitution. A rumour of something that Antony was reported to have said he would do the next year is blown up into flagrant defiance of law. The attack is in the familiar technique of American as well as Roman politics, not to be taken too seriously.

While Octavian had made progress in collecting a private army, he saw he needed senatorial support to legalize his position and to provide him government troops. To carry out this plan Cicero could be of great help. By November he was deluging the elder statesman with letters, all of which he was able to suppress when he came to power so that they do not appear in Cicero's published correspondence. They might have proved embarrassing. Cicero was flattered, intrigued, and temporarily flustered by these advances. "I don't trust the youth," he writes to Atticus. "I am in the dark as to his intentions. . . . Varro doesn't like the young man's plans. I don't agree with him. He has forces on which he can depend. He can count on Decimus Brutus [with troops in northern Italy], and is making no secret of his intentions. He is organizing his men in companies at Capua. He is paying them their bounty money. War seems to be coming nearer and nearer. Do answer this letter." Atticus seems to have replied urging caution, for a fortnight later Cicero writes: "I quite agree with you that if Octavian gets much power the acts of the tyrant will be confirmed much more decisively than they were by the Senate last March. But if he is beaten you can see that Antony will become intolerable. So you can't tell which to prefer."

Cicero finally decided he preferred Octavian. At once the young adventurer was transformed in his eyes into a White Knight battling for a holy cause, while Antony became forthwith an evil fellow, not to be endured. When the elder statesman went to Rome in December 44 the prospect for peace was not hopeless. Antony was in a legal position; legal, his opponents would have said, by duress because of his bodyguard. Still it may be assumed that the Assembly which had supported Cæsar would have voted the provincial commands to Cæsar's marshal irrespective of the bodyguard. And now Antony was on his way to exercise his legal claim to the province which Decimus Brutus, in defiance of the law, was determined not to surrender. In this situation only the extremists were ready to permit their hatred of Antony to carry them into civil war. The moderates, still a majority, hoped the consul would be willing to accept the same semi-constitutional position of pre-eminence at which Pompey had aimed. Such an outcome, they believed, while unsatisfactory, would be better than the misery of armed conflict.

But now they had Cicero and his impassioned oratory to reckon with. For all his uncertainties about Octavian, he believed he saw a way out. His indignation against Antony had aroused the fanaticism that often clouded his judgment. He realized that something more than oratory was needed in the crisis. Speeches, no matter how furious, merely meant " words against weapons," as he wrote to a friend, and words would not avail against " the most abandoned gladiator in the world." Octavian was collecting the weapons. A brilliant opportunity seemed to offer itself to Cicero's excited imagination. He would play off Octavian against Antony until Antony should be destroyed. Then he would put Cæsar's young relative in his place and establish senatorial authority, perhaps with himself as first citizen and director of the policy of the state. " Octavian," he said later, " is to be complimented, distinguished, and extinguished." Unfortunately the sentiment was repeated to the victim of the pun. He did not need the information to see through Cicero's scheme. His retort to the epigram was that he did not propose to give them a chance to get rid of him. He was playing his own game of intrigue, but playing it more cleverly than the older man.

Cicero threw himself into the struggle with all the flaming energy he had shown against Catiline. After twenty years of frustration and humiliation he would make up for past weaknesses by boldly coming to the front as the saviour of his country. In a series of frantic speeches he denounced Antony and extolled Octavian. Stifling his distrust of Cæsar's heir, he assured the Senate he knew all the young man's innermost thoughts and could guarantee his loyalty to the Republic. "Nothing is dearer to him," he thundered, "than the state, nothing more important than your authority, nothing more desirable than the opinion of good men, nothing sweeter than genuine glory. . . . I promise, I undertake, I solemnly engage, Senators, that Octavian will always be such a citizen as he is today and as we should especially wish and pray he should be." We can imagine the complacency with which the ambitious aspirant for power heard the reports of the clean bill of health given him by the man he had taken into camp.

There were many Romans who knew Cicero well enough to distrust his zealous moods of righteous indignation. They had had experience of the frightfulness of civil war. After one of the first engagements a provincial governor was to write: "Think of the desolation of Italy and all the fine soldiers killed." Others felt as he did and were ready to go to almost any length to avoid armed conflict, which so far as they could see would only pull down one potential autocrat to put another in his place.

Marcus Brutus, who had assumed the governorship of Macedonia, was outraged by Cicero's policy. He wrote a sharp letter to his old friend taking him to task for his readiness to exchange the tyranny of Cæsar for the tyranny of Cæsar's heir. Cicero's course, he said, had cut him to the heart. To Atticus he wrote a keen analysis of the elder statesman. "I know," he says, "that Cicero does everything with the best intentions — for what could be clearer to me than his devotion to the Republic? But cautious though he is, he seems to me in certain matters to have acted — how shall I put it? – imprudently, or to make himself popular. For in upholding the republican cause he has deliberately antagonized the powerful Antony. I don't know what to say except the one thing, that the boy's ambition and unscrupulousness have been rather provoked than repressed by Cicero. . . . How strange is the blindness of fear! While taking precautions against what you dread, actually to invite danger and to bring it upon you, though you might perhaps have avoided it altogether! . . . So long as Cicero has people from whom to get what he wants and by whom to be made much of and flattered, he has no aversion to servitude, if it be but tempered by a show of respect. Therefore though Octavian call Cicero 'father,' consult him in everything, praise and thank him, nevertheless the truth will come out that words do not agree with deeds." Time was to vindicate his prophecy.

In the face of the opposition of the moderates who still hoped for an accommodation Cicero pressed the extremist position. He wanted Antony declared a public enemy. He urged an all-out war. He could not carry the Senate with him. Over his bitter opposition delegates were sent to Antony to negotiate on terms. Cicero denounced the majority members as timid souls and prayed for the failure of the peace mission. He was manœuvring Antony into the same position that Cæsar was in before he crossed the Rubicon, with the same alternatives of being destroyed or waging a civil war. The terms Antony proposed were fairly reasonable; certainly a basis for negotiation. The zealous Cicero would have none of them. In his inflamed view they were intolerable. He was violently against any settlement that did not involve Antony's destruction.

By this time the extremists under Cicero's leadership were in the saddle. They had overborne the moderates, as the extremists had overborne the peace party in the critical days before Cæsar crossed the Rubicon. The Senate had been whipped into line. The war was on. Octavian's position had been legalized by senatorial decree, and in accordance with his plans he now commanded troops as the representative of the government. The next step was to move in support of Decimus Brutus against Antony. At first the government troops were successful. Antony was defeated and forced to retreat. But of the two consuls who had held the chief command for the Senate one had fallen, the other had been mortally wounded, and Octavian showed a strange indisposition to join Decimus Brutus in the pursuit. Appian says this was because Brutus was one of the assassins. His attitude involved more than that. Cæsar's heir was approaching a position where he could deal with Antony on approximately equal terms. He needed his rival for a combination against the forces gathering in support of the Senate. His purpose was to impress, not to destroy him.

Cicero became uneasy. Marcus Brutus had troops in Macedonia, Cassius had taken over Syria and had raised an army. Both had acted without legal warrant. "There is a higher law than the Constitution," exclaimed William H. Seward in 1850. Cicero appealed to the higher law when he said in a speech that Cassius had acted "by a decree of Jupiter himself that whatever is salutary for the state should be considered legal and right." As to what was good for the state Cicero believed himself a competent judge. At his suggestion the Senate confirmed Brutus and Cassius in their positions, and then adopted a resolution inviting Brutus to come to the aid of the republican forces in Italy. Brutus ignored it, and Cicero repeatedly wrote urging him to respond to the Senate's call. In one of these letters Cicero shows his misgivings. Octavian was beginning to reach for one of the vacant consulships, which he saw he needed in order to strengthen his position in negotiating with Antony. The fact that he was more than twenty years under the legal age did not disturb him. The Senate could grant a special dispensation for his candidacy. Cicero attributed his ambition to the influence of certain unprincipled persons. Up to this time, he writes to Brutus, Octavian had been wholly governed by his advice — a complacent delusion. Now he is constantly admonishing the young man by letter to abandon his consular ambitions. But he is fearful of the outcome. Argument unsupported by arms gets nowhere in Rome. "Each man," he says, "claims to be powerful in the Republic in proportion to his physical force. Reason, moderation, law, custom, duty — all go for nothing. . . . If Octavian keeps his word and follows my counsel, I think we shall have protection enough. But if the counsels of the disloyal have greater weight than mine, or if the weakness of his age proves unequal to the strain, our whole hope is in you. So fly here, I implore you, and put the last touch to the freedom of a state which you liberated by courage and high spirit." But Brutus had no confidence in the republican leadership, in Cicero or in Octavian. As one of Cæsar's assassins he understood the position in which he would find himself if he transported his troops to Italy. His army would be hopelessly outclassed if the Cæsarian generals combined against him, as they doubtless would. The wiser course, he believed, was to unite his forces with those of Cassius and make a stand for the Republic in the East.

Conditions in Italy were increasingly critical. It had become necessary to impose special taxes to pay the bounties promised by Octavian to his soldiers. Taxes were unpopular then as always. "The greatest difficulty in the Republic," Cicero wrote, "is the want of money. The loyalists daily grow more callous to the call for the property tax. All that was collected by the one per cent income tax, owing to the shameless returns of the wealthy, is exhausted by the bounties given to two legions, leaving nothing for armies in the field." He was learning that unpaid troops without steady rations were not to be depended on.

Besides, Cicero's anxiety about Octavian was mounting. "The bitterest sorrow which is affecting me as I write this," he admitted to Brutus, "is that whereas the Republic accepted me as a surety for that youth, or I might almost say that boy, I seem scarcely able to make my promise good.

. . . However, I shall retain even him, I hope, in spite of many adverse influences. For he seems to me to have a character of his own, though he is at the pliable time of life and there are many prepared to corrupt him." It was not the first time that Cicero, carried away by enthusiasm, had been mistaken in his judgment.

His hopes were soon dashed. In spite of his efforts the Senate had snubbed the young commander. It did not matter. So far as the shrewd Octavian was concerned, his championship of the senatorial cause had been only a temporary expedient. He had much more far-reaching plans. To carry them out he recognized that it would be folly for the two Cæsarian forces, his and Antony's, to destroy each other and leave the field to the large senatorial armies that Brutus and Cassius had assembled beyond the Adriatic. He had been sounding out his realistic rival and had learned that he was ready for a deal. The young man judged that at last he could safely throw off all disguise and boldly apply for the consulship. In July he sent a party of centurions to Rome to carry his demands to the Senate. These included insistence on bonus money for the troops, authorization for him to run for the consulship, and the rescinding of the act under which Antony had been declared a public enemy. This last revealed his hand and foreshadowed the coming coalition. The senators temporized and spoke of Octavian's age as an objection. The soldiers were ready with the reply that age had been waived in many previous instances. When the Senate still hesitated the leader of the delegation threw back his cloak, showing the hilt of his sword, and exclaimed: "This will make him consul if you do not!"

Early in August came the news that Octavian had crossed the Rubicon — the second historic crossing of that stream by armed forces — and was marching on Rome at the head of eight legions. In a panic the Senate sent word that it would comply with his demands. Then it heard of the arrival in port of two legions summoned from Africa to join one that had remained in Rome. With a burst of hope it revoked its resolution. But the troops deserted to Octavian and he entered the city in triumph. There was a rush of senators to make their peace. Among them was Cicero.

"Ah!" exclaimed Octavian ironically, "the last of my friends to welcome me."

A rumour came that two of the legions had just heard they were to be used against the Senate and had revolted against Cæsar's heir. There was a hurried night meeting of senators, who were welcomed by Cicero at the door of the Senate chamber. While they were considering the possibilities of further resistance they learned that the rumour was false and Cicero fled, never again to see his beloved city. He must have received some hint that Octavian had relented. A fragment of a letter of humble thankfulness remains — the last we have from Cicero's pen. "I rejoice doubly," he said, "that you grant leave of absence to Philippus and myself, for it means pardon for the past and indulgence for the future." There is pathos in the fragment — the pathos of a once proud spirit now broken and crushed.

Octavian was elected consul with a relative, Q. Pedius, as colleague, and the Senate, completely cowed, provided for the prosecution of Cæsar's assassins *in absentia*. They were tried and outlawed. Decimus Brutus, fleeing to join Marcus Brutus in Macedonia, was killed on Antony's orders by Celtic brigands who had captured him. Three Cæsarian provincial governors with their forces had joined Antony. Cicero by pleas and arguments had tried to hold them in line for the senatorial cause. A letter to one of them, his young friend Plancus, still moves the reader. In essence it says: "It is not the great Cicero full of honours and renown who speaks. It is the old man who has nothing more to expect from life, who is nearing its end and points out the road to one who is about to enter on it. It is the friend who loves Plancus like a son and whose fatherly affection is perhaps injudicious because it is too wholehearted. For what hope can there be in a state in which everything is held down by the arms of the most violent and headstrong of men; in which neither Senate nor people has any power or control; in which there are neither laws nor law courts — in fact no shadow or trace even of a Constitution?" There is no doubt of Cicero's devotion to liberty and the Republic, no matter how much it was intermingled with his hatred for Antony. But in the existing situation the alternative to Antony was not, as Cicero assumed, liberty under law, but autocratic rule by another man who could command the loyalty of the armed forces.

This condition, recognized by more practical men, made Cicero's appeals to the governors perfectly futile. Even if they had so desired they probably could not have resisted the pressure from their troops. Too many of Cæsar's veterans were among them. Earlier in the campaign when the Senate had urged Octavian to help Decimus Brutus against Antony his troops had shown that they would not join one of Cæsar's assassins against Cæsar's marshal even if their commander had been willing. Decimus Brutus wrote to Cicero: "No one can control Octavian nor can Octavian control his own army — both most disastrous facts." It was not long before Brutus' soldiers were deserting to Antony.

The Cæsarian governors were themselves disaffected. They saw that the Senate was coming increasingly under control of the old crowd that had sided with Pompey against Cæsar. They regarded with apprehension the growing strength of the armies in the East, which might come to the support of the senatorial government that they distrusted. The march of events drove the governors inexorably into Antony's camp. One of them, Lepidus, Cæsar's cavalry commander at the time of the assassination, joined with Antony in November in arranging a conference with Octavian on a little island in a tributary of the Po between Modena and Bologna. The three still did not trust one another and elaborate precautions were taken against treachery. If Appian is to be believed, after the leaders had withdrawn from their escorts they "searched one another carefully to make sure no one had a dagger concealed" — a fitting precaution in view of the bloody work ahead. In a two-day conference they portioned out the Roman world west of the Adriatic among them. Octavian was to give up his consulship. Another Committee of Three was to be established, the Second Triumvirate, with dictatorial powers for five years. The Three still had the armies of Brutus and Cassius in the East to deal with and their restless soldiers were clamouring for money. Nothing less than a very considerable redistribution of wealth would satisfy the proletarians who made up the armed forces. The leaders recognized they had no choice. "To encourage the army with expectation of booty," Appian says, "the generals promised them, besides other gifts, eighteen cities of Italy as colonies — cities which excelled in wealth, in the splendour of their estates and houses — which were to be divided among the soldiers, lands, buildings, and all, just as if they had been captured from an enemy in war." Two famous sufferers from the confiscations later became world figures. The property of Virgil near Mantua was in the territory seized for the soldiers, as was the estate that Horace had inherited from his father at Venusia.

There was a more immediate source of loot. It arose in connection with another policy. If the troops were to be transferred beyond the Adriatic the Three could not take chances of an uprising at home while they were away. They had had a vivid demonstration of the results of Cæsar's policy of clemency. They would not repeat his mistake. Their enemies must be destroyed before they left. If they made the list sufficiently inclusive, after the example set by Sulla, the confiscation of the property of the men proscribed would furnish ready cash to keep the soldiers quiet; and they were "short of money," the ancient historian writes. Some of the men were put on the list, he continues, because they had handsome villas or city residences. It may have been a disagreeable job for the Three. But as Cicero had said many years earlier, men's senses become blunted when they are accustomed to cruelty. The names of some three hundred senators and two thousand wealthy business men were selected. There is no record of any qualms except in one case. Plutarch has given a graphic description of the trading. For two days, he said, Octavian tried to save Cicero, but on the third gave him up. These were the terms agreed upon: Octavian was to abandon Cicero to his fate; Lepidus, his brother Paulus; and Antony, Lucius Cæsar, his uncle on his mother's side. Shakespeare has pictured the scene in a familiar passage:

ANTONY. *These many, then, shall die: their names are pricked.*
OCTAVIUS. *Your brother too must die; consent you, Lepidus?*
LEPIDUS. *I do consent —*
OCTAVIUS. *Prick him down, Antony.*
LEPIDUS. *Upon condition Publius shall not live,*
Who is your sister's son, Mark Antony.
ANTONY. *He shall not live; look, with a spot I damn him.*

While official massacres had become unhappily familiar in the last century of the Republic, later writers shuddered at the cruelty of the Three and especially at the fate of the great man of letters who was involved in the general purge. Writers of the Augustan age, except Livy, were prudently silent on the subject. Augustus himself in his official record of his life preserved in the celebrated inscription at Ankara, Turkey, ignores unpleasant details of his earlier rise to power. But it was observed that after he had established himself as Emperor, he went out of his way to honour Cicero's worthless son. Plutarch tells a story of the Emperor's later life that may have significance. He surprised one of his grandsons reading a book. In alarm the boy hid it under his cloak. Augustus took it from him. It was one of Cicero's. He stood reading it a long time. Then handing it back he said: " A learned man, my boy, a learned man, and a lover of his country."

With the post-Augustan historians there was a disposition to find extenuating circumstances for the young Octavian and to put the chief blame on Antony. Perhaps this had become the official version. "Octavian seems to have taken part in the business," Dio writes, "merely because of his sharing in the authority, since he himself had no need at all to kill a large number, for he was not naturally cruel." "Octavian protested," says another historian, Velleius Paterculus, "but without avail, being but one against two." And he launches into a bitter attack. "You accomplished nothing, Mark Antony," he writes, "—for my indignation compels me to speak—you accomplished nothing by the murder of this great man who once had saved the state. You took from Marcus Cicero a few years of old age, but you did not rob him of his fame and the glory of his deeds and words. He lives and will continue to live in the memory of the ages, while your deed will be execrated." According to Florus, writing early in the second century, "the crimes of the proscriptions were largely the work of Antony and Lepidus. Octavian contented himself with proscribing his adoptive father's murderers, for fear his death might be considered to have been deserved if it had remained unavenged." On the other hand Suetonius, the impartial biographer of Augustus, says that though for some time he tried to prevent a proscription, "yet when it was begun he carried it through with greater severity than either of his associates." He was traditionally thorough.

A devil's advocate could make a case for Antony against Cicero in the conditions then existing. Cicero had been his implacable foe. Repeatedly he had said that if he had been in the conspiracy Antony would not have been left alive. He had called for the legal lynching of his enemy and for his assassination as a tyrant. He had been the head and front of the senatorial war upon Antony and had insisted on having him voted a public enemy. If Cicero had had the power he would have had Antony done to death. It is hardly surprising that Antony should have insisted that his bloodthirsty enemy be put out of the way. We may deplore the fate of one of the outstanding benefactors of civilization.

Sentiment should not blind us to the fact that he invited it.

As to the position of Octavian, it is quite possible that he made an effort on Cicero's behalf. After all, the elder statesman had been his champion before the Senate and now was too broken to be dangerous. But Octavian knew that Cicero had been playing a game and would have been willing to discard him if the occasion had seemed favourable. Antony, he recognized, had received immense provocation. He was much older and more distinguished than Octavian, and more powerful. It would not do to antagonize him. As to the proscriptions in general, the young man was utterly ruthless. The situation was still full of danger. He could not afford to be squeamish.

At the end of the conference the arrangements were announced to the soldiers, who received the news of prospective loot with enthusiasm. The proscription list was suppressed for the time. Later the official justification was posted in Rome. The Three called attention to the fact that Cæsar's policy of conciliation had failed; that the men spared by Cæsar had combined to murder him and to involve the country in civil war; that these men had declared the Three public enemies (not strictly true, for Octavian had not been so declared); that they were about to set out on a war overseas and they did not consider it safe to leave enemies behind to take advantage of their absence and watch for opportunities to make trouble. They thought it better to omit any reference to the detail that mass murder was to be made the instrument for raising necessary funds.

While civilized men cannot condone the purges of either ancient or modern times, by the standards of the age the Three were justified in having their enemies summarily destroyed. In their murders for confiscation of property they themselves felt they were on much more debatable ground, as is evidenced by their significant silence. But their official defence was based on pitiless logic.

Before starting with their troops for Rome the Three sent forward to the city a preliminary list of a dozen or more names of men to be at once put out of the way, including Cicero. The message was directed to Pedius, Octavian's colleague in the consulship. The news of the purge created a panic. But Pedius, who did not know that a longer list was coming, tried to reassure those who thought they might be included. Only these few, he said, were to be executed. It is an incidental tribute to his humane feeling that within twenty-four hours he died, presumably from a heart attack produced by the executions for which he was responsible. When the complete lists were posted, there was a hideous Reign of Terror of which we have vivid accounts in the ancient historians. It has remained a terrible fact through the intervening centuries that civilization always has been thin in spots. Evidently there were educated Romans wearing the toga, the garb of respectability, who were carried in fashionable litters to the theatre and yet had the mental processes of their barbaric ancestors. Just as today there are Europeans wearing evening clothes who drive in limousines to listen to Wagnerian operas, and yet are living mentally in the Stone Age.

In addition to Marcus Cicero himself the Three had proscribed his son Marcus, his brother Quintus, and his nephew the younger Quintus. The son was safe in Macedonia with Brutus, the nephew was in Rome. The brothers were at Marcus' villa at Tusculum when they heard the news. Some of the prominent victims were permitted to live, including Lepidus' brother and Antony's uncle, and many others fled to safety. Cicero had plenty of time to escape. But in the collapse of his world his characteristic indecision had grown and he could not make up his mind what to do. He was worn out and he felt that life held nothing worth while. The brothers decided to go to Marcus' island villa at Astura, to which he had retreated after Tullia's death. From there they could sail to join Brutus in Macedonia.

On the way Quintus Cicero remembered that they had little money with them. He determined to let his older brother continue his flight while he would return to Rome for funds and then hurry after Marcus. With his hot temper and arbitrary disposition he probably had been a harsh master, for his slaves betrayed him – in sharp contrast to the conduct of the slaves of Marcus. His son Quintus, who had behaved like a rotter on various occasions, redeemed himself at the end. He hid his father. When the assassins arrived he refused under torture to reveal the hiding-place. The elder Quintus learned what was going on, came out and surrendered. Each asked that he be killed before the other. The murderers complied with their requests by killing father and son simultaneously.

Marcus embarked at Astura and sailed down the coast a few miles to Capo Cirello. There was a heavy swell and "he could no longer put up with the tossing of the ship," Livy says. Or, as Appian puts it more frankly, "he could not endure the seasickness." Insisting on going ashore, the confused and frantic man started on foot on the long road to Rome. Then, according to Plutarch, "becoming distracted and again changing his mind, he turned aside to his villa at Astura, and there spent the night in terrified and hopeless reflection." The next morning he allowed his slaves to persuade him to go by boat down the coast round Capo Cirello to the port of Gaeta close to his villa at Formiæ, where he might embark again for Macedonia. But he was "weary of flight and of life" and he went ashore to rest at his villa. A flash of his old vanity gave him a moment's comfort. "Let me die," he exclaimed, "in this country I have so often saved." The classic and moving account of the final scene is given by Plutarch with legendary and eerie details:

There was at Gaeta a chapel of Apollo, not far from the sea, from which a flock of crows rose screaming, and made toward Cicero's vessel as it rowed to land, and lighting on both sides of the yardarm, some kept cawing and others pecked the ends of the ropes. This was looked upon by all on board as an omen of evil. Cicero landed and, entering his house, lay lown upon his bed to take some rest. Many of the crows settled about the window, making a dismal cawing. One of them alighted upon the bed where Cicero lay covered, and with its beak tried little by little to draw the cover from his face. His servants seeing this blamed themselves that they should stay to see their master slain and do nothing in his defence, while the brute creatures came to help take care of him in his undeserved troubles. Therefore, partly by entreaty, partly by force, they took him up and carried him in his litter toward the sea.

But in the meantime the assassins were come, Herennius a centurion, and Popillius a tribune, whom Cicero had formerly defended when prosecuted for the murder of his father. Soldiers were with them. Finding the doors locked, they broke them open. When Cicero did not appear, and those in the house said they did not know where he was, it is stated that a young man to whom Cicero had given a liberal education, an emancipated slave of his brother Quintus, named Philologus, informed the tribune that the litter was on its way to the sea through the dark wood. The tribune, taking a few men with him, hurried to the place where he was to come out, while Herennius ran down the path after him. Cicero saw him running and commanded his servants to set down the litter. Then stroking his chin, as he used to do, with his left hand, he looked steadfastly upon his murderers, his person covered with dust, his beard and hair untrimmed, his face haggard with anxiety. So most of those that stood by covered their faces while Herennius slew him. He thrust out his head from the litter and Herennius cut it off. Then by Antony's command he cut off his hands also, by which the Philippics *were written.*

When these members were brought to Rome Antony was holding an Assembly for the choice of public officers; and when he heard it, and saw them, he cried out: " Now let there be an end of our proscriptions! " He commanded the head and hands to be fastened up over the rostra, where the orators spoke; a sight which the Roman people shuddered to behold, and they believed they saw there, not the face of Cicero, but the image of Antony's own soul.

It was on the 7th of December 43 that Cicero died. He lacked less than a month of being sixty-four years old.

The next year the combined Republican forces under Brutus and Cassius were defeated by Antony and Octavian at Philippi in Macedonia. Cassius and then Brutus committed suicide.

A curious fact is noted by Suetonius. He remarks that hardly any of Cæsar's assassins survived him for more than three years or died a natural death. "They were all condemned and they perished in various ways — some by shipwreck, some in battle; some took their own lives with the very dagger with which they had killed Cæsar."

Gradually the Triumvirate disintegrated. First the inconsequential Lepidus was frozen out. In 31 Octavian defeated Antony at Actium and on Antony's suicide the next year became the undisputed ruler of the Roman world. The greatest and most promising democratic experiment of ancient times had failed. It had failed because of the deterioration of the national character under the impact of economic forces that shortsighted selfishness had allowed to get out of hand. The leading men, Tacitus wrote in the next century, preferred immediate ease and safety to the danger of contending for ancient freedom. The Romans had proved unequal to the delicate and difficult task of combining liberty with the organization needed to operate an effective government. They had surrendered freedom for security and order.

Under this security, protected by what the elder Pliny called "the boundless majesty of the Roman peace," Italy and the Empire entered upon a long era of material wellbeing. Greco-Roman civilization gained the opportunity to establish and maintain itself against the waves of barbarism that beat upon its frontiers. This was the achievement of

Augustus and his successors to which the modern world is profoundly indebted. The price was high. Eventually under the new order character withered. The spirit of initiative and independence gave way to servility. In the mordant words of the Roman historian who witnessed the effects of autocracy: " Genius died by the same blow that ended public liberty."

CHAPTER XXV

THE TWO CICEROS

FROM OUTSTANDING contemporaries we have two keen estimates of Cicero as a statesman. The historian Livy, who was sixteen years old at the time of Cicero's death, gives this appraisal: "Cicero lived sixty-three years, so that even if he had not died by violence, his death cannot seem untimely. The rich products of his genius were amply rewarded. He enjoyed years of prosperity. But his long career of good fortune was interrupted from time to time by serious disasters – exile, the ruin of the party he championed, the sad and untimely death of his daughter. Of all these disasters he bore as became a man none except his death. A true judgment might have found this less deserved in that he suffered at the hands of his enemy no more cruel fate than he would himself have inflicted had he been equally fortunate. Yet if one weighs his virtues with his faults, he deserves a place in history as a truly great man, and another Cicero would be required to praise him adequately."

The second judgment comes from Pollio, a Cæsarian soldier who joined Octavian and later became a distinguished man of letters. Pollio's verdict has the greater force because he was in opposition to Cicero. "His numerous and imperishable works," he writes, "make it superfluous to recount the genius and industry of this great man." Summarizing his career he adds: "Would that he had been able to endure prosperity with greater self-control, and adversity with greater fortitude! For whenever either had fallen to his lot he thought it would not change. Hence arose those violent storms of unpopularity and hence his personal enemies had greater confidence in attacking him; for he invited enmity with greater spirit than he fought it. But since no mortal is blessed with perfect virtue, a man must be judged by that virtue on which the greater part of his life and genius has been based. And I should not have thought his end was to be pitied had not he himself thought death so great a misfortune."

With these estimates may be placed the significant omission of Cicero's name by an objective historian of his time. Sallust writes that within his memory "there have appeared two men of towering merit, though of diverse character, Marcus Cato and Gaius Cæsar." The failure to mention Cicero recalls the reply of a French musical critic to a composer who reproached him for falling asleep during a concert: "Sleep also is a criticism."

These contemporary comments point to the weaknesses as well as to the strength of Cicero as a public man. He was too sensitive, too vain, too dominated by personal feeling, too open to impressions, to become a great leader of men. At times he saw both sides of public questions too vividly to enable him to make up his mind, close it to all doubts, and drive ahead. At other times, when his hatreds became engaged — and he was a fierce hater — he would plunge forward recklessly. To steadier men he gave the impression of inconsistency and of being motivated by what Plutarch calls his "passion for glory." From his own standpoint he was not inconsistent. He was working at all times toward what he regarded as good and stable government and the preservation of the Republic. Early in his career he reacted against the brutality and tyranny of the aristocratic regime set up by Sulla and favoured an extension of democratic control. Later what he regarded as the excesses of democracy turned him to ardent support of senatorial pre-eminence. The fact that this meant the perpetuation in power of an incompetent and selfish oligarchy disturbed him at times. It did not swerve him from his course.

Cicero would have appreciated John Morley's remark that "in public life the choice is constantly between two evils and action is one long second best." He would have insisted that he acted in accordance with this maxim. But just here he made some of his greatest blunders. A successful American politician used to say that one of the differences between a politician and a statesman was this: In his necessary compromises a politician would often surrender essential principles. The statesman would surrender less important points, but would recognize that there were certain great principles for which he must put his back to the wall and fight. In such situations Cicero's judgment was often infirm and helped to break down his influence.

He had high ideals of provincial administration and his energetic prosecution of the corrupt provincial governor Verres was a fine effort toward reform. He largely nullified it by his readiness to defend governors who were known scoundrels. His political aim was to create his famous union of the orders, to bring the wealthy business men into an alliance with the aristocrats in the interest of orderly government. In pursuing this policy he was willing to throw justice to the winds and blindly support measures that he believed were scandalous and rotten. In the latter part of his life he lived in an atmosphere of unreality. Always a superb wishful thinker he was obsessed with the idea that if the state could only rid itself of one undesirable man after another the Republic of the previous century could be restored. He was blind to the fact that a situation had developed in which an ambitious commander of troops could dominate the civil authorities. In politics he was a visionary, not a realist. It might be said of him as was said of Edmund Burke, with whom he had much in common: "With his virtues and powers were conjoined defects which largely neutralized their influence. He was too literary to be a philosopher and too philosophic to be a politician."

I have referred to Cicero's kinship to the great eighteenth-century English liberal. Burke, first a defender of the liberties of the American colonists, later a foe to the liberties of the French people, was a conscious Ciceronian. "Cicero," says John Morley, "was ever to him the mightiest of the ancient names." On Cicero he modelled his oratorical style. In his famous prosecution of Warren Hastings for maladministration in India he quoted from Cicero against Verres. Like Cicero a New Man, he forced his way into the governing class. Like Cicero, when he had arrived he bought a great estate for which he went heavily in debt. The house at Beaconsfield, like the mansion on the Palatine, was adorned with art treasures. Burke's early liberalism was overborne finally by the excesses of the French Revolution, just as Cicero's was overborne by his distrust of the common people. The man who sympathized with the American colonists and the exploited millions of India had no word of sympathy for the miseries that provoked the Revolution in France. He utterly failed to grasp its meaning and in revulsion against the French democratic movement he even turned against parliamentary reform in England. With the same blindness Cicero was unmoved by the proletarian wretchedness around him and opposed measures for relief.

Another modern with whom Cicero might be compared is Alexander H. Stephens, Vice President of the Confederacy. Stephens has faded from the minds of the American people, but he was a great figure in his day. In an earlier chapter I have mentioned his letter-writing proclivities. There are striking similarities between him and Cicero besides their addiction to correspondence, which shows both of them, in the words of Stephens's biographer, "furiously longing for the applause of mankind."

Stephens's attitude toward his Confederate chief recalls that of Cicero toward Julius Cæsar. By his emergency war measures Jefferson Davis turned Stephens against him, as Cæsar alienated Cicero. Davis, Stephens thought, had overridden Congress and the Constitution and had made himself an imperial despot. Constitutional liberty, Stephens exclaimed, had ceased to exist. There were no ides of March for the Confederacy. But the Confederate Cicero did much to undermine the support of the key state of Georgia for the Richmond government, and in the disintegrating crisis of 1864–5 the state's influence was directed to destroying the Confederacy. On the same ground the influence of Cicero helped promote the destruction of Cæsar and the Cæsarian government.

But perhaps the nearest parallel to Cicero in our times is found in Guizot, of whom I have previously spoken. Like Cicero, Guizot was an eminent man of letters who tried to play the role of statesman. Historian, orator, letter-writer — his published works in many volumes include all these fields — he was long premier in the parliamentary monarchy of Louis Philippe, which went down in the Revolution of 1848 to be succeeded by the autocracy of the third Napoleon.

Social discontent overthrew the uninspired regime of the bourgeois King. "Guizot," writes E. L. Woodward in his *Three Studies in European Conservatism*, "did not ask how far disorder was the result of material conditions in which liberty was only unchecked opportunity of the strong to exploit the weak" — a precise description of the situation under the liberty of the Roman oligarchy which Cicero so stubbornly defended. We recall Mommsen's words: "Cæsar came to break the intolerable yoke of the aristocracy," and the remark of Ronald Syme of Oxford about the aim of the nobles supported by Cicero and the possessing classes "to perpetuate in Rome their harsh and hopeless rule."

For the six years preceding the overthrow of Louis Philippe, Guizot as premier brought forward no measure of social importance. His timid efforts at social reform were defeated by fear of offending business. Precisely the position taken by Cicero in allowing Roman business men to have their avaricious way.

One of Guizot's supporters, the president of the Chamber of Deputies, once said to the Chamber: "We are here to make laws, not to give work to workmen" — Cicero's position exactly. " In spite of child labor and long working hours," Mr. Woodward writes, " Guizot could say: ' All the great conquests have been made, all the great interests satisfied.' " Under a similar illusion Cicero gave hardly a thought to the three hundred and twenty thousand families on the dole.

Guizot and Cicero were both sincere defenders of liberty. But neither was able to discern the deeper signs of the times. Neither rose to the first rank in statesmanship.

In retrospect we see that Cicero was oblivious of the fundamental difficulties that confronted the Roman Republic. A statesman cannot be expected to be endowed with the wisdom that comes after the event. But the difficulties were not beyond the perception of the more penetrating political intellects of the last century of the Republic, the Gracchus brothers and Cæsar. The significance of certain obvious facts escaped the conventional mind of Cicero. He failed to take account of the economic evils of Roman society, divided, as Mommsen said, into " the world of beggars and the world of the rich." He recognized the feebleness and indifference of the owners of the big estates although he catered to them. He did not understand that the blind arrogance and selfishness of these natural leaders had alienated the loyalty of the soldiers from the state at a time when the needs of imperial defence had shifted authority to the holders of the great commands. He had no conception of the meaning of the rise of an embittered proletarian army representing an embittered world of beggars. Cicero's remedies were surface remedies and his defects as a politician prevented his carrying even these surface remedies to success. His political theories were better than his practical wisdom. It was left to the great organizer Augustus to create a system of government based in part upon theories set forth by the senatorial champion to whose death he had consented.

But if we are fairly to appreciate the man we must realize

that there were two Ciceros. One was Cicero the politician, who never attained the stature he fondly thought he had achieved. The other was Cicero the philosophical man of letters, whose work was destined to influence the world down to the present day. One was the recklessly vindictive Cicero of the *Second Philippic*. The other was the urbanely charming Cicero of the essay *On Friendship*. The political weaknesses of the first Cicero affected his own age. The reflections of the second Cicero have proved an inspiration to mankind. His influential words about true law as " right reason in harmony with Nature," I have already cited. His political writings are full of far-seeing wisdom which he did not know how to apply but to which future generations have listened, although too often with dull ears. It was the duty of a politician, he wrote, to " make the life of men safer and richer." There was no form of state more depraved, in his opinion, than that " in which the richest are accounted best." The way to put the welfare of the state in the best hands was for " a free people to choose the best men to govern them." Autocracy meant the end of freedom, for " in no state except that in which the people's power is supreme has liberty any dwelling-place, and surely nothing can be sweeter than liberty." It was from Cicero that the world first heard the still neglected admonition that " a war is never undertaken by the ideal state except in defence of its honour or its safety," and that war should have " no other object than to secure peace."

Classical scholars glow over the achievement of Cicero in enriching his native tongue and making it fit for use as the common language of Europe. Even in translation we notice his feeling for the right word and the telling phrase — " strain every nerve . . . easily first . . . the breeze of popular favour . . . old wives' tales . . . tried as by fire." His genius went further. An earlier chapter discussed his service to the intellectual leaders from antiquity through the Middle Ages down to the present time. " Without Cicero," writes a British scholar, J. W. Mackail, " the Middle Ages would not have had Augustine or Aquinas; but without him the movement which annulled the Middle Ages would have had neither Mirabeau nor Pitt."

Not only did he popularize ethics and philosophy. He wrote on these subjects in his essays, and on everyday matters in his letters, with such culture, such discrimination, such a rich background, that he lifted the whole level of discussion and thought of the European world. In sum he contributed vastly to the graciousness, the sparkle, the understanding, the urbanity, that are essential factors in civilized intercourse.

Cicero the politician died on that December day two thousand years ago. Cicero the great exponent of humane living still survives.

APPENDIX I

CHRONOLOGY OF CICERO'S LIFE

B C

106 **January 3.** Birth of Marcus Tullius Cicero at family home near Arpinum, sixty miles southeast of Rome. September 30, Birth of Pompey. Roman army reorganized on professional basis the previous year by Marius, self-made man. He conducts victorious war in Africa against Jugurtha, completed in 105, and introduces new system of army training in 104. (First consulship of Marius, 107. Birth of Atticus, 109.)

102 **Age 4.** Birth of Cicero's brother Quintus. Probable year of birth of Julius Cæsar, July 12. (Possibly the year was 100 or 101.) Marius stops German invaders in battle of Aix-en-Provence (Aquæ Sextiæ).

101 **Age 5.** Germans attempt another invasion of Italy through Brenner Pass; routed by Marius and Catulus in battle of the Raudine Plain, north of the Po. Marius becomes national hero.

100 **Age 6.** Sixth consulship of Marius. Rioting in Rome. Tribune Saturninus killed.

99 **Age 7.** Birth of Lucretius, philosophical poet (?).

97 **Age 9.** About this time (date not definitely known) the Ciceros move to Rome. Human sacrifices forbidden by law.

95 **Age 11.** Birth of Cato, reactionary leader, great-grandson of the famous Cato the Censor.

91 **Age 15.** Tribune Drusus attempts reform program including enfranchisement of Italian towns allied to Rome; assassinated. Failure of enfranchisement brings on Italian war (usually called the Social war; i.e., War of the *Socii*, or Allies).

90 **Age 16.** Cicero comes of age, assumes white toga of manhood. War continues. In Rome armed business men, the knights, force a bill through Assembly with drawn daggers in spite of tribunician veto, overriding civil government by violence.

89 **Age 17.** Cicero serves briefly in Italian war. Franchise concessions made which end war the next year. Cicero studies law with Scævola the Augur.

88 **Age 18.** Cicero studies philosophy and attends speeches of leading orators. Eighty thousand Romans, perhaps Italian traders, massacred in Asia Minor (first war with Mithridates); Sulla as consul given eastern command. Refuses to submit when superseded by law by Marius, marches on Rome; Marius flees; another demonstration of ascendancy of armed forces over civil government.

87 **Age 19.** Cicero attends lectures on rhetoric. Sulla departs for Asia; Marius seizes Rome; reign of terror, purge of aristocrats. Birth of Catullus (perhaps in 84) and Sallust.

86 **Age 20.** Cicero begins writing on rhetoric. His *Rhetorical Invention* (*De Inventione Rhetorica*)

is still extant, first of series completed much later. Death of Marius in seventh term as consul.

85–83 **Age 21–3.** Peace in Rome, with Sulla occupied in the East. Cicero devotes himself to studies and declamation. Sulla makes peace in 84, returns to Italy in 83. Second war with Mithridates. Birth of Marcus Junius Brutus, 85, and of Mark Antony, 83.

82 **Age 24.** Sulla establishes himself as dictator with proscription of wealthy business men, third seizure of Rome by armed forces in six years. Cicero attends lectures on public speaking.

81 **Age 25.** Sulla attempts by legislation to assure supremacy of senatorial oligarchy. Cicero's first extant plea in court, for one Quinctius. End of second Mithridatic war.

80 **Age 26.** Cicero's first big case, defence of Roscius of Ameria.

79 **Age 27.** Sulla abdicates. Cicero sets out with his brother and cousin for the grand tour of Greece and Asia Minor, with a stay of several months in Athens for post-graduate work. Meets Atticus in Athens. His first religious experience through initiation into Eleusinian Mysteries.

78 **Age 28.** Cicero travels in Asia Minor, meeting famous speakers, and studies public speaking at Rhodes. Death of Sulla.

77 **Age 29.** Cicero returns to Rome improved in health and in speaking; marries Terentia (?).

76 **Age 30.** Cicero busy in the courts. Elected finance officer (*quæstor*). Probable year of birth of his daughter Tullia, August 5.

75 **Age 31.** Finance officer in Sicily. Discovers tomb of Archimedes at Syracuse.

74 **Age 32.** Returns to Rome and engages in practice of law. Third war with Mithridates; Lucullus in chief command.

73–71 **Age 33–5.** Great slave revolt under Spartacus, gladiator. Spartacus defeated and killed by forces under Crassus in 71. Pompey returning from war in Spain mops up insurrectos. The two generals unite their troops outside of Rome and under pressure Senate waives legal disabilities and permits both to be elected to consulship for 70. During these years Cicero says he was working hard, presumably at his law practice.

70 **Age 36.** Cicero elected commissioner of public works (*ædilis curulis*); prosecutes Verres, corrupt governor of Sicily. Birth of Virgil.

69 **Age 37.** Cicero holds works commissionership. His brother Quintus marries Pomponia, sister of Atticus (?).

68 **Age 38.** Probable year of purchase of villas near Formiæ and Tusculum. Cæsar finance officer in Farther Spain (including Portugal). Death of Cicero's father.

67 **Age 39.** Cicero elected judge (*prætor*). Pompey given command against pirates. Birth of Cicero's nephew Quintus.

66 **Age 40.** Pompey supersedes Lucullus in command for war against Mithridates. Conferring of extraordinary powers for the command supported by Cicero, now judge of extortion court, in speech *For the Manilian Law* before preliminary session of Assembly. Quintus Cicero and Cæsar elected

commissioners of public works. Pompey overwhelms Mithridates.

65 **Age 41.** Cicero prepares for canvass for consulship. Birth of son Marcus, July. First conspiracy involving Catiline. Pompey continues conquest and reorganization of the East, completing work in 62. Birth of Horace, December 8.

64 **Age 42.** Quintus Cicero writes *Handbook of Politics* for his brother. Cicero denounces Catiline, rival candidate, in speech *In the White Toga*; elected consul with Antonius as colleague.

63 **Age 43.** Cicero consul, Cæsar leader of the opposition. Suppression of debtors' protest, headed by Catiline, and execution without trial of five men charged with conspiracy against the government and with plot to burn Rome. Cæsar elected chief pontiff (*pontifex maximus*) and judge with Quintus Cicero. Birth of Octavius (later Augustus) September 23. Marriage of Tullia to Piso.

62 **Age 44.** Catiline and followers killed in battle with state troops. Cicero defends poet Archias in court. Scandal of Clodius at rites of the Good Goddess. Quintus Cicero and Cæsar judges. Pompey returns to Italy at end of year.

61 **Age 45.** Clodius acquitted of sacrilege. Quintus governor of province of Asia, Cæsar of Farther Spain.

60 **Age 46.** Cicero writes history of his consulship in Greek. Cæsar returns from Spain and brings Pompey and Crassus into informal agreement with him to dominate legislation, First Triumvirate.

59 **Age 47.** Cæsar, as consul, puts legislative program through Assembly in spite of opposition of Sen-

ate and political use of omens by his colleague Bibulus to block all legislation. Shorthand reporters introduced into Senate and official record, *Daily Doings* (*Acta Diurna*) posted, to develop into first newspaper. Pompey marries Julia, Cæsar's daughter. Clodius adopted into plebeian family to become eligible for tribuneship, and elected tribune. Birth of Livy.

58 **Age 48.** Clodius drives Cicero into exile in March for having put to death Roman citizens (Catilinarian conspirators) without due process of law. Cæsar sets out as proconsul on first campaign in Gaul. Gangs of Clodius destroy Cicero's mansion on the Palatine and his villas at Tusculum and Formiæ.

57 **Age 49.** Law for recall of Cicero passed, August 4. He reaches Rome September 4. After vexatious delay is compensated by the state for property destroyed by Clodius. Death of Tullia's husband Piso.

56 **Age 50.** Triumvirate renewed at conference at Lucca. Cicero dragooned into its support. Tullia engaged and probably married to Furius Crassipes; soon divorced.

55 **Age 51.** Cæsar builds famous bridge across the Rhine; invades Britain. Cicero writes treatise *On the Character of the Orator* (*De Oratore*). Death of Lucretius (?).

54 **Age 52.** Cæsar's second invasion of Britain. Death of Pompey's wife Julia and of Catullus. Cicero begins book *On the Commonwealth* (*De Re Publica*). Crassus leaves for Asia to build military reputation. Rioting between gangs of Clodius and Milo.

53 **Age 53.** Crassus killed in battle with Parthians at Carrhæ. (Roman standards lost in this battle recovered by Augustus thirty-three years later.) Cicero elected to board of augurs. Rioting continues in Rome.

52 **Age 54.** Clodius killed by Milo's gangsters on the Appian Way. Great revolt in Gaul led by Vercingetorix crushed by Cæsar. Pompey sole consul. Obtains extension for several years of proconsular command of Spanish provinces, with permission to live in Rome. Cicero begins treatise *On the Laws* (*De Legibus*).

51 **Age 55.** Cicero goes to Cilicia as proconsul, accompanied by his brother, son, and nephew. Cæsar completes subjugation of Gaul and spends next year in conciliation and pacification. Pompey as proconsul and senatorial crowd plan to jockey Cæsar out of his command to permit his prosecution in court for illegalities of first consulship and prevent his second election as consul.

50 **Age 56.** Tullia married to Dolabella. Returning from Cilicia, Cicero reaches Brindisi November 25 and goes to his villa at Formiæ before setting out for Rome. December 1, Senate registers its aversion to civil war by voting 320 to 22 that both Cæsar and Pompey lay down commands simultaneously.

49 **Age 57.** War party in saddle carries vote demanding that Cæsar give up proconsulship and declaring martial law. Cæsar crosses Rubicon about January 10–13 by incorrect current calendar, November 20–23 by solar calendar. Rapidly overruns Italy. Pompey retires to Macedonia to raise additional troops. After long hesitation Cicero joins him at Durazzo in June.

48 **Age 58.** Pompey defeated at Pharsalus, flees to Egypt and is murdered. Cicero, not present at Pharsalus, abandons struggle and returns to Brindisi in late October, where he remains until the following September, awaiting Cæsar's pardon. Cæsar involved in war in Egypt and an intrigue with Cleopatra.

47 **Age 59.** Cæsar finishes Egyptian war and after brief stay with Cleopatra wins battle of Zela in Asia Minor, August 2, over son of Mithridates. (*Veni, Vidi, Vici* campaign.) He returns to Italy, greets Cicero cordially; Cicero goes to Tusculum.

46 **Age 60.** Cæsar defeats Pompeians at Thapsus in Africa. Cato commits suicide. Cæsar, reaching Rome at the beginning of September, reforms calendar and starts for Spain. Cicero lives at Rome and at his country places; composes several books, including, in his series on oratory, *Oratorical Divisions* (*De Partitione Oratoria*), *Brutus* or *On Famous Orators* (*Brutus de Claris Oratoribus*) and *Orator* (*Orator*). Divorces Terentia, marries Publilia. Divorce of Tullia and Dolabella.

45 **Age 61.** Death of Tullia in February. Cicero's second religious experience. Writes *Consolation* (*Consolatio*), *Academics* (*Academica*), *Theories of Ethics* (*De Finibus Bonorum et Malorum*). Divorces Publilia. His son goes to Athens for study. Cæsar defeats Pompeians at Munda, Spain, March 17. Returns to Rome in September. Divorce of Quintus and Pomponia.

44 **Age 62.** Cæsar assassinated, March 15. Cicero remaining away from Rome writes, among other works, *Tusculan Disputations* (*Tusculanæ Disputationes*), *On the Nature of the Gods* (*De

Natura Deorum), *On Divination* (*De Divinatione*), *On Old Age* (*De Senectute*), *On Friendship* (*De Amicitia*), and *On Moral Duties* (*De Officiis*), addressed to son at Athens. Octavius (Octavian, Augustus) arrives in Rome and begins contest with Antony for supreme power in the state. Cicero returns to Rome, delivers first speech against Antony in Senate September 2 (*First Philippic*). *Second Philippic*, circulated, not delivered, carries mortal challenge to Antony. In December, Cicero decides to accept Octavian as senatorial champion against Antony.

43 **Age 63.** Cicero persuades Senate to declare war on Antony. Civil war. Birth of Ovid, March 20. Octavian makes deal with Antony against Senate. Lepidus, one of Cæsar's officers, arranges conference with Octavian and Antony; Committee of Three organized (Second Triumvirate) to control the state. Proscription of their enemies and of wealthy men to obtain resources to pay soldiers. The Ciceros on the list. Young Marcus safe in Macedonia. Quintus and his son killed at Rome. Marcus Tullius Cicero reaches his villa at Astura with opportunity to escape by ship to Macedonia. Uncertain what to do, is overtaken by soldiers and killed near Formiæ, December 7.

APPENDIX II

BIOGRAPHIES AND HISTORIES, ANCIENT AND MODERN

BIOGRAPHIES OF CICERO IN ENGLISH

CONYERS MIDDLETON: *The Life of Marcus Tullius Cicero.* 1741.

J. F. HOLLINGS: *The Life of Marcus Tullius Cicero.* 1839.

B. R. ABEKEN: *An Account of the Life and Letters of Cicero.* German edition, 1835; translated under direction of Charles Merivale, 1854.

WILLIAM FORSYTH: *Life of Marcus Tullius Cicero.* 1864.

GASTON BOISSIER: *Cicero and His Friends.* French edition, 1865; translated by A. D. Jones, 1867.

REV. W. LUCAS COLLINS: *Cicero.* 1871. (Ancient Classics for English Readers.)

ANTHONY TROLLOPE: *The Life of Cicero.* 1880.

G. E. JEANS: *The Life and Letters of Marcus Tullius Cicero.* 1880.

EDUARD MUNK: *The Student's Cicero.* Adapted from the German by Rev. W. Y. Fausset, 1889.

J. L. STRACHAN-DAVIDSON: *Cicero and the Fall of the Roman Republic.* 1894. (Heroes of the Nations.)

E. G. SIHLER, *Cicero of Arpinum, a Political and Literary Biography.* 1914.

HANNIS TAYLOR: *Cicero, a Sketch of His Life and Works.* 1916.

TORSTEN PETERSSON: *Cicero, A Biography.* 1920.

JOHN C. ROLFE: *Cicero and His Influence.* 1923. (Our Debt to Greece and Rome.)

Gaston Delayen: *Cicero.* French edition, 1929; translated by Farrell Symons, 1931.

G. C. Richards: *Cicero, A Study.* 1935.

A. F. Witley (A. Forbáth): *The Tremulous Hero, The Age and Life of Cicero.* 1939.

Most of the older biographies are out of print, except the Boissier and the Strachan-Davidson. The Petersson is no longer available. But they occasionally appear in shops specializing in old books. In the last three years I have been so lucky as to pick up all of those listed, except the Hollings. It has been an interesting search from Oxford (where Blackwell's is the great storehouse), Cambridge, and London to Washington, Philadelphia, New York, Boston, Chicago, Kansas City (where I found an old Middleton), Berkeley, and Los Angeles.

To the biographical writings should be added the brilliant introductions to each of the six volumes of R. Y. Tyrrell and L. C. Purser: *The Correspondence of Cicero* (Dublin, 1879–85), which might well be collected in a single volume; the chapter on Cicero in R. S. Conway: *Makers of Europe* (1931); Tenney Frank: *Cicero, Annual Lecture on a Master Mind* (1932); and chapters in Grant Showerman: *Men and Monuments of Ancient Rome* (1937), and in the various literary histories of Rome, especially Frank: *Life and Literature in the Roman Republic* (1930). There are interesting points of view in L. Laurand: *Cicéron est intéressant* (1937), and *Cicéron, vie et œuvres.*

Middleton's (1741) was the only life of Cicero available in English for a century. It is an undiscriminating panegyric and evoked in 1747 a rather keen critical reply in a considerable volume, *The Character and Conduct of Cicero,* by the versatile actor, dramatist, and poet laureate Colley Cibber. Hollings (1839), a small book in a Family Library series, was a popularization of Middleton, which, the author says, was "respectfully consulted." Charles Merivale, author of *History of the Romans under the Empire,* supervised a translation of Abeken in 1854. The German was a scholar whose experience in the diplomatic service was helpful to his understanding of Cicero and his work is still useful. In 1864 William Forsyth, Queen's Counsel, brought out the first competently done biography of Cicero by an Englishman, stressing Cicero's activity as a pleader. Then followed Boissier in French (1865), soon translated into English, so charmingly written that some scholars unjustly criticized it as superficial.

The slight volume by Collins (1871) is a pleasant book by a cultured classicist, an example of condensation without sacrifice of interest. Anthony Trollope, the novelist, in 1880 barged in with a two-volume life which, he complains in his *Autobiography*, was much sniffed at by the professionals. In the same year appeared the Jeans book, in which an abbreviated life is constructed out of selected letters with copious biographical notes. This is the book referred to in Chapter VI, with Cicero's Greek phrases translated into French. Munk's *The Student's Cicero* (1889) is a translation of a section from Munk's elaborate *Geschichte der Römischen Literatur*; a good book, of only 237 pages, with stimulating notes by the translator.

Strachan-Davidson in the Heroes of the Nations series (1894) remains probably the best of the biographies for popular reading. It deals chiefly with Cicero's political career and is written from the standpoint of nineteenth-century British liberalism. Most British historical writers, I may say, have been members of the same upper class to which Cicero belonged, and so naturally and unconsciously have accepted his point of view.

The first life by an American is Sihler's (1914). It is preeminently for scholars, as is Petersson's (1920), the most comprehensive and valuable of the biographies, a mine of information. Both are rather slow reading. Hannis Taylor, lawyer and diplomat, produced his study in 1916. Its unique feature is an anthology of 150 pages of quotations from Cicero. Rolfe's *Cicero and His Influence* (1923), in the series Our Debt to Greece and Rome, is valuable for its discussion of Cicero's influence on thought. The Delayen, of which the translation appeared in 1931, was crowned by the French Academy; it is difficult to understand why. Raymond Poincaré as premier of France wrote a brief approving introductory note. *Cicero, A Study* (1935), by the Reverend G. C. Richards, canon of Durham, is a brief and scholarly popular life which supplements the Strachan-Davidson with chapters on Cicero's writings. "A. F. Witley" is the pen name of a Hungarian doctor, Sándor Forbát, who also uses the equivalent Alex Forbáth. Born in 1890, he is author and editor of several books in English. His *Tremulous Hero* (1939) reflects the modern European liberal attitude.

Other important biographies of the period cover the lives of Julius Cæsar, Marcus Brutus, Mark Antony, and Augustus. I may mention some of these.

Napoleon III was moved to publish a two-volume *History of Julius Cæsar* (English translation, 1866). It deals with the period to the crossing of the Rubicon. While he gives no credit, the work was done by competent ghost writers, especially by Colonel Eugène Stoffel, French army engineer, who excavated the sites of the battles in the Gallic wars. The preface, contributed by the Emperor, indicates that his purpose was to justify his uncle, the first Napoleon, by glorifying Cæsar. Since Napoleon did not finish his work, Stoffel continued it with his *L'Histoire de Jules César — Guerre Civile*. Cæsar's campaigns are considered in *Cæsar*, in the Great Captains series by T. A. Dodge, brevet lieutenant colonel, U. S. Army, retired, a Civil War veteran. The most authoritative discussion of the campaigns is T. Rice Holmes: *Cæsar's Conquest of Gaul* (1899; extensively revised, 1911), and *Ancient Britain and the Invasions of Julius Cæsar* (1907). Among the biographies J. A. Froude wrote a clever but distorted *Cæsar, A Sketch* (second edition, 1896). The standard biography is W. W. Fowler: *Julius Cæsar* (1891), in Heroes of the Nations. Also to be noticed are Sihler: *Annals of Cæsar* (1910); John Buchan: *Julius Cæsar*

(1932), a slight sketch; and Fletcher Pratt: *Hail Cæsar!* (1936).

Max Radin: *Marcus Brutus* (1939) presents a fresh view of the conspirator. Arthur Weigall: *The Life and Times of Marc Antony* appeared in 1931, and Jack Lindsay's Leftist study, *Marc Antony,* in 1937.

The lives of Augustus include J. B. Firth: *Augustus Cæsar and the Organization of the Roman Empire* (1902), in Heroes of the Nations; E. S. Shuckburgh: *Augustus, the Life and Times of the Founder of the Roman Empire* (B.C. 63–A.D. 14) (1903); Mason Hammond: *The Augustan Principate* (1933); A. D. Winspear and L. K. Geweke: *Augustus and the Reconstruction of Roman Government and Society* (1935); B. M. Allen: *Augustus Caesar* (1936); John Buchan: *Augustus* (1937); G. P. Baker: *Augustus and the Golden Age of Rome* (1937). All are competently done. I happen to like especially the Shuckburgh and the Buchan – the last written with Lord Tweedsmuir's characteristic charm. A popular life by a German doctor is Ferdinand Mainzer; *Cæsar's Mantle, the End of the Roman Republic* (translated by Eden and Cedar Paul, 1936).

The standard histories are rich in material for the period. Of especial importance are Theodor Mommsen: *The History of Rome* (5 vols., translated by W. P. Dickson, revised edition, 1894), brilliantly prejudiced for Cæsar and against Cicero; W. E. Heitland: *The Roman Republic* (3 vols., 1909); T. Rice Holmes: *The Roman Republic* (3 vols., 1923), with an excellent chapter on the "Roman World in the Ciceronian Age" and abundant reference notes; F. B. Marsh: *The Founding of the Roman Empire* (1927), and "A History of the Roman World, 146–30 B.C.," *The Cambridge Ancient History* (12 vols., Vol. IX, 1932, and Vol. X, 1934); Tenney Frank: *An Economic Survey of Ancient Rome* (5 vols. and Index, Vol. I, 1933), and *An Economic History of Rome* (second edition, 1928). President Theodore Roosevelt, with a review in the *Outlook,* almost made a best seller of Guglielmo Ferrero: *The Greatness and De-*

cline of Rome (translated by Alfred E. Zimmern, 5 vols., 1909). Scholars think Ferrero was not a fanatic on accuracy. There is much sound sense as well as learning in the almost forgotten George Long: *The Decline of the Roman Republic* (5 vols., Vol. III, 1869, and Vol. IV, 1872). A remarkable study of the period following Cæsar's death is Roland Syme: *The Roman Revolution* (1939). Syme is university lecturer in ancient history at Oxford. C. M. Bowra, Warden of Wadham, characterizes this as "the best book on Roman history that has appeared for many years." Syme takes the view that the struggle which Cicero led against Antony was engineered by Octavian for reasons of personal ambition.

Other useful histories bearing on various aspects of the Ciceronian era are Fowler: *The City-State of the Greeks and Romans* (1893); G. B. Grundy: *A History of the Greek and Roman World* (1925); T. R. Glover: *Democracy in the Ancient World* (1927), and *The Ancient World* (1935); A. N. Sherwin-White: *The Roman Citizenship* (1939); G. H. Stevenson: *Roman Provincial Administration* (1939). An early heretical study of the Catilinarian conspiracy was the essay "Catiline" by E. S. Beesly that appeared in the *Fortnightly Review* (1865) and was included in a small book, *Catiline, Clodius, and Tiberius* (1878, republished 1924). The standard work is E. G. Hardy: *The Catilinarian Conspiracy in Its Context* (1924). I have given some of the economic background in *The New Deal in Old Rome* (1939).

On the side of government and politics are T. M. Taylor: *A Constitutional and Political History of Rome* (1899); F. F. Abbott: *Roman Political Institutions* (1901), and *Roman Politics* (1923); A. H. J. Greenidge: *Roman Public Life* (1901); G. W. Botsford: *The Roman Assemblies* (1909); Léon Homo: *Roman Political Institutions* (1929). Legal aspects are covered by Greenidge: *The Legal Procedure of Cicero's Time* (1901); Strachan-Davidson: *Problems of the Roman Criminal Law* (1912); James Hadley: *Introduction to Roman Law* (1873); Max Radin: *Handbook of*

Roman Law (1927); W. W. Buckland: *The Main Institutions of Roman Private Law* (1931); C. H. McIlwain, *Constitutionalism, Ancient and Modern* (1940); Cyril Bailey, editor: *The Legacy of Rome* (1923); Sir J. E. Sandys, editor: *A Companion to Latin Studies* (third edition, 1935). With these should be included James Bryce: *Studies in History and Jurisprudence* (2 vols., 1901), with comparative studies of Roman and English law.

Interesting books on religion are Fowler: *The Roman Festivals of the Period of the Republic* (1899), *The Religious Experience of the Roman People* (1911), and *Roman Ideas of Deity* (1914); J. B. Carter: *The Religious Life of Ancient Rome* (1911); Franz Cumont: *The Oriental Religions in Roman Paganism* (1911), and *After Life in Roman Paganism* (1922); Cyril Bailey: *Phases in the Religion of Ancient Rome* (1932); Boissier: *La Religion romaine* (2 vols., 1909). On a related subject is Eugene Tavenner: *Studies in Magic from Latin Literature* (1916).

Of the books on the daily life of the people, I have found especially helpful Fowler: *Social Life at Rome in the Age of Cicero* (1909); H. W. Johnston: *The Private Life of the Romans* (revised edition, 1932); T. G. Tucker: *Life in the Roman World of Nero and St. Paul* (1910); Ludwig Friedländer: *Roman Life and Manners under the Empire* (translation of the German seventh edition by L. A. Magnus); Abbott: *Society and Politics in Ancient Rome* (1909), and *The Common People of Ancient Rome* (1911); W. A. Becker: *Gallus, or Roman Scenes in the Time of Augustus* (translated from the German by the Reverend F. Metcalfe; second edition, 1849; republished 1898); F. Poland, E. Reisinger, and R. Wagner: *The Culture of Ancient Greece and Rome* (translated from the German by J. H. Freese, 1926); Grant Showerman: *Rome and the Romans* (1931); F. G. Moore: *The Roman's World* (1936); Jérôme Carcopino: *Daily Life in Ancient Rome* (edited by H. T. Rowell, translated by E. O. Lorimer, 1940); M. Cary and T. J. Haarhoff: *Life and Thought in the Greek and Roman World* (1940).

Ancient Rome — its topography, buildings, and architecture — is treated in S. B. Platner and Thomas Ashby: *A Topographical Dictionary of Ancient Rome* (1929), an elaborate and fascinating volume; Platner: *The Topography and Monuments of Ancient Rome* (1904); J. H. Middleton: *The Remains of Ancient Rome* (2 vols., 1892); Robert Burn: *Ancient Rome and Its Neighbourhood* (1895); E. Rodocanachi: *The Roman Capitol in Ancient and Modern Times* (translated by F. Lawton, 1906); Christian Huelsen: *The Forum and the Palatine* (translated by Helen H. Tanzer, 1928); Thomas Ashby, *The Aqueducts of Ancient Rome* (1935); Rodolfo Lanciani: *Ancient Rome in the Light of Recent Discoveries* (1892), *The Ruins and Excavations of Ancient Rome* (1897), and *Ancient and Modern Rome* (1925); W. J. Anderson and R. P. Spiers: *The Architecture of Ancient Rome, An Account of Its Historical Development* (revised and rewritten by T. Ashby, 1927); D. S. Robertson: *A Handbook of Greek and Roman Architecture* (1929).

Of the classical dictionaries in English, the most useful to me have been *A Dictionary of Greek and Roman Antiquities* by William Smith, William Wayte, and G. E. Marindin (2 vols., 1890); *A Dictionary of Classical Antiquities*, by Oskar Seyffert (translated and revised by Henry Nettleship and J. E. Sandys, 1891); *A Manual of Roman Antiquities*, by William Ramsay (revised by Rodolfo Lanciani, 1901); *Harper's Dictionary of Classical Literature and Antiquities* (edited by H. T. Peck, 1923); Smith: *Dictionary of Greek and Roman Biography and Mythology* (3 vols., 1844); and *Dictionary of Greek and Roman Geography* (2 vols., 1853). Both reprinted 1870.

Those who wish to refer to the ancient writers will find English translations, chiefly in the Loeb Classical Library, of most of the material. Of greatest importance, of course, are the writings of Cicero. A few of these that have not yet appeared in the Loeb Library are in the Bohn translations — *On Rhetorical Invention, On Oratorical Partitions, On the Character of the Orator, On the Best Style of Orators, The Paradoxes,* and several important orations, including the surviving fragments of *In the White Toga.* In addition are Cæsar's *Commentaries on the Gallic War* (about 50), and *The Civil Wars* (perhaps 45, but published after his death); Sallust: *The War with Catiline* (43), and *The War with Jugurtha* (41); Nepos: *Lives of Illustrious Men* (including Atticus) (35); Velleius Paterculus: *Compendium of Roman History* (A.D. 30); Seneca the elder: *Rhetorical Exercises* (*Suasoriæ*) (about A.D. 34); Lucan: *The Civil War* (*Pharsalia*) (A.D. 60–65), a long poem with acute observations on Pompey and Cæsar; Plutarch: *Parallel Lives* (about A.D. 100); Suetonius: *Lives of the Twelve Cæsars* (A.D. 120); Florus: *Epitome of Roman History* (about A.D. 130); Appian: *Roman History* (A.D. 160); Dio Cassius: *Roman History* (after A.D. 230). All these are translated in the Loeb Library except the *Suasoriæ* of Seneca (translation by W. A. Edward, Cambridge University Press). The Bohn Library edition of Cæsar includes the books on the Alexandrian War, the African War, and the Spanish War written by Cæsar's marshals, and not yet translated for the Loeb Library. There are numerous editions of Plutarch. A convenient translation is in three volumes in Everyman's Library.

APPENDIX III

SOME OF THE PROBLEMS

THE average reader, I suspect, finds footnotes disturbing and superfluous. For scholars it hardly seemed worth while to document the references in the text with the familiar passages in Cicero and the other ancient writers. There may be inquisitive persons, however, who would be interested in the reasons for some of the statements made and who might desire to look further into some of the subjects touched on. Such questions as the age of Julius Cæsar, the size of the population of Rome, certain details concerning Cicero's villas, the value of Roman money, the nature of the repeated illnesses of Augustus, illustrate some of the less important matters. The two great controversial issues in the career of Cicero, of course, are those of the conspiracy of Catiline and of the final conflict between Cicero and Mark Antony. On these the reader is entitled to fuller references than can be given in the narrative.

A word about my consultants, Professor Poteat, Professor Walker, and Professor Lord. They have been exceedingly helpful in detecting errors of fact and in trying to save me from what they regard as errors of interpretation. They all, I believe, think that I am unfair in my appraisal of Cicero as an orator. Professor Walker feels my treatment of Cæsar's military qualities is deplorable. Professor Poteat wholly disagrees with my views on Cicero's agnosticism and several other matters. On these points as well as on others I have thought it necessary to recast material to take their arguments into account. In this Appendix some of the discussions with my learned friends have been included. In doing this I fall back on the principle laid down by an old gentleman of Jefferson City, Missouri, who used to say: " I may be mistaken about this and doubtless I am, but I think – ."

In fairness I should warn my readers not to assume my consultants' approval of opinions in the text where their criticisms are not mentioned. Not all of their dissents are set forth in these notes. In other words, I want full credit for all my mistakes.

Under this general scheme the selection of subjects here touched upon is necessarily arbitrary and spotted, rather than complete. The books and articles listed are those I happen to have found the most useful. Additional books would be included in a complete bibliography. I have preferred, however, to confine the list to material which I have myself consulted.

CHAPTER I. *Prologue of Great Names*
CHAPTER II. *A Roman Visits Eighteenth-Century London*
CHAPTER III. *And Finds Himself at Home*

The influence of Cicero in the framing of the American Constitution may be studied in *The Works of John Adams*, edited by his grandson, Charles Francis Adams, Vol. IV, which includes his *Defence of the Constitutions of Government;* in Charles Warren: *The Making of the Constitution;* Gilbert Chinard; *Honest John Adams;* and Van Wyck Brooks: *The Flowering of New England*. The state of eighteenth-century England is presented in W. E. H. Lecky: *A History of England in the Eighteenth Century;* Élie Halévy: *A History of the English People;* the Histories of G. E. Trevelyan and André Maurois; and such biographies as David Cecil: *The Young Melbourne*, and J. C. Long: *Mr. Pitt*.

Page 10. The " smoking kitchen " joke is recounted in Seneca's letter to Lucilius, No. 64. Originally I had followed two English translators, Dr. Gummere in the Loeb edition and

Dr. Barker in the Oxford translation, who use the term: " kitchen chimneys." Professor Poteat and Professor Lord both protested that Roman kitchens had no chimneys, and I suspect they are right. The word " chimney " does not appear in the Latin text. Smith's Dictionary, article " Domus," suggests that the Romans were familiar with the use of flues — attached to the furnaces used in heating public baths — and that it is hard to believe flues were not used in the kitchens of the great houses. Nevertheless none has been discovered by archæologists. The kitchen stoves found at Pompeii were adapted for burning charcoal and had no flues. The fumes escaped from a small window above the hearth. The Italians usually heated their rooms with charcoal-burning braziers. There is no record of suffocation from monoxide gas, except when a room was sealed by a man determined on suicide. This incident indicates that the poisonous nature of the gas was known. In one of his satires (I, v, 71) Horace tells of the cooking in a kitchen where the fire blazed up so the flames licked the roof, and in the same satire (I, v, 80) of a fire of green wood in a stove, the smoke from which brought tears. So I imagine the firemen of Seneca's letter came running because smoke burst out of a kitchen window.

Page 13. Characterization of Clodia: Tyrrell and Purser: *Correspondence of Cicero*, Vol. III, xliii.

Page 14. Servilia's pearl worth $300,000: The value of Roman money can be only approximated in modern terms. Like " real wages," the essential factor was purchasing power, which depended on the things that entered into the ancient standard of living. For comparative purposes we may get a rough idea of the value of Roman coins in gold by considering the weight of the metal that went into them, with the silver-gold ratio 12 to 1. The copper *as* was the lowest denomination. Then came the silver *sestertius*, worth four *asses*, and the silver *denarius*, worth four *sestertii*. I follow Frank: *Economic Survey*, Vol. I, p. 422, who figures the *as* at 1¼ cents, the *sestertius* at 5 cents, and the *denarius* with 4⅜ grams of silver at 20 cents. Frank's computation was made before the devaluation of the dollar. But I believe with the Supreme Court in the gold cases that the price structure was not materially affected by the change in the gold content.

Page 14. Women's struggle for Brutus: Radin: *Marcus Brutus*, pp. 117–18.

Page 16. First plea against taxation without representation: Professor Poteat inquires: "How about the 'secession of plebs' in 494, and the Social War of 91–88?" Tradition records five such secessions between 494 and 287, not all historical. These were parts of a struggle, political, social, and economic, not directed specifically, as I understand them, against the principle of taxation without representation. The Social War was fought to gain the rights of Roman citizenship. The citizen's tax had been abolished in 167, and while the Italian communities feared injustice from new land laws, I do not see that the taxation issue was primarily involved. Credit for the first direct protest of taxation without representation I believe goes to Hortensia.

Page 17. Double standard of morals: M. P. Nilsson: *Imperial Rome*, p. 323. T. R. Glover writes in *Virgil*, p. 203: "Faithfulness in a husband and chastity in a man were neither expected nor particularly admired."

Page 18. Survival of custom of beating parish bounds: Fowler: *Roman Festivals*, p. 127.

Page 23. Aristocrats reaching cabinet positions in England: H. J. Laski, cited by W. S. Greene: *Achievement of Rome* (1938), p. 199.

Pages 26–7. Account of Assemblies and Senate and aristocratic political machine: Marsh: *Roman World*, 17–28.

Page 29. Origin of Roman equivalent to the newspaper: Boissier: *Tacitus and Other Roman Studies* (1906), pp. 195–229.

CHAPTER IV. *The Country Boy of Arpinum*

This book is frankly inconsistent in the spelling of ancient names. In general I have tried to use the modern spelling to give the reader a better idea of the location of places. Thus Brindisi is used instead of Brundisium, Durazzo instead of Dyracchium, Aix-en-Provence instead of Aquæ Sextiæ. But Gaul is used instead of France for obvious reasons, and Arpinum instead of the modern Arpino because the Latin form is associated with Cicero.

On Roman education see A. S. Wilkins: *Roman Education* (1905), and Aubrey Gwynn: *Roman Education from Cicero to Quintilian* (1926).

Page 41. The scribblings on the walls at Pompeii are discussed in August Mau: *Pompeii, Its Life and Art,* and Helen H. Tanzer: *The Common People of Pompeii.*

Page 41. Education throughout the Empire: F. Haverfield: *The Romanization of Roman Britain,* p. 31.

CHAPTER V. *He Moves to the Big City*

Interesting details of physical conditions in Rome may be found in numerous books on the life of the people, especially in Fowler: *Social Life;* Johnston: *Private Life;* Tucker: *Life in the Roman World;* Showerman: *Rome and the Romans;* Moore: *Roman's World;* and Carcopino: *Daily Life.* Carcopino tells of sanitation and comfort stations, pp. 39–41, and cites the evidence on maids attached to taverns, p. 253.

A curious mistake is made by the famous archæologist Rodolfo Lanciani in his *Ancient Rome.* He tells of excavating the site of the ancient potter's field in 1884 and says he was obliged to relieve his gang of workmen from time to time "because the smell from that polluted ground, turned up after a putrefaction of twenty centuries, was absolutely unendurable even to men so hardened to every kind of hardship as my excavators." As chemical action destroys all organic matter in a comparatively few years, the stench that overcame Lanciani's workmen must have come from something fairly recent; a sewer, perhaps. Several Latinists to whom I expressed doubts about Lanciani's statement were unconvinced until they had taken up the question with university chemists.

Page 42. It is pleasant to glance over Platner and Ashby: *Topographical Dictionary,* for information about houses and public buildings.

Page 44. Protection of sun-dried brick walls by whitewash:

I had assumed that these walls were protected by a coating of a marble cement stucco as stated by Middleton: *Remains*, Vol. I, pp. 74–5, and Anderson: *Architecture*, p. 33. But Professor Lord, who has spent much time in Rome and Athens, believes the walls were protected by the cheaper and much more easily managed whitewash. He writes: " In the climate of Rome and Greece a mud brick building will last indefinitely after it is whitewashed. The Pythian Apollo hotel at Delphi is protected in just this way. All you need to do for such a building is to keep a roof on it and whitewash its sides. The Romans did have a sort of marble stucco; a plaster in which marble dust was mixed. It was applied to temples that were built of rough stone, like those, for instance, at Pæstum. You can still see traces of it in the flutes on the columns. Rough limestone covered with this stucco looked like marble. The Romans may have used that on the outside of their houses; I don't believe they did, but they may have. More probably they used just plain whitewash. Under Augustus most of the elaborate houses were made of concrete faced with baked brick. Augustus didn't use marble stucco, but a marble veneer; that is, slabs of marble three-quarters to one inch thick, that covered the brick facing."

Page 47. The cloaca maxima, the mouth of which is familiar to many travellers, is ascribed by tradition to the pre-republican period. Modern archæology has shown that most of the drain was reconstructed in later times, with the mouth assigned to about 100 B.C., Platner and Ashby, op. cit.

Page 48. Illnesses of Augustus are diagnosed as malaria by Mainzer: *Cæsar's Mantle*, p. 137.

Page 49. The population of Rome can be only estimated from various unsatisfactory data — the three hundred and twenty thousand recipients of free grain in Cæsar's time, area of city and possible density of population, number of houses, consumption of grain, etc. No firm conclusion is possible. The number of slaves is estimated from references to the proportion of slaves to free population of Pergamum, a nebulous computation. The question is discussed in Holmes: *Roman Republic*, Vol. I, pp. 360–3; Carcopino: *Daily Life*, pp. 16–21; Friedländer:

Roman Life and Manners, Vol. IV, pp. 17–28; Sandys: *Companion,* pp. 354–6.

Page 50. Wages and cost of living: Frank: *Economic Survey,* Vol. I, pp. 385–6. Slave competition made strikes virtually impossible. In the volumes of the *Economic Survey* few strikes are recorded: occasional strikes of tenant farmers in Egypt and one of workmen in an alabaster quarry; among menders of temple utensils in Jerusalem, where there were few slaves; among bakers in some city of Asia Minor where members of the Bakers' Union were threatened with arrest for sedition; threats of strikes in the building trades in some other Asiatic city and by shipowners at Arles in southern France. A sit-down strike is reported in the mint at Rome in the latter part of the third century of our era under the Emperor Aurelian, who sent troops to drive the strikers out.

Page 54. As to Cicero's opinion of the commoners as undesirable citizens, " I wonder! " Professor Poteat comments. But in letters to Atticus, *Ad Att.* i, 16, 11, he refers to " the wretched starveling mob, the blood-suckers of the treasury "; in *Ad Att.* ii, 1, 8, he speaks of " the dregs of humanity collected by Romulus "; and his brother urges him in a perfectly matter-of-fact way in the *Handbook of Politics* to remember that " this is Rome, a city made up of a combination of nations, in which many snares, much deception, many vices, enter into every department of life." I should say Cicero wasn't exactly crazy over the common people of Rome.

Chapter VI. *Dining Out with Friends*

Page 58. Greek and Roman writers referred to by Cicero are listed by Sihler: *Cicero,* pp. 37–8.

Page 58. The Scipionic circle is discussed by Heitland: *Roman Republic,* Vol. II, pp. 124, 232, 250, 252, and by H. H. Scullard: *History of the Roman World from 753 to 146* B.C., pp. 388, 416, 438.

Page 59. The dinner party given by Lucullus is recorded by Plutarch: *Lucullus,* Ch. xli. It may be worth while to cite the sources of the conversation attributed to Cicero with the customary abbreviations (Letters to Friends, *Ad Fam.*; To Atticus, *Ad Att.*): " A dinner party is my delight," *Ad. Fam.* ix, 26; Metellus, *Ad. Att.* i, 18; Cato, *ibid.*; finance officer in Sicily, *Pro Plancio,* xxvi, 64–5; art of conversation, *De Officiis,* i, 37, sec. 134; Crassus, *Ad. Att.* iv, 13; story of Ennius, *De Oratore,* ii, 68; mistakes stay by one, *De Oratore,* i, 28; books as companions, *De Re Publica,* i, 9. Gossip about the cost of works of art and of luxurious mansions is given by Pliny: *Natural History* (translation in Bohn Library).

Page 62. Immortality, in which neither of them believed: " I don't agree at all, so far as Cicero is concerned," Professor Poteat writes. " The *Somnium Scipionis* seems to present ' civic immortality ' as Cicero's point of view; but in works written after Tullia's death, he often affirms his faith in the continued life of the soul. See, e.g., *Tusc. Disp.*, i, 26–81; v, 38; *Nat. Deorum,* ii, 4; *Amic.*, 13; *Senec.*, 67–85; and especially *Tusc. Disp.*, i, 118." This question comes up in more detail in Chapter xxi, where Cicero's religious views are discussed. Here I merely call attention to Frank's remark in *Life and Literature,* pp. 221–2, that Cicero's mood of mysticism after Tullia's death " probably lasted only a few months," and that he then " returned to his earlier agnosticism "; and to Cumont: *After Life,* p. 31: " beyond doubt Cicero was an agnostic for the greater part of his life."

Page 63. Jews favoured in Palestine: A consultant objects that Cæsar never visited Palestine. Yes, but Josephus tells of his liberal legislation on behalf of the Palestinian Jews. See Holmes: *Roman Republic,* Vol. III, p. 507.

CHAPTER VII. *He Studies Law*

Page 64. The consulship reserved for members of noble families: It is true that the Licinian-Sextian Law of 367 provided that one consul must be a plebeian. But able plebeian families forced their way into the aristocracy. Greenidge says, in *Roman Public Life,* pp. 128–9: " The old nobility had relaxed its exclusive hold on public office but only to give room for the still firmer grasp of a new. This was an aristocracy of mixed origin composed indifferently of the leading patrician and plebeian families."

Page 67. The commentator on Cicero is Frank: *Social Behavior*, p. 109.

Pages 69–70. For Roman legal procedure the standard works are Greenidge: *Legal Procedure*, and Strachan-Davidson: *Problems of the Roman Criminal Law*. The influence of Roman law on English law is considered in Radin: *Roman Law*, p. 478; McIlwain: *Constitutionalism*, Ch. iii; Bryce: *Studies*.

Page 69. Blackstone is chiefly responsible for the widespread but erroneous belief that the modern jury system of England and America derived from the Anglo-Saxons. Our jury developed from Roman origins although not from the jury system of the Republic, which faded under the Empire. The Roman imperial treasury acquired the right to summon members of the community and require them to supply tax information. This practice survived in Charlemagne's time and later in provinces conquered by the Normans. It was taken by the Norman dukes to England. From this procedure came the English jury, which originally was a body of neighbours summoned by some public official to answer questions under oath. Gradually this body became a jury which heard and decided cases. See the exhaustive treatment in W. S. Holdsworth: *History of English Law*, Vol. I, pp. 312 ff., and Sir F. Pollock and F. W. Maitland: *The History of English Law*, Vol. I, pp. 138 ff.

CHAPTER VIII. *His First Big Case*

Page 81. Poor unable to rear children: Appian: *Civil Wars*, I, i, 10.

Page 81. The subject of grain relief is dealt with in my *New Deal in Old Rome*, pp. 109–14; summarized, p. 240.

Page 82. On the mixed population in Rome: Frank is the chief authority, *American Historical Review* (1916), pp. 687–708. His studies are summarized in *Economic History*, pp. 206–18. Certain critics regard his position as extreme. The subject is interestingly reviewed in Nilsson: *Imperial Rome*, Book II, Ch. iv, " The Population Problem "; and in M. E. Park, dissertation: "The Plebs in Cicero's day."

Page 82. Quotations from Gustav Stolper: *This Age of*

Fable, p. 350, and André Maurois: A *History of England*, p. 497.

Page 86. Ready to appear for a scoundrel: as for Fonteius, corrupt governor of Provence, in 69; Murena, guilty of bribery, in 63; Antonius, extortionist in Macedonia, in 59; Rabirius Postumus, extortionist in Egypt, in 54.

Page 86. Cicero's desire to break into the inner circle of the old families: Professor Poteat doubts that he "ever had the real instincts of a social climber." Perhaps I am unfair. But I suspect that his elaborate mansion on the Palatine, his recognition of the dislike of some of the aristocrats, and the way he stuttered in writing to great nobles indicate climbing instincts.

CHAPTER IX. *Post-Graduate Work in Athens*

On education in Athens see J. W. H. Walden: *The Universities of Ancient Greece* (1909).

Page 95. In an unpublished dissertation: "The Personal Property and Sources of Income of Marcus Tullius Cicero" (1941), which the author has kindly lent me, Dr. A. H. Reents gives reasons for supposing that Cicero's income from his books "was not inconsiderable." As a supporting argument he suggests that Tiro, who was associated with Cicero in his literary productions, was able to retire to a farm which he had purchased. It is possible, however, that Cicero was generous to his secretary without regard to possible book royalties.

Dr. B. L. Ullman thinks that literary Romans were more concerned with distinction than with profits. He writes: "Pliny reports in one of his letters that the booksellers told him that his books were in demand. When Pliny concluded from this that he must write something more, I take this to mean that Pliny liked to be in the public eye and not that he received any financial reward. He was a very rich man and the few cents he would have received from the sale of his books would be a mere trifle."

But there were writers not so fortunately situated as Pliny. Juvenal remarks that glory will not feed a starving poet. After Cicero's time the bookselling trade developed to a point where it began to pay modest returns. But authorship was probably no more remunerative in Rome of the first century of our era than it was in eighteenth-century England when authors had to depend on wealthy patrons or government subsidies. The first reference to booksellers' shops is by Catullus, perhaps about 58. Cicero speaks of a bookstore in the Forum in 52. Later we read of shops in Booksellers Row and one or two other streets that stocked Horace, Livy, Cicero, Quintilian, Martial, and other popular authors. It may be assumed that writers received compensation from the sale of their works. Suetonius tells of an author who sold his rights to a bookseller for $800.

The witty and popular poet Martial is so preoccupied with prices and sales that we may guess he received royalties. The critics, he says, may think his poetry is rotten. His bookseller knows better. To a friend who wishes to borrow one of his books he replies by directing him to the shop where it is for sale. Another book he says he must hurry to finish because he needs money. His poems sold at from twenty cents to one dollar a volume and he believes that the bookseller could still make a profit if he would cut the price of one of the cheaper books in half and thus stimulate sales. Nevertheless he complains that the poet's business is a poor one. The world-wide reputation of which he modestly boasts is not productive. His books, he says, are read even in far off Britain. But with what profit to him? His purse never hears about it.

Pages 97–8. For the letters of Cicero, the most convenient translation is that of Shuckburgh, four volumes, in the Bohn Library. The letters are printed in chronological order, with a good index. The Loeb edition prints the letters to Atticus in three volumes, the letters to and from other correspondents, called *Letters to His Friends,* in three more volumes. The collection of twenty-four Marcus Brutus letters, including the important letter of Brutus to Atticus criticizing Cicero, is omitted from the Loeb edition. These letters appear in Shuckburgh. Their authenticity was challenged for a time, but they are now generally accepted.

Page 98. Publisher of letters to Atticus: See Albert Watson: Cicero, *Select Letters,* p. 122. As to the date, Asconius, writing A.D. 54, does not know of them, and they are first quoted by

Seneca, A.D. 66. Tyrrell: *Correspondence,* Vol. I, p. 50, thinks the *Letters to His Friends* and to Atticus were probably published at the same time and edited by the same editor, since " there is evidence of the strict observance of the rule to exclude from one collection letters published in the other." The conclusion does not follow. Tiro and Atticus could have had an understanding.

Pages 99–100. The Petrarch letters may be found in J. H. Robinson and H. W. Rolfe: *Petrarch, The First Modern Scholar and Man of Letters* (1898), beginning at p. 239.

Page 101. Two such Lives have been constructed from the letters, by Abeken and Jeans, referred to in the preceding Appendix.

Pages 102–3. The Eleusinian Mysteries are discusseed in Seyffert: *Dictionary,* under " Eleusinia "; and in Smith: *Dictionary,* under " Eleusinia " and " Mysteria," where the Renan quotation is cited. I assume that Cicero's first religious experience was not lasting. Professor Poteat suggests that his initiation into the Mysteries " planted a seed which later, watered by his tears for Tullia, grew into a noble tree of hope and faith — of which the finest fruit was Book I of the *Tusculan Disputations.*"

Page 105. On the authenticity of the portrait busts I accept the views of Laurand: *Cicéron, vie et œuvres,* pp. 166 ff.

CHAPTER X. *He Becomes a Man of Family*

Pages 112–14. As to Roman marriage and divorce see Radin: *Roman Law,* pp. 114–17; on the right of a divorced woman, if innocent, to recover her dowry, Radin, op. cit., p. 209; Hadley: *Introduction to Roman Law,* p. 147; Smith: *Dictionary,* article " Dos." On the gravity of offences which prevented the recovery, see Ramsay and Lanciani: *Manual,* p. 298, article, " Marriage-Dos."

CHAPTER XI. *The Plunge into Politics*

Page 121. Rome taken by armed forces three times in the previous twelve years: by Sulla in 88, by Marius in 87, by Sulla in 82.

Page 125. Figures on Cicero's success as a pleader are cited by Rolfe: *Cicero,* pp. 75–7.

Pages 127–8. With my denial to Cicero of a place in the top flight of public speakers, all my consultants disagree. Professor Walker writes: " I don't think you are fair to Cicero in what you say of his oratory. You are judging him by present-day standards and your tone implies that these standards are the eternally true standards. But I think oratory is the most ephemeral of the literary arts. Its standards change most. The orator's rank must be judged by the degree in which he conforms to the standards of his own time and by his success in his own generation. By that test Cicero belongs in the top flight whether we like his style or not. If he was not supreme in his own day, who was? " I quite agree that Cicero was supreme in his own day. But I am trying to appraise him by timeless standards, *sub specie æternitatis,* as the old theologians used to say. In spite of passing styles I believe there are standards of simplicity, sincerity, restrained emotion, fine choice of words, dramatic feeling, which are always valid. Gross vituperation may be immensely admired in some epochs. That does not make it great oratory. By the eternal standards Lincoln's Gettysburg Address passes muster; Webster's laboured Ciceronian passages do not.

Page 129. T. S. Jerome: *Aspects of the Study of Roman History* (1923) devotes Ch. iv to " The Use of Invective." The general question of libel and slander is studied by Laura Robinson: dissertation, " Freedom of Speech in the Roman Republic " (1940).

Page 132. Lawyers forbidden to accept fees: An echo of the old Roman statute forbidding fees for legal services has come down into English procedure. A barrister's fee is considered an honorarium or voluntary present made in appreciation of services. On the gown of a junior barrister is a kind of vestigial pocket, the relic of the pocket into which the honorarium was supposed to be slipped when the lawyer wasn't looking. If the fee is not paid the barrister may not sue for it, and as a sort of compensation, neither may he be sued for negligence. On the other hand, a solicitor may sue for his fee.

Pages 132 ff. Cicero's income: On this subject I am indebted to numerous suggestions in Dr. Reents's dissertation, previously mentioned. It is by far the most systematic and painstaking discussion of the sources of Cicero's wealth with which I am familiar. Dr. Reents concludes: " Shrewd business acumen is present alongside showy waste. The ability of earning great sums is seemingly disavowed by an unbending aristocratic pride. Cicero, in his virtues and vices is, after all, a fairly faithful picture of the noble of the post-Sullan Republican regime." — It is Frank who estimates the value of Terentia's apartments at $65,000, *Economic Survey*, Vol. I, p. 371.

Pages 136–8. Villas: Cicero is generally credited with owning eight villas. But with the sale of the villa at Antium, the number owned at one time was reduced to seven. In a letter to Atticus written in 49 (*Ad Att.* ix, 9) he speaks of " the house I possessed at that time at Antium," and again in a letter written in July 45 (*Ad Att.* xiii, 47a) he refers to a letter from Lepidus dated at Antium, " for he was there in a house which I sold him." The only letter written from Antium after this tells of the conference of the conspirators and probably was written from the villa of Brutus, where the conference was held. Laurand thinks Cicero sold the Antium villa to buy the villa at Astura (*Cicéron*, p. 85).

Dr. Reents gives this table of Cicero's estates, with the approximate dates of acquisition. He thinks we can be sure only that the villas were acquired on or before the dates assigned. Thus the ancestral estate near Arpinum is first mentioned in 64, although it must have come to Cicero several years earlier, for his father probably died in 68.

1. Formiæ	before 68	5. Antium	60
2. Tusculum	68	6. Cumæ	56
3. Arpinum	64	7. Astura	45
4. Pompeii	60	8. Puteoli	45

To list the estate at Formiæ as the earliest of Cicero's villas after Arpinum requires, I think, some dubious reading between the lines of Cicero's correspondence. The first villa mentioned in the letters is the Tusculan, in *Ad Att.* i, 5, and i, 6, both written in 68. The Formian is not mentioned until a year later, in *Ad Att.* i, 3, written probably late in 67, and again in *Ad Att.* i, 4, written early in 66. In putting the Formian ahead of the Tusculan Dr. Reents follows C. E. Schmidt: *Ciceros Villen*, p. 23: "Already in the year 67 when Cicero thinks of decorating the Tusculan, acquired in 68, he mentions the Formian as an estate to which he has become somewhat indifferent because he has owned it longer." Schmidt makes this inference from a remark by Cicero that some statues temporarily placed in the Formian villa are to be moved to the Tusculan, and that later when he can afford it he will decorate the Formian. The assumption that the Formian villa came first, on the ground that the incident of the statues shows that Tusculum has supplanted Formiæ in Cicero's affections, is a mere guess. The letters simply show that Cicero owned the Tusculan villa in 68, the Formian in 67. He might well have decided to decorate the villas in the order of their acquisition.

CHAPTER XII. *Leader of the Roman Bar*

Page 139. There were two classes of commissioners of public works who had charge not only of public works, but also of the grain supply and of public games. The Latin term for such a commissioner was *ædilis,* usually Anglicized as ædile. The first ædiles were plebeians. Later a patrician ædileship was established. The officers holding this position on formal occasions sat in ivory state chairs, also used by consuls, judges, and censors. The ivory chair was called a *sella curulis,* and the officers entitled to such chairs were known as curule magistrates. The upper-class ædiles were the curule ædiles. The exclusive right of the patricians to this office soon disappeared and the plebeian and curule ædiles came to have virtually the same authority. But it was the curule ædileship that admitted a family to the nobility. The statement that election to one of the higher or curule magistracies carried with it admission to the nobility is not accurate. Smith's *Dictionary*, article "Nobiles, Nobilitas," points out that while the magistrate's descendants were ennobled, the magistrate himself, if a commoner when elected, occupied a sort of no man's land. He was neither a commoner nor a noble " in the full sense."

Page 140. As to Cicero's belief that a lawyer must take cases as they come, see his speech for Cluentius, 50, in which he says: "It is the greatest possible mistake to suppose that the speeches we barristers have made in court contain our considered and certified opinions; all those speeches reflect the demands of some particular case or emergency, not the personality of the advocate."

Pages 142–3. The character of Roman provincial governors is considered by G. H. Stevenson, in *Cambridge Ancient History,* Vol. IX, Ch. x, and is more fully developed in his book: *Roman Provincial Administration.*

Page 145. Cicero's speech on the Manilian Law was not delivered before the Assembly, for the Assembly merely voted without discussion. It was delivered before the preliminary session, the *contio,* which corresponded in some ways to the Committee of the Whole in the American House of Representatives.

CHAPTER XIII. *The New Man Crashes the Gate*

Page 152. For the development of the Roman party system see Taylor: *Constitutional and Political History,* Ch. ix.

Page 155. Theatre seats assigned to the knights probably in the Gracchan period: Mommsen: *History,* Vol. III, p. 351, and Vol. IV, p. 111; Taylor, op. cit., p. 254. Privilege revoked probably by Sulla and restored by Otho, tribune, in 67; Velleius: *History of Rome,* II, xxxii, 3; Botsford: *Roman Assemblies,* p. 429.

Page 159. First reference to harmony of the orders in speech *For Cluentius,* 152, made in 66.

Page 162. The candidate in charge of the Flaminian Way was Thermus. There is an unsupported and far-fetched guess that he was adopted by a Figulus and was elected under the name of C. Marcius Figulus.

Page 162. The senatorial roving commission (*libera legatio*) had an interesting survival, Professor Lord writes, until Mussolini suppressed the Roman Senate. "Before that time each Roman senator had a watch fob something like a Phi Beta Kappa key which entitled him to travel free on all government-owned railroads and steamship lines. Lanciani told me with a good deal of pride that he could go clear to Africa without paying anything for first-class accommodations, but he added sadly that the privilege did not include meals."

Page 163. The only translation of the *Handbook of Politics* that I have found is in Shuckburgh, Vol. I, Appendix.

CHAPTER XIV. *Cæsar Keeps Him Guessing*

Page 172. It is commonly stated that Rabirius was tried and appealed to the Assembly of the Centuries. But in the later Republic there was no appeal from a regularly constituted court to the Assembly. The court was supposed to be the Assembly's voice. (Strachan-Davidson: *Problems of the Roman Criminal Law*, Vol. II, ch. xv, especially pp. 48–9.) Strachan-Davidson discusses the trial of Rabirius in Ch. xi. See also Cary, in *Cambridge Ancient History*, Vol. IX, p. 490.

Page 172. Red flag on the Janiculum: Professor Poteat observes that "the Assemblies did not function after Tiberius transferred the voting power to the Senate." But see Greenidge: *Roman Public Life*, p. 373: "The survival of the *comitia* into the third century . . . was no mere mass-meeting informally assembled. The stately forms of the Republic were preserved and when the centuries were assembled the red flag still flew from the Janiculum."

Pages 174 ff. On the Catilinarian conspiracy, see especially Hardy: *Catilinarian Conspiracy*; Beesly: *Catiline* (extreme but suggestive); Lindsay: *Mark Antony*; Long: *Decline*, Vol. III; Syme: *Roman Revolution*, pp. 15–17; Walter Allen, Jr.: "In Defense of Catiline," *Classical Journal*, Vol. XXXIV, pp. 70–85; S. L. Mohler: *Sentina Rei Publicæ*; "Campaign Issues, 63 B.C.," *Classical Weekly*, Vol. XXIX, pp. 81–4; B. L. Ullman: "Cicero and Modern Politics," *Classical Journal*, Vol. XXX, pp. 385–402. Cicero's orations must be interpreted in the light of his violent prejudices. Fragments of evidence upon which the case of the debtors and Catiline can be constructed are given in Sallust: *The War with Catiline*.

Page 175. Napoleon's opinion is cited by J. Michelet: *History of the Roman Republic*, p. 331, note.

Page 177. For conjecture on a possible deal between Cæsar and Crassus on one side and Pompey on the other, see Hardy, op. cit., pp. 62, 104.

CHAPTER XV. *Catiline Leads a Debtors' Protest*
The speeches of Manlius, Catiline, Cæsar, Cicero, and Cato and the moving letter from Catiline are quoted by Sallust in *The War with Catiline.* Presumably the quoted speeches convey the substance of what was said. The customary defence of Cicero for his execution of the conspirators is well presented in Strachan-Davidson: *Cicero,* pp. 151–7.

Page 187. One historian who recognizes that the letters contained nothing treasonable is Shuckburgh: A *History of Rome* (1894), p. 703.

Page 188. On the responsibility of Cicero and the Senate Professor Walker writes: "I don't quite like your statement. Cicero had no authority in the case except what the Senate had given him. If, as you say, and I believe, the Senate had no legal authority, neither did Cicero. The legal maxim, *Nemo dat qui non habet,* fits the *Senatus consultum ultimum*" (the decree for martial law). Professor Poteat words his criticism a bit differently: "But the Senate, constitutionally or otherwise, had passed the *Senatus consultum ultimum;* so that Cicero, like a dictator, at least theoretically was responsible to that body." But see Strachan-Davidson, authority on Roman criminal law: *Cicero,* p. 155: "The decree of the Senate could make no difference in the legal responsibility of the consul"; Holmes: *Roman Republic,* Vol. I, p. 274: "The Senate had in strict law no right to decide the question; but Cicero, who relied upon the authority conferred by the ultimate decree, doubtless desired the moral support of the august assembly"; and Greenidge: *Roman Public Life,* pp. 279–80: "After the passing of this decree the responsibility of the Senate ceases; the magistrates act at their own peril and cannot devolve any responsibility for a judicial murder they may have committed in the execution of their instructions by again consulting the Senate on the guilt of their victims or on the method of execution to be employed."

Page 197. On Cicero's argument that the accused men had lost their citizenship see Greenidge: *Roman Public Life*, p. 281: "Cicero's quibble that the Gracchan law only protected the lives of *cives* and that individuals specified by the Senate had been declared *hostes*, is an argument in a circle."

CHAPTER XVI. *Deflation*

Pages 200–1. On the possible corrupt deal between Cicero and Antonius, Long thinks the evidence is bad for Cicero and that his letter to Atticus on the subject is "consistent with his guilt and inconsistent with his innocence"; *Decline*, Vol. III, p. 238.

Page 203. On Pompey's hope through Metellus Nepos to be recalled to deal with Catiline, Professor Poteat writes: "It would be difficult, I think, to prove this." But Plutarch says (*Cato Minor*, 26, 2), that Nepos proposed that Pompey should bring his troops into Italy "under the pretext of saving the city from Catiline." This view is accepted by Strachan-Davidson: *Cicero*, p. 160; Petersson: *Cicero*, p. 295; Holmes: *Roman Republic*, Vol. I, p. 285 and note.

Page 207. "I wonder," Professor Poteat comments regarding the statement that Cicero thought of Cæsar as well as of Pompey as one who might become the leading citizen of the state. My guess, which may be wrong, is based on Cicero's occasional outbursts of admiration for Cæsar, especially in his oration for Marcellus, and his letter to Servius Sulpicius, telling about the speech, *Ad. Fam.* iv, 4, in which he speaks of imagining that he saw before him some fair vision of the Republic rising as it were from the dead.

Page 208. The idea of the *Princeps* is elaborated in Homo: *Political Institutions*, p. 169; Frank: *Life and Literature*, pp. 210–11.

CHAPTER XVII. *The Big Three*

Page 215. In my account of the affair of Clodius I have followed Dio among others, and Professor Poteat properly observes: "You have often cited passages from Dio, one of the most prejudiced of historians!" True, especially in the account of Cicero's speech for Pompey on the Manilian Law, p. 145, in which I speak of Dio's presenting what was "perhaps cynical contemporary opinion." Dio's comment is there represented as being "wholly unfair," but I remark that it reflected a widespread feeling. Dio certainly is prejudiced, but unfortunately his prejudices often have much reason behind them.

Page 222. The reason for Cæsar's manœuvres in obtaining the proconsular command and recruiting troops while he was still consul are discussed by Marsh: *Roman World*, p. 182; his reply to critics, ibid., pp. 391–2.

CHAPTER XVIII. A *Political Gangster in Action*

Page 235. Holmes thinks the first general bill of Clodius did not carry: *Roman Republic*, Vol. I, p. 334, note.

Page 237. That the interdict carried a provision for the destruction of Cicero's property is questioned by Professor Poteat. "It was destroyed," he writes, "yes, but I believe by the arbitrary action of Clodius' minions." My authority is Dio, 38, 17, 6–7: "On his departure the law went into effect. . . . His property was confiscated, his house was razed to the ground." Strachan-Davidson: *Cicero*, p. 235, interprets this as I do, as does Holmes: *Roman Republic*, Vol. I, p. 334. Sihler says, in *Cicero*, p. 205: "The law was like an act of attainder; for the guilty one was declared one who had forfeited everything but mere life."

Pages 239–41. On the gangs of Clodius see Marsh: "The Gangster in Roman Politics," *Classical Journal*, Vol. XXVIII, p. 168.

CHAPTER XIX. *Exponent of Blitzkrieg*

Page 252. On the state of Gaul, see Norman J. DeWitt, dissertation: "Urbanization and the Franchise in Roman Gaul"; Albert Grenier: "*La Gaule romaine,*" in Frank: *Economic Survey*, Vol. III; and Holmes: *Cæsar's Conquest of Gaul*.

Page 257. The letter comparing Cæsar with other commanders is from Colonel E. F. Koenig, U.S.A. Colonel Armstrong's studies are summarized in "Cæsar's Art of War" in the

Classical Weekly, Vol. XXXII, p. 291, and "The Blitzkrieg in Cæsar's Campaigns" in the *Classical Journal*, Vol. XXXVII, p. 138.

Pages 257 ff. On Cæsar's qualities as a soldier I am glad to subjoin the criticism of Professor Walker, who has given the subject especial attention. The text has been modified to meet some of the considerations adduced by Professor Walker, but not nearly enough to meet his general objections. Thus I have been impelled to explain in what sense I think the modern Blitzkrieg is to be differentiated from the surprise attacks which always have been a feature of war and I have tried to show what seems to me to be Colonel Armstrong's contribution as a professional soldier. Here is Professor Walker: "I hope you will forgive my pretty general disapproval of what you have written about Cæsar as general. . . . I agree pretty substantially with what you quote from Adcock and Veith and some of the views of the unnamed 'instructor.' It is amazing that you should think you have discovered that speed is the clue to Cæsar's success. Of course that was a part of the reason, but I venture to say that every writer on Cæsar has spoken of his speed. However, they have spoken of it only as a part of his natural endowment — his genius for organization and his extraordinary ability to get the best out of his men in everything, marching, fighting, endurance of hardships. . . . Surely every general has seen the importance of speed at the right time and has tried to get it. But most of them have not had the personality to get it. Blitzkrieg is not what you call it, a real contribution to the art of war by Cæsar. It is merely a new name for what Cain used on Abel and the Indians constantly practised without benefit of Cæsar. Cæsar no more invented the thing than the namer of appendicitis invented the disease. What did make Cæsar a great general, I think, was his mental speed in grasping the details of a problem, in coming to a decision, and in acting on his decision."

In the text I recognize that various factors entered into Cæsar's success. His service of supply, logistics, as the military men say, was generally well organized; his qualities of leadership and self-control were outstanding. An appraisal is to some extent a matter of perspective and here it seems to me that the professional soldier is apt to have a better comprehension than the layman. The standard work on Cæsar's Gallic campaigns is Holmes: *Cæsar's Conquest of Gaul.* Colonel Armstrong comments that "Holmes knows his Roman history but is lacking in training in strategy and tactics." Dodge's *Cæsar* is a painstaking and intelligent piece of work. The author studied military science in Germany. In the American Civil War he enlisted as a private in the Union Army, finished with the brevet rank of colonel of volunteers, and later served in the regular army, in which he obtained the brevet rank of lieutenant colonel. While acknowledging his indebtedness to Colonel Stoffel, Dodge made his studies on the ground, following Cæsar around the entire Mediterranean basin. Colonel Armstrong writes that Dodge has made "definite contributions in the discussion of tactical and strategic problems." Dodge's analysis of the military qualities of Cæsar in the chapter: "The Man and the Soldier," and his chapter comparing Alexander, Hannibal, and Cæsar, are excellent.

As to Holmes and Dodge, Professor Walker writes: "I hate to see Holmes put in the same list as Dodge. I think I know something about the Gallic campaigns and the literature, and I must relieve my mind. . . . Holmes wrote the one great book about the campaigns. He read and digested everything that had been written by hundreds of other men. He usually gave their arguments so fairly that one could almost dispense with the originals. Then he applied intelligence and common sense to solving doubtful points. . . . Dodge followed Napoleon slavishly for his Gallic campaigns and has no independent value whatever."

For the reorganization of the Roman army and the development of strategy and tactics see H. P. Judson: *Cæsar's Army* (1888), H. M. D. Parker, *The Roman Legion* (1928), and F. E. Adcock: *The Roman Art of War under the Republic* (the Martin Lectures, 1940). Cæsar's own story in his *Commentaries* is good reading in either the Bohn translation or the Loeb. An attractive and handy recent translation is Eugene I. Burdock: *The Gallic War of Julius Cæsar.*

Page 260. As to Cæsar's reserves, the use of a three-line

formation, of which the second and third lines were in the nature of a tactical reserve, antedated Cæsar. Colonel Armstrong's reference is not to this tactical reserve, but to the reserve as defined in the field service regulations, U.S.A.: "The primary mission of the reserve is to enter the action offensively at the proper place and moment to clinch the victory." Cæsar's most striking use of a reserve was in the battle of Pharsalus. He tells about it in the *Civil Wars*, Book 3, Ch. 89, pointing out that the winning of the battle depended upon the effective work of this reserve. For other instances see Dodge: *Cæsar*, p. 748.

Page 260. Of the failure of Cæsar's scouting, the three conspicuous instances are: first, the battle of the Sambre in 57, in which the Gauls were hidden in the woods; Napoleon I criticized Cæsar for permitting himself to be surprised (Holmes: *Conquest of Gaul*, p. 77); second, after the surrender of Noviodunum in 52 the Roman force was surprised by the cavalry of Vercingetorix (Holmes, ibid., p. 138); third, a surprise attack by the cavalry of Vercingetorix just before Alesia; "Cæsar was surprised as completely as in the battle of the Sambre" (Holmes, ibid., p. 168).

Here Professor Walker again registers dissent. "It is not a question," he writes, "whether Cæsar was ever surprised, but whether he used scouts when they should have been used. He did use them on the Sambre. They would have been useless at Noviodunum. The third case is not so clear, but I am sure that Holmes got too imaginative. Cæsar was in no danger and he knew it. The Gallic cavalry never could charge Roman infantry."

Chapter XX. *The Crisis of the Rubicon*

Page 273. That civil war had never entered into Cicero's calculations Professor Poteat "doubts seriously." At least I understand Cicero to have meant this in the passage quoted in the preceding chapters, *Ad Att.* vii, 1: "My idea was this: If I were allied with Pompey I should not hereafter have to take any improper steps in politics; nor if I agreed with Cæsar, should I have to fight with Pompey; their union was so close."

Page 277. The suggestion that Cæsar's winter campaign in

Italy took Pompey by surprise because it was not considered good form to fight in the winter, comes from Colonel Armstrong.

Page 279. Macaulay's comments on Cæsar are quoted by William Lyon Phelps: *Autobiography with Letters*, p. 185, from Sir George Otto Trevelyan: *The Marginal Notes of Lord Macaulay*.

CHAPTER XXI. *Sorrow Intervenes*

Page 290. For Cæsar's rather brief affair with Cleopatra after the fighting in Egypt was over, contrary to the general opinion, see the time-table worked out by Professor Lord in " The Date of Julius Cæsar's Departure from Alexandria," *Journal of Roman Studies*, Vol. XXVIII, pp. 19–40. Cæsar won the battle of the Nile on March 27, 47. Professor Lord believes that after establishing Cleopatra and her brother on the throne, Cæsar lingered with the Egyptian Queen only from the middle to the end of April before setting out on his campaign. There was no time, he thinks, for the voyage up the Nile with Cleopatra reported by later writers. — That Cæsar used the phrase: "*Veni, Vidi, Vici*," in a letter to a friend is reported by Plutarch: *Cæsar*, 50, 2; that the phrase was used in his Pontic triumph in Rome is stated by Suetonius: *The Deified Julius*, 37.

Pages 297 ff. On Cicero's religious experience: Fowler: *Religious Experience*, pp. 384–90.

Page 300. For his religious views, including those expressed in his letters: Boissier: *La Religion romaine*, Vol. I, Ch. ii. On his rationalism: Tavenner: *Studies*, p. 30.

Page 302. Cicero's influence on philosophical thinking: Rolfe, *Cicero*, Chs. vii–xii. The Zielinski quotation is from Richards: *Cicero*, p. 239.

CHAPTER XXII. *The Irrepressible Conflict*

Page 304. Cæsar was in Rome for a few weeks in 49; he was absent throughout 48. He was again in Rome in the autumn of 47, the autumn of 46, and finally from September 45 to March 44.

Page 306. The first really effective police force in Rome was organized by Augustus A.D. 6 (P. K. B. Reynolds: *The Vigiles of*

Imperial Rome, pp. 15, 18). A remark by F. E. Adcock, in *Cambridge Ancient History*, Vol. IX, p. 697, seems to have given currency to the idea that Cæsar was responsible for policing the city, using " troops to reinforce the lictors, the only civil police force known to the Roman state." So A. A. Trever says: " Public order was improved [by Cæsar] by the use of a small armed force to assist the lictors who were, strange to say, the only civil police in the Roman state" (*History of Ancient Civilization*, Vol. II, " The Roman World," p. 235). The only basis for these statements that I can find is Suetonius: *The Deified Julius*, Ch. xliii: " Sometimes he sent his lictors and soldiers " to enforce sumptuary legislation." This is a rather insubstantial basis upon which to generalize.

CHAPTER XXIII. *Colossus of the Narrow World*

Pages 315–17. Cæsar's epilepsy: Dr. C. MacLaurin writes in *Post Mortems*, p. 224: " It is a sort of pleasing paradox to say that supremely great men suffer from epilepsy. It was said of Julius Cæsar, of St. Paul, and of Mohammed. These men are said to have suffered from 'falling sickness,' whatever that may have been; there are plenty of conditions which may make men fall to the ground without being epileptic. Menière's disease, for instance. It is ridiculous to suppose that Julius Cæsar and Napoleon — by common consent the two greatest of the sons of men — should have been subject to a disease which deteriorates the intellect."

Page 321. A short letter from Cicero to Basilus, one of the conspirators, is usually attributed to the day of the assassination. It has been called Cicero's " scream of triumph " over the death of a tyrant. Shuckburgh gives it under the probable date of March 15, 44. It reads: " I congratulate you. For myself I am rejoiced. I love you and have your interests at heart. I want you to love me too and should like to know how you are and what is going on." In a footnote Shuckburgh says: " The note is no doubt written immediately after the assassination; though there is no direct evidence of it, nor do we know anything of Cicero's relations with Basilus to explain why he is selected for congratulation out of all the conspirators. He is only once mentioned before."

The arguments against this date for the letter are convincingly presented by E. T. Merrill, of the University of Chicago, in *Classical Philology*, Vol. VIII, pp. 48–56 (January 1913). The letter is undated. Basilus was only a minor figure in the conspiracy and not one whom Cicero might be expected to single out for a letter of congratulation. The form of the letter, with its use of the singular pronoun and verb forms instead of the plural, suggests a personal favour rather than a public event. The conventional inquiries after Basilus' health and what is going on, hardly fit into a dramatic occasion.

Professor Merrill thinks it likely the letter may have been in the correspondence referred to by Cicero in a letter to Atticus (*Ad. Att.* xi, 5) written in November 48 from Brindisi, where Cicero was awaiting pardon from Cæsar. He asks Atticus to write to Basilus and other friends of Cæsar's to intercede for him. It is quite possible that Basilus did so and that the note usually attributed to the ides of March was merely one of thanks for Basilus' services in 47. Holmes believes Merrill has proved there is no connection between the letter and the assassination (*Roman Republic,* Vol. III, p. 351).

Page 323. Professor Poteat does not agree that it was no part of Antony's policy at this time to stir up mob violence. This criticism, I believe, stems from the generally accepted view of Antony which assumes that he started out with the policy which, as I read the record, he did not adopt at the outset, but to which he was subsequently driven. The facts seem to me to back Syme in his important study: *The Roman Revolution,* p. 105, in saying: "His [Antonius'] own security and the maintenance of order dictated the same salutary policy. By force of argument and personal authority, Antonius brought the session of March 17th to terms of compromise — even to a spirit of concord."

Pages 324 ff. The view taken in this chapter and the next on the probable ambitions of Antony, the conflict between Cicero and Antony, and the motives of the young Octavian is contrary to accepted historical opinion. It is developed by Syme in the book just mentioned. After reading his book, I returned to the ancient sources and was interested to observe how, with preconceptions out, the evidence fell into the general pattern outlined by the Oxford scholar. In studying the Ciceronian period, as I have remarked before, I have been amazed at the readiness of historians to accept frankly political speeches, with all the customary distortions of politics, as authentic records. This is particularly so in the period now under consideration. It might perhaps be thought a tribute to Cicero's oratory that his hysterical *Philippics* have been made the basis of history. They reflect the frame of mind of a political zealot and egotist. As always when his emotions are involved, facts fly out of the window.

Page 329. Professor Poteat writes that he can't agree with my judgment of the *Second Philippic*. I had suspected as much because in the interesting notes to his *Selected Letters of Cicero*, p. 252, he speaks of the *Second Philippic* as "probably the most terrific and scathing oration ever written — Cicero's masterpiece in the field of oratory." Against his view I may quote that of Syme, op. cit., p. 104: "The Philippics, the series of speeches in which he [Cicero] assailed an absent enemy, are an eternal monument of eloquence, of rancour, of misrepresentation. Many of the charges levelled against Antonius — such as unnatural vice or flagrant cowardice — are trivial, ridiculous, or conventional." Juvenal suggests that the "divine" *Second Philippic* was responsible for Cicero's death (*Sat*. x, 120–5).

Chapter XXIV. *Last Crusade*

Page 345. The statement that by the standards of the age the Three were justified in having their enemies summarily destroyed brings another "I don't agree at all" from Professor Poteat. But as Dr. Samuel Crothers once remarked regarding the criticism of Samuel for hewing Agag in pieces before the Lord, the alternative was not religious toleration. "The question of the age was, Shall Samuel hew Agag in pieces, or shall Agag hew Samuel in pieces, and my sympathies are with Samuel." Contemporary opinion was perhaps expressed by Livy in the passage quoted on page 351, that Cicero " suffered at the hands of his enemy no more cruel fate than he would himself have inflicted had he been equally fortunate."

CHAPTER XXV. *The Two Ciceros*

Page 351. The quotations from Livy and Pollio are cited by Seneca the elder in the *Suasoriæ*.

Page 353. The judgment that in pursuing a policy Cicero was ready to support scandalous measures is considered " far too severe " by Professor Poteat, and it may be. But as I pointed out in Chapter xiii Cicero makes the charge against himself in a letter to Atticus (*Ad. Att.* i, 17). The knights were protesting against a proposal under which they would be liable for prosecution if they accepted bribes when serving as jurors. Cicero pleaded their cause before the Senate, speaking impressively, he tells his friend, " considering the shamelessness of the case." Strachan-Davidson speaks of " this monstrous immunity " publicly defended by Cicero. Another case referred to in the same letter was the appeal of the syndicate which had bid too high on the tax-collections of Asia Minor and wanted to have its contract cancelled. Cicero tells Atticus that the case is " scandalous, the demand a disgraceful one," yet he upheld it before the Senate.

Pages 354–5. The discussion of Alexander H. Stephens is based on Burton J. Hendrick: *Statesmen of the Lost Cause*.

Page 355. Guizot is considered by E. L. Woodward: *Three Studies in European Conservatism*.

Page 355. Professor Poteat thinks it would be hard to prove that Cicero allowed Roman knights to have their avaricious way for fear of offending business. In dealing with a politician such as Cicero I believe we are justified in applying the rules of ordinary political behavior. In general Cicero looked to the powerful business crowd for clients and for political support. He showed the politician's attitude in his plea for a big business client (*pro Rab. Post.*, vii, 16), in the speeches referred to in his letter to Atticus cited in the note on page 353, and in his gingerly handling of the business interests in their tax extortions when he was governor of Cilicia. It has been said: " When the harmony of the orders and the natural rights of the provinces had to be weighed against each other, the latter kicked the beam " (Munk: *Student's Cicero*, p. 106.

Page 357. The quotation from Mackail is in his *Latin Literature*, p. 74.

APPENDIX I, *Chronology of Cicero's Life*

Page 359. The date of Cæsar's birth is uncertain. I assume with reservations that he probably was born July 12, 102, and so was four years younger than Cicero. The ancient authorities, Velleius, Suetonius, Plutarch, and Appian, make the year 100. But Mommsen points out (*History*, Vol. IV, p. 278, note) that if the year 100 is accepted, then Cæsar held all the magistracies two years under the legal age, and there is no record of any senatorial dispensation permitting this. He cites other confirmatory evidence, and calls attention to the fact that two of the ancient writers, Plutarch and Appian, are demonstrably mistaken in citations of the age of Pompey.

M. E. Deutsch takes issue with Mommsen, *Transactions of the American Philological Association*, 1914, pp. 17–28. Deutsch believes the date of 100 given by the ancient authorities should be accepted and that we are justified in assuming that Cæsar received a blanket dispensation early in his career that is not mentioned by the historians. He supports this view with collateral arguments, most of which seem rather tenuous. Deutsch's reasoning is adopted in a recent study, Lily Ross Taylor: " Cæsar's Early Career," *Classical Philology*, April 1941, pp. 113 ff. M. Cary in the *Cambridge Ancient History*, Vol. IX, p. 487, says Mommsen's theory rests on " wholly unconvincing grounds " and assumes 100 as the date.

In the temper attending this controversy I think may be detected a certain enthusiasm in rebelling against the discipline of Mommsen, whose tremendous scholarship so long dominated the field. In the group against the Mommsen year 102, besides those already mentioned, are George Long, Sihler, A. E. R. Boak, and G. De Sanctis. Carcopino: *Points de vue sur l'impérialisme romain,* p. 92, suggests the year 101. The arguments that seemed "wholly unconvincing" to Cary have convinced such modern scholars as Eduard Meyer, Fowler, Strachan-Davidson, Heitland, H. Stuart Jones, J. S. Reid, Tenney Frank, and Holmes. There is a full discussion in Holmes: *Roman Republic,* Vol. I, pp. 436–42, in which he concludes: "if we cannot fix the date of Cæsar's birth with mathematical certainty it is in the highest degree probable that he was born in 102 B.C." This seems to me a fair statement. But it must be recognized there is no consensus on the subject.

Page 360. It is probable, although not certain, that Cicero assumed the white toga of manhood at the festival of the Liberalia, March 17, 90, after his sixteenth birthday. Customarily at this period of the Republic boys were considered to come of age at sixteen, and Cicero speaks of entering the Forum — that is, of being on his own — after the death of the orator Crassus in 91 (*Brutus,* 303). The next ceremonial date for receiving the *toga virilis* would have been at the March festival in 90. The Liberalia was the traditional date for the army to be called out and the boys who had just assumed the manhood toga were supposed to present themselves for service (Fowler: *Roman Festivals,* p. 56). They were called *tirones,* equivalent to the American word "draftees."

Page 360. Chronology in *Cambridge Ancient History,* Vol. IX, gives the year of Catullus' birth as 87. Frank, in *Catullus and Horace,* pp. 5–6, argues persuasively for 84.

INDEX

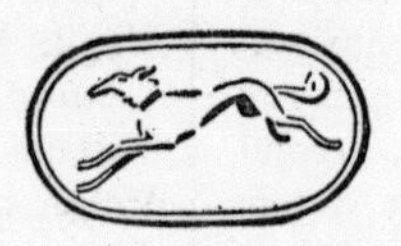

This book is set in Electra, a linotype face designed by W. A. Dwiggins. This face cannot be classified readily as either " modern " or " old-style." It is not based on any historical model, nor does it echo any particular period or style. It avoids the extreme contrast between " thick " and " thin " elements that mark most " modern " faces, and attempts to give a feeling of fluidity, power, and speed. The book was composed, printed, and bound by The Plimpton Press, Norwood, Massachusetts. The typographic and binding designs are by W. A. Dwiggins.

THE TRIUMVIRATE PROLONGED
BOLOGNA
CICERO PROSCRIBED
CROSSING THE RUB
LUCCA
FIESOLE
PISA
DEBTORS' PROTEST UNDER CATILINE
FLAMINIAN WAY
TIBER R.
OSTIA
AST
CORSICA
Tyrrhenia
SARDINIA
CICERO'S ITALY
Medite
(MARE
Darrell Porter